INKLINGS-JAHRBUCH FÜR LITERATUR UND ÄSTHETIK
29. BAND 2011

INKLINGS

JAHRBUCH FÜR LITERATUR UND ÄSTHETIK

29. BAND
2011

Herausgegeben von Dieter Petzold
in Verbindung mit
Adelheid Kegler, Raimund Kern,
Christian Rendel, Elmar Schenkel,
Angelika Schneider, Manfred Siebald

PETER LANG
Frankfurt am Main · Berlin · Bern · Bruxelles · New York · Oxford · Wien

Bibliografische Information der Deutschen Nationalbibliothek
Die Deutsche Nationalbibliothek verzeichnet diese Publikation in
der Deutschen Nationalbibliografie; detaillierte bibliografische
Daten sind im Internet über http://dnb.d-nb.de abrufbar.

Herausgeber: Dieter Petzold
Wissenschaftlicher Beirat:
Adelheid Kegler, Raimund Kern, Christian Rendel,
Elmar Schenkel, Angelika Schneider, Manfred Siebald
INKLINGS ist ein Organ der Inklings Gesellschaft für Literatur
und Ästhetik e.V., Aachen. Mitglieder erhalten das Jahrbuch kostenlos.
Kontakt: Inklings, c/o Irene Oberdörfer, Ringofenweg 6, 47877 Willich;
Tel. 02154-88377; inklings@gmx.de.
Weitere Informationen unter: www.inklings-gesellschaft.de.

Beiträge mit kurzen Zusammenfassungen in deutscher oder englischer
Sprache per E-Mail (inklings.jahrbuch@gmx.net) oder Post erbeten an:
Prof. Dr. Dieter Petzold, Parkstr. 6, 91336 Heroldsbach

Umschlaggrafik:
A. Conan Doyle nach einer zeitgenössischen
Lexikonillustration (bearbeitet).

Gedruckt auf alterungsbeständigem,
säurefreiem Papier.

ISSN 0176-3733
ISBN 978-3-631-62347-3
© Peter Lang GmbH
Internationaler Verlag der Wissenschaften
Frankfurt am Main 2012
Alle Rechte vorbehalten.

Das Werk einschließlich aller seiner Teile ist urheberrechtlich
geschützt. Jede Verwertung außerhalb der engen Grenzen des
Urheberrechtsgesetzes ist ohne Zustimmung des Verlages
unzulässig und strafbar. Das gilt insbesondere für
Vervielfältigungen, Übersetzungen, Mikroverfilmungen und die
Einspeicherung und Verarbeitung in elektronischen Systemen.

www.peterlang.de

INHALT

Vorwort 8

Beiträge zur Tagung "Der andere Conan Doyle"

ELMAR SCHENKEL
Quallen in der Troposphäre: Flug, Phantastik und Moderne in Arthur Conan Doyles "The Horror of the Heights" . .   10

JANA NITTEL
A Lasting Legacy: An Ecocritical Reading of Arthur Conan Doyle's "When the World Screamed"   31

JOANNA KOKOT
Manipulating the Reader: The Strategies of Telling the Story in *The Lost World* by Arthur Conan Doyle   49

STEFAN LAMPADIUS
Evolutionary Ideas in Arthur Conan Doyle's *The Lost World*   68

CATRIONA MCARA
Of Paper Cut-outs and Other Worlds: Cottingley, Collage, Cornell, and Conan Doyle   98

KATI VOIGT
A Mathematician in the Fourth Dimension: Professor Moriarty Travels Through Time   121

STEFAN WELZ
Brüder in Geist und Tat: A. C. Doyle, R. Kipling, R. Haggard und der Burenkrieg   142

Inhalt

TILL KINZEL
Confronting Barbarism and Religion in *The Tragedy of the Korosko* and *The River War*: Arthur Conan Doyle and Winston Churchill on Violence, Empire, and War in the Soudan . . . 168

MARIA FLEISCHHACK
Undershaw 186

Varia

KARL HEPFER
Sir Gawain and the Green Knight: Ein Ritter auf der Suche nach sich selbst 196

RUDOLF DRUX
Zwischen Werkstatt und Labor: Zur poetologischen Paradigmatik des Menschenbildners Prometheus in der Goethezeit 213

ADAM BARKMAN
"No Doubt They Are Substantially Right": C. S. Lewis and the Calvinists 232

CHRISTIAN SCHNEIDER
Disreputable Heroes: A Re-examination of Robert E. Howard and His Literature 253

The Poet's Eye

JULIANE KREPPEL
Resignation oder Widerspruch? Christoph Meckels "Gedicht in Ermangelung eines Besseren" 274

Favourite Authors

DOMINIK BECHER
Edwin Morgans Panoptikum: Stimmen aus dem Werk eines Whittrick 291

Besprechungen

Zu Fantasy Fiction und verwandten Gattungen 308
   Neues von der Fantastikfront (Dieter Petzold) 308
   Einführung in die Einführung (Maike van Delden/Uwe Durst) 311
   Summa phantastica: Darko Suvin und die Science Fiction (Johannes Rüster) 315
   Märchen: Verzauberung und Entzauberung (Elmar Schenkel) 318

Zu einzelnen Autoren 319
   Johann Wolfgang von Goethe (Adelheid Kegler) . . . 319
   Lewis Carroll (Stefan Lampadius/Dieter Petzold) . . 324
   Arthur Conan Doyle und H. G. Wells (John S. Partington) 329
   J. R. R. Tolkien (Thomas Fornet-Ponse/Dieter Petzold) 333
   C. S. Lewis (Josef Schreier) 344
   Michèle Roberts (Susanne Gruss) 350
   Joanne K. Rowling (Franziska Burstyn/Dieter Petzold) 354

Vermischtes 362
   Gewalt in der Kinderliteratur (Maren Bonacker) . . . 362
   Eine kurze Geschichte der englischen Kurzgeschichte (Arno Löffler) 364
   Das lange Leben des Don Quijote (Dieter Petzold) . . 367
   Surrealismus, Futurismus, Spiritismus (Elmar Schenkel) 370
   Walter Benjamin und Mircea Eliade (Elmar Schenkel) 372
   Anthroposophie (Elmar Schenkel) 375
   Ein Freund der Inklings: Stephen Medcalf (Elmar Schenkel) 378
   Das Geheimnis ist immer und überall (Dieter Petzold) 380
   Was ist das Glück? (Elmar Schenkel) 382

Weitere eingegangene Schriften 384

Die Beiträger 386

Personenindex 393

VORWORT

Das diesjährige Symposium, das die Inklings-Gesellschaft zusammen mit dem Institut für Anglistik der Universität Leipzig als *joint venture* am 20. und 21. Mai 2011 in der prächtigen Universitätsbibliothek Albertina in Leipzig veranstaltete, beschäftigte sich mit einem Autor, der auf den ersten Blick nichts mit den Inklings, ja nicht einmal mit fantastischer Literatur zu tun zu haben scheint. Arthur Conan Doyle (1859–1930) ist in die Literaturgeschichte eingegangen als derjenige, der mit seinen Sherlock-Holmes-Geschichten die *Detective Story* wenn nicht erfunden, so doch entscheidend geprägt und popularisiert hat. Aber (um aus dem Programmheft der Tagung zu zitieren) "Conan Doyle hat sich [auch] als Romancier, Historiker, Arzt, Kriminalist, Imperialist, Spiritist und Sportler hervorgetan und über fast alles geschrieben". Die nachfolgenden Beiträge zu dem internationalen Symposium "The Other Arthur Conan Doyle/Der andere Arthur Conan Doyle" korrigieren das gängige Doyle-Bild, indem sie sich "auf den Doyle konzentrieren, der die phantastische Literatur und Science Fiction bereichert hat mit Erzählungen aus Parallelwelten, aus verlorenen Ländern und der Tiefsee, der sich mit den Schrecken der Erde und der Luft, mit Phantomhänden und Mumien beschäftigt hat", der mit Büchern über den Mahdi-Aufstand im Sudan und den Burenkrieg das britische Empire gestärkt und die Echtheit von Elfen-Fotografien verteidigt hat. Ein klein wenig werden aber auch seine Sherlock-Holmes-Geschichten berücksichtigt, allerdings geht es dabei nicht um den berühmten Detektiv, sondern um seinen Widersacher Moriarty, der wie sein Intimfeind Holmes ein literarisches Eigenleben entwickelt hat. Ein Blick auf den wenig erfreulichen Umgang der Nachwelt mit Doyles materieller Hinterlassenschaft rundet die Reihe der Tagungsbeiträge ab.

Wie immer öffnen die übrigen Artikel des Jahrbuchs den Blick auf das weite Spektrum der (im weitesten Sinne) fantastischen Literatur – von dem spätmittelalterlichen Kurzepos *Sir Gawain and the Green Knight* über Gestaltungen des Prometheus-Stoffes in der deutschen und englischen Literatur seit Goethe bis hin zu zwei zeitgenössischen Dichtern – dem Deutschen Christoph Meckel und dem Schotten Edwin Morgan –, die auf je ihre eigene Weise der Realität mit mythologisch-fantastischen Mitteln beizukommen versucht haben. Dazwischen liegen ein Essay über C. S. Lewis' Verhältnis zum Kalvinismus und zu den Kalvinisten sowie eine umsichtige Auseinandersetzung mit einem Autor, über den man in der akademischen Welt trotz (oder wegen) seiner Popularität gern etwas verschämt hinwegsieht: mit Robert E. Howard, dem Erfinder von "Conan, dem Barbaren" und (Mit-)Begründer der *Heroic Fantasy*. Wer sich auf noch weiteren Feldern nicht nur der fantastischen Literatur umsehen möchte, dem sei der Rezensionsteil des Jahrbuchs ans Herz gelegt, in dem vielfältige Forschungen vorgestellt werden, von denen auch diesmal wieder einige von Inklings-Mitgliedern bzw. -Mitarbeitern stammen.

Zu danken ist abschließend den Beiträgern und Rezensenten für ihre Mühen und ihre Kooperationsbereitschaft und Herrn Peter Kramer für die Gestaltung des Layouts.

D. P.

Elmar Schenkel

QUALLEN IN DER TROPOSPHÄRE

Flug, Phantastik und Moderne in Arthur Conan Doyles "The Horror of the Heights"

Im vorliegenden Beitrag werden die phantastischen Erzählungen von Conan Doyle beleuchtet. Im Mittelpunkt steht die Kurzgeschichte "The Horror of the Heights". Sie handelt von einem Fragment, das ein verschollener Pilot hinterlassen hat und in dem er über den Angriff von quallenartigen Wesen in den Lüften berichtet. Diese Geschichte steht an einem Schnittpunkt mehrerer Diskurse: Vorkriegsängste, die sich auf mögliche Luftkriege beziehen, ästhetische Bewegungen wie Vortizismus und eine Frühform des Futurismus, biologisch-evolutionäre Fragen, Ernst Haeckels *Kunstformen der Natur*, die ein neues Interesse an Quallen, Radiolarien und anderen Tiefseewesen auslösten. In der Geschichte ist auch die Rede von einem kopflosen Piloten. Das Bild der Kopflosigkeit verweist auf verwandte Bildlichkeit bei Dante und Kafka. Die Erzählung deutet an, dass Technik/Luftfahrt als eine Form des spirituellen Aufstiegs oder des Schamanismus zum Scheitern verurteilt ist.

In this essay, the unknown Conan Doyle, in particular the writer of phantastic stories, is under scrutiny. After a short survey of his Gothic and supernatural tales, the paper will focus on his 1913 short story "The Horror of the Heights". This story about a fragment written by a lost pilot, who apparently had been attacked by jelly-fish in the troposphere, can be seen to be at the intersection of a number of discourses: the pre-war anxieties about a war in the air, aesthetic movements such as Vorticism and (potential) Futurism, biological and evolutionary questions, Ernst Haeckel's art forms of Nature and the interest it sparked in jelly-fish, radiolaries and other deep-sea creatures. The story also stresses the loss of another pilot's head and this image of the headless body is compared to similar imagery in Dante and Kafka. "The Horror of the Heights" suggests that technology is a form of shamanism or spiritual ascent gone wrong.

Wer den Namen Doyle ausspricht, meint nicht selten Holmes, und umgekehrt. Der britische Autor ist so verwachsen mit seinem Helden wie Frankenstein mit dem namenlosen Ungeheuer, und beide wollten sie ihre Doppelgänger loswerden. Um so größer also das Erstaunen bei vielen Lesern, wenn sie erfahren, dass Sir Arthur Conan Doyle ein Leben und Schreiben außerhalb seines Detektivs führte und dieses gar für wichtiger hielt als jene Geschichten, die für ihn oft nicht mehr als *pot boiler* waren, ähnlich wie die Father-Brown-Erzählungen für Chesterton. Doyles historische Romane, etwa über die Zeit des Hundertjährigen Krieges, werden heute kaum noch gelesen, vielleicht weil sie sich nicht besonders vom damals praktizierten Genre heraushoben. Hunderte anderer Autoren konnten mindestens ebenso gut und detailverliebt die Vergangenheit beschwören, zumal das goldene Mittelalter. Von seinen anderen Romanen wäre zu reden, *Rodney Stone* etwa, in dem es um Dandys, Boxen und die napoleonischen Kriege geht, oder die gewitzten Geschichten um den napoleonischen Brigadier Gérard; Romane wie *The Tragedy of the Korosko* sind allerdings von anderem Kaliber und verdienten größere Beachtung. Doyle war zudem in Prozesse verwickelt, die zum Teil romanhaften Charakter hatten – man lese Julian Barnes' Darstellung der Edalji-Affäre in *Arthur and George* –, er betätigte sich auf imperialer Seite im Burenkrieg, stellte ein Freiwilligenkorps im Ersten Weltkrieg auf, schrieb zahllose Leserbriefe und setzte sich für die Ausrüstung der Marine mit Schwimmwesten ein. Er war ein begeisterter Sportler und trug dazu bei, dass das Skifahren in der Schweiz populär wurde. Er nahm an Autorennen ebenso wie an Séancen teil, und das letzte Jahrzehnt seines Lebens stand im Zeichen seiner spiritistischen Mission. Er verteidigte die Elfen und ihre Fotografinnen aus Yorkshire, ließ sich mit dem Zauberer Houdini ein und verstritt sich mit ihm. Er setzte sich für den als Hochverräter verurteilten Iren Roger Casement ein. Er war Arzt und Boxer, Patriot und Okkultist, gläubiger Rationalist, romantischer Technikfan und Verteidiger der Unschuldigen, oft blind, aber immer mutig: Stoff also für viele biographische Romane, die nicht ausbleiben sollten.

Bei solcher Diversität stellt sich die Frage nach dem einigenden Band. Musste eine solche Person nicht in viele Figuren zerfallen, so wie der Lissabonner Handelskorrespondent Fernando Pessoa (1888–1935) in seinen Heteronymen verschiedene Leben auslebte? Ihn deshalb zu pathologisieren, wie dies etwa Dr. Andrew Norman in seiner Biographie *Arthur Conan Doyle – Beyond Sherlock Holmes* getan hat, indem er Doyle eine von seinem Vater ererbte *delusional disorder* zuschreibt, halte ich für unproduktiv (Norman 172).

Doyle erhielt sich, denke ich, seine Identität durch eine unglaubliche Dynamik, in der rastlos eine Aktivität die andere ablöste. Insbesondere schockiert immer wieder die augenscheinliche Unvereinbarkeit der Rationalität eines Holmes mit der Irrationalität seines Schöpfers. Der lässt Holmes angesichts eines Falles von Vampirismus sogar folgenden bemerkenswerten Satz sprechen: "This agency stands flat-footed upon the ground, and there it must remain. The world is big enough for us. No ghosts need apply" ("The Adventure of the Sussex Vampire" 99).

Doch genau das sollten sie von nun an tun. Ganze Heerscharen von Geistern klopften an die Tür des Erfinders des berühmtesten Detektivs, den die Welt je kannte, insbesondere als er sich im Verlauf des Weltkriegs immer mehr dem Spiritismus näherte. Aber abgesehen davon, dass es mit Holmes' Rationalität auch nicht immer weit her ist – er konnte in Musik schwelgen, in Melancholie und in Kokain –, stellt auch seine eigentliche Arbeit ein Exorzismusprogramm dar, mit dem Vampire ebenso wie geisterhafte Hunde aus der Welt geschafft wurden – als Zeichen einer unerklärlichen Welt, die nicht unerklärt bleiben durfte. Der andere Doyle dagegen machte sich auf eine weltumspannende Mission für eben die Geister, die er gerufen hatte. Hier lebte er das von der Wissenschaft Verdrängte aus, und darin zeigt sich eine erste Verwandtschaft mit Holmes: Scotland Yard nämlich verkörpert ebenso den Positivismus wie es die Wissenschaft tat, und Detektiv und Okkultist sind daher beide gleichermaßen in antagonistischer Stellung zu den Autoritäten ihrer Zeit und Zunft. Vertretung individueller Einsicht gegenüber gesellschaftlichen Mehrheiten ist die eine Seite der Medaille. Die andere

Seite besteht darin, dass beide in einem Feldzug gegen Angst und Unwissenheit begriffen waren. Beide Seiten stehen für die Auseinandersetzung mit Verdrängung, gesellschaftlicher wie weltanschaulicher und psychologischer Art. Zum Bild gehört, dass wer sich mit Verdrängtem auseinandersetzt, sich oft lächerlich macht; darin ging es Doyle nicht anders als Sigmund Freud. Aus heutiger Sicht – weil wir die Hölle verdrängen –, erscheint uns auch das Unterfangen Galileos, Dantes Hölle auszumessen, als eher fragwürdig bis lächerlich.

So ist es auch kein Wunder, dass sich Doyles Interesse an den Erscheinungen des Übernatürlichen schon viel eher, vor oder parallel zu den Sherlock-Holmes-Geschichten, entwickelte. Literarisch drückte sich dieses Interesse in zahlreichen Spuk- und Gespenstergeschichten und in phantastischen Erzählungen aus. Bislang gibt es – bis auf eine französische Dissertation (Michal 2004) – keine umfassende Darstellung und Analyse dieser zahlreichen Erzählungen und Romane.

Doyle schreitet hier den gesamten Kosmos der Phantastik aus, und das heißt eben auch eine Tour durch die menschliche Psyche mit all ihren Abgründen und Ausfällen zu unternehmen. So ist Angst und ihre Überwindung wie in den Sherlock-Holmes-Erzählungen ein leitendes Thema in vielen seiner phantastischen Geschichten. Die Angst bezieht sich zumeist auf etwas Unkontrollierbares. Als solches bieten sich Gegenstände und Menschen mit einem exotisch-kolonialen Hintergrund an ("The Brown Hand", "The Ring of Thoth"). Psyche wie Empire enthalten Impulse und Bewegungen, die vom herrschenden Ich wie der britischen Zentralmacht als Bedrohung empfunden werden. Eine weitere unkontrollierbare Macht wird von der Frau verkörpert oder vom Weiblichen schlechthin ("The Parasite", "John Barrington Cowles"). Die Natur selbst, ob als weiblich konnotiert oder nicht, stellt gleichfalls ein Territorium des Unbeherrschbaren dar – als Erdbeben ("When the Earth Screamed") oder als Ort des Monströsen ("The Blue John Gap", "The Lost World"). Das Innere des Menschen und die äußere Welt bilden oft eine Wechselbeziehung heraus, so dass psychisches Geschehen und phänomenale Wirklichkeit unterscheidbar werden.

Bei einer mesmeristischen Geschichte wie "The Parasite" wird dies besonders sinnfällig. Der Erzähler wird zur Marionette einer weiblichen Mesmeristin aus der Karibik und kann kaum noch einen eigenen Willen und damit ein eigenes Bild seiner Welt erzeugen. Es kann auch zu einem Identitätstausch kommen wie in "The Great Keinplatz Experiment", der allerdings vor allem auf seine grotesk-komischen Elemente reduziert wird. (Keinplatz ist nicht nur der Name einer berühmten deutschen Universitätsstadt, sondern auch die Übersetzung des Wortes "Utopie".) Unbeherrschbarkeit äußert sich oft in Gegenständen. Die *Tücke des Objekts*, wie Friedrich Theodor Vischer sie 1879 bezeichnet hat, lauert in den Dingen und wird unterschiedlich erklärt. Oft hängt die Renitenz oder die Gefahr, die von einem Gegenstand ausgeht, in seiner Vergangenheit. Er wird zum Speicher vergangenen Geschehens, nicht anders als der Phonograph in "The Japanned Box". In "The Leather Funnel" oder in Erzählungen über Mumien ("The Ring of Toth", "Lot No. 249") schlägt die verdrängte Vergangenheit bösartig nicht nur in die Träume, sondern auch in die Realität hinein. Das Objekt wird zu einem Emblem der unbeherrschbaren und unbewältigten Vergangenheit. Die logische Verknüpfung besteht in der Vorstellung, dass Materie geistige Schwingungen speichern kann, sowie in Vorstellungen von Reinkarnation und Rückführungen in frühere Leben. All dies könnte, unter einem psychoanalytischen Gesichtspunkt, als magische Umschreibungen für psychische Sachverhalte gelesen werden. In diesem Sinne handelt es sich bei Doyles phantastischen Erzählungen um Vermessungen des Ich, die auch die unauslotbaren Tiefen und Dimensionen mit einschließen wollen. Ähnlich wie die Erzählungen H. G. Wells', die immer nur unter dem Signum Science Fiction kursieren, ließen sich Doyles Texte als Niederschriften psychischer Erlebnisse dekodieren, die etwa den Fallgeschichten von Neurologen wie A. R. Luria, Oliver Sacks oder Vilaynur S. Ramachandran an die Seite zu stellen wären (vgl. Schenkel, *H. G. Wells* 221–245).

Viele seiner Geschichten lassen sich als Schnittpunkt verschiedener Diskurse lesen und sind angesiedelt zwischen Ästhetik, Psychologie, Politik, Naturwissenschaft und Religion. Als Beispiel möge die Erzählung "The Horror of the Heights" dienen, die im wörtlichen Sinn auch eine "Fallgeschichte" ist.

"The Horror of the Heights"

Im November 1913 veröffentlichte Conan Doyle in *The Strand* eine Erzählung unter dem Titel "The Horror of the Heights". Auf einer Wiese an der Grenze zwischen Kent und Sussex findet man ein fragmentarisches Manuskript, das in der Wissenschaft als "the Joyce-Armstrong Fragment" bekannt wurde. Der Erzähler wehrt sich gegen alle Gerüchte, dass es sich um einen Streich handeln könnte (mit Streichen hatte Doyle ja eine besondere Bekanntschaft, von Harry Houdini und dem Piltdown Man bis hin zu den Elfenfotos):

> The idea that the extraordinary narrative which has been called the Joyce-Armstrong Fragment is an elaborate practical joke evolved by some unknown person, cursed by a perverted and sinister sense of humour, has now been abandoned by all who have examined the matter. ("The Horror of the Heights" 325)

Die Beglaubigungsstrategien sind rhetorische Formen, dem Monströsen und Ungeheuerlichen einen Raum zu geben, sozusagen die Anführungsstriche für das, was nun kommen wird. Noch in der Doppelung des Namens klingt ein wissenschaftlicher Habitus an, etwa das "Michelson-Morley Experiment" (1881/87), durch das die Annahme widerlegt wurde, das Licht bewege sich im Medium des "Äthers". Am 15. September entdeckt ein Farmarbeiter eine Pfeife und ein Notizbuch mit losen Blättern. Er nimmt das Notizbuch, von dem einige Seiten verlorengegangen sind, mit zu einem gebildeten Gentleman in Hartfield (dorthin übrigens, wo wenige Jahre später Winnie-the-Pooh leben wird). Der Aero-Club in London übernimmt den Fall und untersucht das Dokument. Man kennt dessen Autor Joyce-Armstrong als einen der kühnsten Fliegerpioniere, der auch neue Apparaturen erfunden hat, so das "Joyce-Armstrong Gyroscopic Attachment" (326). 1817 war das rotierende Navigationsgerät von Johann Bohnenberger erfunden worden, 1904 wurde es entscheidend verbessert von (man achte auf den Doppelnamen) Hermann Anschütz-Kämpfe. Dieser deutsche Erfinder machte das Gerät kriegsfähig, vor allem für U-Boote, sein amerikanischer Kollege Elmer Sperry machte den Kreiselkompass ebenfalls einsatzfähig (vgl. "Gyroscope"). Das Manuskript ist größtenteils in Tinte geschrieben, die letzten Zeilen allerdings mit Bleistift hingekritzelt. Auf der letzten Seite und dem Umschlag finden sich Spuren von wahrscheinlich menschlichem Blut, sicherlich aber von einem Säugetier ("certainly mammalian", 327). Der letzte Hinweis ist ominös, denn er eröffnet einen neuen Horizont: den der Evolution und des Rätsels. Halten wir fest, dass Joyce-Armstrongs Manuskript von Kampf gezeichnet ist, und zwar, wie man wohl annehmen muss, einem Kampf in der Luft. Es kommt allerdings hinzu, dass man in dem Blut Malariaspuren entdeckt hat. Der zeitgeiststolze Erzähler erwähnt dies hauptsächlich, um auf die technische Modernität hinzuweisen: "a remarkable example of the new weapons which modern science has placed in the hands of our detectives" (327). Der Aspekt des Kampfes bleibt erhalten, wird aber verlagert auf den Angriff der Medizin und der Naturwissenschaften auf die Natur. Allerdings ist der Hinweis auf gelegentliche Fieberattacken, die Joyce-Armstrong aufgrund seiner Malaria erlitt, auch ein Mauseloch für den Erzähler. Wenn alles gelogen sein sollte, so ist es doch wenigstens ein Fiebertraum gewesen. Mit dieser Andeutung sowie der Beschreibung des Piloten beginnt der Boden unter den Füßen des Lesers schwankend zu werden. Wir erfahren, dass Joyce-Armstrong ein Exzentriker war, wohlhabend, er besaß vier Flugzeuge, und er machte im letzten Jahr 170 Flüge. Introvertiert, depressiv, menschenscheu war er, ein Dichter, Träumer, Mechaniker und Erfinder. Ein Kollege hielt ihn für morbid. Die Tatsache, dass er immer ein Gewehr mit ins Flugzeug nahm, ließ nichts Gutes ahnen. Der Fall des Leutnant Myrtle machte ihn nur noch düsterer. Myrtle stürzte bei einem Rekordversuch aus 10 000 m Höhe. Rumpf und Glieder blieben erkennbar, doch sein Kopf war verschwunden. Seither pflegte Joyce-Armstrong mit einem rätselhaften Lächeln zu fragen: "And where, pray, is Myrtle's head?" (327).

In dieser Frage verrätselt sich die Geschichte selbst und erzeugt eine weitere narrative Instabilität. Weiß Joyce-Armstrong mehr als die anderen? Das wird jedenfalls angedeutet in seinen Reaktionen auf Gespräche, die andere Piloten über die Gefahren in der Höhe führen. Er zuckt nur mit den Schultern und gibt selbst keine Auskunft, so als wüsste er mehr. Eine solche Kenntnis schließt der Erzähler auch aus der Tatsache, dass der Pilot vor seinem letzten Flug seine privaten Angelegenheiten bis ins Detail geregelt hatte.

Nun hebt der Binnenerzähler in Form des blutgetränkten, fragmentarischen Tagebuchs an und sogleich beginnt er mit dem, was er den anderen verschwiegen hat. Er vermutet nämlich, dass es in der Luft, jenseits der 30 000-Fuß-Marke, also etwa 10 km, eine andere Welt gibt: "There are jungles of the upper air, and there are worse things than tigers which inhabit them" (329). Von zweien dieser Luftdschungel ist er überzeugt – nämlich über Pau-Biarritz in Frankreich und in Wiltshire direkt über ihm –, einen dritten vermutet er über dem Gebiet Homburg-Wiesbaden (329). Er geht dann die Indizien für eine solche Wildnis über unseren Köpfen durch, vor allem beschäftigt ihn das Verschwinden von Fliegern sowie Myrtles Kopf. Als man Myrtle auffand, war sein Rumpf völlig ölverschmiert. Joyce-Armstrong beschließt sodann einen Aufstieg in diese Höhen, um mehr über den Luftdschungel herauszufinden, auch mit dem Risiko, dabei sein Leben zu verlieren.

Angezogen wie ein Polarforscher, steigt er mit seinem Eindecker auf, spiralförmig (331) geht es über die Ebene von Salisbury in die Höhe. Dabei versteigt er sich auch in eine Hymne auf die moderne Technik und ihre Märtyrer: "If only the early aviators could come back to see the beauty and perfection of the mechanism which have been bought at the cost of their lives!" (332). Spiralig geht es durch das Wolkenmeer (333), dann ist er allein, nur noch einzelne Vogelschwärme ziehen vorüber. Mit den Vögeln sieht er den Menschen nun verbrüdert (333). In einem Luftstrudel unter sich entdeckt er einen fernen weißen Doppeldecker, vermutlich der Morgenpostflug nach London. Der Kompass wird allmählich unzuverlässig (334). Er muss einen Kampf mit unerwartetem Wind aufnehmen und erreicht gegen Mittag die 6-km-Grenze. Der Flug des Menschen kommt ihm erhaben vor, selbstlos, heldenhaft – das Gegenteil von Entartung ("degeneration", 335). Nach diesen erbaulichen und idealisierenden Gedanken sieht er sich plötzlich in Windwirbeln gefangen, die ihn nach unten ziehen, und zwar in die Spitze eines Kegels hinein ("a cone rather than a funnel", 335), doch mit Geschick und Mut gelingt ihm der Wiederaufstieg in der Aufwärtsspirale. Neue Euphorie erfasst ihn, er inhaliert auch aus seinem Sauerstoffbehälter und gerät in einen Rausch. Die Kälte der Höhen erinnert ihn an Ballonaufstiege von Glaisher und Coxwell von 1862. In der Höhe von 10 500 m zieht etwas Rauchendes vorbei, das zischt und explodiert: Meteoriten (336). Er ist sich dessen bewusst, dass er bald das Stratum verlässt, das die Erde vor kosmischen Bomben schützt, das heißt, er ist auf dem Weg in die absolut schutzlose und konfrontative Welt, für die der Mensch nicht geschaffen ist. Bei 13 000 m kreist er ziellos herum auf der Suche nach jenem Dschungel. Nichts zu sehen. Doch dann trübt sich die Luft ein und etwas wie ganz feiner Zigarettenrauch zieht vor ihm her, kranz- und kreisförmig. Als er hindurchfliegt, bemerkt er etwas Öliges – man erinnert sich an Myrtle! Sollte es sich um ein Lebewesen handeln oder eine Spur davon? Oder vielleicht eine Form der Nahrung für andere riesige Lebewesen des Himmels, so wie Plankton für den Wal? Und dann wird er überrumpelt von einer wahrhaftigen Erscheinung: eine riesige glockenförmige Qualle segelt über ihm hinweg, größer als St. Paul's (338). Ganz rosa, aber grün durchädert, pulsiert sie ganz regelmäßig, während sie zwei lange Fangarme mit sich zieht. Nun folgt diesem schönen Geschöpf eine ganze Flotte kleinerer Quallen wie eine Schar von Ballons – alles sehr schön, zart grün-rosa schimmernd, Hunderte von ihnen. Doch hinter und über ihnen tun sich weitere Wesen auf, Luftschlangen, "serpents of the outer air" (339), die sich mit großer Geschwindigkeit drehen und winden. Es sind gespenstige Wesen in Grau oder rauchfarben, in denen er wirkliche Organismen zu sehen scheint. Die schrecklichste Erscheinung ist aber ein violetter Dunst, der aus der Höhe stürzt und immer größer wird. Er ist um ein Vieles körperlicher als die anderen Phänomene. So hat er etwa einen dunklen runden Teller auf beiden Seiten, es sind möglicherweise Augen, zwischen denen sich etwas Weißes erhebt wie ein Geierschnabel. Hinzu kommt, dass es immer wieder die Farbe und die Gestalt ändert. Auf dem Wesen sind drei blasenartige Erhebungen auszumachen, in denen er extrem leichtes Gas vermutet, mit dem der Auf- und Abstieg geregelt wird. Dann der Angriff: das Wesen wickelt ihn ein mit seinen Tentakeln, Joyce-Armstrong schießt und eine der Blasen zerplatzt, so dass das Monster sein Gleichgewicht verliert. Es torkelt davon, und am Ende sieht er nur noch einen violetten Fleck am blauen Himmel.

Spiralförmig geht er nun hinab in der Nähe des Bristol Channel, nahe dem Dorf Ashcombe[1] (341), um zu tanken und dann nach Hause, nach Devizes in Wiltshire, zu fliegen. Das Notizbuch in Tinte endet mit dem Wunsch, noch einmal aufzusteigen und das Rätsel des Luftdschungels zu ergründen. Es folgt eine Lücke und schließlich, mit Bleistift hingeworfen, der Ausruf: "Forty-three thousand feet. I shall never see earth again. They are beneath me, three of them. God help me; it is a dreadful death to die!" (342). Hier endet das Manuskript und der erste Erzähler beschließt den Text mit Hinweisen, wo die Reste des Flugzeugs aufgefunden wurden (in der Nähe des Notizbuchs an der Grenze von Sussex und Kent) sowie mit Rückschlüssen über den Hergang des Absturzes. Er vermutet, dass Joyce-Armstrong aus dem Luftdschungel über Wiltshire Richtung Osten geflohen ist und dabei von den schrecklichen Monstern über dem Fundort verschlungen worden ist:

> The picture of that monoplane skimming down the sky, with the nameless terrors flying as swiftly beneath it and cutting it off always from the earth while they gradually closed in upon their victim, is one upon which a man who valued his sanity would prefer not to dwell. (343)

Es spricht also manches dagegen, sich mit diesem Text zu beschäftigen; wir wollen es aber dennoch wagen. Gerade diese Warnung

---

[1] Ashcombe House in Somerset wurde übrigens später von Peter Gabriel bewohnt, Ashcombe House in Wiltshire von Guy Ritchie und Madonna.

macht ja deutlich, dass wir es mit psychischen Tatbeständen ebenso zu tun haben wie mit einem rätselhaften Flugzeugabsturz.

Das 19. Jahrhundert mit seinem Fortschrittsglauben hatte den Himmel für seine nächsten Schritte in die Zukunft entdeckt, und er schien unendlich offen zu sein wie die Zukunft und das Glück, das man sich durch Technik, Transport und Hygiene erhoffte. Die Freiheit des Himmels stand für den offenen Geschichtsentwurf. Diese neue *frontier* wurde lange vor Kennedy entdeckt. Ich würde behaupten, sie tritt mit den ersten Ballonfahrten nicht zufällig in der Zeit um die Französische Revolution in Erscheinung: sieben Jahre davor waren die Brüder Montgolfier in die Luft gegangen. Es folgten die ersten Flugversuche von Lilienthal (1891) und den Brüdern Wright (1900), schließlich überquerte Blériot 1909 den Ärmelkanal. Zwei Monate später besuchte Franz Kafka die Flugschau von Brescia, an der die berühmtesten Flieger der Zeit teilnehmen, auch Blériot. Während die Volksstimmung aufgeheizt wird und sich Gabriele d'Annunzio als Flieger betätigt und Hymnen auf den Übermenschen der Luft verfasst, schaut Puccini von der Bühne und Kafka macht sich Notizen. Die Franzosen waren die führende Fliegernation in diesen Jahren, gefolgt von den Briten. Die Deutschen hatten sich zu lange mit der Luftschifferei aufgehalten und kamen erst ab 1910 mit Hilfe des Kronprinzen Heinrich in den Tritt. Zwischen 1912 und 1914 wurden dann sämtliche Flugrekorde durch die Deutschen gebrochen (vgl. Wissmann, Vogt). Dieser Kontext ist auch für Doyle wichtig, nicht nur weil er selbst an dem Prinz-Heinrich-Autorennen 1911 von Deutschland nach England teilgenommen und eine kriegerische Stimmung bemerkt hatte (Doyle, *Memories* 271–273). Die deutsche Aufrüstung beunruhigte ihn wie die meisten Bewohner und Politiker des Empire. Und während sich Sherlock Holmes über die Bruce-Partington-Pläne beugen wird, wird Doyle nicht nur Leserbriefe schreiben, sondern auch eine kleine Freiwilligentruppe trainieren. In seiner Autobiographie sieht er eine Zukunft für das Fliegen wie für das Auto – beide Technologien sind ja fast gleichzeitig entstanden. Er erinnert sich an einen gloriosen Aufstieg im Ballon und einen frühen Flug 1911 mit einem Doppeldecker, der gerade noch glimpflich verlief (Doyle,

Memories 250f.) – genug, um sich eine Horrorgeschichte auszudenken. Dafür hatte er natürlich Modelle, insbesondere bei dem von ihm bewunderten Edgar Allan Poe. Er knüpft, wie schon erwähnt, an die Tradition der fragmentarischen Botschaften an, die den Erzähler aus einer anderen Welt erreichen. Größtes Vorbild dürfte hier Poes Erzählung "MS. Found in a Bottle" (1833) sein, in dem ein ähnlich monströser Stoff die Nachwelt durch ein Manuskript erreicht. Inhaltlich gibt es auch Parallelen zu Poes "A Descent into the Maelström" (1841), in dem der Erzähler durch Wasserstrudel in die Tiefe gerissen, dann allerdings dank kalkulatorischer Fähigkeiten wieder nach oben gespült wird. Bei Doyle wimmelt es von Spiralen und Wirbeln in der Luft, und Joyce-Armstrong sieht sich einmal an der nach unten gerichteten Spitze eines Kegels. Wenn Poe Vorgaben gemacht hat, so zielen diese aber auch auf den Beginn des literarischen Modernismus. Gerade diese Bewegungsformen spielen eine große Rolle in der ästhetischen Revolution, die Ezra Pound, der Expressionismus und der Futurismus hervorgebracht haben. Spiralen tauchen in Pounds und Wyndham Lewis' Ideen vom Vortex auf als symbolischer Grundlage des Vortizismus, der Energie, Dynamik und Maschine zu Leitfiguren erhob, und zwar genau in der Zeit, als Doyle seine Geschichte veröffentlichte. Der Vortizismus hatte nur ein kurzes Leben, nämlich von 1913 bis 1915, doch das Konzept der Spirale und des Kegels lebte fort, etwa in W. B. Yeats' geschichtsphilosophischer Mythologie der *Gyres*, wie er sie in seinem okkulten Werk *A Vision* (1925) dargelegt hat. Bei Doyle sehen wir auch die fast erotische Verehrung, die der Flieger für seine Flugmaschine hegt. Er ist ein britischer Vertreter des Flugkultes, der bei Gabriele d'Annunzio und den Futuristen noch ganz andere Dimensionen annehmen sollte (vgl. Ingold 59–61). Aber auch für Joyce-Armstrong ist der Flug ein Mittel, den Menschen weiter und höher hinaus zu tragen, wenn nicht zum Übermenschen zu machen, so doch die damals gefürchtete "Entartung" zu bremsen: "Talk of human degeneration! When has such a story as this been written in the annals of our race?" (335). Die Evolution geht weiter und zwar in die Höhe.

Poes Geschichten erinnern uns jedoch daran, dass die Schauplätze des Monströsen zuvor eher in der Tiefe angesiedelt waren, was etwa auf sein Vorbild S. T. Coleridge ("The Rime of the Ancient Mariner") wie auf seinen eigenen Roman *The Narrative of Arthur Gordon Pym of Nantucket* (1838) verweist. Im 19. Jahrhundert begannen Wissenschaft und Literatur die Schrecken und Schönheiten der Tiefsee zu erkunden (vgl. Schenkel, "Nachrichten aus der Tiefe"). Die britische *Challenger*-Expedition von 1872–76 lieferte Grundlagen der modernen Ozeanographie und drang erstmals in unbekannte Tiefen vor. Mit etwa 4700 neuen Arten kam sie zurück. Wenige Jahre zuvor hatte allerdings schon Jules Verne sich der Tiefe gewidmet mit seinem Roman *Vingt mille lieues sous les mers* (1869–70). Spätere Erzähler, wie etwa Wells, haben die Ungeheuer der Tiefe ausgelotet. Die Höhe blieb zunächst von Ungeheuern verschont – bis zum ersten Jahrzehnt des 20. Jahrhunderts. Dann begann Wells sich mit der Luftfahrt und ihrer militärischen Nutzung zu beschäftigen. 1908 erschien sein Roman über den Luftkrieg: *The War in the Air*, in dem die Deutschen New York bombardieren. 1914 fällt in einem anderen seiner Romane, *The World Set Free*, die erste Atombombe. Es sind also die Menschen, die den Luftraum mit Ungeheuern anfüllen.

Nicht so in Will A. Pages Erzählung "The Air Serpent" (1911), die ein direkter Vorläufer von Doyles Geschichte zu sein scheint. Hier stoßen Piloten in der Höhe von 12 000 m auf ein walgroßes Monster mit sechzig Flügeln, eine Mischung aus Fledermaus und Schlange. In einem Luftkampf stürzt der Maschinist von Bord und fällt in das weitgeöffnete Maul des Bösen hinein. Der Pilot ist nach der Rückkehr vor allem empört, dass sein Rekordflug nicht anerkannt wird, und die Geschichte vom Monster, das Maschinisten verschlingt, glaubt ihm sowieso keiner. Am Schluss seiner Rede an die Gentlemen des Aero Club zieht er die Vertikale von der Tiefsee in die Höhe:

> And then, gentlemen, the world will realize that just as in the farthest depths of the sea, there are strange monsters we have never seen, so in the thin upper strata of

air there are tenuous creatures living in a world of their own, which we have never seen. (Page 7)

Wenn wir uns die von Doyle beschriebenen Monster anschauen, so ähneln sie in der Tat nicht Vögeln oder Drachen, sondern Ungeheuern der Tiefsee: Quallen. Die Beschreibung des Flugs erinnert eher an eine Fahrt mit dem U-Boot durch die Abgründe des Meeres. Die Glockenquallen, deren zarte Transparenz ihre Bedrohlichkeit verbirgt, stehen für eine Ästhetik um die Jahrhundertwende, die sich aus den wunderbaren Erscheinungen der Natur nährte. Der Jugendstil betonte wallende Formen, Schlingmuster, organisch-fließende Gestalten. 1904 veröffentlichte der deutsche Hauptvertreter des Darwinismus, der Jenaer Biologe Ernst Haeckel, den Klassiker *Kunstformen der Natur*. Dieses opulente Werk enthielt die merkwürdigsten Formen der Schöpfung, Radiolarien, Quallen, Panzerkrebse und Igelsterne. Haeckel wollte die ästhetische Komponente der Evolution darstellen und kam damit dem Bedürfnis nach, Technik und Natur zur Einheit zu bringen. Um dieselbe Zeit baute etwa Renée Binet das Eingangstor zur Weltausstellung in Paris 1900 nach dem Vorbild einer Radiolarienzeichnung von Haeckel (Haeckel 27).

Auch Doyle begab sich in einem seiner unbekannt gebliebenen Romane in die Tiefe: *The Maracot Deep* (1929). Gleich zu Anfang wird Haeckels Werk erwähnt:

> I remember that you laughed when I asked him what I ought to read as a preparation, and he said that for serious study I should read the collected edition of his own works, but for relaxation Haeckel's Plankton-Studien. (Doyle, *The Maracot Deep* 7)

Luft und Meer sind demnach austauschbar in "The Horror of the Heights". Aber es ist nicht nur die Tiefsee, die die Bilder eines bewohnten Luftraums liefert. In der Luftfahrt der Neuzeit scheint der Himmel stets rein gewesen zu sein, kartiert und einzig meteorologisch manchmal unberechenbar. Die Ballonfahrer berichten nicht von Ängsten über Wesen, die sie überfallen könnten in der Luft, und Piloten kämpfen mit ganz anderen Problemen als aggressiven

Quallen am Himmel. Doch Doyle nutzt wieder einmal eine große wissenschaftsgeschichtliche Chance, indem er seine Geschichte zu einer Zeit schreibt, als der Luftraum tatsächlich noch kaum bekannt war. Begriffe wie Stratosphäre, Ionosphäre oder Mesosphäre kommen erst später auf. Als Heinrich Hertz 1886 die elektromagnetischen Wellen entdeckte, glaubte er nicht, dass diese über größere Distanzen gehen könnten, weil er noch nichts von der Ionosphäre wusste. Diese wurde erst 1924 nachgewiesen.[2] Das Bild von der Erdatmosphäre war noch sehr mangelhaft (vgl. Walker, passim). So war hier ein idealer neuer Rahmen gegeben für Projektionen aller Art – seien sie biologischer, politischer oder ästhetischer Natur. Doyle greift dabei auf einen alten mythologischen Fundus zurück, um diesen Raum zu besiedeln. Der *horror vacui* wird so schnellstens besetzt mit ältesten Requisiten. Schließlich gab es im Mittelalter und in der frühen Neuzeit die Sichtungen von Luftschiffen oder anderen Wesen im Himmel. Von der Antike bis zur frühen Neuzeit war der Zwischenraum zwischen Erde und Himmel, zwischen Mensch und Gottheit bevölkert mit allerlei Wesen, Omen und Orakeln: Dämonen, Geistern, Engeln, Drachen, langhaarigen Sternen, Feuerzeichen. Und was kam nicht alles von oben herunter: Frösche, Fische, Bratpfannen, Pfeile oder Blut (Warner 98). Der exzentrische Wissenschaftler Charles Fort dokumentierte in seinen Büchern gar Eidechsenregen sowie weitere ungewöhnliche Objekte, die vom Himmel fallen: Seeungeheuer, Meteoriten mit Inschriften und Würmer (Magin 87). Noch war der Raum nicht physikalisch, chemisch und meteorologisch bereinigt, d. h. erklärt. Über unseren Köpfen entfaltete sich eine riesige Rorschach-Landschaft. Nicht selten musste man sich dagegen wehren. Karl der Große soll Gesetze gegen fliegende Sturmdämonen erlassen haben (Behringer/Ott-Koptschalijski 167).

Doyles Erzählung steht am Schnittpunkt verschiedener ideengeschichtlicher Linien und zeigt sich als eine Überlagerung von

---

[2] Guglielmo Marconi störte das Unwissen nicht. 1901 übermittelte er erstmals einen Buchstaben mit Hilfe drahtloser Telegraphie von Cornwall nach Neufundland – über den Umweg der unbekannten Ionosphäre.

ästhetischen, technischen und evolutionären Diskursen. Diese wiederum sehen sich konfrontiert mit atavistischen Erfahrungen, mit denen zuvor nur die Wildnis, der Dschungel oder die Tiefsee aufwarten konnten. Doyle verlagert das Schema des nach unten ins Meer und in die Tiefe projizierten Unbewussten in die Höhe: unten wird oben. Wo einst das Ich war, nämlich auf der Höhe der Dinge, die es im Griff hatte, ist nun Es. Der Aufstieg ist nicht länger räumliche Darstellung von Fortschritt, sondern Ankunft in der Verwirrung. Die Menschen nehmen ihre Probleme mit, wohin sie auch gehen, möge der Ort noch so utopisch oder göttlich sein. Diese Behauptung gilt zumal im Jahre 1913, einer Zeit, in der der Krieg förmlich in der Luft lag. Der Himmel füllte sich damals mit neuartigen, technischen Geräten. Von diesen sieht Joyce-Armstrong einige, etwa die Morgenpost nach London, aber ansonsten ist die Troposphäre von Quallen bewohnt. Sie ähneln weniger Flugzeugen als vielmehr Zeppelinen und Ballons. Mit diesen Formen wird wohl auf die deutsche Gefahr hingewiesen, möglicherweise schwingen noch Erinnerungen mit an Napoleons Versuche, England mit Hilfe einer Armee von Ballons zu erobern.

Die zwei anderen Luftdschungel Europas, von denen Joyce-Armstrong spricht, befinden sich über Homburg-Wiesbaden und Pau-Biarritz. Beide stehen für Kurorte und Sommerfrischen europäischer Kaiser und Fürsten. Wiesbaden nannte sich gerne Kaiserstadt aufgrund der Besuche Wilhelms II., in Biarritz traf sich die mondäne Welt von der Kaiserin Eugénie bis Sisi. Die Orte stehen somit für ein altes aristokratisches Europa, das mit dem Ersten Weltkrieg weggefegt sein wird. Der britische Dschungel liegt dagegen direkt über dem Feld des Royal Flying Corps, das später zur RAF wird. 1912 stürzte dort erstmals ein Flieger ab, doch die Übungen wurden am selben Tag weiter durchgeführt. Es ist möglich, dass Doyle aus dieser Episode seine Inspiration zog. Es kam ihm allerdings auch zupass, dass der Ort neuester Technik sich wenige Kilometer von einem der ältesten sakralen Orte der Welt befindet, nämlich Stonehenge. Von daher lässt sich nun Joyce-Armstrongs Aufstieg auch deuten als eine Art Reprise der Flüge von steinzeitlichen Schamanen. Das würde bedeuten, dass der Pilot über den

Wolken in einen psychischen Raum vorstößt und sich mit Archetypen der Seele auseinanderzusetzen hat, mit inneren und äußeren Dämonen. Der zeitgenössische Okkultismus, allen voran die Theosophie, hatte den Äther in der Tat mit diesen archaischen Wesen wieder besiedelt und sie der populären Literatur als Motive zugeführt (vgl. Lembert). Die schamanistische Version der Symbolik in Doyles Erzählung kann sich auf die Geschichten um Odin beziehen. In der nordischen Mythologie geht Odin auf eine solche Reise in die Höhe, indem er am Weltenbaum Yggdrasil hochklettert und in immer neue Dimensionen vorstößt, um den Met der Weisheit zu finden (vgl. Bates 55–61). Joyce-Armstrong wird in die Höhe getrieben, durch den Wunsch, über die bekannte Welt hinauszukommen, durch Neugier und den Ehrgeiz, Rekorde zu brechen. Aber er will auch wissen, warum die anderen abgestürzt sind und wo Myrtles Kopf sich befindet. Am Weltenbaum haben die Schamanen Markierungen hinterlegt, die ihre Aufstiegshöhe bezeichnen, ähnlich wie es uns die Höhenmesser bei Doyle verraten. Doch im Unterschied zu Odin, der mit seinem achtbeinigen Pferd zurückkehren wird, wirft der Himmel bei Doyle nur eine Leiche aus. Aus schamanistischer Sicht handelt es sich also um eine gescheiterte Initiation und als solche könnte man den Versuch des modernen Menschen betrachten, mit Hilfe von Technik und Wissenschaft den Met der Weisheit zu erreichen. Das Unsterblichkeitsprojekt der Moderne muss scheitern.

Ich möchte zum Schluss zum zentralen Angstsymbol der Geschichte zurückkehren: "And what about Myrtle's head?" Für die englische Geschichte ist die Köpfung seit der Enthauptung von Charles I. ein wiederkehrendes Trauma – in Dickens' *David Copperfield* ist Mr. Dick immer noch besessen von dem historischen Ereignis, und auch in *Alice in Wonderland* ruft die Königin immer wieder: "Kopf ab!" Man kann bis zu den Kelten zurückgehen, um diesen Kult der Enthauptung zu verfolgen. Bekanntlich war der Kopf des Feindes die beste Trophäe und man steckte sie auf Pfählen auf. Das keltisch inspirierte mittelalterliche Gedicht von *Sir Gawayne and the Grene Knight* führt diese Motivik fort. Doyles Geschichte gibt keine Antwort auf den Verbleib von Myrtles Kopf:

ist er in den Körper hineingestoßen worden beim Aufprall oder gibt es bei den höheren Schichten in der Atmosphäre gar einen ähnlichen Trophäenkult? Der Kopf des Piloten war in den frühen Maschinen, in denen er offen saß, natürlich besonders gefährdet. Ähnlich wie die Angst aus der Tiefe der Erde nach oben in den Luftraum verlegt wird, wird nun auch die Angst im Körper verschoben von den Beinen in den Kopf. Oben erwähnte ich, dass Kafka 1909 einer Flugschau in Italien beiwohnte. Über diese Schau von Brescia schrieb er nun seinen ersten Zeitungsartikel.

Kafka schaut auf den Hochadel, der sich wie in alten Zeiten versammelt, auf d'Annunzios Tänzchen vor einem Grafen, die Mode der Frauen, auf die Trinkernase Puccinis, dann wiederum beschreibt er die Schwierigkeiten der Mechaniker, die Apparate zum Fliegen zu bringen, das Warten auf den großen Blériot. Das Ganze findet in einer "künstliche[n] Einöde" (Kafka 70) statt, es gibt nicht mehr die Ablenkung der Sportfelder, ein großer Abstraktionsvorgang ist im Gange, vor dem sich das adlige Getue lächerlich und obsolet abzeichnet. Als Blériot dann auftaucht, fällt Kafka auf, wie fest ihm der Kopf auf dem Hals gewachsen ist (Kafka 71). Als Blériot endlich aufsteigt in seiner Monoplane, sieht alles "mit gerecktem Hals" zu (Kafka 73). Kafka notiert nüchtern: "Was geschieht denn? Hier oben ist 20 M. über der Erde ein Mensch in einem Holzgestell verfangen und wehrt sich gegen eine freiwillig übernommene unsichtbare Gefahr" (Kafka 73). Kafka, so Peter Demetz in seinem Buch über die Flugschau von Brescia, holt die Flieger, "selbst wenn sie haarscharf an einem Rekord vorbeigehen, vom Himmel herunter in die heimische und bürgerliche Welt der Schule und des Büros" (Demetz 120).

Doyle dagegen pflegt den Heroenkult, aber wie Kafka erscheint ihm der Himmel nicht als eine *tabula rasa* des Fortschritts, auf den sich Mensch und Technik endlos einschreiben können. Seine Mittel, den Zweifel, ja die Ausweglosigkeit auszudrücken, sind die Motive des Schauerromans: Monster, Rätsel, Einsamkeit, Kampf in den Lüften, das Erhabene des Luftraums. Beide aber ahnen, dass das Fliegen mit dem Kopf zu tun hat, dass der Kopf als erstes gefordert wird. Kafka betont die Hälse der Zuschauer und die Festigkeit von Blériots Kopf, als wollte er damit sagen, wie gefährdet eben dieser ist und wie notwendig dagegen, ihn zu behalten. Doyle schreibt den verlorenen Kopf dem Flieger Myrtle zu, der durch seinen Namen einen symbolischen Raum aufreißt. Der immergrüne Myrtenstrauch ist in der griechischen Mythologie einerseits der Aphrodite zugeordnet – sie entstieg dem Meer bei ihrer Geburt mit einem Myrtenkranz auf dem Haupt – , und steht daher für Liebe und Brautschaft. Andererseits ist sie in mehreren europäischen Kulturen auch eine Toten- und Unglückspflanze und findet daher gerade auf Friedhöfen ihre Verbreitung (*Handwörterbuch des deutschen Aberglaubens* 714–718). In dieser Ambivalenz spiegelt sich das Abenteuer der Piloten Doyles am Himmel wider. Sie vollziehen eine Einheit zwischen Unten und Oben, aber um den Preis ihres Lebens.

Der Verlust des Kopfes wird in einem berühmten Werk der Weltliteratur, in Dantes *Commedia*, ebenfalls kommentiert. Im Canto XXVIII des *Inferno* geht es nicht um einen Flieger, sondern um einen Dichter. Dante und Vergil stoßen auf einen Menschen, der seinen Kopf wie eine Laterne vor sich herschwenkt. Er stellt sich heraus als der große provenzalische Troubadour Bertran de Born. Er bekennt seine Schuld, denn er habe Vater und Sohn gegeneinander aufgewiegelt: "Weil ich so eng verbundene Personen trennte, trage ich nun – ach ! – mein Hirn getrennt von seinem Ursprung, der in diesem Rumpf liegt" (Dante 437). Aus der Sicht Dantes und des Mittelalters ist die Abtrennung des Kopfes vom Rumpf eine Folge moralischer Verfehlungen. Was aber haben die Flieger bei Doyle getrennt, dass ihnen ein ähnliches Schicksal zuteil wurde? Sie haben Mensch und Erde getrennt und sich nach Art der Schamanen in Räume bewegt, die ihnen als Techniker und moralisch unvorbereitete Wesen nicht zustanden. Auch in Kafkas Text steht diese Gefahr schon einbeschrieben, als Warnung an den Hals Blériots. Arthur Conan Doyle mag als Autor populärer Thriller und Horrorgeschichten durchgehen, im Hinter- und Untergrund seiner Texte stehen allerdings Archetypen bereit, die auch unsere moderne Existenz prägen. Dadurch bleibt er unser Zeitgenosse.

Literaturverzeichnis

Bates, Brian. *The Real Middle Earth: Magic and Mystery in the Dark Ages.* London: Pan Books, 2003.

Behringer, Wolfgang, und Constance Ott-Koptschalijski. *Der Traum vom Fliegen: Zwischen Mythos und Technik.* Frankfurt/M.: S. Fischer, 1991.

Dante Alighieri. *La commedia. Die Göttliche Komödie. I. Inferno/Hölle.* Italienisch/Deutsch. In Prosa übersetzt und kommentiert von Hartmut Köhler. Stuttgart: Reclam, 2010.

Demetz, Peter. *Die Flugschau von Brescia: Kafka, d'Annunzio und die Männer, die vom Himmel fielen.* Wien: Zsolnay, 2002.

Doyle, Sir Arthur Conan. "The Adventure of the Sussex Vampire". *The Case-Book of Sherlock Holmes.* Harmondsworth: Penguin, 1951. 98–115.

—. "The Horror of the Heights". *The Great Tales of Sir Arthur Conan Doyle.* London: Magpie Books, 1993. 325–43.

—. *The Maracot Deep.* London: Pan Books, 1977.

—. *Memories and Adventures.* Ware: Wordsworth, 2007.

"Gyroscope". 27. 4. 2011. <http://en.wikipedia.org/wiki/Gyroscope>.

Haeckel, Ernst. *Kunstformen der Natur.* Prestel: München, New York, 1998.

Handwörterbuch des deutschen Aberglaubens. Hg. von Hanns Bächtold-Stäubli, unter Mitwirkung von Eduard Hoffmann-Krayer. Band 6. Berlin: Walter de Gruyter, 1987.

Ingold, Felix Philipp. *Literatur und Aviatik: Europäische Flugdichtung 1909–1927.* Frankfurt/M.: Suhrkamp, 1980.

Kafka, Franz. *Unterwegs mit Franz Kafka.* Hg. von Sascha Michel. Frankfurt/M.: S. Fischer, 2010.

Lembert, Alexandra. "Nebulöse Gefilde. Äther in der britischen Literatur um 1900". *Äther: Ein Medium der Moderne.* Ed. Albert Kümmel-Schnur und Jens Schröter. Bielefeld: transcript, 2008. 205–222.

Magin, Ulrich. *Der Ritt auf dem Kometen: Über Charles Fort.* Frankfurt/M.: Zweitausendeins, 1997.

Michal, Hélène. *Conan Doyle: De Sherlock Holmes au professeur Challenger.* Rennes: Presses universitaires de Rennes, 2004.

Norman, Andrew. *Arthur Conan Doyle – Beyond Sherlock Holmes.* Stroud: Tempus, 2007.

Page, Will A. "The Air Serpent". *The Red Book Magazine*, April, 1911. 7. 4. 2011. <http://www.strangeark.com/cryptofiction/air-serpent.html>.

Schenkel, Elmar. *H. G. Wells – der Prophet im Labyrinth*. Wien: Zsolnay, 2001.
—. "Nachrichten aus der Tiefe. Unterwasserwelten von der Romantik bis zur Science Fiction". *Alles fließt: Dimensionen des Wassers in Natur und Kultur*. Ed. Elmar Schenkel und Alexandra Lembert. Frankfurt/M.: Peter Lang, 2008. 183–195.
Vogt, Dieter. *Das Jahrhundert des Flugzeugs*. Frankfurt/M.: Insel, 1993.
Walker, Gabrielle. *An Ocean of Air: A Natural History of the Atmosphere*. London: Bloomsbury, 2007.
Warner, Marina. *Phantasmagoria: Spirit Visions, Metaphors, and Media into the Twenty-first Century*. Oxford: OUP, 2006.
Wissmann, Gerhard. *Geschichte der Luftfahrt von Ikarus bis zur Gegenwart*. Berlin: VEB Verlag Technik, 1975.

Jana Nittel

A LASTING LEGACY

An Ecocritical Reading of Arthur Conan Doyle's "When the World Screamed"

SF-key contributors such as Mary Shelley, H. G. Wells, and Arthur Conan Doyle strongly mediated the concerns of their specific moment in history, and were by doing so instrumental in formularising genre templates, themes and conventions. Surveying the critical material on Conan Doyle as a prolific writer of imaginative fiction, it seems that the lasting influence of his oeuvre remains grossly underestimated or simply neglected. This paper proposes a rereading of one of Doyle's seminal science fiction stories utilizing an ecocritical approach that seeks to highlight the topicality and eerie contemporaneity of his conceptions. In the process the following explorations will highlight the degree of influence of Conan Doyle's lesser known stories, e. g. "When the World Screamed" (1928), on that part of the SF corpus that reflects the acknowledged shift to ecological concerns in late twentieth-century anglophone SF material in especially cinematic SF.

Mary Shelley, H. G. Wells, und Arthur Conan Doyle prägten mit ihrem literarischen Schaffen nicht nur maßgeblich die konzeptuelle und strukturelle Entwicklung der Phantastischen und Science Fiction Literatur, sondern verhandelten auch eindrucksvoll die gängigen Ängste und Widersprüche ihrer zeitgeschichtlichen Epoche. Blickt man jedoch auf die wissenschaftliche Diskussion der zahlreichen SF-Werke, so scheint es, dass besonders Arthur Conan Doyles Beitrag in diesem Genre der Vergessenheit anheimgefallen ist. Von einem interdisziplinären Ansatz ausgehend, welcher literarische Texte im Zusammenhang mit ökologischen Aspekten untersucht, unternimmt dieser Beitrag eine kritische Relektüre einer Kurzgeschichte aus Conan Doyles späterer Schaffensperiode. Der Beitrag zeigt die Einflüsse der weniger bekannten Geschichte "When the World Screamed" (1928) auf zeitgenössische filmische SF-Texte auf und verweist auf unveränderte Aktualität von Doyles thematischen und generischen Anliegen.

Arthur Conan Doyle's Legacy
to the World of English-language Science Fiction

In 2002, millions of cinema spectators around the world came to enjoy the computer-animated film *Ice Age*, the first instalment of a series of films, the fourth of which is scheduled for release in 2012. *Ice Age* maps the adventures of a group of Paleolithical mammals faced with the consequences of catastrophic and, presumably, cyclical climatic changes on planet Earth. In one of the various trailers promoting the 2009 release of the sequel *Ice Age: The Return of the Dinosaurs*, now in a 3 D format, the saber-toothed squirrel named Scrat, familiar to ardent followers of the commercially highly successful series as a hapless creature trying to hold on to a disproportionately large acorn, plunges through the cracking permafrost crust into the unknown depths at the planet's centre (cf. "Ice Age 3 – Official Trailer"). Attempting to retrieve his treasure, a recurrent subplot of the first three films, he instantly enrages an unsuspecting Tyrannosaurus rex in the process. The *Ice Age* series is of course only one example of the manifold contemporary renderings, fiction[1] and filmic adaptations[2] alike, of the theme of dinosaurs, cavemen, prehistoric men and animals, in short, the pre-

---

[1] A selected list of classic and contemporary science fiction texts in English that feature prehistoric worlds would include: H. G. Wells' "The Grisly Folk" (1921); Edgar Rice Burroughs' "The Land That Time Forgot" (1927); Philip Barshofsky's "One Prehistoric Night" (1934); John Taine's *Before the Dawn* (1934); Arthur C. Clarke's *2001: A Space Odyssey* (1968); George Gaylord Simpson's *The Dechronization of Sam Magruder* (1984), in addition to Michael Crichton's series *Jurassic Park* (1990) and *The Lost World* (1995).

[2] A selected list of the 'Lost Worlds' of Arthur Conan Doyle in terms of cinematic representations and/or TV serialisations may incorporate *The Lost World* (Harry Hoyt, 1925), a film that is historically important as the first feature-length dinosaur movie; *The Lost World* (Irvin Allen, 1960); *The Lost World* and *Return to the Lost World* (Harry Allen Towers, 1992), a programme sold as a two-part miniseries; *Jurassic Park* (Steven Spielberg, 1993); *The Lost World* (Steven Spielberg, 1997); *Jurassic Park III* (Steven Spielberg, 2001), including a vast number of franchise products such as books, films, comics, and videos; *The Lost World TV Series* (Richard Franklin, 1999–2002) and *The Lost World* (BBC TV Adaptation, 2001), starring Bob Hoskins as Professor Challenger.

historic and 'lost' worlds so vividly explored in the classic science fiction texts *Voyage au centre de la terre* (1864) by Jules Verne and more importantly, Arthur Conan Doyle's (1859–1930) *The Lost World*, which was published in instalments in the *Strand Magazine* in 1912. "[Doyle's] most memorable creation [...] [in *The Lost World*], the maddening, fascinating and [...] memorable Professor George Edward Challenger" (Anon. 5) continues his adventures in a succession of novels and stories, beginning with *The Lost World* (1912) and continuing with "The Poison Belt" (1913), *The Land of Mist* (1926), "When the World Screamed" (1928) and "The Disintegration Machine" (1929).[3]

In his first Challenger novel, *The Lost World*, Conan Doyle succeeds in creating a thematic pattern that has reverberated through a century of the science fiction tradition, further supplementing the artificial 'mega-text', a term Damien Broderick coined for the shared conventions, icons, tropes, and narrative forms – the 'collective intertextuality' that constitute a genre (Luckhurst 182). As a prolific writer Conan Doyle produced an impressive body of work including plays, romances, poetry, non-fiction and historical novels, in addition to his collections of detective stories featuring the most memorable and certainly best known of the epistemological detectives, the 'consulting detective', Sherlock Holmes. The enduring impact of Conan Doyle's detective fiction and of the science fiction stories, which constitute "a third major strand of [his] oeuvre" (Anon. 5), will ensure the author's lasting legacy in the SF[4] canon, who besides being an enthusiastic supporter of many technological advancements of his time was, along with H. G. Wells (1866–1946), often hailed tentatively as one of the founders of the genre in a

---

[3] Further noteworthy SF stories, in addition to the Professor Challenger cycle, include "The American Tale" (1879), "The Los Amigos Fiasco" (1892), "The Great Keinplatz Experiment" (1894), "The Terror of Blue John Gap" (1910), "Through the Veil" (1911), "The Last Galley" (1911), "The Great Brown-Pericord Motor" (1911), "The Horror of the Heights" (1913), "Danger!" (1914) and "The Lift" (1922).
[4] For the remainder of this essay "SF" will replace "Science Fiction".

British literary-historical context. And yet, whatever creative proliferations his extraordinary science fiction stories may have inspired, they seemed to have failed to receive the same academic attention that Conan Doyle's detective fiction stories have enjoyed.

In the last thirty years the field of science fiction literature in English has been enriched by an almost unprecedented increase in critical writing (cf. Hollinger n. p.), indicating a paradigm shift in the production and reception of science fiction texts in the English-speaking world. Albeit highly interdisciplinary and encompassing a multitude of theoretical approaches, for example, feminism, Marxism, psychoanalysis, cultural studies, postcolonialism, posthumanism and utopian studies, the majority of this criticism still remains engaged, at least initially, in incessant debates on how to define a genre that has combined Gothic, realistic, fantasy and utopian writing since its early stages of formation.[5] When surveying some of the most prominent examples of critical writing in the field of science fiction studies one cannot help noticing that the term "Science Fiction" itself conjures up a plethora of contradictory definitions and concepts, culminating in interminable and repetitive outpourings on the literary merit and intellectual properties of a vastly heterogeneous body of writing.[6] Probably one of the most commonly cited examples of this comprised proposition originates from Adam Roberts, a British academic, critic and author of SF, describing the genre as a "particular body of texts that [was] specifically founded in science and the extrapolation of science into the future" (25). In an attempt to highlight the difficulties in agreeing on an integrated chronological narrative of the genre's development,

---

[5] The British Marxist critic Raymond Williams, for example, declared that as part of the genre's development, "[t]raditional appeals ha[d] been exploited with new, or apparently new, material, and the result is neither much better nor much worse than the long line from Horace Walpole through Conan Doyle" (357).
[6] A list of recent compendium publications and collection of critical essays may include: Booker and Thomas (2009); Cunnigham (2002); Gunn, Barr and Candelaria (2009); Bould, Butler, Roberts and Vint (2009); James and Mendlesohn (2004); James (1994) and Stover (2002).

Roberts asks; "Where does science fiction begin?" (37), thus identifying two comprehensive approaches to the question of origin, which in turn reveal a deeply Eurocentric and Western perspective regarding the origins and acceptance of scientific knowledge, science-fictional texts and "their visions of the cosmos" (39):

> Different critics have their own favorite jumping-off points. Some go back no further than a hundred years, to H. G. Wells and Jules Verne, giving SF as a genre a youthfulness to fit its supposedly juvenile, forward-fixated profile. Others insist on searching out 'fantastic' or 'science-fictional' elements in literature as ancient as literature is itself. [...] Stress the relative youth of the mode and you are arguing that SF is a specific artistic response to a very particular set of historical and cultural phenomena; more specifically, you are suggesting that SF could only have arisen in a culture experiencing the Industrial Revolution [...]. Stress the antiquity of SF, on the other hand, and you are arguing instead that SF is a common factor across a wide range of different histories and cultures, that it speaks to something more durable, perhaps something more fundamental in the human make-up, some human desire to imagine worlds other than the one we actually inhabit. (37–8)

In view of Conan Doyle's leanings towards investigations into the paranormal, thought-transference, telepathy and spiritualism in the later years of his life, one might speculate to what extent the hegemonic discourses on science in general, and on acceptable parameters for scientific analysis in particular, have affected further critical interest in his science-fictional texts. According to Andrew Lycett, Doyle saw spiritualism as "a natural extension of science" (125), a belief that may have been widely shared at the beginning of the twentieth century, given its popularity in the English-language countries. And yet, once seen placed at the heart of popular culture and the periphery of cultural production, SF literature or science-fictional texts, far from being restricted to anticipating or re-narrating the technological advances of the Western modern world and their consequences, have increasingly been perceived as centrally relevant in many explorations of contemporary culture and its mediation of social criticism, finding ever greater popularity in higher education syllabi in North American, British and German universities. Born from this greater popularity was the desire to perpetuate a process of recognizing, promoting and positioning SF literature in all its medial forms, in addition to an ongoing process of mediation with regards to its future.

Despite numerous efforts, not all critics and historians of the form are currently satisfied with the level of academic saturation. The SF historian Darren Harris-Fain, for example, argues convincingly in his concluding chapter of *Understanding Contemporary Science Fiction* that genre fiction such as SF, fantasy, crime fiction and westerns are plainly excluded from a range of anthologies that ostensibly strive for greater diversity and the inclusion of a "greater number of women and minority writers" (180). It comes as no surprise then that his observations cannot be discarded easily, as he supports this claim with an empirical analysis of numerous histories of American fiction published in the past twenty years. The fact that SF has supposedly a tendency to "focus less on characterization than on idea – a cardinal sin in the dominant literary aesthetic in English-language fiction since the late 1800s" (Harris-Fain 178) seems to him the most plausible explanation of this neglect. Challenging Harris-Fain's perception of a collectively failed critical recognition of both SF literature and screen SF could turn into a purely intellectual exercise, and yet it is essential for this very reason to occasionally re-evaluate the role and configuration of key contributors such as H. G. Wells and Sir Arthur Conan Doyle. In response to what he identifies as an act of politicization of the genre, the British cultural historian Roger Luckhurst promotes a historicist definition of SF, including screen SF, in addition to the established formalist and conceptual approaches. Since the early epistemic changes continue unabated it is becoming increasingly desirable to incorporate the cultural and literary-historical dimensions of a genre that is unmatched in its degree of intertextuality and self-referentiality, and that arguably continues to perpetuate itself seemingly effortlessly (cf. Luckhurst 1–13). In this respect, responding to George E. Slusser's rhetorical question in the introduction to *The Best Science Fiction of Arthur Conan Doyle* (1981), what Conan Doyle's tales may have to do with SF, is neither straightforward nor simplistic.

'To set the whole world screaming' – Science Fiction and Environmentalism: An Ecocritical Reading of Arthur Conan Doyle's "When the World Screamed" (1928)

In addition to *The Lost World* (1912), which continues to influence, directly or indirectly, a great number of contemporary writers who have in turn helped to resurrect common tropes, topics and conventions in current SF texts in various media, the eerie contemporaneity of "When the World Screamed" (1928), one of Doyle's lesser known stories published two years before his death, calls for renewed critical attention. As a literature of ideas current SF motifs include, for example, aliens, space travel, the colonization of other worlds, the effects of relativity and generic engineering while longstanding SF tropes are, for example, the space opera, time travel, entropy, and ecological issues. In many ways "When the World Screamed" seems to connect Conan Doyle's mediations, arguably more prominent at the end of his life and informed by his era's anxieties regarding the advance of science and the decline of religion, with concerns regarding the contemporary environmental situation, compounded by the consequences of unchecked economically-motivated implementations of technological progress. Adding an ecocritical perspective to the reading of "When the World Screamed" unfolds two further lines of investigation, namely the exploration of discernible ecological aspects within the story and the use of 'anthropomorphism' as a category that can be "considered in relation to ethical questions of the just representation of the non-human, [thus] questioning the complacency of dominant human self-conceptions" (Clark 192).

If the prehistoric theme of many of Conan Doyle's earlier stories echo the controversies surrounding Charles Darwin's ideas of the transmutation of species and of Darwinism, in general, as propounded especially between the 1850s and 1870 (cf. Browne), the time span between the *fin de siècle* to the 1920s, however, constituted a historical moment dominated by the First World War (WW I) as well as the final extension and beginning dissolution of the British Empire. A great number of writers, critics and historians have concentrated their efforts on the descriptions of innocence during the last summer prior to the outbreak of WW I in 1914, a time were "certainties were intact" (Fussell 21). At the time nobody seems to have realised the implications of the technological advancements of warfare and British servicemen at the outbreak of WW I could not imagine the horrors they were about to be exposed to. Bearing in mind that Conan Doyle was deeply affected by the death of his son Kingsley at the end of WW I (Lycett 445) his penultimate SF story transmits allegorically a foreboding that the allure of knowledge might prove fateful for mankind. 1928, the year "When the World Screamed" was first published, thus falls in a period when Britain was still exorcising the horrors of the First World War. It was also a time of great changes and transition from the long-cherished values of Victorian and Edwardian England (1901–1914) to the post-First World War period.

Contrasting the differing methodological approaches of both, the science fiction hero and the detective hero, Van Dover reminds us that "the final two stories, 'When the World Screamed' (1928) and 'The Disintegration Machine' (1929), (which ignore [Doyle's] Spiritualist conversion) might be used to illustrate the hubris of the scientist: Challenger's almost maniac insistence that the earth [acknowledge] him" (98). He classifies Challenger as clearly belonging to the history of science fiction as he, in contrast to the detective hero "plays out how humans might act, morally or immorally, under conditions extrapolated from current scientific understanding or technological conditions" (97). Profoundly influenced by Gaboriau and Poe, Sherlock Holmes's celebrated method of investigation involves a rational and efficient process for detecting crime. The "Baker Street Reasoning" combines logical/deductive and intuitive elements of reasoning, yet Holmes's active "collection and rational analysis of information" (Knight 10) and his solitary investigative inquiries distinguish Conan Doyle's detective from the passive academic figure of Dupin. Thus for Conan Doyle, "truth in science fiction is proved by experience, not analysis" (99). Van Dover argues further that "ironically, the most scientific of the Professor Challenger stories, methodically-speaking, are constructed as a polemic of what might seem an anti-science: spiritualism" (103). The conflicting notions within Conan Doyle's literary output seem therefore allegorically emblematic for the incommensurateness of science's rationality and the crisis of spirituality in the modern world.

In line with the previously established narrative formula of the Challenger stories, "When the World Screamed" begins with a prologue that does not reveal the narrator's identity. Described as an expert in Artesian borings in a first communiqué from Professor Challenger, who seeks to employ him, the anonymous character, later identified as Mr. Peerless Jones, appears to be unable to match the journalistic skills of his predecessor, Edward Malone, leaving him at first glance comparatively ill-equipped to chronicle the events that follow. The same paradoxically named Peerless ('without equal') Jones (one of the most common and ordinary names in England), commands the engineer's expertise and eye that is required to see and narrate the technological and geological details for which Malone could not have been expected to have the correct terminology. If the process of writing and more specifically journalistic writing is defined as an endorsement to document the unfolding occurrences in the most truthful manner, then on an intradiegetical level, doubts regarding the validity of Jones' claims are already implied. A first business meeting is fraught with difficulties, especially when the nature of their shared business is revealed:

> 'Now, Mr. Jones, having obtained your promise of inviolable secrecy, I come to the essential point. It is this – that the world upon which we live is itself a living organism, endowed, as I believe, with a circulation, a respiration, and a nervous system of its own'. Clearly the man was a lunatic. (Doyle 460)

Applying his specialist qualifications, Jones nevertheless embarks on completing Professor Challenger's latest scientific project, to pierce the core of the earth in order to convince the "world" to acknowledge his existence.

> 'You can well imagine then, that the earth has not the least idea of the way in which it is utilized by the human race. It is quite unaware of this fungus growth of vegetation and evolution of tiny animalcules which has collected upon it during its travels round the sound as barnacles gather upon the ancient vessel. That is the present state of affairs, and that is what I propose to alter.' […] 'I propose to let the earth know that there is at least one person, George Edward Challenger, who calls for attention – who, indeed, insists upon attention. It is certainly the first intimation it has ever had of the sort'. (461)

Professor Challenger, arrogant and egocentric by nature, is presented as the quintessential experimental scientist who is convinced of his obligation to explore and experiment without regard to moral or practical consequences. Although Malone relates to Jones at the beginning of the narrative how Challenger's enterprise was initially disguised as a search for petroleum, he seems overtly neither economically motivated nor profit-orientated: "Science seeks knowledge" (463) is his credo, "Let the knowledge lead us where it will, we still must seek it" (463). "With the very efficient aid of Morden and Co" (462) the shaft to the core of the earth has already been drilled at the time of Peerless Jones' arrival.

> 'You will accept my statement without question. We are through the crust. It was exactly fourteen thousand four hundred and forty-two yards thick, or roughly eight miles. In the course of our sinking it may interest you to know that we have exposed a fortune in the matter of coal-beds which would probably in the long run defray the cost of this enterprise. Our chief difficulty has been the springs of water in the lower chalk and Hastings

sands, but these we have overcome. The last stage has now been reached – and the last stage is none other than Mr. Peerless Jones. You, sir, represent the mosquito.' (462)

Jones, as a pragmatic believer in the potential of technology and its commercial benefits, does immediately accept the professor's account and with it his assignation. Although seen as inevitably inferior by Challenger, Jones without being arrogant has confidence in his technical skills and problem-solving abilities, defining his set task as a problem to which he needs to find an answer. Malone, his friend, having chronicled Challenger's previous adventures, holds the latter in high esteem and his friend in the dark, for the information he choose to share with Jones appear at best selective. Despite Challenger's apparent lack of interest in the commercial benefits of his endeavour, the number of exploitable natural resources including coal, clay, chalk and feldspar are comprehensively listed. Challenger mentions coal specifically as being present in sufficient quantities to pay for his experiment, an excavation that in the process leads to the pollution and destruction of the surrounding landscape. On their first visit to the Challenger estate at Hengist Down, in Sussex, Jones and Malone encounter a terrain that is littered with discarded equipment, "a huge piece of machinery which seemed to be the valves and piston of a hydraulic pump projected itself, all rusted, from a clump of furze" (466). The secluded area's infrastructure appears as fundamentally changed, "[a] weather-worn Vauxhall thirty landaulette was awaiting us, and bumped us for six or seven miles over by-paths and lanes which [...] were deeply rutted and showed every sign of heavy traffic" (465–6). A broken lorry lying at the roadside speaks of the roughness of the road and of an environment that has been torn up without a second thought.

Both descend to the bottom of the shaft, to its lowest level, into the depths, so to speak. What they encounter, however, are not prehistoric mammals and the lost worlds of Challenger's earlier ventures, but a layer of skin not unlike the dermis of living organisms. The descriptive details, though, prove inconsistent in terms of terminology and ambiguous, thus enhancing the fantastic qualities of the narrative:

> It was a most extraordinary and terrifying sight. The floor consisted of some greyish material, glazed and shiny, which rose and fell in slow palpitation. The throbs were not direct, but gave the impression of a gentle ripple or rhythms, which ran across the surface [...] 'Does look rather like a skinned animal', said Malone, in an awed whisper. (472)

The reference to 'skin' is deployed analogous to the earth's crust in its layers, but the term is also used to refer to the surface Jones is expected to pierce. Malone's description of their encounter as the earth looking like a 'skinned animal', constitutes a creature that has already been violated as it is without skin. The mentioning of 'grayish material' immediately invites comparison with the term 'grey matter', in other words, brain matter, implying that the brain, heart, or other organs are enclosed or encased in fascia, so-called layers of fibrous tissue that permeate the human body. 'Palpitations' indicate a heartbeat and the 'purple fluids' compare to deoxygenated blood. All in all, Challenger's proposition amounts to an external stimulation of the sensory cortex of the brain.

Although the notion of a planet that might be alive or conscious has long been explored in philosophy, fiction and science, Conan Doyle's stories may have been among the earlier fictional renderings of this idea. The world as a central fictional character is here bestowed with anthropomorphic, animal-like if not humanlike qualities, in other words, it is referred to as a single living organism, being both intelligent and sentient. Such conceptual representations are inextricably linked to pertinent central questions regarding the place and role of humans in the earth's evolution that were widely discussed at the time of writing. Classic concepts and theories on the origin of thought and consciousness that were prominently debated in the first half of the twentieth century include for example the concept of noosphere, denoting the "sphere of mind or intellect" (Samson and Pitt 1). Placed at the intersection of science and philosophy, the genesis of noospheric ideas is attributed to the pioneering work of the French philosopher Pierre Teilhard de Chardin (1881–1955), the French philosopher and mathematician Édouard Le Roy (1870–1954) and the Russian/Ukrainian mineralogist and geochemist Vladimir Vernadsky (1863–1945) (cf. Samon and Pitt 1–10). In their formidable anthology *The Biosphere and Noosphere Reader*, intended as a contribution to the history of the idea of noosphere, Samon and Pitt point out that "the noosphere concept is intrinsically linked to the notion of a continuously evolving planet Earth" (2), whereby "evolution may be conceptualized as consisting of three principal phases, each with a corresponding 'layer': the physical formation of the planet itself (the geosphere), the birth of life (the biosphere) and the emergence of human consciousness and self-reflexivity (the noosphere)" (2). The environmentalist James Lovestock's conceptions of the structure of the earth add to the longstanding and wide debate on humanity's place and fate in the biosphere, which gathers increasingly momentum at the onset of the twenty-first century. He was the first to suggest that the biosphere of the earth acts as a single integrated life-form, when formulating his Gaia Hypothesis in the 1979 publication of *Gaia: A New Look at Life on Earth*. The word 'Gaia', which is ancient Greek for 'Earth' and also refers to the primal goddess and original mother of all being, was befittingly suggested by his friend, the novelist William Golding (Lovelock vii). In seven chapters, Lovelock outlines his holistic approach, which can be seen as a natural development of Darwin's theory of evolution, and has most certainly caused a similar amount of controversy. The idea of conscious and intelligent worlds was also fictionally elaborated on, for example, by the British philosopher and SF author Olaf Stapledon in *Star Maker* (1937), the Polish philosopher, essayist and SF author Stanisław Lem in *Solaris* (1961) and the American astrophysicist and SF author Glen David Brin in *Earth* (1990). More recent examples include the German author Frank Schätzing's SF novel *The Swarm* (2004), which has been translated into 18 languages. The novel features a second intelligent species that has coexisted peacefully with mankind remaining undetected in the depths of the oceans. Eventually it seeks to terminate human life on earth because mankind's activities have created conditions that have begun to affect the delicate equilibrium of organic and inorganic conditions that have fostered and sustained complex life forms and ecosystems.

Similar attributions of sentience and intelligence are implied when the threatened world in the last third of the story develops the ability to anticipate Professor Challenger's imminent attack on its 'cortical regions'. Jones, growing increasingly reluctant to proceed, observes once more:

> It was an amazing sight which lay before us. By some strange telepathy the old planet seemed to know that an unheard-of-liberty was about to be attempted. The exposed surface was like a boiling pot. Great grey bubbles rose and burst with a crackling report. The airspaces and vacuoles below the skin separated and coalesced in an agitated activity. The transverse ripples were stronger and faster in their rhythm than before. A dark purple fluid appeared to pulse in the tortuous anastomoses of channels which lay under the surface. The throb of life was in it all. (477)

Such vivid descriptions of the earth's ensuing activity in the terminology of physiology reinforce the process of personification: the pulsating ripples suggest secreted blood streams, vessels and arteries; the rhythmic movement indicates an increased heartbeat. Morally opposing Professor George Edward Challenger's enterprise since their first descent, yet nevertheless thrusting the dart of technology in the living and thus algesic dermis of the earth, Jones and Malone narrowly escape and reach the surface before the world materialises its "scream". Challenger, the 'brain' of this operation, who repeatedly asserts his own intellectual superiority and sees both as 'subordinates,' escapes equally unscathed.

'The screaming world' in Conan Doyle's story transforms in the narrative from a place to be conquered to a place to be protected –

functioning as a "proleptic promise", to use Luckhurst's term. Its suggestive response, announced by an "exposed surface swirling and revolving" and a "howl in which pain, anger, menace, and the outraged majesty of Nature all blended into one hideous shriek" (Doyle 478) are reminiscent of similarly violent natural events and their effects on technological (human) accomplishments. Earth retaliates against this violent physical assault by expelling the lift cages violently: "Through every vent and every volcano she voiced her indignation" (480). Erupting volcanoes, plutonic indignation and tectonic dislocation conjure up images of roads and dikes broken by earthquakes, crumbling buildings and exploding thermal and nuclear power stations, flooded coast areas, swept-away bridges and tsunamis. Planet Earth as a living organism vents its anger immediately and in terms which cannot be ignored with eco-disasters.

Such eco-apocalyptic representations, if a literal reading might be permitted in this context, was further developed in the Anglophone SF material in the mid-twentieth century, and especially in twenty-first century American cinematic SF. Conan Doyle's metaphorical considerations on the state of the world and mankind following the end of WW I transmute with contemporary debates on the environmental situation and its representation in cultural and literary texts, in Luckhurst's words, are "representations and expressions of the cultural experience of this technological crisis" (170). The nascent ecology movement which formed in the second half of the twentieth century held its first Earth day in 1970s. On that day Stanford University biologist Paul Ehrlich warned that over-consumption, over-population and the threats of nuclear or biological warfare left 'Spaceship Earth' teetering on self-destruction (Luckhurst 170–1). Since the 1970s a number of iconic blockbusters with recurring scenarios and themes, i. e. melting pole caps, flooding, acute temperature drop have been released. These so called disaster narratives or ecologically themed movies[7] in line with the highly popular invasion narratives echoed post-war anxieties in the

---

[7] *Silent Running* (Trumbull, 1972); *Frogs* (Cowan, 1972) and *Phase IV* (Bass, 1973).

US that included ecological catastrophes in recognition of ecological damage, like a new ice age, famine, or drought which indicate a shift to ecological concerns in the English-language SF material.[8] Unfortunately and in light of the recent cataclysmic events in Japan, a number of plot structures of eco-disaster or catastrophe movies in the past ten years take on a rather mimetic character.

As the story draws to an end it seems to imply that to get the whole world talking about his extraordinary adventures was not enough for Challenger, the explorer, scientist and visionary. And so "When the World Screamed" concludes with the ambiguous, rather sardonic and satirical statement that: "To set the whole world screaming was a privilege of Challenger" (480). The trajectory of Conan Doyle's penultimate story which reads at first like a straightforward endorsement of the project of modernity in a time period that was intensely competitive for the development of the sciences, points towards a conceivable shift in the author's perspective with regards to his earlier technological enthusiasm, if not to moments of disillusionment. The word "world" which commonly denotes the whole of human civilization on planet Earth, a thoroughly anthropocentric stance since it sees the natural world entirely in relation to the human (cf. Clark 3), seems to indicate that Doyle's late SF story intends to shed doubt on the validation of curiosity as the quintessential human quality and motor for technological progress. Read in this context, the sequences of Scrat's continuous battle to possess his acorn in the *Ice Age* cycle, including the disastrous consequences of his desire, assume an almost parabolic quality.

---

[8] A list of Hollywood productions since 1980s echoing ecological concerns and the consequences of acute climate and habitat change (feature or animation) should include the following: *The Day the Earth Stood Still* (Wise, 1951); *The Day the Earth Stood Still* – remake (Derrickson, 2008); *Waterworld* (Reynolds, 1995); *The Day After Tomorrow* (Emmerich, 2004); *Ice Age* (Wedge and Saldanha, 2002)/*Ice Age: The Meltdown* (Saldanha, 2006)/*Ice Age: Dawn of the Dinosaurs* (Saldanha and Thurmeier, 2009); *The Happening* (Nelliyattu Shyamalan, 2008) and *Arctic Blast* (Trenchard-Smith, 2010). Some fall into the category of eco-disaster movies.

Works Cited

Anon. "Introduction". *The Lost World and Other Stories*. By Sir Arthur Conan Doyle. London: Wordsworth Classics, 1995. 5–6.

Barry, Peter. *Beginning Theory: An Introduction to Literary and Cultural Theory*. Second Edition. Manchester: MUP, 2002.

Booker, Keith M. and Anne-Marie Thomas, eds. *The Science Fiction Handbook*. Chichester: Wiley-Blackwell, 2009.

Bould, Mark, et al., eds. *The Routledge Companion to Science Fiction*. London: Routledge, 2009.

Browne, Janet. *Darwin's Origins of the Species: A Biography*. London: Atlantic Books, 2007.

Clark, Timothy. *The Cambridge Introduction to Literature and the Environment*. Cambridge: CUP, 2011.

Cunnigham, Jesse G. *Science Fiction*. Gale: Greenhaven Press, 2002.

Doyle, Sir Arthur Conan. "When the World Screamed". *The Lost World and Other Stories*. London: Wordsworth Classics, 1995. 455–80.

Fussell, Paul. *The Great War and Modern Memory*. New York: Oxford UP, 1975.

Gersdorf, Catrin, and Sylvia Mayer. "Nature in literary and cultural studies: defining the subject of ecocriticism – an introduction". *Nature in Literary and Cultural Studies: Transatlantic Conversations on Ecocriticism*. Ed. Catrin Gersdorf and Sylvia Mayer. Amsterdam: Rodopi, 2006. 9–21.

Gunn, James, Marleen S. Barr and Matthew Candelaria, eds. *Reading Science Fiction*. Basingstoke: Palgrave, 2009.

Harris-Fain, Darren. *Understanding Contemporary American Science Fiction: the Age of Maturity, 1970–2000*. Columbia: University of South Carolina Press, 2005.

Hollinger, Veronica. "Contemporary Trends in Science Fiction Criticism, 1980–1999". *Science Fiction Studies* 26 (1999) n. p. 20 May 2011. <http://www.depauw.edu/sfs/backissues/78/hollinger78art.htm>.

Ice Age. Dir. Wedge and Saldanha. US, 2002. Twentieth Century Fox Home Entert. 2004. DVD.

Ice Age 3: Dawn of the Dinosaurs. Dir. Saldanha and Thurmeier. US, 2009. Twentieth Century Fox Home Entert. 2009. DVD.

"Ice Age 3 – Dawn of the Dinosaurs – Official Trailer". 7 May 2011. <http://www.youtube.com/watch?v=W4gvxUlGNAs&feature=player_detailpage>.

James, Edward. *Science Fiction in the 20th Century*. Oxford: Oxford UP, 1994.
James, Edward, and Farah Mendlesohn, eds. *The Cambridge Companion to Science Fiction*. Cambridge: Cambridge UP, 2004.
Knight, Stephen. "The Case of the Great Detective." 1981. *Arthur Conan Doyle: Sherlock Holmes: The Major Stories, with Contemporary Critical Essays*. Ed. J. A. Hodgson. Boston, Mass.: St. Martin's Place, 1994. 368–80.
Lovelock, James. *Gaia: A New Look at Life on Earth*. 1979. Oxford: Oxford UP, 2009.
Luckhurst, Roger. *Science Fiction: A Cultural History of Literature*. Cambridge: Polity Press, 2005.
Lycett, Andrew. The *Man Who Created Sherlock Holmes: The Life and Times of Sir Arthur Conan Doyle*. New York: Free Press, 2007.
Roberts, Adam. *Science Fiction*. London: Routledge, 2006.
Samson, Paul R. and David Pitt. "Introduction: Sketching the Noosphere". *The Biosphere and Noosphere Reader: Global Environment, Society and Change*. Eds. Samson, Paul R. and David Pitt. London: Routledge, 1999. 1–10.
Slusser, George E. "Introduction". *The Best Science Fiction of Arthur Conan Doyle*. Eds. Charles G. Waugh and Martin H. Greenberg. Carbondale: Southern Illinois UP, 1981.
Stover, Leon. *Science Fiction from Wells to Heinlein*. 2002.London: McFarland, 2008.
Van Hover, J. K. *You Know my Method: The Science of the Detective*. Bowling Green: Bowling Green State UP, 1994.
Williams, Raymond. "Science Fiction".1956. *Science Fiction Studies* 15 (1988): 356–60.

Joanna Kokot

MANIPULATING THE READER

The Strategies of Telling the Story in *The Lost World* by Arthur Conan Doyle

The end of the 19th century witnesses the revival of the romance tradition, the new type of fiction being in many respects opposed to the hitherto dominant domestic novel of manners. The story is usually told by a first person narrator, and the narrative situation is often foregrounded. Such is the narration *The Lost World* where the narrator is a reporter commenting not only upon the very act of writing his account but also upon his emotional reactions, thus encouraging the readers to identify with his perspective. The narrative strategies adopted by the writer, too, enhance the readers' engagement in the presented events. The facts are recorded currently by the narrator who is ignorant as to the ending of the adventure; the tale is divided into instalments sent home before the return of the expedition; some of the instalments start with proleptic paragraphs foreshadowing the events revealed only at the and of the chapter – all these function as a source of suspense, and as a literary counterbalance of the non-literary convention of a report ostensibly dominant in the text.

Das Ende des 19. Jahrhunderts erlebte eine Wiedergeburt der nicht- oder pseudo-mimetischen Unterhaltungsliteratur, die in vieler Hinsicht im Gegensatz zum bis dahin dominanten Gesellschaftsroman stand. Die Geschichte wird gewöhnlich von einem Ich-Erzähler präsentiert, wobei die Erzählsituation oft in den Vordergrund gerückt wird. Dies ist auch in The Lost World *der Fall. Dort ist der Erzähler ein Reporter, der nicht nur darlegt, wie er seinen Bericht schreibt, sondern auch seine emotionalen Reaktionen wiedergibt und so den Leser einlädt, sich mit seiner Perspektive zu identifizieren. Auch andere Erzählstrategien verstärken das Interesse des Lesers an den dargestellten Ereignissen. Der Erzähler notiert die Geschehnisse fortlaufend und kennt den Ausgang des Abenteuers selbst noch nicht; die Geschichte wird in Fortsetzungsraten eingeteilt, die vor der Rückkehr der Expedition in die Heimat geschickt werden; einige der*

JOANNA KOKOT, Manipulating the Reader

Berichte beginnen mit proleptischen Absätzen, die auf Ereignisse anspielen, die erst am Ende verraten werden. All diese Mittel erzeugen Spannung und dienen als literarisches Gegengewicht zu den nicht-literarischen Konventionen der Reportage, die in dem Text scheinbar dominieren.

I

At the end of the 19th century the traditional Victorian domestic novel of manners gave way to a new type of fiction that gradually won the appreciation of both contemporary readers and critics. These were the texts referring back to the tradition of the English romance, shorter and dominated by an adventurous action and not by the presentation of every-day life and a broad social background. This change was followed by another – that concerning the conventions of verisimilitude. In the novel of manners verisimilitude was acquired mainly by constructing the fictitious reality in such a way that it might seem a copy of the extra-textual world, where the characters were to resemble "people next door", and the events were such as might occur to the assumed readers. The romance revival changes this status quo. No matter whether a given text proposes a mimetic, antimimetic or fantastic model of the universe,[1] the plot surpasses the range of occurrences known to the (potential) reader from his or her own experience.

---

[1] The terms are used after Andrzej Zgorzelski, who defines the types of literary world models as follows: "*Mimetic literature* [...], while taking for granted the reader's linguistic competence determining his knowledge of the phenomenal reality, presupposes only the *recognition* of its order in the fictional universe. [...] *Antimimetic literature* [...], while taking for granted the reader's linguistic competence determining his knowledge of the phenomenal reality, presupposes the *correction* of the presumably faulty vision of the universe, endowing the fictional world with magical or supernatural dimensions and relating a different *model* of reality, which is presupposed to be a true vision of the universe. [...] *Fantastic literature* [...], while taking for granted the reader's linguistic competence determining his knowledge of the phenomenal reality, presupposes the *confrontation* of its order with a different one, signalling the presupposition by the presentation of both or more orders *within the text*" (32).

However, all this does not mean that the new type of fiction abandons all claims of verisimilitude. The authors, while creating worlds far from the everyday existence of the assumed readers, often refer to information acquired indirectly – from press articles, popular lectures and similar publications. The development of forensic medicine, ballistics, pathologic anatomy and other fields of criminology constitutes the background for many detective tales – it is enough to mention the early-twentieth-century stories and novels about Doctor Thorndyke by R. Austin Freeman, where the detective's arguments are often endorsed by references to recent discoveries in these fields. The scientific romance alludes to the inventions, theories and hypotheses in the fields of physics, technology or chemistry, and even if it does not always popularize their achievements, it speculates about the further vistas that could be opened by these sciences, as well as about the possibilities of life on other planets, the existence of parallel worlds, and even time travels. Geographical discoveries and the experience of other cultures, religions, or even world orders inspire the action of the so-called quest romance, represented for example by H. Rider Haggard's tales set in unexplored areas of the African interior. Even the occult fiction and the vampire stories allude to contemporary scientific or quasi-scientific speculations as, for instance, in Professor Van Helsing's arguments in Bram Stoker's *Dracula* Thus, like in the domestic novel of manners, the border between the intra- and the extra-textual reality is blurred since the laws governing the universe (really or merely hypothetically) are ascribed to the fictitious world model as well.

But these were not the only ways of adding verisimilitude to the presented stories. The uncommonness of the events is often counterbalanced by the commonness of the narrator-character, who is usually a mere observer, often not wholly conscious of the sense and aims of the actions undertaken by the proper hero. While the latter is endowed with unusual qualities, the first person narrator usually does not surpass the average, thus becoming the equivalent of "the people next door" from the novel of manners. Such characters are, for example, the various assistants of Doctor Thorndyke, less educated, less experienced and less observant than their principal, in R. Austin Freeman's detective stories, Edward Malone, treated roughly, both intellectually and physically, by Professor Challenger even at the beginning of Conan Doyle's *The Lost World*, Doctor Watson from Conan Doyle's Sherlock Holmes stories, and even Allan Quatermain, who – even if his profession is rather uncommon among the potential readers of Rider Haggard's tales – incessantly stresses his weaknesses, contrasting them to the extraordinary virtues of his companions. A similar commonness characterizes Jonathan Harker, unexpectedly cast among vampires in Bram Stoker's *Dracula*, Hubbard, the assistant of Doctor Silence from Algernon Blackwood's "Ancient Sorceries", "The Nemesis of Fire" and "The Camp of the Dog", or Jessop, the addressee of Carnacki's narratives (William Hope Hodgson's *Carnacki the Ghost Finder*). Each time it is a character coming from the world known to the assumed readers, thus functioning as a connection between the "frame" world (the outset of the adventures, imitating the readers' reality) and the world of the action proper. The implied reader can identify with this type of character – thus the credibility of the latter is established, no matter how extraordinary the adventures might seem. Thus the adventure story, just like the domestic novel, offers the reader a range of possibilities.

The return to the first person narration itself is common to this type of prose (whereas it was abandoned by the novel of manners quite early in the genre's history). The protagonists of the texts by Freeman, Hodgson, Stoker or Conan Doyle record the events they were witnesses and participants of, either telling about them long after the event, or making notes currently. Often the tale is stylized as a non-literary text – a report, a letter (or a series of letters), a diary or a journal. Bram Stoker's *Dracula* utilizes all kinds of jottings, including press articles and legal documents. The first Sherlock Holmes novel (*A Study in Scarlet*) includes – apart from the retrospective love story – fragments defined as "A Reprint from the Reminiscences of John H. Watson, M. D.". Haggard's novels (*King Solomon's Mines, She*) are accounts of expeditions undertaken by the protagonist-narrators – the accounts themselves being enriched by both the narrator's and the "editor's" footnotes. This is obviously not an automatic adoption of the conventions typical of the beginnings of the novel in England, where the stylization of a tale as a non-literary narrative still stressed the commonplace nature of the events. Here the issue is to counterbalance the extraordinary events with a non-literary, "ordinary" narrative; to play a kind of make-believe game.

A similar game is played when the reasons for the publication of the tale are explained. It often happens that the narrative proper is preceded by forewords, introductions and the like, coming from the fictitious editor, or from the protagonist-narrator himself, commenting upon the publishing of the story. A short preface appears for example in Stoker's *Dracula*, while Haggard's *King Solomon's Mines* and *She* begin with introductions – provided by Allan Quatermain himself and by an anonymous editor respectively – that comment on the shortcomings of the one text and the circumstances of the other text's origins. In *King Solomon's Mines* there even appears a dedication "to all the big and little boys who read it", written ostensibly by the narrator, Alan Quartermain, whereas in another text by the same author – *Allan Quatermain* – the afterword explains the "return" of Allan's jottings to England, even if all the protagonists choose to stay in Zu-Vendis. Jim from Stevenson's *The Treasure Island* puts down the events on the request of his companions, Conan Doyle's Watson often comments on his literary activities, never hiding the fact that his accounts are to be printed to amuse the readers. Thus the first-person narrator not only serves as a means of enhancing the verisimilitude of the tale, but he is often also a self-conscious writer, handling the facts in order to get the reader interested in his tale.

All these features can also be found in *The Lost World* by Arthur Conan Doyle. (Like most of the Sherlock Holmes tales, this text appeared for the first time in *The Strand* in monthly instalments.) It seems worthwhile to take a close look at the narrative strategies adopted by Conan Doyle (and his teller, Malone), as well as at their role in modelling the reading of the novel.

II

The text begins as a conventional love story, and the first person narration seems merely a device used to focus the reader's attention on the protagonist. However, already the ending of the first chapter contains an intriguing remark concerning the reader of Malone's tale:

> And, after all, this opening chapter will seem to the reader to have nothing to do with my narrative; and yet there would be no narrative without it, for it is only when a man goes into the world with the thought that there are heroisms all round him, and with the desire all alive in his heart to follow any which may come within sight of him, and he breaks away as I did from the life he knows, and ventures forth into the wonderful mystic twilight land where lie the great adventures and the great rewards (16–17).

It is significant that the mention of the reader appears together with the announcement of extraordinary events, surpassing the everyday experience of both the narrator-protagonist and – as one can assume – his addressees. Evidently a more or less conventional story of an enamoured young man and an ambitious girl, even if told in the first person, does not demand any additional justification, whereas the tale about "the wonderful mystic twilight land where lie the great adventures and the great rewards" needs to be 'domesticated' by blurring the border between the narrative situation and the world of the assumed readers. However, the mere mention of "the reader" does not yet determine the style of reading proposed for Malone's narrative – the shift from a novel-like narration to that of a report does not take place yet.

Until the voyage into the unknown begins the narrator does not foreground his role as a reporter, even if he plays it as a character. The telling of the occurrences in Challenger's house (together with some details of the scientist's domestic life – note the incident with Mrs Challenger) is still a conventional first person narration;

moreover, from Malone's conversation with McArdle the reader can conclude that the whole story was not recorded to appear in print. Malone's reaction to the editor's wish to publish it is: "I'm longing to, but all I know he gave me in confidence and on condition that I didn't" (64). Also, in the chapter devoted to Percival Waldron's lecture at the Zoological Institute nothing suggests that the text is planned as a newspaper report. Even if McArdle sends Malone there, expecting such a report to follow ("I'll keep space up to midnight" – 65), the continuity on the level of the events with the previous parts of the story rather defines the chapter as a successive stage in a novel narrative.

Even the information defining Malone's role in the expedition concerns the character rather than the narrator, as if the whole tale were recorded only after the adventure had ended – similarly to so many other first person narrations, where the narrative situation remains undefined:

> It was agreed that I should write home full accounts of my adventures in the shape of successive letters to McArdle, and that these should either be edited for the *Gazette* as they arrived, or held back to be published later, according to the wishes of Professor Challenger. (92)

The reader learns that the narrative is a report divided into instalments only at the end of chapter VI, when Malone and his companions set off to explore the unknown. The facts presented at the beginning of the text appear to be a mere introduction to much more extraordinary events, while the purpose of their presentation is merely to make whatever happens next plausible – of which Malone himself is ignorant at the moment of completing this instalment:

> And now, my patient reader, I can address you directly no longer. [...] In the hands of the editor I leave this account of the events which have led up to one of the most remarkable expeditions of all time, so that if I never re-

turn to England there shall be some record as to how the affair came about. (92–93)

The more and more obvious foregrounding of the narrative situation has a similar function. When it becomes clear that Malone's tale is nothing less than a report sent in instalments to the editor of the *Daily Gazette*, the reader will be often reminded of the communicative situation in which it is involved. The narrator not only reveals his role as a reporter on the level of the narrative situation, but also comments on the very fact of recording the events, as he does for example at the end of chapter VI, when he describes the circumstances under which he is writing, e. g., when he is just leaving England ("I am writing these last lines in the saloon of the Booth liner *Francisca*" – 93), or much later, when after the disappearance of his companions he is hastily putting down the events that happened the night before ("To write a letter! Why not? […] I had two completed letters already waiting. I would spend the day in writing the third, which would bring my experiences absolutely up to date" – 226). Thus the extraordinary nature of the events is counterbalanced with the constant reminding of their being recorded, which functions here as a connection between the astounding world hidden in the Amazonian forest and the commonplace one presented in the "introductory" chapters of the tale.

The connection is created also by describing how Malone's jottings reach his "readers". The tale is a special type of report, as it is in fact rather a series of private letters addressed to the *Gazette* editor. The addressee is 'present' in the narration due to phrases like "my dear Mr McArdle" (109), "I leave this material to your own discretion, Mr McArdle" (96–97), etc. These letters/reports are sent to the newspaper editor almost currently, which is commented upon by the narrator himself, when he writes about the ways in which he sends (or rather is going to send) the correspondence to the immediate addressee (through the *Francisca* pilot, the canoe crew, and finally the Indians). Here the very fact of the publishing of the mail is foregrounded, while the reports themselves – as letters sent from a different world to that which is the potential readers' commonplace world – function almost literally as a bridge between the two spheres of reality: the ordinary and the incredible.

Moreover, that bridge is not only constructed between two spheres of the fictitious reality – that known from the first chapters of the text, and that presented in the following chapters. The narration proper in the book edition is preceded by Malone's preface and his acknowledgements expressing gratitude to the co-authors of the illustrations (responsible for the working up of the sketches and photographs made during the course of the expedition), whereas in the first *Strand* instalment the name of Harry Roundtree (the author of conventional, 'fictional' illustrations,[2] a well-known artist from the extra-textual reality) is accompanied by that of Maple White, the character from the presented world (the name of Maple White appears also in the captions of the drawings 'quoted' from his notebook). Thus the barrier between the story and the extra-textual reality is crossed on the level of the implied communication process as well. Of course, it is hard to speak about a hoax arranged by Conan Doyle – after all the tale was published in *The Strand* and not in the *Daily Gazette* (if such a newspaper ever existed), its author is defined as Arthur Conan Doyle (known already to the readers as the author of the Sherlock Holmes cycle),[3] whereas the whole excitement that Challenger's expedition was said to have instigated could be taken at face value only by a reader totally deprived of any

---

[2] These illustrations evidently stress the literary aspect of the tale, constituting a counterbalance for the pseudo-authentic sketches ascribed to Maple White and the photograph-like portraits of the members of the expedition which appear in the *Strand* version of the text. Roundtree's illustrations were left out of the book edition of *The Lost World*, maybe to enhance the illusion of the authenticity of Malone's tale, especially since the original *Strand* Foreword (allegedly of Malone's authorship) ends with the following information: "Mr. E. D. Malone would wish also to express his gratitude to Mr. Patrick L. Forbes, of Rosslyn Hill, Hampstead, for the skill and sympathy with which he has worked up the sketches which were brought from South America, and also to Mr. W. Ransford, of Elm Row, Hampstead, for his valuable expert help in dealing with the photographs" (3).

[3] The April 1912 cover of *The Strand Magazine* bears the following announcements: "Conan Doyle's Great New Serial Begins This Month" and: "Conan Doyle creates a great new character Professor G. E. Challenger in his new serial The Lost World".

contact with reality. Hence we are dealing with a kind of appropriation of a paraliterary genre (a report) by literature.[4] The question is whether the illusion that Malone's narration is a report on a research expedition could be dispelled only through the confrontation of the events presented there with extra-textual reality?

The answer "Yes" might be undermined already by the tongue-in-cheek dedication under the "photographs" in the tale's frontispiece in *The Strand*, and repeated on the cover of the first edition: "Yours *truly* (to tell the conventional *lie*) George Edward Challenger" (emphasis added) – a wink at the reader, playing on the semantic similarity of "truly" and "truthfully". Moreover the question of truth and fiction is touched upon already at the beginning of the text when Tarp Henry comments on Challenger's accident in South America: "My dear chap, things don't happen like that in real life. People don't stumble upon enormous discoveries and then lose their evidence. *Leave that to the novelists*" (65, emphasis added).

And yet a similarly tangled skein of coincidences leads Malone to his participation in the expedition – his proposal to Gladys, her expectations, the task McArdle entrusts him with, the truce between him and the unpredictable Challenger, his presence at Waldron's lecture. In the fictitious reality Malone is a reporter, but from the perspective of the reader he is just a literary character involved in the action consciously and purposefully arranged by the author. If so – what is the style of reading assumed by Conan Doyle's text? And how is this style defined by the narrative strategies adopted by the writer – does the tale of Malone indeed resemble a typical report on a research expedition, where the main stress should fall upon the natural and ethnographic aspects of the endeavour?

---

[4] Similar shifts of the boundaries of literature are discussed by Yuri Tynianov (32–45). It is perhaps worth mentioning that the convention of a report was used in the literary texts by writers contemporary to Conan Doyle – Rudyard Kipling, H. G. Wells or Arthur Machen (in *The Terror*, 1916).

III

In his best-known cycle Conan Doyle creates a narrator who not only functions as the leading character's chronicler, but also openly stylizes his tale as a literary text, manipulating the reader, referring to existing literary conventions, building up suspense so that the final solution of the puzzle would be a surprise for his readers. It is by no means strange that the stories about the detective genius became the subject of a kind of a make-believe game, where Watson is the author of the texts, and his friend is not a fictitious character but a person from the reality of the readers. It is true that in the case of *The Lost World* it would be hard to speak about a similar manipulation of the reader on the level of the narrative situation – the very fact of making notes currently and discontinuously does not allow the perception of the narrator as one who consciously organizes the whole text in the same way as Watson does.

However, this does not mean that on the implied level of communication we do not have to do with strategies allowing the readers from the extra-textual reality to identify with the assumed fictitious 'readers' of Malone's report, as well as with the narrator himself introducing his addressees into the lost world of Jurassic reptiles. Such an identification is even written into Malone's tale itself – the 'readers' are to share with him, even if only on the level of word patterns, the wonders, dangers, discoveries and revelations that the expedition team experienced:

> And now my readers, if ever I have any, I have brought you up the broad river and through the screen of rushes, and down the great tunnel, and up the long slope of palm trees, and through the bamboo brake, and across the plain of tree-ferns. (127)

It is important that the 'reality' is presented from the perspective of a character who is not a scientist. At the very beginning of his tale Malone comments upon his total ignorance as to the intricacies of contemporary natural theories, as well as upon his inability to comprehend the texts which present those theories. While reading Challenger's article he complains: "Most of the matter might have been written in Chinese for any definite meaning that it conveyed to my brain" (25). Even in his description of the journey through the Amazon estuary – as he admits – all the names of the animals and plants come from the professors; he himself displays total ignorance as to the world of the flora and fauna already at Professor Challenger's home, mistaking crocodiles for alligators or misidentifying a fragment of a pterodactyl's skeleton as the bones of a monstrous bat.

True, the plot of Conan Doyle's tale alludes to the controversies in natural sciences, vivid at the times when the book was written, which constitute an important frame of reference here (Frazer 66–74). Challenger himself, while identifying the creature in Maple White's drawing as well as the animal whose bone he shows to Malone, refers to "an excellent monograph by my gifted friend, Ray Lankester" (52), the author being a non-fictitious person, and Tarp Henry mentions "Weissmann".[5] Fragments of Mr Waldron's lecture on the origins of life on the Earth are quoted. There is also an attempt to explain in a scientific way the very existence of the "lost world" which survived due to its isolation and the preservation of the original conditions:

> What is the result? Why, the ordinary laws of nature are suspended. The various checks which influence the struggle for existence in the world at large are all neutralized or altered. Creatures survive which would otherwise disappear. (59–60)

However, even the pending problem of the unknown factor which allowed the predators to survive in such a limited area (as well as that of the coexistence of the Jurassic reptiles and ape-men, never raised by the two professors) suggests that the novel itself does not function as a mere illustration of a scientific theory. Malone does not

---

[5] Ray Lankester was the author of a book entitled *Extinct Animals* (London 1905). August Weismann (spelled with one 's'), a dogmatic Darwinian, was a professor of zoology at the University of Freiburg.

quote any of the learned disputes led by his companions, whereas the scene the background of which might be the theory of atavism is reported by Lord Roxton in the half-distanced, half-mocking style so typical of him. The similarity between the chief apeman and Challenger appears to be simply amusing, even if the state in which the explorers found themselves is not amusing at all:

> This old ape-man – he was their chief – was a sort of red Challenger, with every one of our friend's beauty points, only just a trifle more so. He had the short body, the big shoulders, the round chest, no neck, a great ruddy frill of a beard, the tufted eyebrows, the "What do you want, damn you!" look about the eyes, and the whole catalogue. (232)

A similar function is fulfilled by Challenger's remarks on the alleged intellectual superiority of the chief ape-man – the professor is evidently embarrassed by the similarity, and not provoked to provide purely scientific comments. Atavism, or "race memory", is referred to a couple of other times in the text, never in the strictly scientific context. Its understanding does not surpass the popular stereotypes – for example, when Malone's sixth sense is explained by his being a Celt, or when, at the very beginning of the tale, Malone comments upon the relations between men and women and his knowledge of these:

> Where the real sex feeling begins, timidity and distrust are its companions, *heritage* from old wicked days when love and violence went often hand in hand. The bent head, the averted eye, the faltering voice, the wincing figure – these, and not the unshrinking gaze and frank reply, are the true signals of passion. Even in my short life I had learned as much as that – or had *inherited* it in the *race-memory* which we call instinct. (10, emphasis added)

Even from the point of view of Professor Challenger, the initiator of the expedition, the aim of the journey does not lie in proving any scientific theory in contention at that time. It is merely to prove that there is a place on the Earth where the prehistoric creatures, hitherto considered extinct, have survived. After all, the trophy brought back to England is not a surviving ape-man (that would be a sensational proof that the theory of evolution is valid), but a young pterodactyl! The hypothesis that there may be places where the relics of the prehistoric species have survived is not the most revolutionary one (if we remember the discoveries concerning the Australian fauna) – what counts is the sensational rather than scientific aspect of the expedition. That sensational aspect is foregrounded even by the Professor's behaviour (he refuses to provide the location of Maple White Land), as well as the discretion of Malone himself, drawing maps suspended in a geographical void. The account of the meeting in Queen's Hall 'quoted' in the novel is not provided by a scientist, but by another reporter, Macdona, again emphasizing the sensational aspect of the event.

Thus what is foregrounded is adventure, while the world traversed by the explorers is defined, already in the first descriptions, as "a land of wonders", as it could be perceived by a common observer (after all Malone is one), who is neither a scientist in search of natural trophies, nor an adventurer well versed with such surroundings:

> For a *fairyland* it was – the most *wonderful* that the imagination of man could conceive. The thick vegetation met overhead, inner lacing into a natural pergola, and through this tunnel of verdure in a golden twilight flowed the green, pellucid river, beautiful in itself, but *marvellous* from the strange tints thrown by the vivid light from above filtered and tempered in its fall. Clear as crystal, motionless as a sheet of glass, green as the edge of an iceberg, it stretched in front of us under its leafy archway, every stroke of our paddles sending a thousand ripples across its shining surface. It was a fitting avenue to a *land of wonders*. (60, emphasis added)

What is most important in this description is the beauty of the landscape, its glamour, its distinctness from everyday experience. All these find their analogy in the very language used by the narrator and its literary devices (alliterations, epithets, rhythm). All this is far from the matter-of-factness of a scientist's lecture (even if such devices might characterize a popular report or a travel journal of those times).

Adventure thus is not only present on the level of action, but also on the level of the narration. And foregrounding the narrative situation still enhances the suspense, serving as a means of manipulating the process of reading.

IV

The convention of jottings put down currently, when the distance between the time of events and that of the narrative situation is small, might have been known to Conan Doyle's readers, familiar – for example – with Bram Stoker's *Dracula*, published several years before *The Lost World*. The result of such a narrative strategy is always the uncertainty as to the further fate of the protagonist-narrator. The first-person narration in such a case is not a guarantee of his or her survival. It is enough to mention Lucy Westenra, whose diary is a substantial part of the *Dracula* narrative, and who eventually becomes the vampire's victim.

A similar uncertainty as to the final fate of the protagonist is created in Conan Doyle's text. Already the second address of Malone to his readers (when the reporter and his companions are on board of the *Francisca*) leaves no doubts as to the fact that the story is not written down from a greater time distance and that the narrator is ignorant as to the ending of the adventure. The expedition to the Amazonian jungle appears to be a journey into the unknown both from the perspective of Malone-character and Malone-narrator.

The discontinuity of the report is stressed by the information concerning the sending of the subsequent instalments. These may explain the printing of a given fragment, but they do not guarantee the continuation of the adventures, or at least the identity of the teller. For example, at the end of chapter XII, when Malone sends his letter after the loss of his companions, he writes: "And now you will understand, my dear Mr McArdle, how this communication reaches you, and you will also know the truth, in case you never hear again from your unfortunate correspondent" (227). Exactly the same could be said about the 'readers' of the report – a particular instalment can reach its destination, the question is however whether there will be more.

The way in which the events are told also foregrounds the discontinuity of the account. In fact Malone's jottings refer to two types of narration – that of a letter and that of a journal – while each chapter is a successive entry, and a successive unit of the record. The journal-like entries resemble notes made currently, they follow the chronology of the events and do not anticipate later facts. Sometimes there appear even authorial comments like: "I write this from day to day" (270), "I will describe", "I will tell" (276). This is true of those chapters-instalments which are not planned by Malone to be dispatched to England soon. However, if an instalment is the last of the set which is to be sent to the addressee – McArdle – it is composed in a different way. It opens with an proleptic introduction, announcing some dramatic events, which will constitute the climax of this stage of the plot.

For the first time such an anticipatory preparation appears at the beginning of Chapter VII, when Malone consciously delays the account concerning the mysterious letter with Challenger's instructions. Instead of narrating the episode he provides the reader with detailed information about his companions. And the sensational nature of the events so postponed in telling is prompted by the narrator's own words: "Before I reach the surprising events of that date [...]" (96). The chapter ends with announcing the intention to send the report by canoe. At the beginning of the following chapter – which from the point of view of Malone is a closed unit, as this part of his report will be sent to the *Daily Gazette* through one of the Indians – the information about the discovery of the plateau appears:

> Our friends at home may well rejoice with us, for we are at our goal, and up to a point, at least, we have shown that the statement of Professor Challenger can be verified. We have not, it is true, ascended the plateau, but it lies before us. (110)

But this information concerns the fact which will only close the whole sequence of events narrated in this part of the tale. Similar announcements of future events appear at the beginning of Chapters IX, X and XII, when Malone writes his reports waiting for a messenger. Chapter IX, when the renegade Gomez imprisons the travellers on the plateau, is opened by the following words: "A dreadful thing has happened to us. Who could have foreseen it? I cannot foresee any end to our troubles. It may be that we are condemned to spend our whole lives in this strange, inaccessible place" (129). The first paragraph of Chapter XII ends with the words announcing Malone's nocturnal escapade and the disappearance of his companions: "That little glow of self-satisfaction, that added measure of self-confidence, were to lead me on that very night to the most dreadful experience of my life, ending with a shock which turns my heart sick when I think of it" (206). Chapter X opens with the statement: "The most wonderful things have happened and are continually happening to us" (162). A similar announcement appears in Chapter XV, even if here the information about the happy ending of the adventure does not open the whole chapter, but that fragment of it which is written from a greater time perspective, after reaching the plain:

> So far I have written each of the foregoing events as it occurred. Now I am rounding off my narrative from the old camp, where Zambo has waited so long, with all our difficulties and dangers left like a dream behind us upon the summit of those vast ruddy crags which tower above our heads. We have descended in safety, though in a most unexpected fashion (151).

Here, too, "the rounding off" of the jottings, together with the proleptic opening, takes place when they are prepared to be sent (Malone mentions this fact at the end of the chapter). In each case the reader has to wait almost until the very end of the chapter to learn all the details of what happened, what wonders and what horrors occurred on the plateau. The narration, as it were, describes a circle – the anticipatory preparation at the beginning of the chapter finds its retroactive execution only at its end.

Moreover, the tension itself is graded not only due to the proleptic introductory paragraphs in some of the chapters, but also by the ignorance (or feigned ignorance) of the teller as to the nature and the causes of some of the events. This is the case, for example, in the episode when a pterodactyl appears for the first time over the camp near the plateau. The creature is recognized as a Jurassic reptile by Professor Challenger only, the others are uncertain as to its identity. The uncertainty is stressed by Malone's words: "I give you the incident as it occurred and you will know as much as I do" (127), thus making the readers of the report share it. At the beginning of Chapter X Malone assumes the mask of a naive narrator. The explorers notice prints at first defined as the tracks of a huge bird (168), then the mark of a five-fingered hand undermines the original hypothesis (169), eventually the riddle is solved when Malone and his companions reach the iguanodons' clearing (170).

Thus the addressees of Malone's report (both the immediate addressee, McArdle, and the hypothetical readers of the *Daily Gazette*, as well as the readers of Conan Doyle's text) are manipulated into emotional engagement in whatever the narrator experiences at a given stage of the story, into sharing his anxieties, fears, or expectations – as his knowledge at a given stage of the plot development is no greater than that of his addressees. Just like the events are the source of suspense from the character-narrator's perspective, so the narration itself constitutes the source of suspense for the assumed readers.

V

And it is that emotional engagement, and not merely scientific and philosophical problems, or even verisimilitude that appears to be dominant in Conan Doyle's text. The tension between plausibility and fictionality, as well as the foregrounding of the adventure, makes science a starting point for literature and literary imagination. We may speak here about "the romance of science", when a scientific expedition appears to be fascinating even to someone who – like Malone and the readers – is no scientist at all. It is no coincidence that Conan Doyle uses a similar strategy here as in his Sherlock Holmes stories: the first-person narrator is not a specialist, only a companion of one; and yet he not only gets involved in the latter's activities, but he engages his readers in them as well.

Works Cited

Doyle, Arthur Conan. *The Lost World: Being an account of the recent amazing adventures of Professor George E. Challenger, Lord John Roxton, Professor Summerlee, and Mr. E. D. Malone of the "Daily Gazette"*. London etc.: Hodder and Stoughton, n. d. [1912].

Fraser, Robert. *Victorian Quest Romance: Stevenson, Haggard, Kipling and Conan Doyle*. Plymouth: Northcote House, 1998.

Tynianow, Jurij. *Fakt literacki*. Tr. Ewa Korpała-Kirszak. Warszawa: PIW, 1978.

Zgorzelski, Andrzej. *Born of the Fantastic*. Gdańsk: Wydawnictwo Uniwersytetu Gdańskiego, 2004.

Stefan Lampadius

EVOLUTIONARY IDEAS IN ARTHUR CONAN DOYLE'S *THE LOST WORLD*

Doyle's novel *The Lost World* (1912) is one of his most influential works, establishing dinosaurs in fiction and inspiring later science fiction, but also giving birth to Professor Challenger, one of the most memorable scientists in literature. Doyle's scientific romance combines a thrilling adventure plot with scientific concepts and debates of his time, particularly ideas on evolution. Professor Challenger is not only an expert in evolutionary science but also a man of action, organizing an expedition to a strange plateau in the Amazon rain forest, which turns out to be a lost world with dinosaurs and ape-men. Prehistory comes alive, and like actors in a living natural history museum extinct species participate again in the struggle for survival. Through his fictional microcosm Doyle locates ancient creatures and modern man in the meta-narrative of evolution, drawing inspiration from a wide range of sources, including earlier science fiction, travel accounts and fossil finds near his Sussex home, but especially the innovative fusion of palaeontology and Darwinism and ideas of a 'missing link' at the turn of the century. This paper explores evolutionary ideas, their scientific basis and ambivalent narrative reflection in *The Lost World*, providing greater insight into Arthur Conan Doyle as science fiction writer and the literary discourse on evolution.

Doyles Roman The Lost World *(1912) ist eines seiner einflussreichsten Werke, das nicht nur spätere Science Fiction inspirierte, sondern mit Professor Challenger auch einen der bemerkenswertesten Wissenschaftler der Literaturgeschichte erschuf. Doyles* scientific romance *verschmilzt die Handlung eines Abenteuerromans mit wissenschaftlichen Konzepten und Debatten seiner Zeit, besonders in Bezug auf die Evolutionstheorie. Professor Challenger ist nicht nur ein führender Evolutionsbiologe, sondern auch ein Mann der Tat, der eine Expedition zu einem Bergplateau im südamerikanischen Regenwald organisiert, welches sich als eine vergessene Welt mit Dinosauriern und Affenmenschen herausstellt. In diesem fiktionalen*

Mikrokosmos erweckt der Autor Urgeschichte zu neuem Leben und verankert ausgestorbene Tiere und den modernen Menschen im Metanarrativ der Evolution. Doyle nutzte für seinen Roman eine Vielzahl unterschiedlicher Quellen – frühe Science Fiction, Reiseberichte und Fossilienfunde nahe seines Wohnorts, besonders aber die innovative Verbindung von Paläontologie und Darwinismus und Vorstellungen eines Missing Link *um die Jahrhundertwende. Dieser Aufsatz untersucht Ideen zur Evolution, ihre wissenschaftliche Basis und ambivalente erzählerische Umsetzung in* The Lost World, *um Arthur Conan Doyle als Science-Fiction-Autor und den literarischen Diskurs zur Evolutionslehre näher zu beleuchten.*

◇

Hardly anyone who lived in Britain at the time of Conan Doyle was not somehow influenced in his worldview by the rise of evolutionary theory. For a curious medical student like Doyle this was even more the case, because evolution was not just another new scientific theory but embodied a new, fresh spirit that was not afraid of traditional authorities in its search for the origins of the living world. Looking back to his years as a student, Doyle writes in his memoirs *Memories and Adventures* (1924):

> It is to be remembered that these were the years when Huxley, Tyndall, Darwin, Herbert Spencer and John Stuart Mill were our chief philosophers, and that even the man in the street felt the strong sweeping current of their thought, while to the young student, eager and impressionable, it was overwhelming. [...] A gap had opened between our fathers and ourselves so suddenly and completely that when a Gladstone wrote to uphold the Gadarene swine, or the six days of Creation, the youngest student rightly tittered over his arguments, and it did not need a Huxley to demolish them. (31–32)

Doyle's interest in evolution continued after his study of medicine and can be found in several of his works, first of all in his first science fiction novel *The Lost World* (1912). This paper wants to explore evolutionary ideas in Doyle's *Lost World*, especially through the discussion of characterization, the geographical setting, the dinosaurs and the ape-men in relation to scientific theories at the time.

In Darwin's Footsteps – Professor Challenger as Darwin's Successor

Already at the beginning of the *The Lost World* it becomes obvious that evolution will be of some importance in the book. The scientific protagonist Professor Challenger is introduced as a leading zoologist of his time, who has published works such as 'Outlines of Vertebrate Evolution' (11), and when the first-person narrator of the novel, the journalist Edward Malone, wants to find out more about Challenger, he learns that the professor is currently engaged in "something about Weissmann and Evolution" (13). Malone reads an article titled "Weissmann *versus* Darwin" (13), which reports of a lecture by Prof. Challenger that ended in great uproar, not least due to the very emotional presentation by the professor. The mention of Darwin and the influential German evolutionist Weismann (misspelled by Doyle, but clearly identifiable in the novel) at the centre of a heated debate not only foreshadows later evolutionary ideas in the novel but also points to the status of Darwinism in the early 20th century.

While the idea of evolution had been largely accepted in the Western scientific world by the late 19th century, details of Darwin's ideas on reproduction were already contested by biologists of his time. In the 1880s, several new theories on heredity through cells were proposed which contradicted Darwin's concept of pangenesis, which claimed that "pangenes or gemmules from different parts of a body collected in the reproductive cells and were transmitted to offspring" (Mai 394). Eventually the 'germ plasm theory' by the German evolutionary biologist August Weismann gained more acceptance than Darwin's concept. In contrast to Darwin, Weismann stated that hereditary information could not flow from somatic cells to germ cells and that the so-called germ plasm is the only carrier of genetic information from parent to offspring, which contradicted a heritability of acquired characteristics (cf. Mai 394, 560), an idea that was popular among early evolutionists such as Erasmus Darwin and Jean-Baptiste Lamarck. Weismann also supported the idea of a selfish DNA (although in different terms) that uses organisms to replicate itself, a concept that has recently been popularized by the evolutionist Richard Dawkins (Mai 478). Doyle's Prof. Challenger is apparently very critical of Weismann's germ plasm theory; however, such scientific details are not relevant to understanding *The Lost World* (in contrast to some hard science fiction of the late 20th century)[1], but rather give an air of scientific competence to its author and its leading character. Prof. Challenger even considers himself on par with Darwin and makes boisterous claims such as: "'You persecute the prophets! Galileo, Darwin and I.'" (*LW* 45), in defense of his scientific theories against the apparent ignorance of the public. For Challenger, science is a revolutionary and emotional matter, and his outspokenness reminds the reader somewhat of T. H. Huxley (known as 'Darwin's Bulldog' due to his staunch defense of Darwin's theory), whom Doyle greatly admired as a student (cf. Stashower 50).

In order to get access to Professor Challenger, Malone pretends to be very interested in the Darwin-versus-Weismann debate and writes to him: "As a humble student of Nature, I have always taken the most profound interest in your speculations as to the differences between Darwin and Weissmann" (14), and he continues with a question regarding some detail. Challenger takes the bait, the trick pays off and later Malone finds himself on an expedition to a lost world somewhere on a mysterious South American plateau, together with the leader Prof. Challenger and his companions Prof. Summerlee and Lord Roxton.

By the early 20th century unknown, mysterious places on earth had become very rare, or as the editor of Malone's newspaper says, "The big blank spaces in the map are all being filled in, and there's

---

[1] The mention of different evolutionists in *The Lost World* is more than name-dropping, however, and Robert Fraser, for instance, considers the mention of Weismann as a foreshadowing of the theme of degeneration in the novel (cf. Fraser 69–70).

no room for romance anywhere" (10). In 1910 Doyle made a similar remark during a speech at the Royal Society Club, raising the question of "where the romance writer was to turn when he wanted to draw any vague and not too clearly defined region" (qtd. in Doyle, *Annotated*, x). Interior Africa, South America and the Artic regions still offered some blank spaces on the world map and were therefore favourite settings for such adventure stories at the time,[2] but I would argue that Doyle's choice of a plateau in South America as the main setting for *The Lost World* was closely linked to actual scientific research and to evolutionary ideas in the novel.

Apart from offering blank spaces on the map, which could be filled with the writer's imagination, South America has also been tremendously important for scientific research, especially zoology. Some of the best-known evolutionary theorists, such as Charles Darwin, Alfred Russel Wallace and Henry Walter Bates, spent much time in South America and gained valuable new insights into the workings of nature. Arthur Conan Doyle was not only aware of this fact, but explicitly presents these scientists as precursors of Challenger's expedition in South America. Challenger thinks these scientific explorers left unfinished business there and declares his first journey to South America as a continuation of their research, during which he accidentally found the path to the lost world:

---

[2] For influential adventure stories set in interior Africa see, e. g., H. Rider Haggard's novels *King Solomon's Mines* (1885) and *She: A History of Adventure* (1887), which became founding texts of a popular Lost World genre in English literature (with precursors in utopian and satirical literature and Jules Vernes' fiction). Several scientific romances were set in the Antarctic region in the early 20th century, from Frank Saville's *Beyond the Great South Wall: The Secret of the Antarctic* (1901) to Edgar Rice Burroughs' *The Land That Time Forgot* (1918), in which dinosaurs and prehistoric men are discovered on the fictional island of Caprona (later explained in evolutionary terms in Burroughs' Caspak trilogy). In the context of *The Lost World*, the most interesting novel set in South America is probably Frank Aubrey's *The Devil-Tree of El Dorado* (1897), which uses a mysterious mountain plateau as a lost world setting (Mount Roraima as potential El Dorado), including prehistoric men and a giant, carnivorous monster tree. For an overview of the Lost World genre and the various geographical settings used, see Becker (1992).

'In the first place, you are probably aware that two years ago I made a journey to South America – one which will be classical in the scientific history of the world? The object of my journey was to verify some conclusions of Wallace and of Bates, which could only be done by observing their reported facts under the same conditions in which they had themselves noted them. If my expedition had no other results it would still have been noteworthy, but a curious incident occurred to me while there which opened up an entirely fresh line of inquiry.' (*LW* 26)

Doyle's novel emphasizes the fact that many biological findings of the 19th century were based on trying field work, which demanded a brave and upright man in the best imperial tradition, blending imperial and scientific romance:

[B]oth Summerlee and Challenger possessed that highest type of bravery, the bravery of the scientific mind. Theirs was the spirit which upheld Darwin among the gauchos of the Argentine or Wallace among the headhunters of Malaya. (*LW* 68)

Through references to Darwin and Wallace, who served science in a similar wild setting as Challenger's expedition, Doyle underlines that the scientist as a brave adventurer is not a literary invention, but that his main character is based on historical forerunners, whose dedication to new scientific insight was a physical and intellectual challenge.[3] Furthermore, South America was very important for

---

[3] Doyle's Prof. Challenger can be considered a speaking name in this context, challenging nature and his contemporaries through his scientific theories, adventurous expeditions and forceful manner. Furthermore, the name reminds the reader of the seminal 'Challenger expedition' (1872–76) that started the science of oceanography, especially given the fact that a participating zoologist had been one of Doyle's teachers at university (cf. Doyle in Orel 4). However, another one of his professors at Edinburgh served (partly) as model for the fictional Professor Chal-

the development of evolutionary ideas, including Charles Darwin's *Origin of Species* (1859).

Darwin's travels in and around South America for more than three years provided many ideas on animals and humans that would lead to his later theory of evolution. Moreover, fossils found in South America confronted Darwin with prehistoric, extinct species, which posed new questions on the supposed immutability of the natural world and possible causes for its change. According to Christopher McGowan, the discovery and interpretation of South American fossils paved the way for evolutionary ideas and directly influenced Darwin:

> [W]hat interested Darwin most about these strange South American fossils was their obvious affinities with animals still living there today. In his autobiography, written almost two decades after the *Origin of Species* (1859), Darwin cited these fossils as one of the key pieces of evidence that made him realize species were not immutable. It is probably no coincidence that Darwin started to write his first notebook on the question of the origin of new species at about the time he discussed the South American fossils with Owen. (McGowan 162)

The Mr. Owen mentioned above was the very Richard Owen who coined the word 'dinosaur' (meaning terrible/great lizard) in 1842, and who became one of the greatest opponents of Darwin's theory of evolution, trying to prove an unbridgeable gap between apes and humans (Mai 388).

---

lenger, namely the physiologist William Rutherford, who sported a similarly impressive voice, beard, chest and no-nonsense attitude as Doyle's protagonist (cf. ibid. 5; Lycett 51). Furthermore, several of Doyle's biographers have emphasized that Challenger can be partly seen as an alter ego of Arthur Conan Doyle himself (cf. Coren 139; Lycett 333; Pearsall 129), who "showed a fondness and enthusiasm for Challenger that contrasted sharply with his feelings for Holmes" (Stashower 276).

South America was not only a catalytic place for Darwin's *Origins of Species* (1859) and *The Descent of Man* (1871) but also for other proponents of evolution, such as Alfred Russel Wallace, who is mentioned in *The Lost World* three times (26, 45, 68). Unfortunately for Wallace, his own work on evolution was overshadowed by Darwin's writing with the appearance of the *Origin of Species*. Darwin's book was probably rushed to anticipate the publication of Wallace's own theory of evolution (Amigoni 117), which he developed in the 1850s independently of Darwin and which was partly based on his research in South America. It becomes apparent that Doyle's choice of South America for his scientific romance provides links to the history of science that Africa or the Arctic regions could not offer to such an extent. Moreover, South and Central America offer many distinct and isolated habitats (the Galápagos Islands are a well-known example), and in *The Lost World* the main setting is one of these ecological islands in the form of a mountain plateau, which was modelled on real South American plateaus such as the famous Mount Roraima.

In the late 1830s the German botanist Schomburgk discovered a strange region in Venezuela with many isolated flat-topped mountains (Doyle, *Annotated* x) and his descriptions inspired several Victorian scientists to explore them. One of the most fascinating mountain plateaus was Mount Roraima, at the point where the borders of Venezuela, Guyana and Brazil meet. Soon speculations came up as to what mysterious new or old species could be found on this isolated plane, cut off from the rain forest by huge, steep rock walls. In 1877, the newspaper *The Spectator* described Mount Roraima as "one of the greatest marvels and mysteries of the Earth", and called upon British explorers to lift this mystery (Ibex Earth). In 1884, the British botanist Everard im Thurn successfully ascended to the top of the table mountain and indeed found hitherto unknown species (although no dinosaurs or ape-men), and Doyle probably attended one of his lectures in 1885 (Doyle, *Annotated* x). The idea that such elevated islands could harbour extinct species is later extrapolated in *The Lost World* through the plateau as an evolutionary time bubble, for example when Prof. Challenger explains:

'[T]he ordinary laws of Nature are suspended. The various checks which influence the struggle for existence in the world at large are all neutralized or altered. Creatures survive which would otherwise disappear. [...] They have been artificially conserved by those strange accidental conditions.' (*LW* 35)

To make his dinosaur paradise plausible, Doyle not only extrapolates on the time-scale but also extends the spatial dimension of existing plateaus to an "area, as large perhaps as Sussex" (35), adapting natural phenomena to the needs of his fiction. Another important source for the exotic setting of *The Lost World* was the British officer Percy Harrison Fawcett, who had just come back from a visit to mysterious plateaus in 1910 and was consulted on South America by Doyle. In retrospect, Fawcett took a lot of credit for *The Lost World*, claiming that his descriptions eventually led to the creation of the novel (cf. Fawcett in Orel 165). Fawcett was certainly only one of many influences on *The Lost World*, and other previous and contemporary explorers inspired Doyle as much as the latest palaeontology or previous works of literature.

Walking with Dinosaurs – Prehistoric Monsters and the Long Arm of Evolution

Extinct species, including impressive Jurassic reptiles, can already be found in Jules Verne's *Journey to the Center of the Earth* (1864), in which two explorers descend deep into the earth and meet primeval beasts such as an Ichthyosaurus, fighting a Plesiosaurus in a subterranean sea.[4] By the time of Verne's novel dinosaurs had already become part of the public imagination, and while early

---

[4] In his *Memories and Adventures* (1924), Doyle reports his sighting of a similar-looking creature on a voyage in the Mediterranean Sea. Near the Greek Island of Aegina, he and his wife saw an animal "exactly like a young ichthyosaurus", and Doyle concludes this anecdote with: "This old world has got some surprises for us yet" (229).

finds of dinosaur remains were usually attributed to giant humans or other mythical monsters (sometimes thought to have been destroyed with the biblical flood), the ancient lizards had received considerable scientific attention by the middle of the 19th century (cf. McGowan; Debus, *Prehistoric Monsters*). At that time, the study of dinosaurs was closely linked to geology, the first science which undermined the biblical idea of creation some thousand years ago, which to some degree paved the way for Darwinism (ibid.). But already before Darwin, the discovery of such impressive extinct species led to new speculations about the natural order.

Charles Lyell, the most influential geologist of the 19th century and later a close friend of Darwin, speculated that Jurassic reptiles might reappear in slightly different form and that natural change was cyclical rather than directed towards man (Debus, *Prehistoric Monsters* 246ff.). The 19th century findings from geology and biology greatly extended the human time scale and moved humankind from the beginning and centre of creation to a much later and potentially peripheral position in the new timeline of the world. This paradigmatic shift has provided fertile grounds for science fiction, offering different new perspectives on the human condition and the future of mankind. Doyle's *Lost World* shows how modern science, especially evolutionary thinking, both questions and reaffirms the ontological status of mankind, for example through his juxtaposition of modern man with prehistoric creatures such as dinosaurs.

The Victorian approach to dinosaurs was ambiguous and oscillated between unease and reassurance.[5] On the one hand, the ex-

---

[5] The same can be said regarding the reception of the theory of evolution, which led to either high hopes for constant natural improvement or even a cultural evolution (e. g. T. H. Huxley, in some texts by H. G. Wells) or the fear of degeneration (e. g. in H. G. Wells' *Time Machine* and many other late-Victorian texts). The middle and late 19th century saw a number of different evolutionary ideas, sometimes coinciding with Darwin's ideas (e. g. Herbert Spencer), but often synthesising and extending Darwin's theory with various social theories and concerns. As Glendening has aptly pointed out: "In late Victorian fiction and society "Darwinism" represents an assemblage of ideas and tendencies that took on many and often contrary forms. […] Victorians' translation of Darwin's idea from the biological to social realm, relentless from the first, led to varied and conflicted applications" (Gledening 14).

istence of dinosaurs millions of years ago contradicted the biblical version of natural history, and these "Dragons of the prime, That tare each other in their slime" as Tennyson put it in his poem *In Memoriam* (56: 22–23) were fearful beasts and their depiction in scientific books easily outgunned the medieval monsters of the bestiaries. On the other hand, the dinosaur could be seen as a confirmation of the progressive Victorian world view, because the extinction of these prehistoric monsters fitted well into the idea of natural progress from physical to mental power, in which the modern British man was surely the peak and most impressive specimen, ruling large parts of the globe. The dinosaur became one of the wonders of the world that the British had discovered, classified and put on show, in books or even in London's Crystal Palace, where they became a great public attraction from 1854 onwards (cf. Debus, *Prehistoric Monsters* 108ff.).[6]

In *The Lost World* Doyle in turn takes an ambiguous approach to the Victorian idea of the dinosaur. On the one hand, we find the homely idea of the 'great lizards' as anachronistic beasts, who naturally had to give way to more flexible species, but on the other hand, in Doyle's prehistoric setting the competition of species has not yet been decided in favour of modern man. While the influence of Darwin is only slightly visible in Jules Verne's *Journey to the Center of the Earth*, the portrayal of the dinosaurs in *The Lost World* is clearly influenced by evolutionary ideas. As Pilot and Rodin have shown in the appendix of *The Annotated Lost World* (257–59), Doyle drew heavily on Ray Lankester's *Extinct Animals* (1905) in his depiction of dinosaurs and other prehistoric creatures in his novel. Lankester not only provided Doyle with great ideas and pictures of prehistoric animals, and is gratefully mentioned as a friend of Prof. Challenger

---

[6] For the inauguration of the life-sized dinosaur models, the management of Crystal Palace held a banquet with leading scientists (e. g. Richard Owen) on New Year's Eve 1853 inside an Iguanodon model (cf. Freeman 3), where the party broke into a song at midnight, with the humorous lines: "For monsters wise our Saurians are / And wisely shall they reign / To speed sound knowledge near and far / They've come to life again" (qtd. in Freeman 3).

in the *The Lost World*, but was also an important theorist of evolution. He tried to synthesise the concepts of natural selection and genetics, an approach which became known as 'neo-Darwinism' (cf. Debus, *Prehistoric Monsters* 191). In a study on early evolutionary theory, Robert England calls Lankester even "perhaps the most important turn-of-the-century neo-Darwinist in Britain" (281), and Lankester's evolutionary thinking is also visible in his *Extinct Animals*, especially when he tries to explain why certain species like dinosaurs have died out:

> It seems that a small brain may serve very well to guide the great animal machine in established ways, but in order to learn new things in its own lifetime an animal must have a big brain indeed, a very big brain. And the kind of animal which can learn – that is to say, can be educated – will, in the long run, beat the kind which has too small a brain to be capable of learning. (Lankester 151)

Lankester later continues: "Very probably this small size of the brain of great extinct animals has to do with the fact of their ceasing to exist. Animals with bigger and ever increasing brains outdid them in the struggle for existence" (209). This theory can clearly be found in Doyle's novel when Challenger and Summerlee discuss the reason why the dinosaurs have died out everywhere outside the plateau:

> Both were agreed that the monsters were practically brainless, that there was no room for reason in their tiny cranial cavities, and that if they have disappeared from the rest of the world it was assuredly on account of their own stupidity, which made it impossible for them to adapt themselves to changing conditions. (*LW* 131)

In line with this idea, the plateau in Doyle's novel is not a place where the laws of evolution are suspended but where evolution has stood still because environmental conditions in this isolated world have not changed.[7] Interestingly, the absence of dinosaurs in England is presented as proof for this evolutionary perspective when the explorers realize that the beasts on the plateau are old acquaintances from English fossil sites, such as the iguanodon:

> 'Iguanodons,' said Summerlee. 'You'll find their footmarks all over the Hastings sands, in Kent, and in Sussex. The South of England was alive with them when there was plenty of good lush green-stuff to keep them going. Conditions have changed, and the beasts died. Here it seems that the conditions have not changed, and the beasts have lived.' (*LW* 102)

This homely point of reference is not far-fetched, considering that for much of the 19th century, Britain was the most important place for early palaeontology and the discovery of dinosaurs, following Mary Anning's important discoveries in Lyme Regis in the 1820s (cf. McGowan; Debus). Accordingly, the actual appearance of the terrible lizards is not a totally alien experience for Doyle's explorers, and their statements reflect the author's personal interest in the prehistory of Britain. History was a great interest of Conan Doyle's, reflected in many of his works (first of all his historical novels), but in the early 20th century he became especially interested in prehistory,[8] palaeontology and dinosaurs (cf. Lycett 327; Batory/Sar-

---

[7] Several facts in the novel contradict the idea of a totally unchanged environment on the plateau, especially the existence of the ape-men and the Indians and their inevitable impact. Later, the reader even learns that many iguanodons "were kept as tame herds by their owners" (162), pointing to the potential of human ascendancy. Nevertheless, it seems that the balance of power between the different species on the plateau did not really shift before the intrusion of the Challenger expedition, which destroys the equilibrium.

[8] *The Lost World* was not Doyle's first story that involves a prehistoric creature, suddenly appearing in the modern world. In his short story "The Terror of the Blue John Gap" (1910) the English countryside is terrified by a monstrous cave bear, whose existence and strange appearance is finally explained in evolutionary terms. Debus considers Doyle's short story even as "the earliest tale concerning a prehistoric beast which also incorporated distinctive evolutionary messages" (Debus, *Di-*

jeant). According to Batory and Sarjeant, especially the "discovery in 1909 of Iguanodon footprints in the Wealden Beds at Crowborough, Sussex, excited the attention of Sir Arthur Conan Doyle and served as a stimulus to his writing of *The Lost World*" (13). Arthur Conan Doyle even had casts made from these dinosaur tracks for his Sussex home and used a photograph of such an iguanodon footprint for the illustration of *The Lost World* (cf. Batory/Sarjeant, 15–17). In the novel, Challenger is immediately reminded of the Wealden footprints when he sees them on the plateau (100) and links them to British research on prehistoric beasts. Typical for Doyle's explorers, initial awe changes quickly into scientific scrutiny, suggesting that the goal of Challenger's quest romance is largely the quest for new scientific knowledge, for which ancient monsters must be studied rather than slain.

On the other hand, the exciting shiver that the illustrations or sculptures of dinosaurs would have caused in many Victorian observers gives way to a mortal fear in Doyle's novel, because the ancient beasts are unaware of their supposed evolutionary inferiority and do not mind having British gentlemen for breakfast. As the palaeontologist Jose Luis Sanz has pointed out, a fictionalized lost world is "a place where humans are not the dominant species and in which mankind is scarcely able to survive against the enormous beasts of the past" (qtd. in Debus 40), and Doyle's narrative is no exception to this rule. The lack of a large, central brain makes the dinosaurs harder to kill in the novel, and modern British weapons, which had won wars against many natives in remote corners of the Empire, are quite useless against the dinosaurs. The mortal danger through the ancient beasts greatly contributes to the excitement and sometimes Gothic qualities of Doyle's novel. However, with ingenuity and the help of the native Indians, the European intruders to the Jurassic world can survive the great lizards, confirming the idea

---

nosaurs 40). Already as a schoolboy, Conan Doyle was fascinated by prehistoric artifacts such as fossils that could be found in excavation sites near his school (cf. Doyle, *Letters* 560).

of the 'Great Chain of Being' in evolutionary wrapping. But the dinosaurs are not the only new competitors in the struggle of survival for Challenger and company – another threat is posed by the 'missing links' of the ape-men, also living on the plateau.

The Missing Link – Between Apes and Men

The question of the 'missing link' has been posed since Darwin's theory of evolution, especially since he argued that human and apes are biologically closely related in his study *The Descent of Man* (1871). Already in the 19th century, theories regarding the nature of the 'missing link' have been put forward by evolutionists, for example by the German Ernst Haeckel, who thought that an "ape man without speech" was the penultimate phase of human evolution to modern man (Spangenburg 136). The apparent lack of evidence for a prehistoric ape-man was (and still is) held against the theory of evolution, but with new finds in the 1890s, like the so-called Java Man, speculations regarding 'missing links' as anthropoid intermediates between apes and Homo sapiens intensified at the turn to the 20th century (Spangenburg 130ff.).

It is noteworthy that Doyle's missing link differs somewhat from the theories of the time and previous finds of prehistoric men, like the Java Man.[9] Through his sharp and pointy teeth, Doyle's ape-man instantly evokes the notion of a dangerous predator, an impression that is later confirmed by the cruel and blood-thirsty actions of the ape-men against the Indians living on the plateau as well. Moreover, the ape-men have a much brighter skin than expected, something that immediately provokes the scientific mind of Prof. Challenger:

> 'This is a whiskered and colourless type, the latter characteristic pointing to the fact that he spends his days in arboreal seclusion. The question which we have to face

---

[9] Regarding other fictional treatments of the missing link, before and after Doyle, and the influence of the accounts of explorers on this idea, see De Paolo 25ff.

is whether he approaches more closely to the ape or the man. In the latter case, he may well approximate to what the vulgar have called the 'missing link'. The solution of this problem is our immediate duty.' (*LW* 120–21)

Challenger and Summerlee instantly recognize the importance of a live 'missing link' for science and especially evolutionary theory, and Challenger presents this discovery as one of the great merits of his expedition when he is back in London, because the ape-men "might be looked upon as an advance upon the pithecanthropus of Java, and as coming therefore nearer than any known form to that hypothetical creation, the missing link" (179). However, before Doyle's scientists can classify them, they have to fight them first, since the ape-men do not think that the modern intruders are their superiors. When Prof. Challenger gets kidnapped by the prehistoric men, they become rather unpopular with the expedition party, or as Lord Roxton says: "Ape-men – that's what they are – Missin' Links, and I wish they had stayed missin'" (138). When the party finds Challenger, the direct comparison between the professor and the ape-men is rather striking for the narrator:

> 'I couldn't have believed it if I hadn't seen it with my own eyes. This old ape-man – he was their chief – was a sort of red Challenger, with every one of our friend's beauty points, only just a trifle more so. He had the short body, the big shoulders, the round chest, no neck, a great ruddy frill of a beard, the tufted eyebrows, the "What do *you* want, damn you!" look about the eyes, and the whole catalogue. When the ape-man stood by Challenger and put his paw on his shoulder, the thing was complete. Summerlee was a bit hysterical, and he laughed till he cried. The ape-men laughed too – or at least they put up the devil of a cacklin' – and they set to work to drag us off through the forest.' (*LW* 138)

This passage is one of many in Doyle's novel that undermine the imperialist pretension of modern man as the peak of nature or the

British scientist and explorer as some kind of demigod. Brian Stableford even argues that the narrative style of Doyle's novel is "always close to self-parody", due to Doyle's ambiguous relation to the genre of the "boys' books", which often were "a celebration of courage, toughness, honour and veiled misogyny" (87). To portray a scientist ironically as an ape already had some tradition at that time, especially the evolutionists Charles Darwin and T. H. Huxley had repeatedly been depicted this way, but in the case of Challenger the idea is hardly to ridicule the theory of evolution, but to question the assumed superiority of the professor. Challenger thinks of himself as a superman, while he constantly refers to other people as inferior and hardly more intelligent than anthropoid apes. Challenger is not a 'mad scientist', in the sense of Shelley's Frankenstein or H. G. Wells's Dr. Moreau, but he is certainly not as rational as he likes to think. Contrary to his boastful self-image as a very reasonable man, he has a strong animalistic side with little self-control, a tendency to violent outbreaks and a primeval appearance. The idea that the human veil of culture and civilization can hide an amoral ape (who is only waiting to break out) can be found in several late-Victorian fictions, for example in Stevenson's *Jekyll and Hyde* (1886).[10]

Challenger's similarity with the ape-men, however, does not make him more friendly towards them. On the contrary, he sets on a mission to exterminate them after they have proven their violent nature and lack of morality to the British visitors. In one of

---

[10] In contrast to *Jekyll and Hyde*, and several other late-Victorian narratives featuring evolutionary ideas and lost worlds, the Gothic elements are, however, not dominant in *The Lost World*. Although Doyle's novel contains, for instance, allusions to the danger of degeneration, a strong irony undermines the Gothic qualities, the scientific world view reassures the protagonists and the novel has a rather happy ending. For a very different reading of Challenger's depiction between man and ape, see e. g. Jaffe, who claims, "[b]y combining these qualities, Challenger is the best of pre-historic man and the best of modern man" and "a perpetual reminder of qualities that the middle class has forgotten ever existed" (97); while Coren thinks that "*The Lost World* is so written as to emphasize the hero's greatness" (139). For a psychoanalytic reading of Challenger's ambivalent character, see Howard 115–19.

the most disturbing passages of *The Lost World*, the extermination of the 'missing links' is celebrated in social Darwinist language by Challenger, and justified as an intervention into progressive evolution:[11]

> At last man was to be supreme and the man-beast to find forever his allotted place. [...] Challenger's eyes were shining with the lust of slaughter. 'We have been privileged,' he cried, strutting about like a gamecock, 'to be present at one of the typical decisive battles of history – the battles which have determined the fate of the world. [...] By this strange turn of fate we have seen and helped to decide even such a contest. Now upon this plateau the future must ever be for man.' (*LW* 159)

Again, these exclamations must be seen in the context of Doyle's tongue-in-cheek style and unfavourable depiction of Challenger (including his occasional bloodlust), which prevent a simplistic reading of *The Lost World* mainly as an imperial romance that justifies British colonization and a social Darwinist world view. On the other hand, the notion that so-called higher species or races have the right or even the duty to show the so-called inferior ones 'their place' was common in Europe of that time (culminating in a global catastrophe with the rise of fascism). *The Lost World* can be considered representative of Arthur Conan Doyle's complex world view between a defense of imperialism and a great scepticism regarding

---

[11] Progressive evolution is a linear model, in which evolution is thought to move "toward some preordained goal", usually seen in "the increased independence from and control over the environment" (Mai 437). Although largely absent in Darwin's writing, this concept can often be found in the theories of his contemporaries (e. g. Herbert Spencer) and disciples (e. g. T. H. Huxley and Ernst Haeckel), and I would argue that this concept contributed to the growing public acceptance of the theory of evolution, because it reinstated modern man as the 'peak of creation' by synthesising religious and scientific ideas on the common ground of anthropocentrism and the need for meaning. Moreover, the idea of progressive evolution has been tremendously fertile for science fiction, especially regarding the idea of posthumanism, intelligent machines and superorganisms.

power and establishment. Doyle not only followed contemporary debates on evolution, human ancestry and related claims but contributed to this discourse through his science fiction novel in an original and often ironic way. In the context of the missing link and Doyle's interest in evolution, a peculiar discovery at the time of *The Lost World* is noteworthy – a scientific fraud that first supported and later undermined the evolutionary idea of a common descent.

The Strange Case of the Piltdown Man – Doyle vs. Evolution?

In 1912, the year in which *The Lost World* was first serialized and published as a book, the long-sought 'missing link' was finally discovered in a gravel pit at the English village of Piltdown. According to Russell's study *The Piltdown Man* (2003), the excavated remains corresponded very well with the idea that the missing link must have an ape-like body and jaw but a comparatively large skull:

> These pieces fitted the basic theory of evolution being propounded at the time for modern man had, it was argued, developed from the apes because of an expansion in brain capacity. The remains recovered from Piltdown confirmed this hypothesis, showing that it was the evolution of thought, and subsequent enlargement of the brain, that defined early humans. A huge media storm greeted the presentation of these remains to the Geological Society on 18 December 1912. The finds were hailed as one of the most important archaeological discoveries *ever*, something that would irrevocably alter our perception of who we are and where we came from. (Russell 18–19)

Since then, these and later finds by Charles Dawson have been declared as authentic by scientific authorities such as Grafton Elliot Smith and Arthur Smith Woodward, but have also been suspected to be forgeries by others. In 1953 it was finally established through fluorine absorption dating that the Piltdown Man was a fraud, which the London *Star* declared as the biggest scientific hoax of the century (cf. Russell 8). Later analysis showed that the remains actually came from a 500-year-old human and a juvenile orangutan (cf. Mai 414), so the Piltdown Man was indeed between man and ape, but surely not in any scientific sense.

Regarding *The Lost World*, there seems to be more than just a temporal coincidence of the appearance of the important missing link in Doyle's science fiction novel and in English soil in the same year. The Piltdown Man was discovered only a few miles from Conan Doyle's Sussex home, he was really interested in palaeontology and he knew some of the scientists involved quite well. Moreover, Doyle had already proven his talent for forging evidence with the photographs in the book edition of *The Lost World* (in this case acknowledged); and in the context of the faked Piltdown Man, the following sentence from his novel might read as a not even subtle hint: "'If you are clever and know your business you can fake a bone as easily as you can a photograph'" (38).[12]

In 1983 the suspicions against Doyle were condensed into a theory by John Winslow and Alfred Meyer in their academic paper "The Perpetrator at Piltdown", published in the influential journal *Science*. In this essay, Arthur Conan Doyle is declared to be the mastermind behind the so-called Piltdown Hoax, and Winslow and Meyer present this theory like a Sherlock Holmes story, building on Doyle's literary reputation and his scepticism regarding science in relation to his faith in spiritualism. It seems only logical to the authors that Doyle is the perpetrator, considering the apparent evidence:

---

[12] The best-known fake photograph in *The Lost World* shows Doyle disguised as Prof. Challenger and some of his friends as the rest of the expedition. Doyle went to great lengths in providing authenticity through faked photographs as illustrations for his story, using, for example, pictures from Lankester's *Extinct Animals*, as Pilot and Rodin have demonstrated in their *Annotated Lost World* (247-52). Even concerning Doyle's photograph of the dinosaur footprint from Wealden, Batory and Sarjeant have to conclude that such evidence cannot be found in any major collection and that "the track which Doyle found has never been mentioned in any scientific publication" (18).

He was a man who loved hoaxes, adventure, and danger; a writer gifted at manipulating complex plots; and perhaps most important of all, one who bore a grudge against the British science establishment. He was none other than the creator of Sherlock Holmes: Sir Arthur Conan Doyle. That Doyle has not been implicated in the hoax before now not only is a testament to the skill with which he appears to have perpetrated it, but it also explains why the case against him is circumstantial, intricate, even convoluted. For to be on Doyle's trail is in a sense to be on the trail of the world's greatest fictional detective himself: Sherlock Holmes. (Winslow/Meyer 34)

Most of the arguments in this essay have been refuted since then. The major point, that Doyle wanted to damage Ray Lankester's reputation because Lankester was a "dedicated Darwinian evolutionist" (Winslow/Meyer 40) and critical of spiritualism, is not convincing for a number of reasons. First of all, Doyle and Lankester were good friends at that time and Doyle made it clear that Lankester's ideas of prehistoric animals had been very helpful for writing *The Lost World* (Russell 226). Secondly, even at the time when Doyle had become a firm believer in spiritualism, he did not question the theory of evolution, and thirdly, Doyle cannot be considered a zealous spiritualist yet in 1912 (ibid.). The fact that it took more than forty years to prove that the Piltdown Man was a forgery also speaks against Winslow's and Meyer's theory, although they claim that Doyle tried to unveil the fraud in subtle ways, which were not correctly understood by the public.

Winslow and Meyer use several parallels between *The Lost World* and the forgery of the Piltdown Man against Doyle, concluding that "the Piltdown hoax was inspired by, or developed hand-in-hand with, the plot of *The Lost World*" (Winslow/Meyer 39). Portraying Doyle as a treacherous enemy of modern science, and especially Darwinism, they declare Doyle's major intention: "If science swallowed a scientific fraud like Piltdown Man, then all of science, especially the destructive and arrogant evolutionists, whom Doyle called the Materialists, could be condemned" (Winslow/Meyer 41).

"The Perpetrator at Piltdown" is a good example of the occasional polemics against Doyle and the dubious claim that Doyle's growing belief in spiritualism must mean that he disliked modern science and would try to damage its reputation if he could. Evidence to the contrary can already be found in the evolutionary scientist Alfred Russel Wallace (featuring as one of Challenger's precursors in *The Lost World*) as a famous example that shows that beliefs in evolution and spirituality are not mutually exclusive. In an interview on spiritualism from 1919, Doyle even cites Wallace as a witness to the spiritual cause; however, he does not show a grudge against other evolutionists, but rather regrets that they did not do research in spiritual communications: "It is true that Darwin, Huxley, Spencer, and others rejected them, but without adequate examination" (Doyle in Orel 242).

In his book *Piltdown Man: The Secret Life of Charles Dawson* (2003), Miles Russell presents a new theory on the link between Conan Doyle and the Piltdown hoax. Like some previous critics, he thinks that Dawson's discovery of the Piltdown man and Doyle's writing of *The Lost World* in pretty much the same time and place is not just a coincidence, but in contrast to Winslow and Meyer he sees Doyle not as the perpetrator of the Piltdown hoax. Instead, he considers Doyle's science fiction novel as an unintentional inspiration for Dawson's fabrication of the missing link in form of the Piltdown man. Russell presents the following scenario:

> Dawson, whilst searching for 'the big 'find' which never seems to come along', presumably listened to the details of Doyle's novel at the Windlesham lunch in November 1911 with glee. Here was the basis for the 'big find'; the discovery that would launch him from local to international academic recognition. All he had to do, if he were to successfully remove suspicion that Doyle's novel had preeminence over his find, was to push the initial date of Eoanthropus' discovery back to 1908. (Russell 229)

In creationist texts, the forgery of the Piltdown Man is still being used as witness to the supposed wickedness of evolutionary scientists and to proclaim the theory of evolution a fraud and inferior to religious ideas of creation.[13] In any case, the search for the so-called missing link is an ongoing quest in palaeontology and evolutionary science, and science fiction, such as Doyle's *Lost World*, has closely followed the scientific debates and contributed to them in its own, imaginative way.

The Lost World Revisited

Arthur Conan Doyle's *Lost World* has become an influential work of literature and inspired several later works. Thirteen years after the publication of the novel, *The Lost World* was released as a film in 1925, adapting Doyle's narrative in its own original way. There are a number of differences between the novel and the movie, mainly due to the different media, target audiences and necessary narrative compression. The *Lost World* movie focuses much more on the dinosaurs, especially their struggle for survival as a constant mortal battle among the different dinosaur species (with a rampaging Allosaurus as the leitmotif of beastly brutality), while the ape-men are reduced to one individual who follows the expedition in a kind of sub-plot. The ending is also more dramatic, because instead of a small pterodactyl, the explorers bring a much bigger Brontosaurus to London to prove that their story is true. However, due to an accident while unloading the dinosaur from the ship, the terrible lizard can escape and enjoys itself in the centre of London, somewhat reminding of Charles Dickens's early ironic vision of a dinosaur in the streets of London at the beginning of his novel *Bleak House* (1853). Similar to the unofficial sequel *King Kong* from 1933 (also featuring a lost world with dinosaurs, savages and an intelligent ape, and produced by the same lead animator), people panic in the film adap-

---

[13] Ironically, a world co-inhabited by humans and dinosaurs is presented as historical fact in the American 'Creation Museum', in which the creationist group 'Answers in Genesis' presents a biblical counter-scenario to the theory of evolution.

tation of Doyle's novel, especially when the ancient beast begins to destroy buildings. In the end it is its excessive weight that ends the nightmare, because when the monster wants to cross Tower Bridge the bridge breaks and the dinosaur falls into the river (and swims away). This ironic twist in the film seems to repeat the traditional assumption that the dinosaurs were too big for their own good and therefore bound to lose in the evolutionary race in the long run.

Some other works shall be mentioned in the context of Conan Doyle's legacy through *The Lost World*, namely the modern adaptations *Dinosaur Summer* (1998) by Greg Bear, *Return to the Lost World* (2010) by Steve Barlow and Steve Skidmore, and Michael Crichton's *The Lost World* (1995). In *Dinosaur Summer* dinosaurs are not only experienced through books and films but have become a common circus attraction, soon after the return of Prof. Challenger's expedition. The original *Lost World* narrative is presented as a factual report, which "began the big dinosaur craze. Everybody sent teams into El Grande and started catching dinos and exporting them for zoos and circuses" (23). However, the use of the dinosaurs as public attractions has led to their demise and unpopularity within a few decades, and in 1947 a new expedition is formed to return the animals of the last dinosaur circus to the famous plateau of Doyle's novel. The teenage protagonist Peter is able to join the expedition party, as his father is the accompanying journalist for *National Geographic*, and the team even includes Willis O'Brien, the famous animator who brought the dinosaurs alive in the first *Lost World* film. Considering Greg Bear's great interest in Darwinism (his 1999 novel *Darwin's Radio* has become a key text regarding evolution in fiction), it is not surprising that evolutionary ideas also feature in his modern adaptation of Doyle's narrative. In *Dinosaur Summer* Challenger's expedition did indeed provide proof of the theory of evolution and embarrassed the clergy, because "[i]t's bad press to claim Darwin is a fool and other extinct animals never existed, and then along comes Challenger ..." (61). In Bear's story, the South American plateau also provides evidence of the evolutionary transition of dinosaurs to birds, already proposed in the 19th century by T. H. Huxley but greatly substantiated by findings in the late 20th century.

Very similar to Doyle's novel, the mountain plateau is a unique microcosm that provides insight into the workings of nature, and the protagonists "can observe directly the evolution of reptilian lizard into dinosaur, dinosaur into bird, bird into the tiniest and most beautiful of jewels, as well as into the fiercest predator of all" (53). Greg Bear invented several new species for his novel (366–67), such as a 'Stratoraptor velox', inter- and extrapolating from various prehistoric species and thereby extending the narrative of evolution through his fiction. *Dinosaur Summer* also demonstrates great ecological awareness, and instead of hunting down prehistoric species as Prof. Challenger did, the expedition party prefers to preserve and watch them, with their adventure inspiring a possible new blockbuster film, "*Return to the Lost World*! Technicolor!" (362).[14]

Return to the Lost World is also the title of a recent pastiche of Doyle's novel by Steve Barlow and Steve Skidmore. Set in the year 1933, the protagonist of *Return to the Lost World* is Prof. Challenger's grandson, 14-year-old Luke Challenger, who has inherited the adventurous and scientific spirit of his grandfather. The reader learns that while no one believed Prof. Challenger's dinosaur story anymore soon after his expedition, he became very successful with his high-tech company Challenger Industries. His resourceful grandson Luke wants to find his mother, who has gone missing on her return to the Lost World, and has to fight evil Germans and other threats on the way. Of course, Luke has read Doyle's novel about the Challenger expedition time and again, and Luke's father bears a grudge against Conan Doyle because: "The famous Challenger Expedition to the Lost World! As soon as that blasted scribbler Conan Doyle got hold of that story, it was all over the place.

---

[14] Several new film adaptation of Doyle' novel have actually been made since then, with movie versions released in 1960, 1992 and 1998, including a *Return to the Lost World*, which was released as a sequel to the 1992 film in the same year. Doyle's novel even provided inspiration for a whopping 66 episodes of the TV series *Sir Arthur Conan Doyle's The Lost World* (1999–2002) and a two-part BBC film (2001), which is much closer to the original narrative than the TV series and one of the better adaptations.

He should have stuck to writing about that fat-headed detective!" (47). Nevertheless, Luke's knowledge of Doyle's works proves very helpful in reaching the plateau and surviving the adventure in this juvenile science fiction pastiche of *The Lost World*.

While *Dinosaur Summer* provides an ecological sequel to Doyle's novel, and *Return to the Lost World* shows its fertility as a literary inspiration even in the 21st century, Michael Crichton's *Lost World* (1995) is the most orginal and influential text that has been inspired by Doyle's *Lost World*, especially in its regard for scientific and evolutionary concerns. As the sequel to his seminal novel *Jurassic Park* (1990), it continues Crichton's highly successful Jurassic story, which brought dinosaurs back into mainstream fiction about eighty years after Doyle's seminal novel[15] – a real 'dinosaur mania', greatly amplified through Steven Spielberg's film adaptations. To find a natural, prehistoric lost world on earth, which is still possible in Doyle's novel at the beginning of the 20th century, had become basically impossible at the end of the 20th century. Accordingly, Crichton's modern reincarnation of the lost world is artificial, and created through the latest genetic engineering. A company specialized in genetic technology has managed to recreate dinosaurs from DNA found in the blood sucked by prehistoric mosquitoes, which became trapped in resin and subsequently fossilized in amber. For research, but also in order to recover the costs, the resurrected dinosaurs are kept in a kind of theme park, in which the Lost World adventure shall become a commercial operation. The ancient lizards, however, turn out to be much more intelligent than expected and use a technical failure to escape and spread havoc. In

---

[15] The emphasis is on mainstream fiction, since dinosaurs did not at all disappear from literature after Doyle's *Lost World*. From the works of Edgar Rice Burroughs (shortly after Doyle) to numerous stories involving time and space travel, dinosaurs certainly had their niche in science fiction literature; for details, see Debus, *Dinosaurs*. Many ideas in Crichton's Jurassic Park novels can be found in previous stories, including the idea of bio-engineering dinosaurs (already in 1929) and the use of fossilized DNA for their artificial resurrection (cf. Debus, *Dinosaurs* 126ff.), but none of these stories had the public impact of Michael Crichton's dinosaur fiction and their cinematic adaptations.

The Lost World, Crichton emphasizes the evolutionary aspects in this scenario even more than in its prequel *Jurassic Park*, and the novel opens with a meeting of leading scientists who listen to a talk on the connection between complexity theory and evolution. A palaeobiologist reveals that he knows of the secret Central American island that had been turned into the artificial Lost World, which seems to have become a term in evolutionary science:

> "What if the dinosaurs did not become extinct? What if they still exist? Somewhere in an isolated spot on the planet."
> "You're talking about a Lost World," Malcolm said, and heads in the room nodded knowingly. Scientists at the Institute had developed a shorthand for referring to common evolutionary scenarios. They spoke of the Field of Bullets, the Gambler's Ruin, the Game of Life, the Lost World, the Red Queen, and Black Noise. These were well-defined ways of thinking about evolution. But they were all –
> "No," Levine said stubbornly. "I am speaking literally."
> (Crichton 426)

They return to the Jurassic Park and find a second secret island on which some dinosaurs have survived the apocalyptic ending of the first novel. In the chapter 'Problems of Evolution', major characters of *The Lost World* discuss issues regarding Darwin's theory and it is suggested that the study of the recreated dinosaurs can bring new insight into evolution. The insight turns out to be a concept of cultural evolution, as it had already been proposed by T. H. Huxley and others, and in its modern version socialisation and culture are described as a kind of virtual DNA. This concept takes a middle position in the nature versus nurture debate regarding evolution, but the novel ends on a very sceptical note regarding the power of scientific theories to grasp reality:

> "Human beings are so destructive," Malcolm said. "I sometimes think we're a kind of plague, that will scrub

the earth clean. We destroy things so well that I sometimes think, maybe that's our function. Maybe every few eons, some animal comes along that kills off the rest of the world, clears the decks, and lets evolution proceed to its next phase." [...]
Thorne said, "I wouldn't take any of it too seriously. It's just theories. Human beings can't help making them, but the fact is that theories are just fantasies. And they change. [...]"
"A hundred years from now, people will look back at us and laugh. [...] They'll have a good laugh, because by then there will be newer and better fantasies." (Crichton 800–01)

As Malcom points out in the novel, at the end of the 20th century sometimes the whole world seems to be lost, considering how difficult humans make survival for many other species. The scepticism regarding the human position in nature is much greater in Crichton's novel *Lost World* than in Arthur Conan Doyle's book, and this suspicion extends to science, one of the greatest sources of scepticism in the first place. By moving scientific theories such as evolution close to fiction at the end of the novel, Crichton's *Lost World* poses the question of how far science is part of a grand narrative that humans need to explain their origin and destination. It certainly makes an exciting story, be it as the 'Greatest Show on Earth', as Richard Dawkins has called his latest book on evolution, or as a scientific adventure story of a prehistoric world, as in Doyle's groundbreaking science fiction novel. Maybe life is too complex to fully understand it, but it seems certain that mankind will never cease to find explanations for its nature, and that good stories will pave that way.

Works Cited

Amigoni, David. "Evolution". *Routledge Companion to Literature and Science*. Eds. Bruce Clarke with Manuela Rossini. London: Routledge, 2010. 112–23.

Barlow, Steve, and Steve Skidmore. *Return to the Lost World*. London: Usborne, 2010.
Batory, R. Dana, and William A. S. Sarjeant. "Sussex Iguanodon Footprints and the Writing of *The Lost World.*" *Dinosaur Tracks and Traces*. Eds. David D. Gillette and Martin G. Lockley. Cambridge: Cambridge University Press, 1989. 1–18.
Bear, Greg. *Dinosaur Summer*. London: HarperCollins, 1998.
Becker, Allienne R. *Lost Worlds Romance: From Dawn till Dusk*. London: Greenwood Press, 1992.
Crichton, Michael. *Jurassic World* [containing *Jurassic Park* and *The Lost World*]. New York: Knopf, 1997.
Coren, Michael. *Conan Doyle*. London: Bloomsbury, 1995.
Davies, Howard. "*The Lost World*: Conan Doyle and the Suspense of Evolution". *Nineteenth-Century Suspense: From Poe to Conan Doyle*. Ed. Clive Bloom. London: Macmillan, 1988. 107–119.
De Paolo, Charles. *Human Prehistory in Fiction*. Jefferson: McFarland, 2003.
Debus, Allen A. *Dinosaurs in Fantastic Fiction: A Thematic Survey*. Jefferson: McFarland, 2006.
—. *Prehistoric Monsters: The Real and Imagined Creatures of the Past That We Love to Fear.* Jefferson: McFarland, 2010.
Doyle, Arthur Conan. *The Annotated Lost World*. Eds. Roy Pilot and Alvin Rodin. Indianapolis: Wessex Press, 1996.
—. *The Lost World* [1912]. Ed. Ian Duncan. Oxford: Oxford University Press; 1998.
—. *Memories and Adventures*. London: Hodder and Stoughton, 1924.
England, Richard. "Natural Selection, Teleology, and the Logos: From Darwin to the Oxford Neo-Darwinists, 1859–1909". *Osiris* 16 (2001): 270–87.
Fraser, Robert. *Victorian Quest Romance: Stevenson, Haggard, Kipling, Conan Doyle*. Plymouth: Northcote House, 1998.
Freeman, Michael. *Victorians and the Prehistoric: Tracks to a Lost World*. New Haven: Yale University Press, 2004.
Glendening, John. *The Evolutionary Imagination in Late-Victorian Novels: An Entangled Bank*. Aldershot: Ashgate, 2007.
Ibex Earth. "The 2011 'Lost World' Expeditions". *Ibexearth.com*. 15 May 2011. <http://www.ibexearth.com/2011-lost-world-project-expeditions.html>
Jaffe, Jacqueline A. *Arthur Conan Doyle*. Boston: Twayne, 1987.

Lankester, Ray E. *Extinct Animals.* New York: Henry Holt, 1905.
Lellenberg, Jon L., et al., eds. *Arthur Conan Doyle: A Life in Letters.* London: Harper Perennial, 2008.
Lycett, Andrew. *Conan Doyle: The Man Who Created Sherlock Holmes.* London: Weidenfeld & Nicolson, 2007.
Mai, Larry L., Marcus Young Owl, and M. Patricia Kersting. *The Cambridge Dictionary of Human Biology and Evolution.* Cambridge: Cambridge University Press, 2005.
McGowan, Christopher. *The Dragon Seekers: How an Extraordinary Circle of Fossilists Discovered the Dinosaurs and Paved the Way for Darwin.* Cambridge: Perseus Publishing, 2001.
Orel, Harold. *Sir Arthur Conan Doyle: Interviews and Recollections.* Houndmills: Macmillan, 1997.
Pearsall, Ronald. *Conan Doyle: A Biographical Solution.* Glasgow: Drew, 1989.
Russell, Miles. *Piltdown Man: The Secret Life of Charles Dawson.* Stroud: Tempus, 2003.
Spangenburg, Ray, and Diane Kit Moser. *Modern Science, 1896–1945.* Rev. ed. New York: Facts On File, 2004.
Stableford, Brian M. *Scientific Romance in Britain, 1890–1950.* London: Fourth Estate, 1985.
Stashower, Daniel. *Teller of Tales: The Life of Arthur Conan Doyle.* London: Allen Lane, 2000.
Tennyson, Alfred. "In Memoriam A. H. H.". [1850]. *The Norton Anthology of Poetry.* 5th ed. Eds. Ferguson, Margaret et al. New York: Norton, 2005. 996–1004.
The Lost World [1925]. Dir. Harry Hoyt. Prod. First National Pictures. Eureka, 2001. DVD.
Winslow, John Hathaway, and Alfred Meyer. "The Perpetrator at Piltdown". *Science* 83 (Sept. 1983): 32–43. *Clarke University.* 17 May 2011. <http://www.clarku.edu/~piltdown/map_prim_suspects/DOYLE/Doyle_prosecution/perp_pilt.html>

Catriona McAra

OF PAPER CUT-OUTS AND OTHER WORLDS

Cottingley, Collage, Cornell, and Conan Doyle

The Cottingley Fairy Photographs have challenged and mystified critics and commentators for close to a century now. This article proposes to reread Sir Arthur Conan Doyle's documentation of the Cottingley affair in his book *The Coming of the Fairies* (1922) through refocusing the emphasis onto the role of the not-so-innocent paper cut-out. An art historical interpretation of the affair enables a consideration of both the contemporaneous avant-garde techniques and the visual culture of the period, which in turn raise discussion about the nature of hoaxes, questions of representation, and strategies of fakery. Finally, this article considers the Cottingley photographs as a model or precept for the creation of more recent art and design including that of Su Blackwell and Tessa Farmer.

Seit nahezu einem Jahrhundert haben die Feen-Fotos von Cottingley Kritiker und Kommentatoren Rätsel aufgegeben. In diesem Artikel soll Sir Arthur Conan Doyles Dokumentation der Cottingley-Affäre in seinem Buch The Coming of the Fairies *(1922) neu gelesen werden, indem das Augenmerk auf die Rolle der nicht-so-unschuldigen Ausschneidefiguren gerichtet wird. Eine kunstgeschichtliche Interpretation ermöglicht eine Betrachtung sowohl der damaligen neuen Techniken als auch der visuellen Kultur der Epoche, was wiederum Fragen nach dem Wesen von Scherzen und Strategien des Fälschens aufwirft. Abschließend betrachtet der Artikel die Fotografien von Cottingley als Anregungen für jüngere Kunst und Design, insbesondere von Su Blackwell und Tessa Farmer.*

◇

Fig. 1: Elsie Wright, Frances and the Fairies, July 1917

> Frances eyed me with amusement. "From where I was, I could see hatpins holding up the figures" [...] My world shifted a little [...]. Hatpins. Of course. (Cooper, *Cottingley Fairies* 169)

> The Cottingley Fairy Photographs reveal how Conan Doyle's scientific positivism compelled him to interpret the photograph as a document of an external reality, whereas the young girls themselves [...] understood the medium's deep relation to fantasy and other worlds and made it the mirror of their dreams. (Warner 234)

Introduction

The Cottingley hoax of 1917/20 has enchanted and disenchanted scholars, writers, and artists for close to a century now. The case has had much ink splattered over it, filled to bursting with trickery, deception, lies, and illusion – the stuff of all good stories. Indeed it is fascinating how the whole affair ran away with its own imagination and has been misrepresented in the subsequent scholarly and popular literature. This 'true story' involves two young cousins, Elsie Wright and Frances Griffiths, who, during the First World War, took photographs of what appeared to be fairies in the beck at the back of their garden in the Yorkshire Village of Cottingley near Bardford. The photographs might have faded into a private family joke, had they not attracted the attention of two literary and theosophical luminaries, Edward L. Gardner (1870–1970) and Sir Arthur Conan Doyle (1859–1930), who commissioned more photographs and brought the case to the public's attention.

A key moment in the many post-Doyle narratives occurred in 1978 when the magician James Randi and his accomplice Fred Gettings exposed the fairies which appear in the first photograph, taken in July 1917, as having a direct source in an illustration by Claude Arthur Shepperson (1867–1921) to accompany a poem 'A Spell for a Fairy' by Alfred Noyes (1880–1958) in the *Princess Mary Gift Book* published three years earlier in 1914 (Cooper, *Cottingley Fairies* 137). Gettings and Randi's discovery followed an important television interview in 1976 with the perpetrators Frances Way (née Griffiths) (1907–1986) and Elsie Hill (née Wright) (1901–1988). This programme was hosted by the journalist and politician Austin Mitchell (b.1934) who presented his rather blunt theory of the Cottingley fairies: "Cut-outs. Fakes. Painted on maybe. Conan Doyle was an old man" (118). The "paper cut-out theory" was consolidated in several articles in the mid–1980s: most famously in Joe Cooper's articles for a journal of supernatural phenomenon called *The Unexplained* (1982–1983), as well as in Geoffrey Crawley's articles for the *British Journal of Photography* (1982–86), and the protagonists' own admissions in *The Times* newspaper (9 April 1983). Dwelling on the revelations, the elderly Wright stated elsewhere: "I am sorry someone has stabbed all our fairies with hatpins" (176).

This article proposes to re-read Conan Doyle's documentation of the Cottingley affair in his book *The Coming of the Fairies* (1922) through refocusing the emphasis onto the role of the not-so-innocent paper cut-out. By repositioning the art work in the centre stage, this article will reconstruct some of the key visual narrative moments related to the affair, as well as hinting at an underlying psychoanalytic subtext in the shape of case studies by Sigmund Freud (1856–1930), a contemporary of Doyle. This article will also attempt to re-present some of the different accounts of the story including: that of Doyle's accomplice, the Theosophy chairman Gardner in his book *Fairies: The Cottingley Photographs and their Sequel* (1947/1957), the University of Leeds' Professor Joe Cooper's *The Case of the Cottingley Fairies* (1990/1997), and finally the posthumous comments by Frances Griffiths, *Reflections on the Cottingley Fairies: Frances Griffiths in her Own Words*, as edited by her daughter Christine Lynch (2009) after appearing on the *Antiques Road Show* (4 January 2009). The recent publication of this latter text is especially significant because it enables a third reappraisal of the evidence for a new generation. Reading between the strings of binaries associated with the differing perspectives on the Cottingley case: empiricism versus interpretation, reality versus illusion, truth versus fakery, science versus art, the paper cut-out emerges as the true jamming force in the works. One might argue that by shifting emphasis back onto the materiality of these paper fairy-cut outs and by highlighting them as a masquerade or *trompe l'oeil*, one can reveal the true crux of this fairy tale: Gardner and Doyle publically confounded by, or implicated in, the magical illusionism achieved by the creative conflation of such simple materials as paper and hat pins, frozen in a moment by modern photographic technology. This paper also wishes to reconsider the five Cottingley photographs as art historical documents by placing them in dialogue with the visual culture of the period. Here I will use them to access select aesthetic debates which were taking place in avantgarde circles on the Continent around this time. Finally, I wish to reinterpret them more broadly as important source materials for recent artistic practices.

Doyle's Intervention

Though the first two Cottingley photographs were taken in July and September of 1917, the case really begins with the high-profile involvement of Doyle who commissioned the final three photographs in the summer of 1920. By this point, the first two were an insignificant, blurry memory for Wright and her younger cousin Griffiths, but by Christmas that year they had been projected into the public domain. The whole affair would doubtfully have attracted the same notoriety if Doyle had not got involved and stamped his well-known name on the debate. It is significant that his first published thoughts on the photographs appeared in the *Strand* journal of December 1920 and March 1921, the same journal which had previously carried his most famous of fictions. Many have noted that Doyle tends to be confused in the popular imagination with his literary character Sherlock Holmes (Owen 61, Saler 613). However, the author himself was keen to distance himself from his literary creation. His growing involvement with Spiritualism, Theosophy, and, later, the Cottingley mystery may have been several methods of achieving such emancipation through escaping into the realm of the fantastic. The investigative techniques which he endowed his best-known protagonist with were put to the test when discussing the other-worldly evidence for fairies in his documentation of 1920–1922. Critics are often prompted to question how someone as rational-minded to create the logical personality of Holmes could have been so easily deceived (Wilson xi). For both Doyle and Gardner, not only did their professional reputations rest on being proven correct but they believed that proof of the spirit world relied on the truth of these photographs. Cooper makes a valid point concerning the public view of such an investigation into fairies by two adult males:

> To raise the question of a belief in fairies, with most people, is to invite ridicule. The very term 'a fairy story' suggests some sort of fabrication, and the whole idea of nature spirits […] is linked with childhood and fiction (15).

This is echoed by Carol G. Silver who suggests that the lack of sound scientific evidence in the Cottingley case drove fairies back underground during a historical moment of emerging modern technologies (9). Associating oneself with the supposed femininity, childishness, and irrationality represented by fairies was a risky business for a late Victorian/early Edwardian gentleman. Though committed to publishing a documentation of the occurrences, it is interesting to note how little Doyle got involved in the scandal physically, often sending Gardner on research trips to Cottingley on his behalf, after agreeing that Gardner would handle the "personal side of the matter" while Doyle departed for Australia (Cooper, 45). One is tempted to suggest that Doyle knowingly participated in the hoax, though there is not space here to develop this argument.

Modernity: Collage and Photomontage

Today there is little doubt that Wright and Griffiths' photographs were faked. To a twenty-first century, 'cut and paste' generation familiar with manipulated digital photography and computer-generated imagery, the cut-outs appear illustrated, almost cartoon-like as cardboard dolls or paper puppets. In 1917, photography was almost a century old, having been invented around 1827 by Joseph Nicéphore Niépce (1765–1833) and Louis-Jacques-Mandé Daguerre (1787–1851). Animation was, meanwhile, still an experimental medium, having developed from the motion photography of Eadweard Muybridge (1830–1904) and Étienne-Jules Marey (1830–1904), and from Victorian optical toys such as the zoetrope and fluttering thaumatrope. It was a medium still associated with phantasmagorias, magic and optical illusions by such early practitioners as Georges Méliès (1861–1938) (see Warner 2006). Though shadow art had been popular throughout the nineteenth century, and though animated shorts were extant by 1917, it would still be a few years until the first paper cut-out silhouette fairy tale animations of Lotte Reiniger (1899–1981), such as *Cinderella* (1922) and *Die Abenteuer des Prinzen Achmed* (1923–26), and two decades until the first animated feature-length fairy tale film, Walt Disney's *Snow White and the Seven Dwarves* (1937) was issued. One must remember that the Edwardian public was transfixed by the Cottingley images and rigorously debated their authenticity. One striking feature of all the literature surrounding the hoax is the proliferation of camera lenses, magnifying glasses, retouched images and lantern lectures which were used to focus the evidence. For instance, one lantern operator, managing a lecture which Gardner was presenting in Wakefield, was astonished to observe no trickery at work in the images he was showing for his lecture on an enlarged screen (Gardner 23). Doyle deduced that any image enlarged to this scale "would show the least trace of a scissors irregularity or of any artificial detail," and concluded: "The lines were always beautifully fine and unbroken" (92). Elsewhere, he mentions a "strong lens" used to inspect the photographs in detail (57), again prompting the reader to make inevitable analogies with the detective's magnifying glass. Both Doyle and Gardner refer to the consultation with the photography expert Howard Snelling; the eye of the expert always being regarded as definitive evidence.

Another suspicious idea which emerges in the Cottingley fairy literature is the seemingly naive reliance on the good will of everyone involved. For example, Doyle pondered Wright's ability as a draughtsman and whether she thus had the necessary abilities to hand-craft the fairies: "This naturally demanded caution, though the girl's own frank nature is, I understand, sufficient guarantee" (57). The insistence on the moral hierarchy provided an easy excuse in the deflection of suspicions of fakery. This was certainly the complaint of one notable critic, Maurice Hewlett, writing in the literary journal *John O' London Weekly*, as cited in Doyle's narrative:

> [...] why does [Sir Arthur] believe it? Because the young ladies tell him that they are genuine. Alas! [...] Which is the harder of belief, the faking of a photograph or the objective existence of winged beings eighteen inches high? Undoubtedly, to a plain man, the latter; but assume the former. (84–6)

Hewlett's complaint shifts the discussion from the moral dilemma to the issue which is really at stake here; the believability of the photographs. His exasperation with the photographic fakery continues into interesting territory:

> They are not well rendered by any means. They are stiff compared with, let us say, the whirling gnomes on the outside wrapper of *Punch*. They have little of the wild, irresponsible vagary of a butterfly [...] The photographs are too small to enable me to decide whether they are painted on cardboard or modelled in the round [...]. (87)

Intriguingly, the *Punch* front cover which Hewlett is likely referring to were those of 1849 designed by none other than Richard "Dicky" Doyle (1824–83), Conan Doyle's uncle. Hewlett's comment is matched by another creative criticism and speculation from Major Hall Edwards:

> The picture in question could be faked in two ways. Either the little figures were stuck upon cardboard, cut-out and placed close to the sitter [...] or the original photograph, without 'fairies,' may have had stuck on it the figures of fairies cut from some publication. This would then be rephotographed. (78–9)

This was certainly a technique which would later be employed by the Surrealist artist Max Ernst (1891–1976) for his three collage novels: *La femme 100 têtes* (1929), *Rêve d'une Petite Fille Qui Voulut Entrer au Carmel* (1930), and *Une Semaine de Bonté* (1934).

After assembling and pasting his collages from cut-out illustrations from nineteenth century scientific journals such as *La nature*, and book illustrations such as reproductions of engravings by Gustave Doré (1832–83) (Spies 509), Ernst would re-photograph the result to create a more seamless, other worldly domain – the 'sur' of Sur-realism itself suggesting a fantastical domain above or beyond reality. Surrealism historically followed Pablo Picasso (1881–1973)

Fig. 2: Max Ernst, collage illustration from
Rêve d'une Petite Fille Qui Voulut Entrer au Carmel
(The Little Girl Dreams of Taking the Veil), 1930.
© ADAGP, Paris, and DACS, London 2011

and Georges Braque's (1882–1963) Cubist *papier collé* technique which involved a play with glue and pasted papers in order to question the limits of representation 1910–14. Prior to Surrealism, Ernst was associated with the German Dada movement, which was roughly contemporaneous with the Cottingley photographs in Edwardian England. While this is not to suggest that there was a specific dialogue between the two, a visual comparison indicates some striking coincidences and overlap between Cottingley and avant-garde debates of the period. S. F. Sanderson has previously suggested the potential use of photomontage in the Cottingley hoax (92) but makes no link with developments in modern art. In discussion of the Berlin Dada photomontage technique by artists such as Hannah Höch (1889–1978), Brigid Doherty traces the invention of photomontage to wartime souvenir oleographs where families would cut the faces out of photographs of their loved ones and paste them onto devotional, patriotic clippings from the media (90). However, a recent paper by Hanna Rose Shell suggests that the American artist and naturalist Abbott Handerson Thayer (1849–1921) may have been the instigator of this photomontage fashion as early as the 1890s, significantly using the technique to capture camouflaged flora and fauna in woodland settings (2011). Either way, the Cottingley hoax of 1917 would have been a ripe historical moment for such an aesthetic occurrence, seeing as photomontage was already a trend.

If one dwells further on the modern technology of cameras, one finds that they played a dovetailing role alongside the cut-outs in the artificial construction of the so-called 'truth.' The ubiquitous line appears again and again throughout the literature: "Oh Frances, Frances, the fairies are on the plate – they are on the plate" (Doyle 43), suggesting that the two cousins celebrated the successful two-dimensional capture of their made-up species. Many critics have complained of nine-year old Griffiths' apparent lack of interest in the fairies in the first photograph which Gardner elaborately defended by claiming that sixteen year-old Wright's operation of the Midg quarter-plate camera gadget was more of novelty for Griffiths than the fairies in front of her (17). One remembers that Gardner sought expert advice in the shape of Snelling who was happy to go on the record with his view that the photographs were: "entirely genuine, unfaked photographs of single exposure, open-air work [...] there is no trace whatever of studio work involving card or paper models, dark backgrounds, painted figures, etc." (cited in Doyle 54, Cooper, *Cottingley Fairies* 80). Though a second opinion was sought from Kodak, the company initially declined to publish their comments, simply stating that the pictures showed fairies and therefore could not be real (Sanderson 93). Later Kodak claimed that the first two photographs showed paper dolls while the final three had been subject to a double exposure (Cooper, *Cottingley Fairies* 80).

Believers were, meanwhile, interested in the "aura" of the two girls (Doyle 17), with Gardner claiming that "Frances was mediumistic, which means she had loosely knit ectoplasmic material in her body" (19). The play of light is reminiscent of other examples of spirit photography such as Albert von Schrenck-Notzing's (1862–1929) representations of ectoplasm (c.1913). However, one could suggest that the fairies in the Cottingley photographs appear illuminated because of the reflective play of light on the cut-out paper's surface, particularly the opaque cut-outs in the first four photographs. The photographs themselves were analysed as being low in quality, either over or under-exposed, indicating an amateur's operation. And yet the question of the children's skill in the art of photography recurs in the Cottingley literature. Wright had spent some time working for a photographer at Manningham Lane, Bradford in 1916 (Cooper 111), not to forget the fact that she was already a skilled painter and draughtsman. She would go on to work briefly for a jeweller and a Christmas card company, both of which would have honed her eye for design detail and her ability as a craftsperson (Doyle 56–7, Sanderson 101). However, the fairy tale writer Arthur Machen (1863–1947), for one, remained less convinced, calling the Cottingley fairies fakes and "the product of a third-rate artistic conception" (cited in Silver, 192).

Paper Cut-Outs

We now turn to the heart of the matter. It is at this juncture that the present account of the event comes clean and wilfully accepts the Cottingley affair as a hoax, albeit a very artistic one. Griffiths' posthumously published comments are arguably at their most revealing when it comes to analysing the paper cut-outs in detail. In her *Reflections* she describes how the hoax was achieved. In doing so, the paper-cut out emerges as a recurrent motif for the fakery and illusion associated with the case. As Cooper, Crawley, Gettings, and Randi had already suspected, her older cousin Wright would copy the fairies from books like the *Princess Mary's Gift Book*, then carefully and very precisely cut them out and "conceal" them somewhere secret until they were ready to be photographed (Lynch 54). Next they would compose the delicate cut-outs in suitable places around the beck using long hatpins, presumably purchased at their local haberdashery, for support. The mechanics of the propping must have required a painstaking and time-consuming arrangement. Once the photograph had been taken and the fairy image captured, Griffiths further describes how they "destroyed all the evidence tearing up the cut-outs bit by bit and floating them down the beck and poking the hatpins into the earth" (55). Gardner and Cooper explain that Wright's father would search the girls' rooms and wastepaper basket and go back to the beck where the photographs were taken, actively looking for evidence of "scraps of paper cuttings" (Gardner 15, Cooper 238–40). His search was fruitless, the evidence having long disintegrated or been covered up. The remainder of the trick involved the construction of an elaborate and convincing narrative, namely a harmless white lie on the part of the two girls which they quickly lost control of after the involvement of such adult authorities as Doyle.

On the other hand, one suspects that Doyle may have been aware of his own celebrity and used this respect to his advantage by extending the hoax he knew these girls could no longer admit to. Cooper adds that by holding onto the lie, the girls may have become enchanted by their own fabrication and "terminally arrived at a state of chronic self-delusion" (*Cottingley Fairies*, 131). Griffiths admits that when it came to the second set of photographs commissioned by Gardner and Doyle in the summer of 1920, she was "feeling horribly uncomfortable about the cut-outs. It wasn't a joke anymore. People were taking it too seriously and it had all got out of hand" (Lynch 53). What seems to have especially worried Griffiths was the fact that for the second set Wright had "prepared only two cut-out fairies. 'One for me and one for you' she said" (*ibid.*). Two photographs were therefore all that could have been achieved for the second set, in spite of the new, technologically advanced cameo cameras gifted to them by Gardner and Doyle. However, this is the moment in Griffiths' narrative which leaves a little door open for the imagination, because *three* photographs were taken in the summer of 1920. The final photograph, often referred to as *The Fairy Bower* or *Fairy Sunbath*, is undoubtedly the most obscure and the most transparent representation of a fairy. Its authenticity has proven controversial. Doyle attributes it to Wright but Griffiths later claimed that she took it on a whim, and maintained that it was the only genuine photograph of fairies while all the other ones had been photographs of cut-outs (Lynch 57–58).

In thinking about the visual culture of the early twentieth century era as a backdrop to this paper cut-out affair, it is worth noting that the size of the Cottingley fairies is roughly equivalent to picture-book illustrations from this period, most notably the aforementioned *Princess Mary's Giftbook*. One should remember that this was the so-called "Golden Age" of picture-books when the gnarled, "goblin master" illustrations of Arthur Rackham (1867–1939), Edmund Dulac (1882–1953), and visionary paintings of Richard Dadd (1817–86) such as *The Faery Feller's Masterstroke* (1855–64) were still at their height as an Edwardian hangover from the Victorian obsessions (Cooper, *Cottingley Fairies* 21, 29; Owen 52). Moreover, the scrapbook collecting hobby was still very popular – embossed, chromolithographic scraps could be collected, cut out, assembled, pasted and overlaid, creating new visual worlds instantaneously. This was true too of dried or artificial flower arrangements, shadow puppets, toy theatres, and paper fashion dolls which could be dressed up by cutting out and folding over the tabs to create new stylish garments. Such material demonstrates that children of Griffiths and Wright's generation were no strangers to a pair of scissors and cut-out imagery. Furthermore, both book illustrations and scraps regularly depicted fairy creatures and nursery rhyme characters.

This was similarly the case with much commercial advertising of this era, which employed cherubim and other winged beings to do chores such as bathing and washing – many hands making light work. Many commentators, including Harry Houdini (Erik Weisz, 1874–1926) and Doyle's biographer, Charles Higham, have stylistically linked the Cottingley fairies to an advert for candles by Messrs Price and Sons (Houdini 124, Cooper, *Cottingley Fairies* 138–9). Another complaint which Doyle acknowledged was that the fairies' hairstyles were too Parisian-looking in the flapper bobbed-style to be natural as fairy hair supposedly would be (27). As the narrative theorist Susan Stewart reminds us, there was a cultural obsession with the miniature around this time (37–69) though she discusses domestic bibelots rather than nature spirits of the Cottingley variety. One of Stewart's key examples is the work of the American Surrealist-associated artist Joseph Cornell (1903–1972), who inherited and appropriated the Victorian miniature after seeing the collages of

Ernst from 1931 onwards. Cornell's box assemblage *Nouveaux contes des fees: Poison Box* (1948), for instance, includes paper cut-outs from an illustrated fairy tale book by Madame de Ségur. Cornell also appeared in a staged photographic collaboration with Ernst Beadle, where Cornell is depicted rescuing a fairy from a gigantic bolder in Central Park.

Though there is little evidence in Cornell's works and correspondence to suggest that he was directly acquainted with the literature of Doyle, as a child Cornell did see Conan Doyle's friend Houdini perform in New York. American magazines had been quick to review *The Coming of the Fairies* in such articles as 'Poor Sherlock Holmes – Hopelessly Crazy' as early as 1922 (Baker xix). Gardner also went on a tour of the United States in 1927 when Cornell could have heard about the high-profile Cottingley fairies. There is certainly a cornucopia of fairy creatures and butterfly fauna inhabiting his box assemblages which chimes with the artistic endeavours of Wright. The poet Carter Radcliff reads Cornell's cherishing of fairies and fairy tales as his 'nympholepsy': "a species of demonic enthusiasm or *possession* supposed to seize upon one who had accidentally looked upon a nymph," a sexual repression which employs fairies, or kitsch aesthetics and memorabilia more broadly, as a form of defence; symbols which celebrate the pre-pubescent and apparently safe nostalgic world of the childhood nursery (48–9). This may further explain Cornell's obsessive collecting habit; the profusion of objects and cut-outs from postcards and magazines as examples of the Freudian fetish. Freud's 'Dora analysis,' notably entitled a 'Fragment of an Analysis of a Case Study of Hysteria' (1905), serves as a useful reference point here, particularly in its discussion of 'nymphs' in the woods as a representation of the female genitalia. Again the proliferation of fluttering cluttering cut-outs, suggests a sense of overlap which one also finds in the layering of the forest – also the natural background of the Cottingley photographs – the undergrowth from which the fairy creatures would emerge. Hannah Decker has described for us the visual culture of the late nineteenth century, an aesthetic that Cornell nostalgically employs:

Fig. 3: Ernst Beadle and Joseph Cornell,
Joseph Cornell in Central Park, 1948.
© The Joseph and Robert Cornell Memorial Foundation/
DACS, London/VAGA, New York 2011

> Conventional art of the day, which was popularized for the masses through photographs in magazines, so frequently depicted women as scantily clad tree nymphs, dancing or sprawled on the ground, that one would think the woods were full of them! [...] the nymphs of the woods and streams sent the scientific message that once women escaped from civilized men's rule they reverted back to their wild and sex-crazed nature. (Decker 200)

Decker presents this idea in relation to the "nymphs in the woods" metaphor from Dora's second dream. In discussing a "symbolic geography of sex," Freud reminds us that the word 'nymphae' is the medical term for "the 'labia minora' which lie in the background of the 'thick wood' of the pubic hair" (Freud 139). Doyle pretended to defend the girls' fairy sightings by arguing that only pre-pubescent children are endowed with the magical ability to see them (154). In his writings he compulsively worried about Wright's ability to take the second set of photographs in 1920 seeing as she was now three years older than the first set of 1917 when she was sixteen, and had apparently since gone through "womanhood" (105). *The Coming of the Fairies* might thus be read as a coming of age tale. Nicola Brown has shifted emphasis back onto the girls and feminine fantasy following the misappropriation of the photographs' publication (63). Alex Owen's article is similarly illuminating on the issue of girlhood and femininity, arguing that the photographs serve as a "fragment of childhood which Conan Doyle appropriated" (79). Such appropriation involves a fictionalisation or exaggeration of the evidence. For Cornell and Doyle, as well as Ernst, at certain moments the magical potential of *feés* and little girls or transitional, pubescent *femmes-enfants* (child-women) become conflated and confused as fantastic worlds overlap. Often there is an emphasis on a cluttered visuality and textuality which enables an overlay and underlay between worlds through an intermedial cut and paste approach in both the art and literature associated with the Cottingley affair.

Cottingley: A True Story?

This article now turns its attention to more historically recent manifestations of the Cottingley fairies and paper cut-outs in art, design, and film. In Charles Sturridge's (b.1951) film *Fairy Tale: A True Story* (1997) the supposed innocence of childhood is emphasised by making Wright twelve rather than sixteen, thus making the girls closer in age. The film is self-consciously interpretative in Sturridge's stated aim to create a new fairy tale rather than a historically accurate account of the thoroughly documented events. Though Cooper's advice was sought in research for the film, the final result is an embellished re-imagining of the events rather than a faithful reading of Doyle's text. Here the children even meet Doyle's friend Houdini (played by Harvey Keitel), so that the theme of the magician who never gives away his or her secrets can be used. At times the film verges on being clichéd, false and unsubtle: Keitel's blatant prosthetic nose, a ghost-child brother of Wright who haunts the house, a comedy-villain journalist, and a misjudged magic-show montage which overlays trickery and illusionism, somewhat unnecessarily, to heighten the tension. However, there are moments where the film is more useful to the creative dimension of the present discussion, particularly the reporter's discovery and piecing together of the paper cut-outs in Wright's ghost-brother's sketch-pad portfolio. In another well-researched scene, Doyle (played by Peter O'Toole) displays his father Charles Altamont Doyle's (1832–93) fairy drawings and paintings as further evidence for fairies. This play with representation is echoed in Wright's drawings of fairies which her schoolteacher exhibits to the nosey journalist. Though the fairies are 'real' in their play by actors, Sturridge acknowledges Wright's artistic talent and the materiality of the paper cut-outs. And like Griffiths' version of events, Sturridge leaves the story a little open – Wright's trick is never fully explained. This is not to overlook the playful trickery and 'magic' of the film medium itself which enables the multiplicity of overlapping visual worlds, much like the collages and animations encountered earlier. Furthermore, though this film is based on a 'real story,' it is dramatized and seems to question its own believability. Houdini's published comments thus become relevant here in his claim that those who had had a mediumistic experience often "over-stepped their bounds and resorted to trickery in an effort to convince" (Houdini 141).

Fig. 4: Su Blackwell, *Alice: A Mad Tea Party*, 2007.
© Su Blackwell 2011. Photograph by Andrew Meredith

Cottingley in Contemporary Art

The paper cut-out tradition has been revived in the twenty-first century in hand-made artist's books in craft fairs all over the world, but perhaps most notably in the recycled book-sculptures of the English craftsperson Su Blackwell (b.1975). Through a mixture of delicate cut-outs, origami techniques, Cornellian inspired box-like assemblages or through using the book itself as a prop for many of these works, Blackwell is able to construct new Cottingley-inspired narratives, which often play on well-known fairy tales such as 'Little Red Riding Hood' and *Alice's Adventures in Wonderland*. Interestingly, 'Alice' was the pseudonym that Doyle used for Griffiths in his *Strand* article of 1920, perhaps after Lewis Carroll's heroine of his children's classic of 1865 where Wonderland is the fantastic setting. Blackwell's manipulation of her medium likewise demonstrates the otherworldly quality of paper cut-outs (Heyenda 57).

Fig. 5: Tessa Farmer, detail of *Swarm*, 2003–2004,
plant roots and insects, dimensions variable-insect scale
© Tessa Farmer

Elsewhere, the Rackhamesque illustrator Brian Froud (b.1947) has taken a more parodic approach, satirising the fairy sightings and hat pinning through his suggestively titled *Lady Cottington's Pressed Fairy Book* (1994). Containing illustrations of fairy figures squashed in the collector's mock pressed collection of specimens, the album claims to be a facsimile belonging to a historical figure who Doyle championed. One thinks of a butterfly entomologist pinning the paper-thin wings of their captured specimens.

The latter is more literally figured in the work of the English artist Tessa Farmer (b.1978) whose microscopic sculptures conjure the possibility of oxymoronic 'real fakes.' In the Cottingley literature, Gardner attempts a "straightforward" narrative of events (9) until the end of his book which goes into the minutiae of fairy creatures as if they were scientific specimens. He also claims the Cottingley fairies to have evolved from butterflies rather than mammalian origins (Silver 54). Such ideas can be observed in Farmer's practice which plays on ideas of a hoaxed reality with fairies that appear entomologically accurate as if they had evolved from insects as their own unique species. Using natural found objects, Farmer's knowledge of entomology was enhanced during her residency in the Natural History Museum in London where she was able to study specimens in detail under the microscope (see Arnaud and Neal). Here she was particularly drawn to a type of parasitic wasp known as *Mymaridae* or 'fairy flies' on account of their miniscule size. Like Gardner and Doyle's Theosophical beliefs, such work creates an interesting conflation of science and the fairy tale. Moreover, in an article for *Antennae* magazine, Alistair Robinson and Marie Irving were right to reproduce the first Cottingley photograph in discussion of Farmer's work (Irving/Robinson 13). Farmer's representative, Danielle Arnaud, has explained to me that in order for Farmer to conjure the fairies, the artist has to actively believe in them herself. Farmer draws influence from Doyle's uncle Richard, particularly an illustration called *The Triumphal March of the Elf King by Night* (1870) which involves similarly mischievous fairies colonising larger insects and animals as their hosts.

An even more intriguing coincidence is that Farmer is the great granddaughter of the writer Arthur Machen (1863–1947), a fact she learnt years after she began making the fairies but now appears very fitting for her practice. This generational aspect occurs again and again between Charles Altamont Doyle and his son Arthur, who would find proof for the fairies his father so rigorously believed in and faithfully attempted to represent (Baker, xix), between Gardner and his son Leslie, who would continue to defend his father's estate and beliefs, and between Griffiths and her daughter Christine Lynch who would publish the tales' 'ending' on her mother's behalf. Again one finds a metaphor of layering, this time genealogically.

Conclusion

Displacing attention back onto the paper-cut out has enabled this article to question the nature of representation, and to sift through the layering of narratives associated with the Cottingley affair to create a fluttering, cluttering intertext. It has also enabled a visual contextualising of the photographs, caught between a historical moment of fading Edwardian visual culture and the technologically progressive, modern avant-garde, and an exploration of the appropriation of the cut-outs as a precept or model for more contemporary modes of art and design. This article has undeniably accepted Elsie Wright's paper fairies as a hoax but claims them as art works. Both Wright's fairies and Doyle's account are representations of the on-going debate between this world of mundane reality and a fantastic, other-worldly domain beyond. Though the photographs were found to be single exposure, the illusion was construed by a double means: the assemblage of paper cut-outs and the use of photography to seal the composition which the cut-outs achieved; paper on paper, art on art, text on text. Though Wright liked to claim in later life that the fairies were "figments of our imagination" (Cooper 101) the missing fragment in the tale, which leaves room for suggestion, was Griffiths' comment that the last of the five photographs, her *Fairy Bower* image, was genuine, snapped on impulse whilst questioning Wright on how they were going to confess to their trickery. Frances Griffiths' posthumous account un-fixes our judgement and tears through the possibility of definitively closing the mysterious case of the Cottingley paper cut-outs and the other worlds beyond.

Works Cited

Arnaud, D., and J. Neal. *Little Savages: Tessa Farmer*. London: Parabola, 2007.

Baker, Michael. *The Doyle Diary: The Last Great Conan Doyle Mystery with a Holmesian Investigation into the Strange and Curious Case of Charles Altamont Doyle*. London: Paddington Press, 1978.

Brown, Nicola. "'There are fairies at the bottom of our garden': Fairies, Fantasy and Photography". *Textual Practice*, Vol. 10, Issue 1 (1996): 57–82.

Cooper, Joe. *The Case of the Cottingley Fairies*. London: Simon and Schuster, 1997.

Crawley, Geoffrey. "That Astonishing Affair of the Cottingley Fairies". *British Journal of Photography* 129 (December 1982–April 1983): 1406–14.

Decker, Hannah. *Freud, Dora and Vienna 1900*. New York: The Free Press, Macmillan, 1991.

Doherty, Brigid. "Berlin". *Dada: Zurich, Berlin, Hanover, Cologne, New York, Paris*. New York: Museum of Modern Art, 2005. 84–112.

Doyle, Arthur Conan. *The Coming of the Fairies*. University of Nebraska Press, 2006.

Freud, Sigmund. 'Fragment of an Analysis of a Case of Hysteria'. *Case Histories 1: 'Dora' and 'Little Hans'*. Ed. James Strachey and Angela Richards. Harmondsworth: Penguin, 1977. 44–164.

Froud, B., and T. Jones. *Lady Cottington's Pressed Fairy Book*. Pavilion Books, 1994.

Gardner, Edward L. *Fairies: The Cottingley Photographs and Their Sequel*. London: The Theosophical Publishing House, 1957.

Griffiths, Frances. *Reflections on the Cottingley Fairies: Frances Griffiths – In Her Own Words with additional material by her daughter Christine*. Ed. Christine Lynch. Belfast: J. M. J. Publications, 2009.

Heyenda, L, R. Ryan, and N. Avella. *Paper Cutting: Contemporary Artists, Timeless Craft*. San Francisco: Chronicle Books, 2011.

Houdini, Harry. *A Magician Among the Spirits*. New York: Harpers and Brothers, 1924.

Irving, M., and A. Robinson. "Entirely Plausible Hybrids of Humans and Insects". *Antennae* 1/3 (2007): 13–15.

Owen, Alex. "'Borderline Forms": Arthur Conan Doyle, Albion's Daughters, and the Politics of the Cottingley Fairies'. *History Workshop Journal* 38 (1994): 48–85.

"Photographs Confounded Conan Doyle: Cottingley Fairies a Fake, Says Woman". *The Times*. (9 April, 1983).

Radcliff, Carter. "Mechanic of the Ineffable". *Joseph Cornell*. Exhibition Catalogue. Ed. Kynaston McShine. New York: Museum of Modern Art, 1980. 43–67.

Saler, Michael. "Clap if You Believe in Sherlock Holmes: Mass Culture and the Re-Enchantment of Modernity, c. 1890–c. 1940". *The Historical Journal* 46 (2003): 599–622.
Sanderson, S. F. "The Cottingley Fairy Photographs: A Reappraisal of the Evidence". *Folklore* 84/2 (Summer 1973): 89–103.
Shell, Hannah Rose. "Skins of Nature and Emulsion". Unpublished research paper presented at *Taxidermy: Animal Skin, Colonial Practice* workshop at the Natural History Museum, London, 2011.
Silver, Carole G. *Strange and Secret Peoples: Fairies and Victorian Consciousness*. New York and Oxford: Oxford UP, 1999.
Spies, Werner. *Max Ernst, Collages: The Invention of a Surrealist Universe*. London: Thames and Hudson, 1988.
Stewart, Susan. *On Longing: Narratives of the Miniature, the Gigantic, the Souvenir, the Collection*. Durham: Duke UP, 1993.
Warner, Marina. *Phantasmagoria: Spirit Visions, Metaphors, and Media into the Twenty-First Century*. Oxford UP, 2006.
Wilson, Colin. "Foreword". *The Case of the Cottingley Fairies*. By Joe Cooper. London: Simon and Schuster, 1997. xi–xii.

Kati Voigt

A MATHEMATICIAN IN THE FOURTH DIMENSION

Professor Moriarty Travels Through Time

Professor Moriarty is often considered the arch villain of Sherlock Holmes. Nevertheless, he only appears in two stories – "The Final Problem" and *The Valley of Fear*. Although he is mentioned in five other stories, it is a rather low number considering a canon of about sixty stories dealing with the famous detective. Numerous authors have tried to find the missing parts in Moriarty's biography. However, nobody has ever pondered over the question of why Arthur Conan Doyle chose Professor Moriarty to rid himself of Sherlock Holmes. Is there a connection between the spiritualist and the mathematician other than their developing aversion to Sherlock Holmes? In addition, what is actually known about Professor Moriarty – either from the Canon or from research done by others? Did he really die at the Reichenbach Falls and which significant knowledge in the field of mathematics and physics did he possess in addition to binominal theorems and asteroids? Besides trying to answer these questions, this paper gives three examples of authors that have been inspired by Professor Moriarty and which unravel the truth behind this mysterious man. Interestingly enough, they all send him on a journey through time.

Professor Moriarty wird oft als Erzfeind von Sherlock Holmes bezeichnet. Er tritt aber nur in zwei Geschichten in Erscheinung – "The Final Problem" und The Valley of Fear. *Obwohl er in fünf weiteren Geschichten erwähnt wird, ist dies eine eher kleine Anzahl wenn ein Kanon von sechzig Geschichten betrachtet wird, die von dem berühmten Detektiv handeln. Eine Vielzahl an Autoren hat versucht, die fehlenden Stücke in Moriartys Biographys zu finden. Jedoch hat bis jetzt noch niemand über die Frage nachgedacht, warum Arthur Conan Doyle Professor Moriarty auswählte, um sich von Sherlock Holmes zu befreien. Gibt es außer der wachsenden Abneigung Sherlock Holmes' gegenüber eine weitere Verbindung zwischen dem Spiritualisten und dem Mathematiker? Was ist überhaupt über Professor Mori-*

arty bekannt – entweder aus dem Kanon oder durch Recherchen anderer? Starb er wirklich bei den Reichenbachfällen und welches bedeutsame Wissen innerhalb der Mathematik und Physik hatte er zusätzlich zum Binomischen Lehrsatz und zu Asteroiden? Dieser Artikel versucht Antworten zu diesen Fragen zu finden. Darüber hinaus gibt er drei Beispiele für Autoren, welche sich von Professor Moriarty inspirieren ließen und die Wahrheit hinter diesem mysteriösen Mann enträtseln. Interessanterweise schicken ihn alle drei auf eine Reise durch die Zeit.

Arthur Conan Doyle – Sherlock Holmes and Spiritualism

"The characters in this book are real persons. Any resemblance to fictitious characters, living or dead, is purely accidental" (Shreffler, "Introduction" 1).

At the turn of the 19th century, readers impatiently awaited new stories about Sherlock Holmes. They simply could not get enough of him. Dr. Watson patiently collected and published the cases, his literary agent Doyle, however, soon grew tired of the detective and planned his death. He wrote in a letter to his mother, "I am weary of his name" (Doyle, *Annotated* 15) and "I think [...] of slaying Holmes [...] and winding him up for good. He takes my mind from better things." (Doyle, *Annotated* 14). After Doyle finally rid himself of his most famous client, his 'death' being recorded in "The Final Problem" in December 1893, more than twenty thousand readers cancelled their subscriptions to the *Strand Magazine* (Doyle, *Major Stories* 10; Higham 114). People even protested and mourned openly (Higham 114). Doyle, however, was relieved to be free of his tedious hero because he "could devote himself again to higher literary pursuits" (Doyle, *Major Stories* 10). In his diary he simply wrote "Killed Holmes" (Doyle, *Annotated* 15).

In order to kill Holmes, however, Doyle needed an apt and able man. A mathematician seemed to be the worthy opponent for Sherlock Holmes. The reason is hidden in Doyle's belief in spiritualism. Doyle's interest in this belief began in 1887 (Jaffe 122). In the beginning, he was still very sceptical because he failed to find a scientific proof for it (Jaffe 122, 124–25). Nonetheless, he eventually came around to believe it himself and embraced it without further questioning. Even when confronted with deceiving mediums, dishonest séances and scientific proof of the contrary, "Doyle simply retorted that as there are dishonest people, so of course there must be dishonest Spiritualists" (Jaffe 125). Although disagreeing with Doyle on some aspects, his friend Harry Houdini once said "He believes that it is possible and that he can communicate with the dead. [...] There is no doubt that Sir Arthur is sincere in his belief and it is this sincerity which has been one of the fundamentals of our friendship" (Polidoro 23).

The Fourth Dimension – Mathematicians explain Spiritualism

Doyle attended numerous talks on the topic and it is only natural to assume that it was during one of the conferences that he was introduced to Professor Moriarty. Whether it was a meeting by spiritualists or by mathematicians is uncertain. Nonetheless, the topic was undoubtedly connected to the fourth dimension. A higher dimension has to exist for spiritualists which we cannot perceive or understand in order to talk to deceased people. Whereas spiritualists *believe* in another dimension, mathematicians *know* that there are more dimensions than the three known to us. They can even provide solid arguments for spiritualism. Therefore, Doyle and Moriarty must have met during a talk which combined spiritualistic beliefs with mathematical reasoning. Although this talk is not listed in any chronicles the argumentation can be reconstructed as follows.

First of all, spiritualists have to know that there *is* a fourth dimension. One of the earliest scientists to discuss this matter was Gustav Theodor Fechner (1801–1887). He was a German physicist and experimental psychologist of the early 19th century and taught at the University of Leipzig. In his essay "Der Raum hat vier Dimensionen" (1846) he tries to prove that a fourth dimension is possible. For his argument he has his readers imagine that a little man lives on a sheet of paper and, therefore, knows only two dimensions, namely breadth and length. He has never even heard of something called height, because he cannot perceive it. Fechner now reasons that just like that little man does not know anything of a third dimension, humans do not know anything of a fourth dimension – not because it does not exist, but because they simply cannot perceive it. With this reasoning, Fechner provides solid argumentation for a dimension beyond understanding.

Furthermore, spiritualists have to have at least some notion of how they would perceive an object from the fourth dimension. Charles Howard Hinton (1853–1907), a mathematician and science fiction author at the end of the 19th century, tried to imagine four dimensional objects and how people would perceive them in our three-dimensional world. His most famous creation of a four dimensional object and its perception in the third dimension is the tesseract which was used, for example, in "– And He Built a Crooked House –" (1941) by Robert A. Heinlein. Hinton's ideas how objects from another dimension may appear to other dimensional creatures were also used by Edwin A. Abbott (1838–1926), although in a much simpler way. The protagonist in Abbott's novella *Flatland* (1884) is a two-dimensional square that lives on a plane. One day the square is visited by a sphere from the third dimension. At first, the square cannot see anything. However, as soon as the sphere touches the square's world, he sees a single point. As the sphere moves, as it were, through the surface of Flatland, the point evolves into a small circle which becomes larger and larger until it reaches the diameter of the sphere. Then the circle becomes smaller again until it is a point once more and then it simply vanishes.

These are the mathematical outlines of a fourth dimension and how it would be perceived by other-dimensional beings. Yet, what does this have to do with Spiritualism? Hinton explains, as can be seen in Abbott's *Flatland*, that an object or a creature of a higher dimension can appear and disappear at any time and any place within the lower dimension (17). Add to that the idea in Abbott's *Flatland* that the square hears the sphere's voice only in its head because it talks out of another dimension. These descriptions of a fourth dimension would be a perfect explanation for ghosts appearing and disappearing, uncanny happenings like moving objects, and voices only a medium can hear – basically everything that is supposed to happen at a séance. It also shows how close the beliefs of spiritualists and the theories of mathematicians were at the time of Arthur Conan Doyle and how spiritualism could be explained by mathematics! Therefore, Doyle must have known from the first moment that the mathematician he met during those talks was highly intellectual and that he was his best chance to rid himself of Holmes.

Professor James Moriarty – Inside and Outside the Canon

Doyle must have been fascinated by Moriarty. This quality of Moriarty is supported by Watson's writings where the Professor is "one of the most compelling figures" (Watt and Green 175). Nevertheless we do not know a lot about this intriguing man. John Bowers correctly observes that "just as for Archimedes, our knowledge of the life of James Moriarty is derived from a biography of someone else" (17). This is further complicated by the fact that "despite how large he looms in the mythology of Holmes [...], Moriarty plays a surprisingly small role in the Canon" (Riley and McAllister 124). Out of 60 stories, he is only featured directly in two – "The Final Problem" and *The Valley of Fear* – and briefly mentioned in five other stories, namely: "The Norwood Builder"[1], "The Missing Three-Quarter"[2],

---

[1] In "The Norwood Builder", Holmes complains that "from the point of view of the criminal expert [...] London has become a singularly uninteresting city since the death of the late lamented Professor Moriarty" (781) and continues to explain, "with that man in the field, one's morning paper presented infinite possibilities. Often it was only the smallest trace, Watson, the faintest indication, and yet it was enough to tell me that the great malignant brain was there, as the gentlest tremors of the edges of the web remind one of the foul spider which lurks in the centre" (781).

[2] In "The Missing Three-Quarter", Holmes comments on Dr. Leslie Armstrong's reluctance to help him in a case and rather compliments him in saying "I have not seen a man who, if he turns his talents that way, was more calculated to fill the gap left by the illustrious Moriarty" (1001).

"The Illustrious Client"[3], "His Last Bow"[4], and "The Empty House"[5].

Professor Moriarty is introduced to the Canon in "The Final Problem", and this is the only time that he is actively involved in the plot. In *The Valley of Fear* he is the always-present evil that awaits its turn in the background. Moriarty's first name is James, which is only mentioned once in the whole Canon, namely in "The Empty House" (777). His appearance is described as follows:

> He is extremely tall and thin, his forehead domes out in a white curve, and his two eyes are deeply sunken in his head. He is clean-shaven, pale, and ascetic-looking, retaining something of the professor in his features. His shoulders are rounded from much study, and his face protrudes forward and is forever slowly oscillating from side to side in a curiously reptilian fashion. He peered at me with great curiosity in his puckered eyes. ("The Final Problem" 741)

We also know that Professor Moriarty is "a man of good birth and excellent education, endowed by nature with a phenomenal mathematical faculty" and that "his career has been an extraordinary one" ("The Final Problem" 739). At a very early age he wrote a trea-

---

[3] In "The Illustrious Client", Holmes remarks that "if your man is more dangerous than the late Professor Moriarty, or than the living Colonel Sebastian Moran, then he is indeed worth meeting" (514).

[4] In "His Last Bow", Holmes observes that the criminal Von Bork is not the first who wants to get level with him and that "it was a favourite ditty of the late lamented Professor Moriarty" (505).

[5] In "The Empty House", the reader learns, firstly, that Professor Moriarty's first name is James – this is the only time that the Professor's Christian name is ever mentioned (777). Secondly, Professor Moriarty ordered the blind German mechanic Von Herder to construct an air-gun, "an admirable and unique weapon" which is "noiseless and of tremendous power" (775–776), and which is the reason that in later versions he is often shown with a walking stick containing the air-gun. And thirdly, Holmes states again his opinion that the Professor "had one of the great brains of the century" (777).

tise upon the binomial theorem and he is "the celebrated author of *The Dynamics of an Asteroid*" (The Valley of Fear 6) which was not understood by other scientists. Nevertheless, his treatise won him a "mathematical chair at one of [the] smaller universities" ("The Final Problem" 739). However, Moriarty soon turned his talents to a criminal career. Holmes calls him "the Napoleon of crime" and adds that Moriarty "is the organizer of half that is evil and of nearly all that is undetected in this great city" ("The Final Problem" 740). But no matter how guilty the Professor might be, "so aloof is he from general suspicion, so immune from criticism, so admirable in his management and self-effacement, that for those very words that you have uttered he could hale you to a court and emerge with your year's pension as a solatium for his wounded character" (*The Valley of Fear* 6). This shows that the Professor is "a very respectable, learned, and talented sort of man" (*The Valley of Fear* 15). In *The Valley of Fear*, we also learn more about his personal background. From "The Final Problem" we already know that he has a brother named Colonel James Moriarty (737). Now, we hear that the Professor is unmarried, that "his younger brother is a station master in the west of England", that he earns "seven hundred a year" and that he owns a picture by Greuze (*The Valley of Fear* 16). Unfortunately, the information we can gather from Dr. Watson's writings is not reliable in respect to Professor Moriarty's family. First of all, it is rather curious that two brothers in one family are supposed to have the same Christian name – James. Secondly, it is not apparent whether Colonel James Moriarty and the mentioned younger brother are in fact two different brothers or actually the same person.

The lack of information on Professor Moriarty within the Canon and mysterious flaws in Dr. Watson's accounts about him have inspired other authors to make further investigations. They tried to find hidden clues in the text and used other background information to fill in the gaps of Moriarty's life. Whole articles and chapters are written about those assertions.[6] For all of them, it is

---

[6] See for example Bowers; Canton; T. H. Hall; McKie; Rennison; Schaefer; Shreffler.

obvious that Moriarty is of Irish descent (Bowers 17–18; Trevor Hall 8; Shreffler 263), most likely from County Kerry (Shreffler 263; Canton 20), although one author claims that Moriarty's family lived "in Greystone, a small town on the coastal road between Dublin and Wicklow" (Rennison 67). Moriarty was born in 1846 (Trevor Hall 7; Shreffler 264) at "the end of October or the beginning of November" (Shreffler 265), though Bowers suggests very convincingly that his birth year is 1840 (17–18) and Rennison beliefs that 1849 is the correct year (67). Moriarty comes from a Roman Catholic family (Bowers 17), entered the Junior Seminary (Bowers 17) and attended either Queen's College in Cork (Bowers 18) or Trinity College in Dublin (Trevor Hall 10). However, Rennison remarks that "as a Catholic, Moriarty was unable to enter Trinity College, Dublin, which was an exclusively Protestant establishment" (68). Therefore, he attended the newly founded University College, Dublin (Rennison 68). It was during that time, that he wrote his famous treatise which "was actually dedicated to Carl Gottfried Neumann, a professor at the University of Leipzig" (Rennison 68). His father was Barnardo Eagle, a travelling conjurer, who was "suggestively referred to as 'The Napoleon of Wizards'" (Shreffler 263). At a comparatively early age, Moriarty became a Professor of Mathematics at one of the smaller universities ("The Final Problem" 739). This university is believed to be Durham (Rennison 68; Shreffler 265; Trevor Hall 12; Rennison 68).

It is often claimed that Moriarty is a pseudonym to hide the identity of another man and much speculation has been done about the possible role model for Moriarty. Charles Frederick Higham, for instance, claims that Moriarty's Christian name comes from the editor of *The Cornhill*, James Payn, because he is said to have had "Moriarty's spidery figure, deathly complexion, and pallid brow" (113). Higham also suggests that Moriarty's surname is taken from the criminal George Moriarty because Doyle had read about him in the *Times* after his arrival in London (34). Although Holmes connects Professor Moriarty with Jonathan Wild (*The Valley of Fear* 18; Riley and McAllister 125), Moriarty is often associated with Adam Worth (Mortimer; Higham 113; Rennison 66). Firstly, Worth was called 'the Napoleon of the criminal world' (Macintyre 7) and, secondly, he stole a famous portrait painting of Georgiana, Duchess of Devonshire, from Thomas Agnew's gallery (Mortimer; Macintyre 2–3; Higham 114; Rennison 66). As we know, Moriarty owns a stolen painting called 'La Jeune à l'Agneau', and it is said to be a pun on Agnew's gallery (Mortimer). Looking at Moriarty's mathematical and astronomical talents, Doyle's friend Major-General Alfred Wilks Drayson is a possibility (Doyle, *The Valley of Fear* 18; Higham 113). The private joke is that professional astronomers refused to take Drayson's theories seriously. Doyle used this and claimed that the scientific press was not able to understand Moriarty's work on the asteroid (Doyle, *Valley of Fear* 18). Professor Moriarty may also be based on the American astronomer Simon Newcomb, because their biographical background is almost identical (Schaefer 31–32), or on the mathematician and astronomer Karl Friedrich Gauss (Schaefer 31; Shreffler 266–267), who had written an important paper on the dynamics of the asteroid Ceres (Teets and Whitehead). Other potential models include (1) Reverend Thomas Kay, S. J., the Prefect of Discipline at Doyle's school Stonyhurst because he looked like Moriarty (Doyle, *The Valley of Fear* 181), (2) the Rothschild family who had enormous power in England and a likeness of body type to him (Canton 18), and (3) "two eponymous fellow-students at Stonyhurst, one an infant prodigy in mathematics, the other a future Irish Lord Justice of notable lack of scruple" (Doyle, *The Valley of Fear* 174). Rennison states that "Moriarty was no fictional creation nor was he one of the names Watson used to hide another's identity. Moriarty was very much a real person and he was to haunt Holmes for most of the 1880s" (Rennison 66). Nonetheless, considering all the possible prototypes for Professor Moriarty, Rolf Canton justly argues that "a blend of notable persons is quite a reasonable possibility for the Moriarty we love to hate" (Canton 18). After all, even Arthur Conan Doyle would not let Watson write about such a dangerous man as Professor Moriarty without fictionalizing him to some extent.

In the whole Canon it is emphasized that Professor Moriarty is Sherlock Holmes' intellectual equal and both seem to be "two forces [that] oppose each other in perfect equality" (Canton 4). Considering "Newton's Laws of Motion in physics: for every action there is an equal and opposite reaction" (Canton 4) it is not surprising to find those "two titans in battle, one the genius for good and the other an equal genius for evil" (Canton 4). In "The Final Problem", it finally came to this combat between Holmes and Moriarty at the Reichenbach Falls and both fell over the rim into the abyss. Watson writes that "any attempt at recovering the bodies was absolutely hopeless, and there, deep down in that dreadful cauldron of swirling water and seething foam, will lie for all time the most dangerous criminal and the foremost champion of the law of their generation" ("The Final Problem" 755). In "The Empty House", however, Sherlock Holmes returns. The question is – why could not Moriarty have survived as well? First of all, Holmes tells Watson "I am not a fanciful person, but I give you my word that I seemed to hear Moriarty's voice screaming at me out of the abyss" (*The Empty House* 766). Secondly, Moriarty's body was never found. Thirdly, maybe the newspaper letter by Colonel Moriarty was a hoax, "since the signature is 'James Moriarty' – the same as the professor's" (McKie). Therefore, can we really be certain that Moriarty died on 4 May, 1891 falling down the Reichenbach Falls in Switzerland? Since Professor Moriarty, being an extraordinary mathematician, knew that a fourth dimension exists, he must have been aware of the possibility of time travel as well. Therefore, he could have saved himself by the means of time travel.

Time Travel – Its Science and its Paradoxes

But what exactly is time travel and how is it achieved? Earlier in this paper the idea of a fourth dimension was already established. While Fechner argues for a fourth dimension, he is using time to explain his idea. He describes that if the sheet of paper, with the little man on it, is moved through the third dimension the little man will experience everything connected to this third dimension. For example, the light beams will change the colour of the little man. He may be red and smooth in the beginning but will turn blue and wrinkled at the end. The little man knows nothing of light beams because they are beyond his two dimensions. But he will perceive the change gradually. Therefore, he will think that something like 'time' exists and that 'time' changes everything. What does that mean for humans? Humans are beings in a three-dimensional world and the world moves through a four-dimensional space. This movement is not felt as such but experienced as a temporal element of life. Thus, Fechner is not only one of the first to introduce a spatial fourth dimension but he also was one of the earliest to connect time to this concept.

Of course, the person to popularize the idea of time being the fourth dimension was H. G. Wells (1866–1946). In his scientific romance *The Time Machine*, published in 1895, he uses a similar argument to Fechner's. In the beginning, the Time Traveller tells his dinner guests that a cube cannot truly exist if it had only length, breadth, and thickness. In order to be real, it has to last in time as well (Wells 4). Therefore, "any real body must have extension in four directions: it must have Length, Breadth, Thickness, and – Duration" (Wells 4–5). He goes on to explain that "there is no difference between Time and any of the three dimensions of Space except that our consciousness moves along it" (Wells 5–6). To clarify his theory he gives the following example:

> For instance, here is a portrait of a man at eight years old, another at fifteen, another at seventeen, another at twenty-three, and so on. All these are evidently sections, as it were, Three-Dimensional representations of his Four-Dimensioned being, which is a fixed and unalterable thing. (Wells 6–7)

This argument can be considered to be the real foundation of time travel. Although it took thirteen years, it was introduced in mathematics and physics by Hermann Minkowski (1864–1909) (Nahin 157). He described in his paper "Raum und Zeit", which he presented in 1908, his concept of *spacetime*. In it he combines time and space into one single dimension and argues that they cannot be separated (Minkowski 1909). This notion was completely new to science which always viewed space and time independently. Albert Einstein (1879–1955) later appreciated the "power and conceptual beauty" (Nahin 152) of this spacetime dimension and used it in his general relativity theory in 1916 (Nahin 152). Most scientists now agree that Einstein's theory of relativity makes time travel into the future theoretically possible (Barksdale 75; Pickover 16; von Rauchhaupt; Nahin 18).

In general, time travel occurs when the "traveler's journey as judged by the traveler's clock takes a different amount of time than the journey does as judged by the clocks of those who do not take the journey" (Dowden and Bradley; Hunter and Joel; Nahin 25). For example, if Jane travels for one hour according to her own clock but for two hours measured by her friends, who stayed at home, then this would be time travel (Hunter and Joel). The first scientifically observed time travel took place in October 1971. Joseph Hafele und Richard Keating, two American physicists, flew with airliners eastwards once around the world. Back at home they discovered that for them time had not gone by as fast as for the people in Washington. They had travelled into the future – although only 60 nanoseconds (von Rauchhaupt). According to Einstein's theory, if an astronaut were to travel with almost the speed of light the effect witnessed by Hafele and Keating would be considerably stronger. He would not grow as old as his twin brother on earth. However he would never be able to return to the point in time where they are the same age (von Rauchhaupt).

Plainly, as soon as the past is involved, time travel becomes problematic if not even impossible (Dowden and Bradley; Hunter and Joel; Pickover 16). However, "the general theory [...] does allow time travel to the past under certain conditions" (Nahin 18). In 1949, the mathematician Kurt Gödel (1906–1978) found an explanation of how mass-energy cannot only move through space but also *backward in time* (Nahin 19). Gödel's theory was not intended to explain time travel to the past and is, therefore, very technical and theoretical. In addition, in contrast to travels to the future, travels to the past have not yet been proven in the slightest way. Nevertheless, it is much more interesting to study.

First of all, there is the question of whether we can affect the past or not. Would we know whether someone changed something or would everything seem normal to us? For example, in Ray Bradbury's classic "A Sound of Thunder" (1952) only the time travellers realise that the future has changed. For everyone else, everything seems to be normal. And if someone affects the past could that not already have been part of our reality and the time traveler only did what he had already done? This idea is discussed in Audrey Niffenegger's *The Time Traveler's Wife* (2003). Or would time travel create multiple universes which would co-exist but be different from the point of the time traveller's arrival onwards? This would eventually lead to alternative histories like Philip K. Dick's *The Man in the High Castle* (1962). Second, time travel, especially to the past, involves numerous paradoxes which mostly result from problems with causation. Let us consider three of them. First the grandfather paradox which is the most popular (Hunter; Aparta 98; Barksdale 103). Suppose a time traveler goes back in time and kills his grandfather before the time traveler's father is conceived. Then, one of the time traveler's parents does not exist and, therefore, the time traveler cannot be born. If he is not born, how can he go back in time to kill his grandfather (Nahin 48)? The grandfather paradox also explains why nobody can kill himself in the past. Second, the predestination paradox (Aparta 102) or sexual paradox (Nahin 319). It is conceptually the opposite of the grandfather paradox. This involves a time traveller who goes back in time, marries his own mother and, therefore, becomes his own father (Nahin 319). How is that possible? Or rather, is that possible? To reason it out is almost as mind-boggling as the question: "What was first, the hen or the egg?" Third, and last, the ontological paradox (Aparta 101) or closed time loop (Nahin 304). It is closely connected to the predestination paradox. Larry Dwyer uses this paradox to offer a possible reason for his time traveller's journey:

> In our time travel story it just may be that the traveler's interest in going back to ancient Egypt is stimulated by recently discovered documents, found near Cairo, con-

taining the diary of a person claiming to be a time traveler, whereupon our hero, realizing it is himself, immediately begins [...] the construction of a rocket in order to 'fulfill his destiny'. (Nahin 304)

Both events for themselves make perfect sense: "(1) he builds a time machine and goes back to the past because of the discovered diary, and (2) the diary is discovered because he goes back to the past" (Nahin 304). Combined, however, they form an argument that, because of its circularity, is highly confusing.

Professor Moriarty Travels Through Time

Professor Moriarty must have known these theories long before science actually proclaimed them. According to Edgar W. Smith "it is impossible to escape the conclusion that Moriarty, long before Albert Einstein, glimpsed the awful potentialities of the formula E equals mc2" (quoted in Trevor Hall 1). He goes one step further proclaiming that "the title of Professor Einstein's Special Theory of Relativity, *Zur Elektrodynamik Bewegter Koerper* ('On the Electrodynamics of Moving Bodies'), first published in *Ann. d. Physik*, June, 1905, was suggestively imitative of the title of Dr. Moriarty's *The Dynamics of an Asteroid*, which was certainly in print as early as 1888" (Trevor Hall 1–2). Therefore, Professor Moriarty was able to explain and even use time travel even before Einstein. Robert Lee Hall's *Exit Sherlock Holmes* (1977), David Dvorkin's *Time for Sherlock Holmes* (1983) and Anne Lear's short story "The Adventure of the Global Traveller" (1978) all depict Moriarty's knowledge of time travel and include some problems of time travel mentioned above as well.

Robert Lee Hall's *Exit Sherlock Holmes* (1977) is supposedly an unpublished case of Sherlock Holmes. Years after his last case, Holmes reveals that Moriarty is still alive. Therefore, the detective wants to disappear but warns that nobody is supposed to know about Moriarty. Later, Watson learns that Holmes has a secret laboratory in the basement of Baker Street. One of the rooms contains a strange-looking cage. Moriarty gains entrance to the room and explains that he is Holmes' "equal in the Eastern art of baritsu, which teaches one how to fall as well as fight" (Robert Lee Hall 46). He broke his left leg in three places, his arm in two, cracked several ribs and had numerous bruises but he was still alive. At seeing the cage, he gets into a fit, destroys it and sets the room on fire. Watson barely escapes the flames and meets Wiggins, one of the boys that ran errands for Holmes. Together, they start a search for Holmes. After finally finding him, Holmes tells Watson that he comes from 300 years into the future, just like Moriarty does. Watson asks Holmes if it is odd for him to find that he is "a famous historical character" (Robert Lee Hall 223). Holmes answers that he did not know Sherlock Holmes because "either [he] had to be born before history could be altered to include Sherlock Holmes, or, what is more likely, that there are infinite branchings of history, and [Moriarty and he] were thrown back into but one of them" (Robert Lee Hall 223–24). This, of course, corresponds with the question concerning multiple universes. Holmes goes on to explain that the cage was one of several time machines he had built in order to get Moriarty back to the future. In the end, and with the help of Watson, Holmes manages to get the Professor together with himself into one of the cages and both disappear.

The short story "The Adventure of the Global Traveller" (1978) by Anne Lear starts with the fictional author explaining that she only wanted to find out who the Third Murderer in *Macbeth* really was. During her search she finds some notes which appear to be very old. She starts to read them and discovers that it is a letter written by none other than Professor Moriarty. Moriarty explains that he was at the height of his power and influence but that he was always chased by Sherlock Holmes. Therefore, he and Colonel Moran "led Holmes into a trap at the Reichenbach Falls" (Lear 71). Holmes, however, escaped. Moriarty had taken precautions for this event. He had set up a net which was to be released by Colonel Moran in the case that Moriarty and not Holmes fell. Landing on the net, a dummy was released tricking Holmes into believing that Moriarty had fallen into the depths of the falls. Moriarty then took on the character of an experimental mathematician and began to research time and time travel. He invented the Time Machine in form of a bicycle and showed it to some friends. One of them, a writer named Wells, thought it very interesting. During one of his time travels, the time machine broke, blasted into nothingness and Moriarty landed on a seventeenth-century stage. Someone asked him "But who did bid thee join with us?" (Lear 73) and Moriarty recognized the line as one from Shakespeare's *Macbeth*. Fortunately, he remembered the lines and played the third murderer. Shakespeare liked Moriarty's improvisation on stage and inserted the lines into his play. He ends the letter by asking the detective "The first time the Third Murderer's lines were ever spoken, *they were delivered from memory*. Pray, Mr. Holmes, who wrote them?" (Lear 76). This is a perfect example of the ontological paradox because (1) Moriarty going back in time and remembering the lines of Macbeth and (2) Shakespeare including the lines after Moriarty's performance make perfect sense for themselves. Together, however, they are dizzying.

David Dvorkin's *Time for Sherlock Holmes* (1983) is again supposedly written by Watson himself. Holmes finds the elixir of youth but does not share this knowledge with the world. He and Watson retire to Sussex and live a remote live. Early in the 1990s however, the Prime Minister is murdered. Holmes explains that Moriarty did not die at the Reichenbach Falls because "a mannequin, dressed in clothing like Moriarty's, were substituted for him and Moriarty himself was drawn to safety" (Dvorkin 34). Holmes also reveals that Moriarty stole H. G. Wells' time machine. However, it broke during the process and it seems that Moriarty has only now been able to repair it. Holmes and Watson pursue Moriarty to Chicago where they contact a Lily Cantrell. Watson is reminded of another Lily Cantrell he once had a romantic relationship with in San Francisco during the 1880s. One day, however, Lily had simply disappeared. Holmes and Watson learn that Lily Cantrell has been blackmailed by Moriarty and is now occasionally working for him. Watson is instructed to keep Lily company until Moriarty contacts her again. Despite the age difference, Watson and Lily soon fall in love and Lily tells him that she was named after her grandmother's great-grandmother.

When Lily has to meet Moriarty again, Watson accompanies her alone because he cannot find Holmes. He is captured by Moriarty who reveals his plan to kill the US President with an atomic bomb and that Lily has betrayed Watson. In the end, Holmes rescues Watson, spoils Moriarty's plan and tells Watson that Lily has always been on their side.

Now, this would have been a good end. Unfortunately, Dvorkin continues the story. Moriarty survived and, because the Time Machine is broken, he now travels uncontrollably through time and space. Due to his evil nature, he is drawn to the assassination of important leaders, for example John F. Kennedy or Martin Luther King, and briefly appears during those events. Although Holmes and the others can speculate on the time of Moriarty's reappearance, they do not know where he will land and who is going to be assassinated. For a few decades, they continue their lives as normally as possible in Sussex. Watson and Lily then move to London, go on to live on a space station before finally settling on Mars. They are only sporadically in contact with Holmes. When a new political leader arises on Mars, Moriarty is drawn to him. He kills the politician and captures Lily. In the end, a disguised Holmes rules Mars for some decades, always increasing his power and importance. This eventually draws the time travelling Moriarty to him which solves the problem of where Moriarty will land and who will be assassinated. Instead of killing Holmes, Moriarty is killed himself. Lily, in the meantime, is transported back to San Francisco in the 1880s. She is taken in by a family who introduces her to "a young doctor fresh from England [...]. His name was John Hamish Watson" (Dvorkin 183). They start a relationship and she gets pregnant. Before disappearing again into some other time and space, Lily realizes that "there *was* only one Lily Cantrell, after all, and it was she" (Dvorkin 183) because her baby "would have grandchildren [...] and one of them in turn would eventually have a granddaughter named Lily Cantrell after her" (Dvorkin 200). This is a good example of the predestination paradox. Can the Lily from the past and the Lily from the present really be the same person? When, then, did their existence start and can one live without the other?

Conclusion

To sum up. It is not the least surprising that Doyle chose Professor Moriarty as the arch villain for Sherlock Holmes. The spiritualist must have found the mathematical reasoning for a fourth dimension very intriguing because – in some part – it was able to explain aspects of spiritualism. Therefore, a mathematician seemed to be the perfect match for the consulting detective. The lack of information about the professor inspired others to fill in the gaps. Some tried to complete his biography; others created a new life for him outside the Canon. In three stories, Moriarty travels through time which is not as surprising as it seems. After all, mathematicians and physicists laid the foundation for time travel and Moriarty seems to have known it well in advance. The accounts of a time-travelling Moriarty also directly or indirectly exemplify different aspects of time travel: in Robert Lee Hall's *Exit Sherlock Holmes* we find the theory of multiple universes, in Anne Lear's "The Adventure of the Global Traveller" the ontological paradox is used and in David Dvorkin's *Time for Sherlock Holmes* a good example for the predestination paradox is given. Although not in accordance to one another, they do coincide in the fact that Professor Moriarty did not die at the Reichenbach Falls but travelled through time instead. In conclusion, Professor Moriarty is a very fascinating character. Although he plays a surprisingly small role, he is an inspiration for numerous authors and scientists who either tried to find out more about him or who gave him a new life outside the Canon. Apparently, they all followed the advice given by Sherlock Holmes in *The Valley of Fear:*

> "Sometime when you have a year or two to spare I commend to you the study of Professor Moriarty." (19)

Works Cited

Abbott, Edwin A. *Flatland: A Romance of Many Dimensions*. 1884. New York: Penguin Books, 1998.

Aparta, Krystian. *Conventional Models of Time and Their Extensions in Science Fiction*. Master of Arts Thesis, 2006. 4 Feb. 2011. <http://www.timetravel.110mb.com/Aparta_Models_of_Time.pdf>.

Barksdale, Ethelbert C. *Enchanted Paths and Magic Words: The Quantum Mind and Time Travel in Science and in Literery Myth*. New York: Peter Lang, 1998.

Bowers, John F. "James Moriarty: A Forgotten Mathematician". *new scientist* 124. 1696/1697 (1989): 17–19.

Canton, Rolf J. *The Moriarty Principle: An Irregular Look at Sherlock Holmes*. Lakeville, MN: Galde Press, 1997.

Dowden, Bradley. *Time. Internet Encyclopedia of Philosophy*, 2001. 4 Feb. 2011. <http://www.iep.utm.edu/time/>.

Doyle, Arthur C. *The Annotated Sherlock Holmes. Volume I: The Four Novels and the Fifty-Six Short Stories Complete*. Ed. William S. Baring-Gould. New York: Clarkson N. Potter, 1967.

—. *The Valley of Fear*. 1915. Ed. Owen Dudley Edwards. Oxford: Oxford University Press, 1993.

—. *Sherlock Holmes: The Major Stories with Contemporary Critical Essays*. Ed. John A. Hodgson. Boston: Bedford Books, 1994.

—. "His Last Bow". 1917. *Sherlock Holmes: The Complete Novels and Stories. Volume II*. 1986. New York: Bantam Books, 2003. 491–507.

—. "The Adventure of the Empty House". 1903. *Sherlock Holmes: The Complete Novels and Stories. Volume I*. 1986. New York: Bantam Books, 2003. 759–81.

—. "The Adventure of the Illustrious Client". 1924. *Sherlock Holmes: The Complete Novels and Stories. Volume II*. 1986. New York: Bantam Books, 2003. 512–38.

—. "The Adventure of the Missing Three-Quarter". 1904. *Sherlock Holmes: The Complete Novels and Stories. Volume I*. 1986. New York: Bantam Books, 2003. 987–1009.

—. "The Adventure of the Norwood Builder". 1903. *Sherlock Holmes: The Complete Novels and Stories. Volume I*. 1986. New York: Bantam Books, 2003. 781–805.

—. "The Final Problem". 1893. *Sherlock Holmes: The Complete Novels and Stories. Volume I*. 1986. New York: Bantam Books, 2003. 736–55.

Dvorkin, David. *Time for Sherlock Holmes*. New York: Dodd, Mead & Company, 1983.
Fechner, Gustav T. "Der Raum hat vier Dimensionen". *Vier Paradoxa*. Leipzig: Leopold Boß, 1846. 15–40.
Hall, Robert Lee. *Exit Sherlock Holmes: The Great Detective's Final Days*. 1977. London: Sphere Books Limited, 1979.
Hall, Trevor H. *Sherlock Holmes and His Creator*. London: Duckworth, 1978.
Higham, Charles F. *The Adventures of Conan Doyle: The Life of the Creator of Sherlock Holmes*. New York: Norton, 1976.
Hinton, Charles H. "What is the Fourth Dimension?" 1884. *Speculations on the Fourth Dimension: Selected Writings of Charles H. Hinton*. Ed. Rudy B. v. Rucker. New York: Dover Publications, 1980. 1–22.
Hunter, Joel. *Time Travel. Internet Encyclopedia of Philosophy*, 2004. 4 Feb. 2011. <http://www.iep.utm.edu/timetrav/>.
Jaffe, Jacqueline A. *Arthur Conan Doyle*. Boston: Twayne, 1987.
Lear, Anne. "The Adventure of the Global Traveler". 1978. *Sherlock Holmes Through Time and Space*. 1984. Ed. Isaac Asimov, Martin H. Greenberg, and Charles G. Waugh. New York: Bluejay Books, 1985. 67–76.
Macintyre, Ben. *The Napoleon of Crime: The Life and Times of Adam Worth, the Real Moriarty*. London: HarperCollins, 1997.
McKie, David. *Sherlock Holmes: The Truth at Last: What really happened at the Reichenbach Falls? The Guardian*, 2001. 13 Apr. 2011. <http://www.guardian.co.uk/books/2001/apr/26/arthurconandoyle>.
Minkowski, Hermann. *Raum und Zeit*. Leipzig: Teubner, 1909.
Mortimer, John. *To Catch a Thief*, 1997. 30 Apr. 2011. <http://www.nytimes.com/books/97/08/24/reviews/970824.24mortimt.html?_r=2>.
Nahin, Paul J. *Time Machines: Time Travel in Physics, Metaphysics, and Science Fiction*. 1993. 2nd., revised ed. New York: AIP Press, 1999.
Pickover, Clifford. *Traveling Through Time. NovA Online*, 2000. *Time Travel*. 7 May 2011. <http://www.pbs.org/wgbh/nova/time/through.html>.
Polidoro, Massimo. *Final Séance: The Strange Friendship Between Houdini and Conan Doyle*. Amherst, NY: Prometheus Books, 2001.
Rauchhaupt, Ulf von. *Raum und Zeit: Sind Zeitreisen möglich? Physik & Chemie – Wissen – FAZ.NET*, 2010. 7 May 2011. <http://www.faz.net/s/Rub163D8A6908014952B0FB3DB178F372D4/Doc~

E~429A061D340B40109B440109CEFC572D~ATpl~Ecommon~Scontent.html>.

Rennison, Nick. *Sherlock Holmes: The Unauthorized Biography*. New York: Grove Press, 2005.

Riley, Dick, and Pam McAllister. *The Bedside, Bathtub & Armchair Companion to Sherlock Holmes*. New York: Continuum, 2001.

Schaefer, Bradley E. "Sherlock Holmes and some astronomical connections". *Journal of the British Astronomical Association* 103.1 (1993): 30–34.

Shreffler, Philip A. "Introduction". *Sherlock Holmes by Gas-Lamp: Highlights from the First Four Decades of the Baker Street Journal*. Ed. Philip A. Shreffler. New York: Fordham University Press, 1989. 1–7.

—. "Moriarty: A Life Study". *Sherlock Holmes by Gas-Lamp: Highlights from the First Four Decades of the Baker Street Journal*. Ed. Philip A. Shreffler. New York: Fordham University Press, 1989. 263–70.

Teets, Donald, and Karen Whitehead. "The Discovery of Ceres: How Gauss Became Famous". *Mathematics Magazine* 72.2 (1999): 83–93.

Watt, Peter R., and Joseph Green. *The Alternative Sherlock Holmes: Pastiches, Parodies, and Copies*. Aldershot: Ashgate, 2003.

Wells, Herbert G. *The Time Machine*. 1895. Ed. Dieter Hamblock. Stuttgart: Reclam, 2004.

Stefan Welz

BRÜDER IN GEIST UND TAT

A. C. Doyle, R. Kipling, R. Haggard und der Burenkrieg

Der Aufsatz soll einen wichtigen biographischen Zusammenhang im Leben des britischen Schriftstellers Arthur Conan Doyle erhellen, der zu dessen Lebzeiten große Beachtung fand und seinen Ruf maßgeblich prägte, heute aber weitgehend in den Hintergrund getreten ist: Conan Doyles leidenschaftlicher Einsatz für die Sache des *British Empire*. Vor dem Hintergrund von Doyles Schriften zum Burenkrieg werden drei Aspekte besondere Beachtung finden: die Möglichkeiten und Grenzen seiner gleichzeitigen Beschäftigung mit Literatur und Geschichte; die Geistesverwandtschaft, die ihn mit Rudyard Kipling, Rider Haggard und anderen zeitgenössischen Empire-Sympathisanten aus Literatur und Politik verband sowie sein Anteil an der Entwicklung der englischen Propagandaliteratur mit einem Vorausblick auf die Zeit des Ersten Weltkriegs.

The article is aimed at illuminating Arthur Conan Doyle's passionate support of the British Empire. At the turn from the 19th to the 20th century Doyle's imperialistic convictions were seen as an indispensable part of his personality. Today, however, this commitment is generally forgotten and overshadowed by his magnificent literary character of Sherlock Holmes. Doyle's writings on the Boer War will serve as a textual basis for discussing three aspects: the possibilities and limits of his parallel interest in literature and history; the things he had in common with other imperialist writers such as Rudyard Kipling and Rider Haggard; and his share in the rise of contemporary propaganda literature.

◇

Wenn es darum geht, aus der Perspektive des 21. Jahrhunderts dem 'anderen' Conan Doyle nachzuspüren, ergibt sich schon bald ein Paradoxon, denn der aus heutiger Sicht 'andere' Conan Doyle war in vielerlei Hinsicht der 'eigentliche' Conan Doyle seiner Zeit. Mit anderen Worten: In Großbritannien um die Wende vom 19. zum 20. Jahrhundert galt Arthur Conan Doyle als weithin geschätzte öffentliche Persönlichkeit, als aktiver Politiker und Patriot, als Streiter für Gerechtigkeit, als respektabler Mediziner, Journalist und Sportler – und daneben auch als ein bekannter Verfasser von Kurzgeschichten und Romanen. Doyles politische Karriere war zwar eher bescheiden – er stellte sich zweimal erfolglos zur Wahl als Parlamentsabgeordneter –, dennoch tat er sich neben Rudyard Kipling als einer der einflussreichsten Meinungsmacher des imperialistischen Zeitalters hervor. Allerdings verkörperte er weniger den Typ des Jingoisten als den des Gentleman mit "a chivalric spirit of fairplay" (Lycett 248). In jedem Fall gehörte der gebürtige Schotte zu jener Gruppe namhafter Briten, die selbstlos und beflissen am Aufbau und Unterhalt des *British Empire* mitwirkten. Selbst Conan Doyles Besitz an südafrikanischen Bergbauaktien kann dieses Bild der Uneigennützigkeit kaum beschädigen (Lycett 248). Seine Popularität als Schriftsteller erwarb Doyle nicht zuletzt dadurch, dass seine literarischen Schriften ein breites zeitgenössisches Interessenspektrum bedienten. Sie vereinten Detektiv- und Abenteuergeschichten, historische Romane, Romanzen und Gedichte, denen populärhistorische Abhandlungen und journalistische Beiträge an die Seite gestellt waren. Als eine derart vielseitige Persönlichkeit mit unterschiedlichen Betätigungsfeldern steht Conan Doyle exemplarisch für die spätviktorianische Werte- und Geisteswelt. Die Inschrift auf seinem Grabstein in Minstead/New Forest, Hampshire zeigt noch einmal die Verehrung, die ihm von seinen Zeitgenossen und Geistesverwandten in Form einer hierarchischen Wertung der Lebensleistung entgegengebracht wurde:

>   STEEL TRUE
>   BLADE STRAIGHT
>   ARTHUR CONAN DOYLE
>   KNIGHT
>   PATRIOT, PHYSICIAN & MAN OF LETTERS
>   ("Conan Doyle Dead")

Stefan Welz, Brüder in Geist und Tat

Der Burenkrieg zwischen Fiktion und Realität

Der zweite Burenkrieg, der von Seiten der Afrikaander *Die Tweede Vryheidsoorlog* (Der Zweite Freiheitskrieg) genannt wurde, brach im Jahr 1899 aus und dauerte bis 1902. Im Ergebnis kamen die beiden Afrikaander-Republiken Oranje-Freistaat und Transvaal (Südafrikanische Republik) mit der Perspektive einer begrenzten Selbstverwaltung unter britische Kontrolle. Nach Jahrzehnten des Konflikts, der mit der britischen Annexion der holländischen Kap-Kolonie im Jahr 1806 seinen Anfang nahm, widersetzten sich die Burenrepubliken aktiv den verstärkten Kolonisierungsversuchen der Briten, denen es am Ende des 19. Jahrhunderts vor allem um die Ausbeutung der reichen Ressourcen an Gold und Diamanten im Grenzgebiet zu den beiden damals unabhängigen Staaten ging. Obwohl Großbritannien den Siedlerrepubliken in den 1850er Jahren die Unabhängigkeit garantiert hatte – im Fall von Transvaal wurde sie nach dem kurzen Ohana Krieg sogar noch einmal bestätigt –, führten die Diamantenfunde in den 1860er Jahren, das Schüren von Spannungen sowie die resolute Expansionspolitik von Cecil Rhodes (1853–1902), Premierminister der Kap-Kolonie zwischen 1890 und 1896, und Alfred Milner (1854–1925), *High Commissioner* der Kap-Kolonie, unausweichlich zum Krieg. Der begann am 11. Oktober mit dem Angriff der Buren auf die britische Kolonie Natal, nachdem ein von Präsident Krüger gestelltes Ultimatum, in dem der Rückzug zusätzlicher britischer Truppenkontingente aus der Region gefordert wurde, ohne Reaktion abgelaufen war.

Die Buren waren europäische Siedler von mehrheitlich niederländischer, deutscher oder französischer Abstammung. Sie waren gut ausgerüstete Gewehrschützen, die ebenso unorthodoxe wie effiziente Kriegsstrategien entwickelten. Die Briten glaubten sich zu Kriegsbeginn mit ihren Rekruten aus den südafrikanischen Gebieten und regulären Truppen (ein großer Anteil davon kam aus anderen Teilen des Empire wie Irland, Kanada und Australien) zahlenmäßig überlegen. Tatsächlich war die Übermacht der Briten so groß, dass weithin die Ansicht dominierte, es werde ein Krieg von kurzer Dauer und des geringen Aufwands sein. Doch die Auseinandersetzung wurde erbittert über zweieinhalb Jahre hinweg geführt und kostete viele Menschenleben. Der Burenkrieg war die bedeutendste militärische Auseinandersetzung, in die das *British Empire* seit der *Mutiny* in Indien im Jahr

Arthur Conan Doyle um 1902

1857/58 verwickelt war. Allerdings hatte dieser Krieg einen gänzlich anderen Charakter, denn zum ersten Mal waren die Briten mit dem militärischen Widerstand weißer, nicht-britischer Siedler konfrontiert. Dies hatte unmittelbare Konsequenzen für die internationale Wahrnehmung des Konflikts in Europa und den Vereinigten Staaten von Amerika, wo die meisten Nationen mit der Sache der Buren sympathisierten.[1] Der Krieg brach in einem Moment aus, als die Angst vor einem möglichen Niedergang des *British Empire* – eine eher gefühlsmäßig als rational begründbare Wahrnehmung der

---

[1] Gemeinsam mit den Buren kämpften schwedische, deutsche, russische und holländische Freiwilligenverbände.

Situation – im Mutterland umging. Derartige Ängste hatten mit den Veränderungen im internationalen Machtgefüge zu tun und spiegelten nicht zuletzt die inneren Probleme Großbritanniens jener Zeit wider, wie die anhaltenden wirtschaftlichen Schwierigkeiten, die Debatte um das Selbstbestimmungsrecht Irlands (*Irish Home Rule*), die Frauen- und Wahlrechtsfrage sowie eine gewisse kulturelle Erschöpfung.

Schon vor Ausbruch des Krieges beschäftigte sich Conan Doyle mit dem Thema Südafrika. Er hatte offenbar intensiv die Geschichte der Region studiert und wichtige Aspekte der aktuellen Situation mit verschiedenen einflussreichen Politikern und Regierungsvertretern des *War Office* erörtert. Er schrieb engagierte Artikel für *The Times* und plante, zusammen mit seinem Bruder Innes (1873–1919) den Winter 1899 in Südafrika zu verbringen. Doch angesichts der aktuellen Entwicklung entschied er sich anderweitig. Unterstützt von Archie Langman, einem Freund der Familie, beabsichtigte er, der regulären militärischen Formation der *Middlesex Yeomanry* beizutreten, die als Teil der *Imperial Yeomanry* dafür prädestiniert war, in Südafrika zum Einsatz zu kommen. Jedoch verweigerten ihm die Militärs den aktiven Dienst (Lycett 250). Es war Langlands betuchter Vater John, dem Conan Doyle schließlich doch einen Einsatz als Arzt im ersten privaten Feldlazarett für britische Truppen in Südafrika verdankte. Einrichtungen wie das von John Langland privat finanzierte Lazarett wurden erforderlich, da das *Royal Army Medical Corps* größte Schwierigkeiten hatte, mit der angespannten Situation in Südafrika zurechtzukommen (Lycett 251). Als Conan Doyle am 21. März 1900 in Cape Town eintraf, waren die Buren allerdings schon im Rückzug begriffen. Für die Briten sah der Krieg zu diesem Zeitpunkt wesentlich günstiger aus als noch im Dezember 1899, als sie drei entscheidende Niederlagen hintereinander hinnehmen mussten, was als Schlagzeile von der 'Black Week' durch die englische Presse ging. Doyle diente in Bloemfontein bis Juni 1900.

Arthur Conan Doyle verfasste zwei historisch-politische Schriften über Südafrika. Im Jahr 1900 veröffentlichte er eine erste, noch stark historisch geprägte Abhandlung unter dem Titel

The Great Boer War. Darin bot er einen historischen Zugang zur aktuellen Situation, die er, angereichert durch Insider-Wissen und Augenzeugenberichte von der Entwicklung des Kriegs in den ersten Monaten nach Ausbruch, zu einer Gesamtdarstellung verdichtete. Aufschlussreich ist, dass er den historischen Überblick des einleitenden Teils noch zuzeiten schrieb, als er in England war (Lycett 257). Während seines dreimonatigen Aufenthalts in Südafrika machte das Projekt große Fortschritte. Doyle konnte auf seinen Vorstudien ebenso aufbauen wie auf den unmittelbaren Erfahrungen und Berichten, die ihm während seines Lazarettdienstes zugetragen wurden. Hinzu kam seine erfahrene Technik in der Darstellung historischer Sachverhalte, die er in seinen zahlreichen Geschichtsromanen am Ende der 1880er und während der 1890er Jahre eingehend erprobt hatte.[2] Ton und Duktus waren jetzt jedoch anders als in den fiktionalen Texten; wenngleich noch immer literarisch angelegt und unterhaltsam, so dominiert doch das Ernsthafte und Argumentative. Doyle entwickelte die Thematik aus der Perspektive des unparteiischen Geschichtsschreibers, muss aber selbst einschränkend eingestehen: "It is difficult to reach that height of philosophic detachment which enables the historian to deal absolutely impartially where his own country is a party to the quarrel" (*Great Boer War* 19). Er reicherte seine Darstellung mit Fakten, Auszügen aus offiziellen Dokumenten und Berichten ihm persönlich bekannter Politiker, Journalisten und Kirchenvertreter an, darunter auch Winston Churchill, dem er in der Einleitung zur Abhandlung seinen besonderen Dank ausspricht. Während seines Dienstes im Feldlazarett hatte Conan Doyle zweifellos die Augenzeugenberichte verwundeter Offiziere und Soldaten gehört, die er gleichfalls als authentisches Quellenmaterial verwendete. Insgesamt geht Doyle aber noch vergleichsweise unbeschwert

---

[2] In kurzer Abfolge entstanden in diesem Zeitraum die historischen Romane *Micah Clarke* (1888), *The White Company* (1891), *The Great Shadow* (1892), *The Refugees* (1893), *Rodney Stone* (1896) und *Uncle Bernac* (1897), die überwiegend von Themen der englischen, aber auch französischen Geschichte insbesondere des 18. Jahrhunderts handelten.

zu Werke, das heißt, er schrieb noch nicht explizit unter einem Rechtfertigungsdruck angesichts der schon bald einsetzenden ausländischen Kritik und Kommentare.

Conan Doyles erste Abhandlung über den Burenkrieg war eine gut informierte und weitgehend ausgewogene Studie, wohlmeinend gegenüber beiden Seiten und vernünftig in der Argumentation. Im Geiste eines Anwalts der Gerechtigkeit und eines fairen Sportlers stellt Doyle den Fall der Burenrepubliken gegen das *British Empire* zur Debatte. Die entscheidende Frage, auf die ihm zufolge der Konflikt hinauslief, sei der Gegensatz von Vernunft und Gerechtigkeit gegenüber emotionalen Beweggründen (48). Gelegentlich macht Conan Doyle sich sogar die Position der Buren zu eigen und kritisiert mit rhetorischer Schärfe die Unzulänglichkeiten und Fehler der Empire-Administration, die er mehr als einmal nicht auf der Höhe des Geschehens sah. Den Buren wiederum gestand Doyle Qualitäten wie Willenskraft, Sinn für das Gemeinwesen, Entschlossenheit sowie einen starken Unabhängigkeitswillen zu (11/12). Diese Qualitäten ließen die Buren zu einem würdigen Gegner werden. Fast im gleichen Atemzug jedoch werden die Buren als konservativ, fortschrittsfeindlich und durch und durch anti-britisch denunziert. Von diesen negativen Charakteristika leitete Conan Doyle einen Teil der Rechtmäßigkeit der britischen Ansprüche her. Denn nicht nur hätten die Briten ein historisches Recht auf das Land durch Eroberung und Erwerb (13/14), vielmehr seien die britische Justiz und die Garantie der Freiheit, was die gleichen Rechte für alle einschließt, die stärkeren Argumente in der gegenwärtigen Konfliktsituation (15).

Diese Argumentationsstrategie war allerdings nicht frei von Widersprüchen, denn ein historischer Rückblick auf die Staatsform der Afrikaander-Republiken zeigt sehr wohl, dass freiheitliche und demokratische Prozeduren angewendet wurden, wenngleich nur unter den Buren. (Beispielsweise kam der Friedensschluss von 1902 auf Seiten der Buren erst durch eine allgemeine Abstimmung zustande.) Die wiederholt von den Briten angeführte Schutzpflicht gegenüber der einheimischen Bevölkerung vor der Willkür der Siedler erscheint bisweilen fragwürdig, wenn diese Schutzbedürftigen ausnahmslos als Wilde und selbst noch in Doyles gemäßigtem Text als "hideous aborigines, lowest of the human race" (6) erscheinen. Dabei gilt es festzuhalten, dass ein derartiges Vokabular zum gängigen imperialistischen Diskurs jener Zeit gehörte. Innerhalb von Doyles Argumentationsstrategie tauchen ökonomische Beweggründe wie Ressourcenkontrolle erst an zweiter Stelle auf. Sie wurden zwar nicht verschwiegen, wohl aber von der Frage nach dem Status der *Uitlanders* überlagert, einer kosmopolitischen Gruppe von Arbeitskräften, die in der südafrikanischen Minenindustrie beschäftigt waren und den Buren in deren eigenen Gebieten zahlenmäßig den Rang abzulaufen drohten.

Im Verlauf der historischen Studie wird mit Blick auf die anfänglichen spektakulären Niederlagen der Briten Doyles ernste Besorgnis deutlich, dass das Empire nicht mehr länger den Anforderungen der modernen Welt gewachsen sei. Das Beispiel des effizienten Widerstandes der Buren, deren Entschlossenheit und deren Guerillataktik schienen Doyle als Vorboten einer neuen Ära, auf die das Empire mit seinen veralteten Grundsätzen und den sich selbst genügenden Netzwerken sowie angesichts unzureichender militärischer Ausrüstung schlecht vorbereitet war: "... for they [the Boers] drove home the fact – only too badly learned by us – that it is the rifle and not the drill which makes the soldier" (24).

Doyles *The Great Boer War* hatte einen bemerkenswerten Erfolg. Noch während der Kriegsjahre erlebte das Buch zahlreiche, mehrfach aktualisierte Auflagen. Da Conan Doyle das Manuskript bereits kurze Zeit nach seiner Rückkehr aus Südafrika veröffentlichte,[3] konnte er über den weiteren Verlauf des Kriegsgeschehens nur mutmaßen. In der Folgezeit überarbeitete er den Text beständig und stellte aktualisierende Vorworte voran. Auf diese Art

---

[3] Doyle hatte seine Ausführungen mit einem Schlusskapitel unter der Überschrift "The End of War" versehen, obwohl der Krieg zu diesem Zeitpunkt noch nicht beendet war. Daran schloss sich ein polemischer Essay zu "Some Military Lessons of the War" an, der kurz vor der Publikation der Abhandlung Ende September 1900 gesondert im *Cornhill Magazin* abgedruckt wurde. Die Erstauflage von *The Great Boer War* erschien im Verlag Smith, Elder (Lycett 359–61).

und Weise schuf er eine Form von *work in progress*. Folgerichtig zeigt dann auch eine Ausgabe mit Vorwort vom September des Jahres 1902 eine geistige und stilistische Nähe zu seiner zweiten Publikation über den Burenkrieg, die unter dem Titel *The War in South Africa: Its Causes and Conduct* im gleichen Jahr erschien, aber bereits als Idee im November 1901 mit dem Verlagshaus Smith, Elder abgesprochen wurde. Der Übergang von der ersten Abhandlung, ursprünglich geschrieben im ersten Kriegsjahr, zur zweiten, die einige Monate vor Kriegsende erschien, zeigt sich als beredtes Beispiel für Doyles Wandel vom literarischen zum patriotischen Geschichtsschreiber, der schließlich einem selbst ernannten Advokaten des *British Empire* glich.

Noch während des Kriegsverlaufs und auch nach dem formalen Friedensabkommen von Vereeniging am 31. März 1902 erhoben die Buren Anschuldigungen gegen die britischen Truppen wegen begangener Kriegsverbrechen. Den Briten wurden unter anderem das systematische Abbrennen von Farmen (*scorched earth policy*), die Teilnahme an Folterungen und das Errichten von Konzentrationslagern vorgeworfen. Die Vorwürfe lösten weltweite Reaktionen aus, die in den meisten Fällen äußerst kritisch ausfielen. Aus diplomatischen Gründen erfolgte von Seiten der britischen Regierung keine offizielle Stellungnahme zu den Anschuldigungen. Conan Doyle kritisierte diese passive Haltung, für die er "either arrogance or apathy" als mögliche Gründe anführte, wie er im Vorwort zu der zweiten Schrift sagte. Mit seiner Abhandlung zum Burenkrieg *The War in South Africa: Its Causes and Conduct* vom Januar 1902 ergriff er schließlich selbst die Initiative, um die Sache des Empire in Südafrika zu verteidigen:[4]

> In view of the persistent slanders to which our politicians and our soldiers have been equally exposed, it

---

[4] In seiner Biographie *Conan Doyle: The Man Who Created Sherlock Holmes* weist Andrew Lycett darauf hin, dass Doyle bei dem Vorhaben nicht nur vom Verleger Reginald Smith, sondern auch von einflussreichen Kreisen bis hin zum britischen Geheimdienst mit Material und finanzieller Hilfe unterstützt worden sei (vgl. 271/72).

becomes a duty which we owe to our national honour to lay the facts before the world. I wish someone more competent, and with some official authority, had undertaken the task, which I have tried to do as best I might from an independent standpoint. (*The War in South Africa* 2)

Im Burenkrieg von 1899–1902 zeigte sich erstmals eine neue Qualität der Kriegsführung, die für das folgende Jahrhundert bestimmend werden sollte: Neben den Schlachtgeschehen vor Ort erfolgte eine aktive Auseinandersetzung um die öffentliche Meinung hinsichtlich der Ursachen, Ziele und Praktiken in diesem Krieg. Daher haben Historiker den Burenkrieg als ersten großen Medienkrieg[5] mit massivem Propagandaeinsatz von beiden Seiten charakterisiert. In diesen modernen Kontext ordnet sich Conan Doyles zweite Abhandlung zum Burenkrieg ein. Dass es sich dabei um einen Propagandatext handelt, wird bereits im Vorwort deutlich, denn Doyle wollte den 60 000 Wörter umfassenden Text in alle europäischen Sprachen übersetzen lassen, mit dem Ziel "to send a free copy to every deputy and every newspaper on the Continent and in America" (*The War in South Africa* 2). Conan Doyle stellte sich allen erhobenen Anschuldigungen in einer exakten und systematischen Art und Weise. So widmete er beispielsweise ein ganzes Kapitel (Chapter VII) den Vorwürfen hinsichtlich der Errichtung von Konzentrationslagern und verteidigte diese Lager als "camps of refuge for women and children, where, out of reach, as we hoped, of all harm, they could await the return of peace" (*The War in South Africa* 62). Er zitierte zahlreiche Augenzeugen, die den humanen Charakter der Lager bestätigen sollten, und listete sogar die Bestandteile der täglichen Nahrungsmittelrationen auf. Die hohe

---

[5] Matthew Sweet verweist in seiner Studie *Inventing the Victorians* darauf, dass erstmalig Filmaufnahmen vom Kriegsgeschehen gezeigt wurden, wobei allerdings vieles davon in Hampstead Heath mit geschwärzten Schauspielern nachgestellt war (Sweet 52).

Sterblichkeit in den Lagern schrieb er weniger einer schlechten Behandlung als grassierenden Krankheiten wie Masern zu.

Conan Doyles Abhandlung *The War in South Africa: Its Causes and Conduct* fiel trotz der nunmehr möglichen Überschaubarkeit des gesamten Kriegsverlaufs weniger ausgewogen und stilistisch ausgefeilt aus als die vorhergehende Publikation *The Great Boer War*, der zahlreiche Passagen für die neue Schrift entnommen worden waren. Dennoch wurde auch die zweite Abhandlung in Großbritannien sehr populär und erlebte innerhalb weniger Monate sechzehn Auflagen. Neben dem allgegenwärtigen polemischen Gestus erscheinen die Verteidigung der Sache des Empire und die Entkräftung der weltweiten Kritik an den britischen Kriegspraktiken als dominierende Motivation. Doyle sieht den Krieg als ein Ereignis, das dem Empire einen neuen Zusammenhalt verliehen habe. Gleichzeitig übt er vehemente Kritik an der kritischen Haltung Deutschlands, dem neuen Gegenspieler des britischen Weltreiches (vgl. *The War in South Africa*, Chapter X). Obwohl im Vergleich der beiden Abhandlungen ein stilistisches Abgleiten von einer überwiegend literarisch-historischen Behandlung der südafrikanischen Thematik in eine propagandistische unübersehbar ist, wurden Conan Doyles übrige literarische Arbeiten dadurch nicht kompromittiert. Die erfolgreiche Sherlock-Holmes Geschichte *The Hound of the Baskervilles* (1902) wie auch die Erzählungen um den napoleonischen Husaren Etienne Gerard (*The Adventure of Gerard*, 1903) – Arbeiten, mit denen Conan Doyle während der Jahre des Burenkriegs beschäftigt war – sind der Kontinuität seines literarischen Gesamtschaffens verpflichtet. Diese offenbar bewusst praktizierte Parallelität unterschiedlicher Textsorten, die die Qualität von Doyles literarischem Schaffen sicherte, wird im Vergleich mit Rudyard Kiplings (1865–1936) tendenziösen Texten jener Jahre besonders deutlich.

In Anerkennung seiner Unterstützung für die Sache des Empire wurde Conan Doyle vom König Edward VII. am 24. Oktober 1902 in den Adelsstand erhoben. Die Abhandlung *The War in South Africa: Its Causes and Conduct* war zweifellos der ausschlaggebende Grund für diese Entscheidung, die zusätzlich mit der Ernennung zum *Deputy-Lieutenant of Surrey* verbunden war. Es spricht für Doyles uneigennütziges Pflichtbewusstsein wie auch für seine menschliche Bescheidenheit, dass er erst von seiner Mutter zur Annahme der Ehrung bewegt werden musste (Lycett 272).

Conan Doyles leidenschaftliches Eintreten für den britischen Imperialismus lässt sich nicht auf sein Engagement im Burenkrieg reduzieren, sondern steht im Zusammenhang mit seinen politischen Überzeugungen, seinen Afrika-Erfahrungen und seinem ausgeprägten Gerechtigkeitssinn. Erste Eindrücke vom schwarzen Kontinent konnte er schon kurz nach Abschluss seiner Medizinstudien an der University of Edinburgh (1876–81) als Schiffsarzt auf der *SS Mayumba* an der afrikanischen Westküste sammeln. 1895 bereiste Conan Doyle Ägypten und den Sudan – ein Aufenthalt, den er später für eine *white lie* nutzte, als er angebliche Kriegserfahrung geltend machte, um seine Chancen bei der Rekrutierung für den Burenkrieg zu erhöhen (Lycett, 250/51).

Im Jahr 1909 schrieb Conan Doyle erneut eine längere Abhandlung zu Afrika, in der er die kolonialen Gräuel in Belgisch-Kongo attackierte. Das Buch unter dem Titel *The Crime of the Congo* behandelte die Grausamkeiten, die in der afrikanischen Kolonie im Namen des belgischen Königs Leopold II. begangen wurden. Sie bot anschauliche Beschreibungen von Gewalttaten gegen die einheimische Bevölkerung und belegte dies mit Fotos von verstümmelten Menschen. Der belgische König, der über den Kongo viele Jahre lang als Privatbesitz verfügte, war zuvorderst an der profitablen Ausbeutung der natürlichen Ressourcen interessiert. Teile der einheimischen Bevölkerung wurden in ein System der Zwangsarbeit gepresst, und bald gab es Gerüchte von abscheulichen Verbrechen an der einheimischen Bevölkerung. Der Journalist Edmund Dene Morel (1873–1924) und der Diplomat Roger Casement (1864–1916) gründeten im Jahr 1904 die *Congo Reform Association,* der auch Conan Doyle beigetreten ist. Deren Ziel war es, die internationale Aufmerksamkeit auf die Zustände in der afrikanischen Kolonie zu lenken und dadurch den Betroffenen zu helfen. Conan Doyle beließ es nicht beim Verfassen der Schrift, sondern nahm Kontakte zu Zeitungen auf und appellierte an die Mächtigen der Welt wie den amerikanischen Präsidenten Theodore Roosevelt und den deutschen Kaiser Wilhelm II., ihren Einfluss geltend zu machen. Während einer dreimonatigen Vortragsreise referierte er zu diesem Thema (vgl. Lycett 315–17). Die Bemühungen der Kongo-Reformbewegung waren letztlich erfolgreich. Im Jahr 1908 trat Leopold II. die Verwaltung der Kolonie an die belgische Regierung ab.

Kontinuität in seinen Überzeugungen bewies Conan Doyle auch noch Jahre nach den Kriegereignissen, als er 1928 ein weiteres Mal Südafrika bereiste. Obwohl es eine Vortragsreise als Spiritualist war, die ihn zu zahlreichen Stationen von Südafrika bis Kenya führte, schimmern durch die Aufzeichnungen, die er unter dem Titel *Our African Winter* (1929) herausgab, immer wieder Erinnerungen an die Zeit des Burenkriegs hindurch. Als aufmerksamer Beobachter und Sympathisant des Empire verfolgte er auch die aktuelle Entwicklung in Südafrika aus kritischer Perspektive. In dem tagebuchartigen Reisebericht, dem kein Verkaufserfolg beschieden war, gewinnt Doyle seine plaudernde, unaufgeregte Darstellungsgabe zurück, wenngleich er nichts von seinen imperialistischen Überzeugungen aufgegeben hat. Allerdings vermischen sich nunmehr politische Ansichten und spiritualistische Weltsicht, so dass für ihn die Geschicke des Empire einer Vorhersehung zu folgen scheinen. Besonders aufschlussreich ist Doyles Report über seinen Besuch in Bloemfontein und ein Foto aus dem Jahr 1928, auf dem er sich demonstrativ von dem *Boer War Memorial* in Bloemfontein abwendet, das an die 26 000 Frauen und Kinder auf Seiten der Buren erinnert, die in britischen Konzentrationslagern ums Leben gekommen waren.[6]

---

[6] *Our African Winter* 65/66. – Das Foto befindet sich in der Arthur Conan Doyle Collection Lancelyn Green Bequest, Portsmouth City Council und ist abgebildet in Andrew Lycetts Doyle-Biographie zwischen den Seiten 400/401.

Imperialismus als Geisteshaltung:
Doyle, Kipling und Haggard

Conan Doyles literaturhistorische Reputation hat durch sein proimperialistisches Engagement im Burenkrieg weniger gelitten als die anderer vergleichbarer Autoren. Das verdankt sich seiner wenngleich nicht unparteilichen, so doch insgesamt sachlichen Behandlung des Sujets und seinem stetig wachsenden Ruhm als Verfasser der Sherlock-Holmes-Geschichten, die sein übriges literarisches Werk bis heute weitgehend in den Schatten stellen. Neben Conan Doyle gab es eine Reihe von namhaften britischen Autoren, die bei unterschiedlichen Lebensläufen und charakterlichen Zügen ähnliche politische Überzeugungen teilten und sich für das Empire im Allgemeinen und für den Burenkrieg im Besonderen öffentlich engagierten. Einer der prominentesten war Rudyard Kipling, die zu jener Zeit einflussreichste literarische und moralische Stimme des Empire. Ein weiterer illustrer Vertreter dieser Geisteshaltung war Rider Haggard (1856–1925). Mit seinen Abenteuergeschichten für ein jugendliches Lesepublikum wurde er zu einem viel gelesenen Autor seiner Zeit und mit dem Erfolgsroman *King Solomon's Mines* zum Begründer des literarischen Genres der *Lost World*-Erzählungen. Auch Edgar Wallace (1875–1932), der als Kriegskorrespondent der *Daily Mail* im Burenkrieg tätig war, gehört zu diesem Kreis, wenngleich er zur jüngeren Generation der imperialistischen Autoren zählt. Seine eigentlichen Propagandatexte schrieb Wallace dann auch über den Ersten Weltkrieg. Weiterhin haben John Buchan (1875–1940) – später 1. Baron Tweedsmuir – und Winston Churchill (1874–1965) zum Thema Südafrika geschrieben. Ersterer begann in den Jahren des Burenkriegs seine diplomatische und politische Karriere als Privatsekretär von Alfred Milner und trat mit der Abhandlung *The African Colony* (1903) und dem späteren Südafrika-Roman *Prester John* (1910) hervor; letzterer arbeitete zu Kriegsbeginn als Kriegskorrespondent für die *Morning Post* in Südafrika und schrieb nach der Rückkehr nach England zwei Bände (*London to Ladysmith via Pretoria* und *Ian Hamilton's March*) über seine spektakulären südafrikanischen Kriegserfahrungen, die später zusammen unter dem Titel *The Boer War* nachgedruckt wurden. Als Politiker und Administratoren waren Buchan und Churchill ganz unmittelbarer in die politischen Geschehnisse jener Zeit eingebunden. Bei allen aufgezählten Autoren fällt auf, dass sie – mit Ausnahme von Churchill – neben politisch-historischen Abhandlungen auch Detektivromane, Spionageromane und Abenteuerroman verfasst haben. Das lässt eine ursächliche Verbindung zwischen den reichen Biographien und derartigen sujet- und handlungsorientierten Erzählmustern vermuten, wenngleich sich die Wechselbeziehungen und Übergänge zwischen den fiktionalen und dokumentarisch-historischen Textsorten von Fall zu Fall unterschiedlich darstellen.

Die meisten Gemeinsamkeiten verbinden Arthur Conan Doyle und Rudyard Kipling: Sie waren geborene Männer des Empire, der eine als Schotte, der andere als Anglo-Inder, wie die britischen Staatsbürger genannt wurden, die auf dem Subkontinent lebten und arbeiteten. Beide waren ebenso überzeugte Männer des Empire, denen höchste Ehrungen angetragen wurden. Beide waren äußerst erfolgreiche Autoren und genossen die Anerkennung eines großen Publikums. Neben ihrer Schriftstellerei konnten beide auf respektable Berufe verweisen, der eine als Arzt, der andere als Journalist. Beide gehörten Freimaurer-Logen an. Beide hatten den Verlust eines Sohnes im Ersten Weltkrieg zu beklagen. Kipling war Conan Doyles erklärter Lieblingsdichter (Lycett, 249) – eine Vorliebe, mit der Doyle nicht allein stand. Auch der junge Edgar Wallace bemühte sich während seines Südafrika-Aufenthalts eifrig, um mit dem Kriegsberichterstatter Kipling in Kontakt zu kommen, und hatte dabei Erfolg. Noch am Ende des 19. Jahrhunderts waren Männer aller sozialen Schichten stolz, sich in geistiger Verwandtschaft mit Rudyard Kipling zu wissen. Doch schon wenige Jahre später galt das vormals gefeierte Idol mit seinen übertriebenen, bisweilen geradezu hysterischen Tiraden einer Mehrheit von Briten als suspekt. Kipling lieferte nun bestenfalls Vorlagen für Karikaturen. Insbesondere die neue jüngere Generation, die sich maßgeblich von den Jugendidealen der Elterngeneration distanzierte, konnte mit dem alternden Jingoisten nichts mehr anfangen.

Sofort nach Ausbruch des Burenkriegs mischten sich Conan Doyle und Kipling aktiv in die Geschehnisse ein. Kipling schrieb Zeitungsartikel und Gedichte, um Geld für einen Unterstützungsfond für Soldatenfrauen zu sammeln. Sein Gedicht "The Absent-Minded Beggar", das es als populäre Ballade bis in die Music Hall schaffte, zeugt davon, wie sehr Kipling in jenen Jahren die literarische Qualität seines Schaffens der ideologischen Botschaft unterordnete: "When you've shouted 'Rule Britania', when you've sung 'God Save the Queen', / When you've finished killing Kruger with your mouth, / Will you kindly drop a shilling in my little tambourine / For a gentleman in khaki ordered South?" (Kipling 366). Conan Doyle wiederum hatte bereits vor Kriegsausbruch Artikel zur Südafrika-Thematik verfasst. In seine literarischen Texte ließ er allerdings kaum etwas von der aktuellen Stimmung einfließen. Da beide Männer praktisch veranlagt waren, zögerten sie nicht, auch auf anderen Feldern als dem der Schriftstellerei die Kriegsbemühungen des Empire zu unterstützen. Kipling stellte einen Freiwilligenverband auf und förderte das Schießtraining unweit seines Wohnhauses in Sussex (Ricketts, 260); auch Conan Doyle bemühte sich um die Formierung einer bewaffneten Miliz, was er als militärische Konsequenz aus dem Burenkrieg als unabdingbar für den Fortbestand des Empire ansah. Diese nahm innerhalb kurzer Zeit als *Undershaw Rifle Club* Gestalt an. Zweimal wöchentlich wurde mit geladenen Ortsansässigen trainiert. Stolz verkündete Doyle: "that in a couple of years there would 'not be a carter, cabman, peasant, or shop boy in the place who will not be a marksman'" (Lycett 262).

Wie so häufig, wenn die Grenzen zwischen Privatem und Öffentlichem verwischen, kamen bei beiden Kriegsenthusiasten neben den imperialistischen Überzeugungen auch persönliche Beweggründe für ihr Engagement ins Spiel. In den 1890er Jahren befand sich Conan Doyle in der unangenehmen Situation, zwischen der Verantwortung für seine kranke Frau Louise (1857–1906) und seiner leidenschaftlichen Liebe für Jean Leckie (1874–1940) hin und her gerissen zu sein. In jenen Jahren schien es ihm unmöglich, die Affäre mit der jüngeren Frau öffentlich auszuleben. Kipling wiederum war 1899 aufgrund einer schweren Lungenentzündung nur knapp dem Tod entgangen und hatte obendrein seine sechsjährige Tochter Josephine verloren, die im März 1899 ebenfalls an Lungenentzündung verstorben war. Der Schmerz über den Verlust trieb Kipling zu einem kompensierenden Aktivismus an. In einer wesentlichen Frage wichen beide Männer voneinander ab: Trotz einiger harscher Artikel in den Jahren des Ersten Weltkriegs ließ sich Conan Doyle nicht zu der aggressiven Germanophobie eines Kipling verleiten, sei es aus seiner humanistischen Geisteshaltung und einem eigenen Interesse an deutscher Kultur heraus oder aus Rücksicht auf die deutschfreundliche Einstellung seiner Geliebten und späteren zweiten Frau Jean.

Ein weiterer Imperialist von vergleichbarer Geisteshaltung war Henry Rider Haggard. Zu Zeiten des zweiten Burenkriegs war er als allseits geschätzter Unterhaltungsschriftsteller etabliert, der vor allem die jüngere Generation mit exotischen Abenteuererzählungen vom afrikanischen Kontinent faszinierte. Haggard, der die Zulassungsprüfung für den Militär- und Zivildienst des Empire nicht bestanden hatte, wurde 1875 Sekretär von Sir Henry Bulwer (1836–1914), *Lieutenant-Governor* der britischen Südafrika-Kolonie Natal. Im Verlauf seines sechsjährigen Aufenthalts diente Haggard auch Sir Theophilus Shepstone (1817–1893), *Special Commissioner* für Transvaal. In dieser Funktion war Haggard im April 1877 bei der offiziellen Verkündung der britischen Annexion dieser Burenrepublik in Pretoria anwesend. Eine Anekdote besagt, dass er stellvertretend für einen ausgefallenen Beamten die Union Flag gehisst und einen Teil der Proklamation verlesen haben soll. 1879 kehrte Haggard nach England zurück, nicht nur, um endlich sesshaft zu werden, sondern auch, um eine Schriftstellerkarriere zu beginnen. Eines seiner ersten veröffentlichten Bücher trägt den Titel *Cetywayo and His White Neighbours; Remarks on Recent Events in Zululand, Natal, and the Transvaal* (1882) und erzählt von Begebenheiten, die er selbst erlebt hat. Allerdings fand die Publikation, abgesehen vom englischsprachigen Südafrika, keinen größeren Anklang. In einer Einleitung brachte Haggard seine Besorgnis über die Vernachlässigung Südafrikas und die Inkompetenz mancher Empire-Administration und Entscheidungsträger in London zum Ausdruck – nur allzu bekannte Themen, die auch 20 Jahre später nichts von ihrer Gültigkeit eingebüßt hatten:

> The position of South Africa with reference to the Mother Country is somewhat different to that of her sister Colonies, in that she is regarded, not so much with apathy tinged with dislike, as with downright disgust. This feeling has its foundation in the many troubles and expenses in which this country has been recently involved, through local complications in the Cape, Zululand, and the Transvaal: and indeed is little to be wondered at. [...] Now, if there is any country dependent on England that requires the application to the conduct of its affairs of a firm, considered, and consistent policy, that country is South Africa. Boers and Natives are quite incapable of realising the political necessities of any of our parties, or of understanding why their true interests should be sacrificed in order to minister to those necessities. It is our wavering and uncertain policy, as applied to peoples, who look upon every hesitating step as a sign of fear and failing dominion that, in conjunction with previous postponement and neglect, has really caused our troubles in South Africa. For so long as the affairs of that country are influenced by amateurs and sentimentalists, who have no real interest in it, and whose knowledge of its circumstances and conditions of life is gleaned from a few blue-""books, superficially got up to enable the reader to indite theoretical articles to the "Nineteenth Century", or deliver inaccurate speeches in the House of Commons – for so long will those troubles continue. (Haggard)

Es überrascht nicht, dass sich Haggard auch in den Debatten des zweiten Burenkriegs positionierte. Mit seinen unmittelbaren Erfahrungen und profunden Kenntnissen der Materie meldete er sich mit pro-imperialistischen Schriften wie *The Last Boer War* (1899) and *The New South Africa* (1900) zu Wort. Doch ein nachhaltigerer Einfluss ging von seinen Romanen und Kurzgeschichten aus. *King Solomon's Mines*[7] (1885) brachte Haggard den literarischen Durchbruch. An diesen Erfolg schlossen sich Bücher ähnlicher Machart an: *She* (1887), *Allan Quatermain* (1887), *The Pearl Maiden* (1903) und *Ayesha* (1905), Romane, die, wie Nichoals Daly anmerkt, Europa gar nicht wirklich verlassen, sondern eher eine europäische Fantasie bedienen, "that is not in the end about Africa" (Daly 54). In den Jahren des Burenkriegs erschienen dann allerdings doch Erzählungen mit mehr oder weniger deutlichem Südafrika-Bezug: *The Spring of Lion* (1899), *Elissa; the Doom of Zimbabwe* (1899); *Black Heart and White Heart; a Zulu Idyll* (1900). Die Botschaft, die von all diesen literarischen Texten ausgeht, ist eindeutig: Sie spricht von männlichen Abenteurern wie Allan Quartermain, deren moralische Qualitäten und Ehrbegriffe sie berechtigt, in die Geschicke anderer Völker einzugreifen. Das hindert Haggard allerdings nicht daran, seinen britischen Helden den "edlen Wilden" an die Seite zu stellen.

Haggard war Kipling seit dessen Ankunft in London 1889 freundschaftlich verbunden, was bis zu seinem Tod anhielt. Teilten sie in jüngeren Jahren ihre Begeisterung für das Empire, so hegten beide im Alter ausgeprägt konservative Anschauungen, die in Kiplings Fall anti-semitische und anti-deutsche, in Haggards Fall einen stark anti-bolschewistischen Zug annahmen (Ricketts 352). Haggards Ader für das Spiritualistische hätte ihn zu einem Freund Doyles machen können, jedoch unterhielt er lieber seine lebenslange Freundschaft zu Kipling. Gleich Kipling und Doyle war Haggard aktiv im Dienst des Empire tätig, das er ausgiebig bereiste. Er verschrieb sich landwirtschaftlichen Reformen und war Mitglied zahlreicher Regierungskommissionen auf diesem Gebiet. Seine Schrif-

---

[7] Der populäre Roman *King Solomon's Mines* wird bisweilen als das erste Buch des *Lost World*-Genre gesehen. Ob Doyle wirklich davon beeinflusst worden war, ist nur zu vermuten. Allerdings hatte er den Roman *She* – Haggards Bestseller – abgelehnt.

ten zu diesem Thema fußten nicht zuletzt auf den Erfahrungen, die er in Südafrika gesammelt hatte. Für seine Verdienste wurde Haggard 1912 geadelt. 1919 bekam er zusätzlich den Titel *Knight Commander of the Order of the British Empire* zuerkannt.

Doyle, Kipling, Haggard und andere imperialistische Autoren pflegten und propagierten einen gemeinsamen Empire-Diskurs, der sich trotz der ihm eigenen Stereotypen und Klischees nicht auf eine Auflistung von Exotik und Kriegstaten reduzieren lässt. Obwohl die individuellen Erzählstrategien dieser Schriftsteller sehr unterschiedlich ausfallen konnten, schrieben sie mit ihren diversen Text eine Masterstory fort, die das geistige Gerüst für ein idealisiertes Empire-Modell war. Zwischen den fiktionalen und den historischdokumentarischen Texten lassen sich thematische und ideologische Gemeinsamkeiten erkennen. Beide Formen verbreiten imperialistische Werte und schaffen ein verbindendes Ideal. Der imperialistische Diskurs jener Jahre entfaltete demnach seine volle Wirkung erst in der Vermischung von Idealisierung, Fiktionalisierung und Dokumentarisierung kolonialer Themen. Diese Art von ideologiegebundener Literaturproduktion unterschied sich erheblich von dem bedeutungsoffenen, symbolträchtigen Schreiben, das Joseph Conrad in seinem Roman *Heart of Darkness* (1899) praktizierte. Die subversive Qualität von Conrads Text bildete in der weit verbreiteten imperialistischen Affirmativität der Literatur jener Zeit die Ausnahme – ein Status, der durch die damalige Nichtakzeptanz von Conrad als englischer Autor noch bekräftigt wird.

Die Geburtstunde des Propagandakriegs

Als Conan Doyle im Herbst des Jahres 1899 beabsichtigte, sich freiwillig zum Kriegsdienst für den Burenkrieg zu melden, zeigte sich die Militäradministration ablehnend. Auch Conan Doyles bahnbrechender Kriegserfindung – ein Gewehradapter, der es ermöglichen sollte, durch Anpassung der ballistische Kurve die Buren in ihren Verstecken mit gezieltem Gewehrfeuer auszuschalten – erfuhr sehr zur Empörung des Erfinders eine resolute Zurückweisung der Militärexperten:

> He [Doyle] was hoping to solve a battlefield problem which he imagined would be significant in South Africa. What is the use of direct rifle fire, he argued, when your opponent, the Boers, can always hide behind cover or in trenches. His solution was a small apparatus which a soldier could attach to his gun and which would allow him to raise the trajectory of his fire and rain down bullets on the enemy. He experimented with a prototype around Fresham Pond, four miles from Undershaw. But when he sent the War Office details of his research into how, as he put it, to turn a rifle into a howitzer, he was shocked to be rebuffed by them – so shocked, in fact, that he wrote to *The Times* to complain about 'the curt treatment which inventors receive at the hands of the authorities.' (Lycett 252)

In den Folgejahren und insbesondere während des Ersten Weltkriegs meldete sich Doyle mit weiteren militärischen Innovationen zu Wort. In Erinnerung an den Burenkrieg forderte er Feldstecher für Artillerieoffiziere, da diese in den damaligen Schlachten wiederholt die eigene Infanterie unter Beschuss genommen hatten. Das von ihm nach seiner Rückkehr aus Südafrika angeregte paramilitärische Training, mit dem er auf die veränderten Kriegsmethoden der Buren reagieren wollte, war darauf ausgerichtet, einem Feind zu begegnen, der sich nicht an die traditionellen Kriegsregeln hielt. In den ersten Kriegswochen des Jahres 1914 schlug Doyle angesichts schwerer Verluste auf See einen aufblasbaren Schwimmgurt als Standardausrüstung für die Marine vor. Die Militärs griffen die Idee auf und rüsteten die Matrosen mit aufblasbaren Gummihalskrausen aus, eine Idee, aus der letztlich die Schwimmweste entwickelt wurde. Auch die Ausstattung von Kriegsschiffen mit Rettungsbooten ging auf Conan Doyles Initiative zurück. Ob er allerdings als erster die Möglichkeit einer Seeblockade Englands vorhergesehen hat, ist angesichts des historischen Beispiels der Kontinentalblockade zu Zeiten der Napoleonischen Kriege fragwürdig. Conan Doyles beständige Interventionen wurde von großen Teilen der Empire-Administration und innerhalb der verknöcherten militärischen Strukturen als Nadelstiche empfunden, die sie in ihrer Routine aufzustören drohten. Doyle wie auch Kipling setzten den zutage tretenden Unzulänglichkeiten in der britischen Armee ihre idealisierte Vorstellung von einer schlagkräftigen und willensstarken modernen Militärorganisation entgegen. Die Lobeshymnen, die Doyle auf die irischen und Kipling auf die australischen Verbände im Burenkrieg anstimmten, sollten vor diesem Hintergrund von Engagement und Kritik gesehen werden (Lycett 256; Ricketts 265). Aus der Perspektive eines *New Imperialism* erschien diese moderne Armee als Garant für den Fortbestand und die Zukunft des Empire. Doch ein solcher Enthusiasmus, gepaart mit Privatinitiative, wurde von offizieller Seite wenig geschätzt. Das Kriegsministerium fürchtete, eher zur Zielscheibe als zum Nutznießer eines so populären Autors wie Conan Doyle zu werden (vgl. Lycett 251).

Mit Ausbruch des ersten Weltkriegs sollte sich die reservierte Haltung der Militärs gegenüber Schriftstellern grundlegend ändern. In militärischen und Regierungskreisen hatte man spätestens seit der Medienschlacht des Burenkriegs erkannt, dass eine bewaffnete Auseinandersetzung gerade auch in der öffentlichen Meinung gewonnen werden musste. Und so berief schon Anfang September 1914 der liberale Politiker und Journalist Charles Masterman (1873–1927) in seiner Funktion als Chef der neu eingerichteten Abteilung für Kriegspropaganda ein Geheimtreffen mit führenden Schriftstellern des Landes ein. Dabei sollten Möglichkeiten diskutiert werden, wie die literarischen Meinungsmacher die Kriegsanstrengungen Großbritanniens unterstützen könnten. Unter den Teilnehmern dieses Treffens befanden sich über zwanzig namhafte Schriftsteller, darunter – neben Conan Doyle – William Archer (1856–1924), Arnold Bennett (1867–1931), J. M. Barrie (1860–1937), G. K. Chesterton (1874–1936), John Galsworthy (1867–1933), Thomas Hardy (1840–1928), Rudyard Kipling (1865–1936), Ford Madox Ford (1873–1939), John Masefield (1887–1967), Sir Henry Newbolt (1862–1938), Gilbert Parker (1862–1932), G. M. Trevelyan (1876–1962) und H. G. Wells (1866–1946). Alle teilnehmenden Autoren unterzeichneten eine

Erklärung über den gerechten Charakter des Krieges und stimmten einer strikten Geheimhaltung zu. Erst 1935 wurden die Aktivitäten des *War Propaganda Bureau* der allgemeinen Öffentlichkeit bekannt. Zahlreiche der eingeschworenen Autoren teilten und propagierten in ihren Schriften und Büchern die regierungsoffizielle Sicht auf die Kriegsgeschehnisse, was aber nicht bedeutete, dass sie sich jeglicher Kritik an der eigenen Regierung enthielten.

Das britische *War Propaganda Bureau* (WPB) wurde mit Beginn des I. Weltkrieges im Londoner Wellington House eingerichtet. Seine Aufgabe bestand darin, die britischen Kriegsanstrengungen durch gezielte Desinformation und Meinungsmanipulation über den Kriegsgegner zu unterstützen. Charles Masterman verfügte aus seiner journalistischen Zusammenarbeit mit Ford Madox Ford bei der *English Review* über ausgezeichnete Kontakte zur Londoner Kunst- und Intellektuellenszene. Auch in der Politik konnte sich der umtriebige Masterman eines verzweigten Netzwerks bedienen. So verband ihn eine besonders enge Freundschaft mit Winston Churchill. Eins der vorrangigsten Ziele des Propagandabüros war die Kriegseinbindung der Vereinigten Staaten auf Seiten der *Entente*. Zu diesem Zweck wurden Lesereisen und Gemäldeausstellungen in den USA organisiert und Kunstmäzene in die Pflicht genommen. Mastermans *Bureau* mutierte schließlich zum *Department of Information* unter der Leitung von John Buchan, bevor es sich ab 1918 zum noch größeren *Ministry of Information* auswuchs. Das spricht für die enorme Bedeutung, die der Propaganda im Kriegswesen nunmehr beigemessen wurde.

Conan Doyle fühlte sich mit seinen fünfundfünfzig Jahren noch nicht zu alt, um am Ersten Weltkrieg aktiv teilzunehmen. Doch trotz eines Briefes an das Kriegsministerium, in dem er auf die symbolische Vorbildwirkung eines solchen Akts verwies, wurde sein Ersuchen abgelehnt. Wie schon im Burenkrieg, so gab sich Doyle auch diesmal nicht mit dem abschlägigen Bescheid zufrieden. Er belebte seine Idee der Bürgermilizen neu und organisierte Verteidigungseinheiten aus Freiwilligen, was allerdings nicht den Vorstellungen des Kriegsministeriums entsprach. Doyle war schließlich zufrieden, in eine neu gebildete Reservistenkompanie aufgenommen zu werden, die Teil des Sechsten Königlichen Freiwilligen Regiments von Sussex war (Lycett 354/55). Obwohl ihm ein Kommandoposten angetragen worden war, bevorzugte es, während des gesamten Kriegs in dieser Einheit als Soldat zu dienen. Im familiären Umfeld musste Doyle in jenen Jahren schmerzliche Verluste hinnehmen. Sein Sohn Kingsley, der 1916 in der Schlacht an der Somme verwundet worden war, starb im Oktober 1917 an den Folgen einer Pneumonie, die sich im Zusammenhang mit seiner Verwundung entwickelt hatte. Auch der *Brigadier-General* Innes Doyle erlag im Februar 1919 einer schweren Lungenentzündung. Diese Schicksalsschläge verstärkten Conan Doyles spiritualistische Neigungen.

Waren die Militärs an Conan Doyles Wehrbereitschaft nur wenig interessiert, so waren sie es umso mehr hinsichtlich seiner schriftstellerischen Fähigkeiten. 1914 verfasste Conan Doyle ein erstes Pamphlet unter dem Titel *To Arms!*, um die Rekrutierungsbemühungen der Armee zu unterstützen. Das *War Propaganda Bureau* organisierte für Doyle einen Frontbesuch. Im Ergebnis wurde ein weiteres Pamphlet unter dem Titel *A Visit to the Three Fronts* (1916) veröffentlicht. Doyle verfolgte auch die alltägliche journalistische Arbeit, indem er für die Zeitung *Daily Chronicle* Kommentare zu den Kriegereignissen schrieb. Diese enthielten heftige anti-deutsche Attacken. Während der Kriegsjahre schrieb Conan Doyle seine sechsbändige Geschichte der britischen Kriegsaktivitäten in Frankreich und Flandern. Es war eine ebenso detaillierte wie anekdotisch weitschweifige Geschichtsdarstellung, die nicht nach dem Geschmack vieler führender Militärs ausfiel. Doyle wollte so genau und korrekt wie nur irgend möglich sein und bemühte sich um eine große Anzahl von Quellen, zu denen ihm bisweilen der Zugang verwehrt wurde. Dennoch schlich sich über die Vielzahl der Materialien Unausgewogenheit ein. Die wohlmeinende, aber viel zu umfangreich ausgefallene Abhandlung wurde weder in Kennerkreisen anerkannt, noch ein Verkaufserfolg. Andere wie John Buchan liefen ihm den Rang ab. Hinzu kam, dass das Lesepublikum in Zeiten von Telegrammdepeschen und Kinopräsentation Neuigkeiten von der Front wollte und keine ausladenden historischen Erklärungen. Und auch späterhin, in der Ernüchterung der Nachkriegsjahre, konnte die aufwendige Arbeit keine höhere Aufmerksamkeit erzielen (Lycett, 357/58).

Vielleicht ist Arthur Conan Doyle hinsichtlich seiner Ambitionen als Krieghistoriograph Opfer einer Entwicklung geworden, die er selbst mit initiiert hatte. Der Übergang von der historischen Darstellung zur Propagandaschrift, von der argumentativen Analyse zum Rhetorischen und Unterhaltsamen hatte letztlich den Wert einer akribischen, faktenorientierten Abhandlung in den Hintergrund treten lassen und der Polemik und Fiktionalisierung Tür und Tor geöffnet. Unterhaltung statt Bildung war auch hier ein Resultat der sich verschiebenden Perspektive innerhalb der modernen Massengesellschaft. John Buchans Spionageroman *The Thirty-Nine Steps* (1915), der sich großer Popularität unter den britischen Frontsoldaten des Ersten Weltkriegs erfreute, kann als ein typisches Beispiel dafür gelten.

Literaturverzeichnis

"Conan Doyle Dead From Heart Attack". *New York Times*, 8 July 1930.
Daly, Nicholas. *Modernism, Romance and the Fin de Siècle: Popular Fiction and British Culture.* Cambridge: Cambridge UP, 2004.
Doyle, Arthur Conan. *The Great Boer War.* London: Thomas Nelson & Sons, 1903.
—. *Our African Winter.* London: Duckworth, 2001.
—. *The War in South Africa. Its Causes and Conducts.* 1902. 15. Juli 2011. <http://www.gutenberg.org/catalog/world/readfile?fk_files=1538431>.
Haggard, Rider. *Cetywayo and His White Neighbours; Remarks on Recent Events in Zululand, Natal, and the Transvaal.* 1882. 14. Juli 2011. <http://www.gutenberg.org/catalog/world/readfile?fk_files=1471688>.
Hopkins, Eric: *Charles Masterman (1873–1927) Politician and Journalist: 'The Splendid Failure'.* New York: Edwin Mellen, 1999.
Kipling, Rudyard. *The Complete Verse.* London: Kyle Cathie, 2002.
Lycett, Andrew. *Conan Doyle: The Man Who Created Sherlock Holmes.* London: Weidenfeld & Nicolson, 2007.

Pakenham, Thomas. *The Scramble for Africa: White Man's Conquest of the Dark Continent from 1876–1912*. New York: Avon Books, 1992.
—. *The Boer War.* London: Weidenfeld & Nicholson, 1997.
Ricketts, Harry. *Rudyard Kipling: A Life.* New York: Carroll & Graf, 2000.
Sweet, Matthew. *Inventing the Victorians.* London: Faber & Faber, 2001.

Till Kinzel

CONFRONTING BARBARISM AND RELIGION IN *THE TRAGEDY OF THE KOROSKO* AND *THE RIVER WAR*

Arthur Conan Doyle and Winston Churchill on Violence, Empire, and War in the Soudan

The Soudan plays a surprisingly great role in British fictions of empire. Its setting proved particularly fertile for fictional and historiographical considerations on the clash of civilisations, as British imperialism was confronted with a militant form of Islam, the so-called Mahdism. This posed both a military and religious or cultural challenge. The imperial imagination was fuelled by the threat to peace, order and security emanating from Mahdism which was perceived as a force outside civilization. Both Arthur Conan Doyle's *The Tragedy of the Korosko* (1898) and Winston S. Churchill's *The River War* (1899; 1902) offer fascinating readings of this confrontation with barbarism and religion, including a moderate self-criticism of Western superiority.

In der britischen Erzählliteratur zum Empire spielt der Sudan eine erstaunlich große Rolle. Er erwies sich als besonders fruchtbar für literarische und historiographische Überlegungen zum Zusammenprall der Zivilisationen, weil sich dort der britische Imperialismus mit einer militanten Form des Islam, dem so genannten Mahdismus, konfrontiert sah, was eine militärische wie auch religiöse und kulturelle Herausforderung darstellte. Was die Schriftsteller beschäftigte, war die Bedrohung von Frieden, Ordnung und Sicherheit, die vom Mahdismus ausging, der als eine Kraft außerhalb der Zivilisation wahrgenommen wurde. Sowohl Arthur Conan Doyles The Tragedy of the Korosko *(1898) als auch Winston S. Churchills* The River War *(1899; 1902) bieten faszinierende Deutungen dieser Konfrontation mit Barbarei und religiösem Eifertum – was auch verhaltene Zweifel an der westlichen Überlegenheit einschließt.*

Introduction: The Soudan in British Fiction

Violent conflicts of various kinds are the stuff of literature. In 19th century Britain, at the highpoint of imperialism, war was not only the subject of historical inquiry. It was a stark reality, even though not in Britain itself but rather in various places around the globe on the margins of the empire. The Crimea, India, South Africa, New Zealand and the Soudan can be mentioned as prime examples of places where the British "warrior race" (Lawrence James) engaged in warfare to consolidate the empire, to repress rebellion, to further, perhaps, the progress of civilization by establishing law and order, or to check other foreign nations' imperial ambitions. The great role that imperial warfare played in British culture is indicated by the existence of a wide range of literary works dealing with war. In particular, it is the literature for children, particularly young boys, that has to be mentioned here. Writers as productive as G. A. Henty (1832–1902), e. g., provided a host of adventure stories as war novels which even became school readings (see Flotow 51, 52–64; Kullmann 194). Apart from novels set in various other places and times, Henty also published two novels set in the Soudan, *The Dash for Khartoum* (1892), and *With Kitchener in the Soudan* (1902). Other novelists also chose the same subject, e. g., George Manville Fenn, Henty's disciple and biographer, wrote *In the Mahdi's Grasp* (1899) and R. M. Ballantyne (of *Coral Island* fame) a novel called *Blue Lights, or Hot Work in the Soudan* (1888), to mention just a few.[1]

To these works, all of which are novels expressly written for young people, two other books need to be added that offer a view of the Soudan and of the struggles and conflicts taking place in this region which was widely perceived to be a borderland of civilization, where one would either have to "wait for the barbarians" or to actively seek them out. Arthur Conan Doyle, who was deeply interested in Africa, as his later activities on behalf of the Congo but also his interest in the Boer War show, wrote *The Tragedy of the Ko-*

---

[1] On all these writers of juvenile fiction see the informative entries in Sutherland.

rosko as his fictional confrontation with the threat and thrill of the encounter with Islamic fundamentalism. It was thus to be expected that renewed interest in the novel would follow the events of 9/11 (cf. Steyn 212–213).

On a different note, combining historiography and autobiography, Winston Churchill produced a kind of modern classic of instant historiography to the literature on the Soudan – *The River War*, published in 1899 in two volumes and shortly afterwards in an abridged and partly rewritten one-volume edition that would become the basis for all later reprints.[2] Both writers offer an account of events in the Soudan, whether fictional or real, that convey the thrill and adventure, the danger and cruelty in the space between two rival empires. The standard term of reference for the kind of fanatic Muslims following the Mahdi and his successor at the time was 'Dervishes', a term both Conan Doyle and Churchill use as a matter of course. Surprisingly, this meaning is not recorded in the Oxford English Dictionary which merely gives the following definition: "A Mohammedan friar, who has taken vows of poverty and austere life. Of these there are various orders, some of whom are know from their fantastic practices as *dancing* or *whirling*, and as *howling dervishes*." The writers of imperial fictions and military travelogues, it would seem, applied the term 'dervish' with its rather specific meaning as a kind of shorthand for the phenomenon of Mahdism and Islamic fanaticism in general without troubling too much about its actual content in terms of religious history.

Arthur Conan Doyle's The Tragedy of the Korosko

Arthur Conan Doyle's concern for issues of colonialism is evident on various fronts. E. g., he was one of those who were extremely critical of Belgian colonial practices in the Congo (Hochschild 271–272). It seems fair to say that Conan Doyle was generally re-

---

[2] After many years of editorial work, Professor James Muller from the University of Alaska at Anchorage is finally publishing the first comprehensive and critical edition of the complete text of *The River War*. It is scheduled to appear later this year.

garded as a pro-empire writer, as shown, e. g., by his propagandistic defence of the Boer War (Lycett 271–272), for which he earned his knighthood (Lycett 274). His short novel *The Tragedy of the Korosko*, first published in serialized form and then as a book in 1898, has, as far as I can see, not received any sustained critical attention at all, apart from being credited to have made the "terrifying Dervishes [...] familiar to British novel readers" (Ashley, *Henty* 252). There is only one other reference by Robert Darby that is emphatically noncommendatory.[3] *The Tragedy of the Korosko*, he claims, "is a most hackneyed and predictable adventure tale" (Darby 132). The only interesting part of the book, Darby adds, are the discussions on international politics between a retired English colonel and a Frenchman (Darby 133). One might add that the story would also lend itself admirably to an interpretation in the light of Edward Said's orientalism thesis, offering, as it does, some standard operating procedures of describing the oriental "Other".

In the winter of 1895 to 1896, Conan Doyle travelled to Egypt and made a trip up the Nile; he felt there were unjustifiable risks involved as the tourists came fairly close to the enemy (Doyle, *Memories* 110). When contemplating the landscape "within the area of the Mahdi forces" with the "Southern sky all slashed with the red streaks", this seemed to Conan Doyle "symbolical of that smouldering barbaric force which lies there" (quoted in Miller 180). In a diary entry for January 16, 1896, Doyle (*Life in Letters* 366) wrote "If I were a Dervish general, I would undertake to carry off a Cook's excursion party with the greatest ease" (cf. Doyle, *Memories* 110). This kind of tactical thinking he later developed in what would become *The Tragedy of the Korosko*, a novel that would then provide the basis for a play and still later a film (both called *The Fires of Fate*; I have not been able to find out anything more about either of these). Conan Doyle called *The Tragedy of the Korosko* "a book of sensation" with a "philosophical basis". His intention seems to have been to "make the man in the bus realise what a Dervish means, as he

---

[3] Brantlinger, e. g., completely ignores *The Tragedy of the Korosko*.

never did before" (Doyle, *Life in Letters* 378). How does Arthur Conan Doyle go about this business of explaining the Dervishes, which also means: the Muslim fanatics, to the ordinary Englishman? How does he, to put it differently, construct the Dervish as the Other of the English as a civilized people?

The narrative construction is as follows: the unnamed narrator begins by explaining why the following story never made it to the news, implying that there were imperative reasons for withholding the story from the public. The oddly self-effacing narrator reports the story after claiming authentication from various sources, most particularly some actual participants in the adventure. One participant, Mr James Stephens, did not write up his own version of the events, according to the narrator, but the fact that this person did not make any comments on the proofs submitted to him is taken as evidence for the veracity of the tale to follow. Thus the reader is given the impression that the tale is based on facts which "have now been thrown into narrative form" (Doyle, *Korosko* 3)[4], though it remains unclear by whom.

The tourist party learns from a dragoman, a tourist guide, who is half Syrian, half Copt, that they will visit a place which is "on the very edge of civilisation" or "at the very end of civilisation" (9, 12). It will be possible to see the country of the Dervishes from the top of the rock of Abousir, from which the tourists will return to Wadi Halfa, at which place, according to Winston Churchill, the "sharp line between civilisation and savagery was drawn" (Churchill, *River War* 98). This concept is again and again brought up in Conan Doyle's text, sometimes still more radicalised, as in the American tourist's words that they are "on the very edge of any kind of law and order", where the absence of every kind of order in the dervish empire is summarily taken to be a matter of fact, even though at this point in time it must be mere speculation (16).

The troubling things to come are foreshadowed in the words of Miss Sadie who talks of "standing on the beautiful edge of a

---

[4] Subsequent page numbers in brackets refer to this text.

live volcano" (12). The position of the observer will, however, be quickly turned into that of a involuntary "participant" or victim. How real then is the danger posed by the Dervishes? Conan Doyle presents us with the whole spectrum of possible approaches to the issue which makes his novel astonishingly polyphonous. There are, e. g., those who ignore or even deny the very existence of any danger. Thus, one Frenchman, M. Fardet, presented as a veritable caricature, most emphatically denies the existence of the Dervishes: "Dervishes, Mr. Headingly! There are no Dervishes. They do not exist" (13). He even goes so far as to suggest that the Dervishes are an "invention of Lord Cromer in the year 1885", an interpretation that is allegedly based on "well-informed papers in France" (13–14). It surely does not come as a surprise that this very Frenchman, when the tourists are about to be captured by the Dervishes, waves his hand and cries in a defeatist and subservient manner, "*Vive le Khalifa! Vive le Mahdi!*" (38–39).

Concerning the Dervishes we learn from a discussion between an American, Mr. Headingly, an Englishman named Cecil Brown and a retired colonel, Cochrane Cochrane[5], how they appear to the English before even one actual Dervish has been encountered. The Dervishes are here made out to be entirely different, a kind of absolute Other, for "they are not amenable to the same motives as other people". Many are said to be "anxious to meet death", which, by implication, no Englishman with knowledge about his enlightened self-interest would do. In short, the Dervishes illustrate a more general point about the connection of barbarism and religion: "They exist as a *reductio ad absurdum* of all bigotry – a proof of how surely it leads towards blank barbarism", as one of the interlocutors says (17).

The desert areas beyond Wadi Halfa are described in such a way as to suggest timelessness; they will not be affected by anything men can do: "And beyond this one point of civilisation and of comfort

---

[5] His name is reminiscent of the great British naval hero of the early 19th century, Lord Thomas Cochrane.

there lay the limitless, savage, unchangeable desert, straw-coloured and dreamlike in the moonlight, mottled over with the black shadows of the hills" (21). The timelessness which is here associated with the desert as a place but also with the Orient turns out to be true in another sense, for when the Dervishes finally come to get the tourists, we learn that "this little group of modern types [...] had fallen into the rough clutch of the seventh century – for in all save the rifles in their hands there was nothing to distinguish these men from the desert warriors who first carried the crescent flag out of Arabia" (39). The fanatical Dervishes are thus made out to be essentially the same as their forbears at the time of Islam's expansion in its early period; they are in fact essentialized as orientals in so many words: "The East does not change, and the dervish raiders were not less brave, less cruel, or less fanatical than their forebears" (39). As Leonard Ashley has noted, the distinction between enemy and friend typically goes hand in hand with calling the enemies fanatical and the friends dedicated in imperial fictions of the time (Ashley, *Henty* 252). Orientalist readings find ample support for their general claims – such as the descriptions of the "savages": "fierce head"; "fierce eyes"; "small, brown and wiry, with little, vicious eyes, and thin, cruel lips" (39); "sinister eyes" (52); "monster of cruelty and fanaticism" (57).

However, there are also odd moments of reversal that draw the seemingly clear-cut distinctions between civilized Westerners and the savage orientals into question. Thus, when the tourists are about to be taken, one of them, "the fat clergyman from Birmingham", comes out of his "cataleptic trance" and wakes "into strenuous and heroic energy" (38). The following action is expressly authenticated by the narrative voice as the most vivid image that one "who helped to draw up this narrative" had experienced: "he broke into a *wild* shout, and, catching up a stick, he struck right and left among the Arabs with a *fury* that was more *savage* than their own" (38, emphasis added). The clergyman is also the only one who is actually bound, "for the Arabs, understanding that he was a clergyman, and accustomed to associate religion with violence, had looked upon his outburst as quite natural, and regarded him now as the most dangerous and enterprising of their captives" (43). Thus, the clergyman actually becomes an almost exact replica of a Dervish, thus providing further evidence for the speed with which members of Western civilisation can be transformed, or transform themselves, into their "Others".

The veneer of civilisation appears to be rather thin, even though there is a repeated insistence on the sharp distinction between civilisation and savagery/barbarism. There is no guarantee that civilisation will prevail in its confrontation with savagery, for savagery is not in fact civilisation's absolute Other but, as it were, internally present as a threat and temptation, or to put it neutrally, as a possibility. Thus, one of the tourists, a diplomat, is physically assaulted by "hideous" savages; this provokes him so much that "this man about town, this finished product of the nineteenth century, dropped his life traditions and became a savage facing a savage" (53–54). And already two pages earlier the colonel had growled "savagely" (52).

In contrast, despite their use of "brutal and unreasoning violence" (38), the savages of the novel are not without nobility. And even in their religion, primitive as it appears to the Europeans, it is interesting to note that a considerable number of the tourists are more or less secularists, for whom Christianity is no longer a living faith. When they are instructed by a mullah in the teachings of Islam the narrator says that this mullah "broke away into one of those dogmatic texts which pass in every creed as an argument" (84).

Winston Churchill's The River War[6]

After lengthy attempts, Winston Churchill, then an officer in the 4th Hussars stationed in India, managed to get an appointment by the War Office to join the expedition army in Egypt with the 21st

---

[6] My remarks are based on the text of the second, abridged version of Churchill's book from 1902. The necessary bibliographical information on this, and all the other books written by Churchill, is provided by Langworth's indispensable *Connoisseur's Guide to the Books of Sir Winston Churchill*.

Lancers – in the face of strong opposition by brigadier general and Sirdar Kitchener, to be sure (Churchill, *Early Life* 162–167). The War Office wrote to him as follows:

> You have been attached as a supernumerary Lieutenant to the 21st Lancers for the Soudan Campaign. You are to report at once at the Abassiyeh barracks, Cairo, to the Regimental Headquarters. It is understood that you will proceed at your own expense and that in the event of your being killed or wounded in the impending operations, or for any other reason, no charge of any kind will fall on British Army funds. (Churchill, *Early Life* 167)

Churchill, always keen to improve his financial situation, was also engaged to write columns for the *Morning Post* and in addition he reports that the "President of the Psychical Research Society extracted rather unseasonably a promise from me after dinner to 'communicate' with him, should anything unfortunate occur" (*Early Life* 167). When he reached Egypt, there already was what has been described as a "ragged platoon of fifteen journalists". Among these was G. A. Henty, the author not only of *The Dash for Khartoum*, considered one of Henty's best works (cf. Ashley, *Henty* 200–202), but also of the later novel *With Kitchener in the Soudan: A Story of Atbara and Omdurman* (1903). Henty, as one of the most prominent Victorian war correspondents since the Crimean War, was reporting on the war for the *Standard* (Green 255).

Churchill presented an account of his experiences in the Soudan in a number of different books. The first and most comprehensive account is to be found in the rare first edition of *The River War*. The most accessible version of *The River War*, however, is the one first printed in 1902 and later re-printed various times. Churchill revised this edition and in particular cut some important passages that he now deemed inappropriate for an ambitious young politician, the career on which he would soon afterwards embark. Also of importance is Churchill's autobiographical book *My Early*

Life, which contains valuable information on the process of writing *The River War*. Most important, from a literary point of view, is Churchill's self-confident alignment with the historiographical tradition of Gibbon and Macaulay (Weidhorn 229, 234). The works of these two historians were among the many books he devoured while stationed in Bangalore, India (Churchill, *Early Life* 111–112; cf. Holley 89–92; 140–162; R. S. Churchill, *Winston S. Churchill* 307–309) and which he also included in the library of the hero of his only novel, the eponymous *Savrola* (Churchill, *Savrola* 34; cf. 212). On the importance of Gibbon and Macaulay for his own historiography he states:

> I affected a combination of the styles of Macaulay and Gibbon, the staccato antitheses of the former and the rolling sentences and genitival endings of the latter; and I stuck in a bit of my own from time to time. I began to see that writing, especially narrative, was not only an affair of sentences, but of paragraphs. Indeed I thought the paragraph no less important than the sentence. (Churchill, *Early Life* 211)

Churchill's reading of these classics of historiography built on his already rather pronounced interest in English history while at school, even though then he failed to warm to "the dullest, driest pemmicanised forms [of history] like *The Student's Hume*" (Churchill, *Early Life* 110).

Churchill begins his account of what he terms "the River War" by describing that part of Africa through which the Nile flows. The Nile offers the only way for commerce to reach markets outside, but it is also the only way by which "European civilisation can penetrate the inner darkness", as he writes (*River War* 1). The Soudan which Churchill deals with, however, is not the "real Soudan" to the south which is "moist, undulating, and exuberant". He talks of another Soudan, "the Soudan of the soldier", which has "tasted the blood of brave men" and "stretches with apparent indefiniteness over the face of the continent". In his description of the land and its peoples, Churchill first introduces the notion of barbarism. He notes the presence of two main races in the land, the "aboriginal natives" and the "Arab settlers" (*River War* 7).

In the context of this paper, I would like to focus particularly on Churchill's references to religion, as these seem to shed light on his overall evaluation of the conflict. In 1897, Churchill had already become acquainted with some form of Islam in the border regions of Afghanistan which were then the object of British imperial concern. In his first published book, *The Story of the Malakand Field Force* (1898), he already compared Islam unfavourably to Christianity, highlighting the generally "modifying influence on men's passions" of Christianity and ascribing to Islam the effect of increasing, "instead of lessening, the fury of intolerance" (Churchill, *Malakand* 25). He goes on to explain that "this form of madness" (i. e., intolerance) is due to the fact that Islam was "originally propagated by the sword" (Churchill, *Malakand* 25). Churchill's first book also introduced the imperial theme, for already here he talks of "that ceaseless struggle for Empire which seems to be the perpetual inheritance of our race" (Churchill, *Malakand* 12).

Churchill's understanding of history always had been averse to the view, often associated with Herbert Butterfield and his criticism of the so-called Whig interpretation of history, that the historian should not, in the words of Churchill's former research assistant, Maurice Ashley, "make any moral judgements at all but should leave them to the Almighty who knows all the circumstances and can search the hearts of men" (Ashley 19). This evaluative attitude shows in his rhetoric, as the most cursory reading of *The River War* shows, even though Ashley (22) claims that here Churchill "does not attempt to draw an elaborate moral because he profoundly believes that history speaks for itself".[7]

---

[7] Ashley gives the following summary of Churchill's general method in his early books: "First he decides his subject and his broad theme. He envisages the grandeur of the story, the qualities and weaknesses of the men whom he characterizes; he sets the scene; he develops his account chapter by chapter – each chapter being of a more or less equal length; he embodies the documentation at appropriate points in the

When Churchill joined the armed forces in the Soudan, some major operations had already started, including a fierce battle that destroyed the Mahdi's lieutenant's army, so what was still missing was "the advance 200 miles southward to the Dervish capital and the decisive battle with the whole strength of the Dervish Empire". As Churchill writes, he "was deeply anxious to share in this" (Churchill, *Early Life* 161). The fascination Churchill felt for the actual warfaring experience is mirrored in his enthusiastic sentences evaluating the events of the war in the Soudan written more than thirty years later: "Nothing like the Battle of Omdurman will ever be seen again. It was the last link in the long chain of those spectacular conflicts whose vivid and majestic splendour has done so much to invest war with glamour" (Churchill, *Early Life* 171).

The military conflict described by Churchill is clearly considered as a conflict between two empires. These empires are similar in being empires, but they are, or so it seems, very different in terms of the actual way these empires are ruled. Churchill expressly paints a picture of military government as the worst kind of despotism, reserving for the Dervish empire the harshest criticism available: "Of the military dominions which history records, the Dervish Empire was probably the worst" (Churchill, *River War* 69).

In the battle of Omdurman on the 2nd of September 1898, the "authority of the Khalifa and the strength of his army were for ever broken" (Churchill, *River War* 327). The British and Egyptian forces gained a complete victory but at night only one "brigade remained in the city to complete the establishment of law and order – a business", as Churchill ominously adds, "which was fortunately hidden by the shades of night" (Churchill, *River War* 306). Thus the violent nature of the establishment of law and order is covered up – both by the night's darkness and by Churchill's poetic diction. In one of his despatches written shortly after the events, Churchill had expressly mentioned that he would not report "all the horrors,

---

narrative; he reaches valid conclusions, marshalling the arguments of both sides" (22).

as the taste for realism is one which should not be greatly encouraged" (Woods 119). We learn elsewhere that hundreds of Dervishes "had been killed in Omdurman the night after the battle, when the Sudanese troops had exacted their own revenge on the Mahdists" (Green 265). Churchill's own romantic view of war did not prevent him from visiting the battlefield three days after the engagement. His comparative descriptions of the deaths of British and Dervish soldiers deserves to be quoted in full, as it indicates his attempt, imperialist and nationalist that he definitely was (see Emmert; Toye), to do justice even to the fanatical Dervishes:

> I have tried to gild war, and to solace myself for the loss of dear and gallant friends, with the thought that a soldier's death for a cause he believes in will count for much, whatever may be beyond this world. When the soldier of a civilised power is killed in action his limbs are composed and his body is borne by friendly arms reverently to the grave. The wail of fifes, the roll of drums, the triumphant words of the Funeral Service, all divest the act of its squalor, and the spectator sympathises with, perhaps almost envies, the comrade who has found his honourable exit. But there was nothing *dulce et decorum* about the Dervish dead. Nothing of the dignity of unconquerable manhood. All was filthy corruption. Yet these were as brave men as ever walked the earth. The conviction was borne in on me that their claim beyond the grave in respect of a valiant death was as good as that which any of our countrymen could make. The thought may not be original. It may happily be untrue. It was certainly most unwelcome. (Woods 126)

The history of the Dervishes, he realizes, will now only be preserved by their conquerors and their bones will be the only remaining monuments. Churchill's respect for the valour of the Dervishes now lying in the field, "those valiant warriors of a false faith and of a fallen dominion", as he calls them in one of his despatches, leads him to add reflections that do not bode well for the empire of the victors as well, for the "Dervish host was scattered and destroyed. Their end, however, only anticipates that of the victors, for Time, which laughs at Science, as Science laughs at Valour, will in due course contemptuously brush both combatants away" (Woods 128). *Sic transit gloria mundi.*

About ten years later, Churchill published an account of another African journey, this time through Uganda and from there following the Nile downwards. Moving from the equatorial regions to the North, he juxtaposes the "regions of abundant rainfall, the Equatorial luxuriance, of docile [!] people, of gorgeous birds and butterflies and flowers" to the "stern realms of sinister and forbidding aspect, where nature is cruel and sterile, where man is fanatical and often rifle-armed" (Churchill, *African Journey* 131). When he finally reaches the very places where the River War was fought, Churchill feels called upon to note the "steady and remarkable progress in every sphere of governmental activity in every province of the Soudan", now that "the Dervish domination was irretrievably shattered on the field of Omdurman" (Churchill, *African Journey* 136). The onslaught of barbarism, it seems, has been successfully repulsed: "Order has been established, and is successfully, though precariously, maintained even in the remotest parts of Kordofan." Likewise, agricultural improvements have considerably increased the country's wealth, according to Churchill, and slavery has been abolished. Even the religious conflict seems to have been attenuated, for now, "without affronting the religion or seriously disturbing the customs of the people, a measure of education and craftsmanship has been introduced" (Churchill, *African Journey* 136). Once the Dervish version of Islam is defeated, the British empire can begin to exert its beneficent influence, it seems. As Manfred Weidhorn claims in the most important study published on Churchill's writings, Churchill did not really grow out of the parochialism of British imperialism so that "he could not dramatize, as do Conrad, Forster, and others, the horrific discovery on the frontiers of empire of the savage within the self and within the European imperialist venture"

(233). Churchill's worldview may have been in part restricted, as Weidhorn suggests, because he did not know anything much in the way of modern literature (except for Kipling). It could therefore be said that "Churchill remained blithely unaware of his own blindness" (Weidhorn 233).

Comparison and Conclusion

At the same time, the British empire's confrontation with the Mahdist rebellion presented a challenge to interrogate and negotiate the complexities implied in a kind of clash of civilizations at the high point of British imperialism. How far could British self-criticism go in the face of adversity? Both Conan Doyle and Churchill respond to the Mahdist challenge in their works published shortly before the turn of the century. Whereas Conan Doyle employs fiction to present a politically charged adventure with Mahdist hijackers of Western tourists exploring "the very edge of civilization", Churchill, as soldier, war correspondent and imperial politician to be, presents a lively and intriguing account of the ultimate suppression of the Mahdi rebellion by Kitchener in 1898. His magisterial book *The River War*, sometimes compared to Thucydides' *History of the Peloponnesian War*, offers highly pertinent reflections on how an utterly alien world was described, presented and evaluated by (to a certain extent) self-critical representatives of British imperialism. Both Conan Doyle and Churchill engaged in story-telling that was meant to shed light on a world of "barbarism and religion" that appeared to be the complete Other of their own civilization. Edward Gibbon famously stated that in his *History of the Decline and Fall of the Roman Empire* he had "described the triumph of barbarism and religion" (Gibbon 1068). In analogy, one could say that both Conan Doyle and Churchill describe what amounts to a triumph over barbarism and religion. However, their undoubted sympathy for the British empire did not preclude some kind of understanding, tenuous though it may have been, of the relativity of their position *sub specie aeternitatis* and in light of the fact that the gap between civilisation and barbarism is neither as unbridgeable nor as stable as one would like to think (cf. Weidhorn 34). In this regard one might say that Arthur Conan Doyle, no less a staunch defender of the British empire than Winston Churchill, presents a somewhat more self-critically subtle portrait of the clash of civilisations that took place on the margins of two empires in the last years of the 19th century.

Works Cited

Ashley, Leonard R. N. *George Alfred Henty and the Victorian Mind*. San Francisco: International Scholars Publications, 1999.
Ashley, Maurice. *Churchill as Historian*. New York: Scribner, 1968.
Brantlinger, Patrick. *Rule of Darkness: British Literature and Imperialism, 1830–1914*. Ithaca: Cornell University Press.
Brendon, Piers. *The Decline and Fall of the British Empire, 1781–1997*. New York: Knopf, 2008.
Churchill, Randolph S. *Winston S. Churchill I: Youth, 1874–1900*. Boston: Houghton Mifflin, 1966.
Churchill, Winston S. *My African Journey*. London: Heron Books, n. d.
—. *My Early Life, 1874–1904*. New York: Touchstone, 1996.
—. *The Story of the Malakand Field Force*. Teddington: Echo Library, 2007.
—. *The River War: An Account of the Reconquest of the Sudan*. Mineola: Dover, 2006.
—. *Savrola: A Tale of the Revolution in Laurania*. London: Leo Cooper, 1990.
Darby, Robert. "Captivity and Captivation: Gullivers in Brobdingnag". *Eighteenth-Century Life* 27:3 (2003): 124–139.
Doyle, Arthur Conan. *A Life in Letters*. Ed. Jon Ellenberg, Daniel Stashower, and Charles Folley. London: Harperpress, 2007.
—. *Memories and Adventures*. Ed. David Stuart Davies, Ware: Wordsworth, 2007.
—. *The Tragedy of the Korosko*. London: Hesperus, 2003.
Emmert, Kirk. *Winston S. Churchill on Empire*. Durham, NC: Carolina Academic Press, 1989.
Este, Carlo d': *Churchill Warlord: A Life of Winston Churchill at War, 1874–1945*. New York: Harper, 2008.

Flotow, Dorothea. *Told in Gallant Stories: Erinnerungsbilder des Krieges in britischen Kinder- und Jugendromanen 1870–1939.* Würzburg: Königshausen & Neumann, 2007.

Gibbon, Edward. *The Decline and Fall of the Roman Empire.* Vol. 3. Ed. David Womersley. London: Penguin, 1995.

Green, Dominic. *Three Empires on the Nile: The Victorian Jihad, 1869–1899.* New York: Free Press, 2007.

Henty, G. A. *The Dash for Khartoum: A Tale of the Nile Expedition.* London: Blackie & Son, n. d.. 22. Juni 2011. <http://www.gutenberg.org/files/21986/21986-h/21986-h.htm>.

—. *With Kitchener in the Soudan: A Story of Atbara and Omdurman.* London, 1902.

Hochschild, Adam. *King Leopold's Ghost: A Story of Greed, Terror, and Heroism in Colonial Africa.* Boston: Houghton Mifflin, 1998.

Holley, Darrell. *Churchill's Literary Allusions: An Index to the Education of a Soldier, Statesman and Litterateur.* Jefferson, NC and London: McFarland, 1987.

James, Lawrence. *The Rise and Fall of the British Empire.* London: Abacus, 1998.

—. *Warrior Race: The British Experience of War from Roman Times to the Present.* London: Little, Brown, 2001.

Kullmann, Thomas. *Englische Kinder- und Jugendliteratur: Eine Einführung.* Berlin: Erich Schmidt, 2008.

Langworth, Richard M. *A Connoisseur's Guide to the Books of Sir Winston Churchill.* Revised edition. London-Washington: Brassey's, 2000.

Lycett, Andrew. *Conan Doyle: The Man Who Created Sherlock Holmes.* London: Weidenfeld & Nicolson, 2007.

Miller, Russell. *The Adventures of Arthur Conan Doyle: A Biography.* New York: Thomas Dunne, 2008.

Russell, Douglas S. *Winston Churchill, Soldier: The Military Life of a Gentleman at War.* London: Conway, 2006.

Steyn, Mark. *America Alone: The End of the World As We Know It.* Washington: Regnery, 2006.

Sutherland, John. *The Longman Companion of Victorian Fiction.* Harlow: Pearson/Longman, 2009.

Toye, Richard. *Churchill's Empire: The World That Made Him and the World He Made.* New York: Henry Holt, 2010.

Valiunas, Algis. *Churchill's Military Histories: A Rhetorical Analysis.* Lanham: Rowman & Littlefield, 2002.

Weidhorn, Manfred. *Sword and Pen: A Survey of the Writings of Sir Winston Churchill*. Albuquerque: University of New Mexico Press, 1974.
Woods, Frederick, ed. *Young Winston's Wars: The Original Despatches of Winston S. Churchill, War Correspondent, 1897–1900*. London: Leo Cooper, 1972.

Maria Fleischhack

UNDERSHAW

In 1895, Arthur Conan Doyle decided to build a house. His wife Louise (also known as Touie) had suffered severely from tuberculosis and her doctors had given her very little time to live. The author had his new home built in Hindhead, a small village in Surrey. Undershaw would not only be a great family home, but also an ideal place for his wife to recover. Every detail was created according to his wishes and Doyle spent ten of his most productive years there. A century later, Undershaw is falling apart, and the Undershaw Preservation Trust was founded in a desperate bid to save the historical house.

1895 beschloss Arthur Conan Doyle, ein Haus zu bauen. Seine Frau Louise (auch Touie genannt) war schwer an Tuberkulose erkrankt, und ihre Ärzte hatten ihr nur eine kurze Lebenszeit vorausgesagt. Der Schriftsteller ließ sein neues Heim in Hindhead, einem kleinen Dorf in der Grafschaft Surrey, bauen. Undershaw sollte nicht nur ein wundervolles Familienheim werden, sondern auch ein idealer Ort der Genesung für seine Frau. Jedes Detail wurde nach seinen Wünschen ausgeführt, und Doyle verbrachte zehn seiner produktivsten Jahre dort. Nach gut hundert Jahren ist Undershaw am Verfallen, und der Undershaw Preservation Trust macht verzweifelte Anstrengungen, die historische Stätte zu erhalten.

◇

In the spring of 1895, Arthur Conan Doyle met Grant Allen, who had quite recently suffered from tuberculosis. Allen talked about Hindhead, a little village in Surrey, where he had resided to write essays for the *English Illustrated Magazine* and recovered from his illness (Lycett 227). Apparently the air was so clean there that it was known as 'Little Switzerland', and it was not too far from London, but isolated enough to be entirely relaxing (Doyle 107). Doyle, after travelling the world with his wife, trying to find a suitable climate for Lousie to recover in, remarks in his autobiography: "It was quite a new idea to me that we might actually live with impunity in England once more, and it was a pleasant thought after resigning oneself to a life which was unnatural to both of us at foreign health resorts" (Doyle 107). Just weeks later Doyle purchased about four acres of land in Hindhead, with the intention to build a house on it for his family (Lycett 227).

Hindhead is situated on a hill, roughly 890 foot high, so Doyle could be sure that the mist which would form down in the valley would not reach his property and that a fresh breeze would always surround the place, which was yet sheltered from rough winds by large fir trees (Lycett 228). These conditions were essential for Louise's health, and Doyle wanted to make sure that their new home would provide everything neccessary to help her with her recovery. In his autobiography, Doyle explains the name he gave the house, once it was finished: "Undershaw – a new word, I think, and yet one which described it exactly in good Anglo-Saxon, since it stood under a hanging grove of trees" (Doyle 123).

Before leaving for Egypt, a popular place to winter for Europeans because of its mild climate, Doyle consulted his friend Henry Ball,[1] an architect and fellow spiritualist (Doyle 71), and commissioned him to build the house according to his wishes (Lycett 236).

Doyle's father had been an architect, and several elements in the house reflect Doyle's knowledge in the field. The land was slightly sloping down, so he had it levelled into several terraces; on the uppermost the house itself was built, while several further terraces formed the large lawn to the south of the house on which he would later build a tennis court.

However, Doyle had made sure that not only his wife would enjoy the new family home. In 1895 he wrote to his mother: "As to my own amusements there I am within an hour of town and an hour from Portsmouth I have golf, good cricket, my own billiard table,

---

[1] There is a constant confusion about the first name of Undershaw's architect. Lycett refers to the architect as Henry Ball, while Doyle himself only calls him Mr Ball and Julian Barnes writes about Stanley Ball. Several newspaper articles confuse Ball with Joseph Henry Bell, Doyle's former teacher and inspiration for Sherlock Holmes.

excellent society, a large lake to fish in not far off, riding if I choose to take it up, and some of the most splendid walks and scenery that could be possibly conceived" (Lellenberg 353).

The construction of the interior of the house strongly reflects the purpose for which Doyle had the house built. The steps on the main staircase were very shallow, so Touie could walk them up easily. Furthermore, the large windows facing south, with a view down into the valley and not another house in sight allowed Touie to enjoy the sunshine and the view without having to sit outside. The dining room as well as Doyle's study also faced south (Hardman). Every room had a fireplace and the doors opened both ways as to allow Touie to move in between rooms without greater difficulty (McKay). To ensure constant access to electricity, Doyle had Henry Ball build an electricity plant next to the house.

Apart from the practical aspects, Doyle also modelled the house after an Austrian hunting lodge, with deer antlers at the side of the house. A coach house and stable block were build close to the house and a tennis court was created below the veranda. Even though Doyle was not particularly fond of riding, he acquired several horses. A garage housed not only a car, but also a motorcycle and several bicycles (Barnes, 252). A large stained glass window displayed the family crests of his and his wife's families, created by Doyle himself. (Fig. 1)

After having to wait another year until the house was built, Grant Allen offered the Doyle family his own residence in Hindhead from where they could supervise the contruction of the house and already profit from the healing air of the village. Arthur Conan Doyle, his wife Touie and their two children Mary and Kingsley moved into the 7500 square feet house on 19 October 1987 (Lycett 239).

The decision to move to Hindhead proved to be a good one, as Touie recovered quite a bit and Doyle, after having had a writer's block, started to write again, working on several projects at the same time (Lycett 237), amongst them *The Hound of the Baskervilles* (published in 1902) and, bowing to public pressure as well as to his impecunity, also *The Return of Sherlock Holmes*.

Fig. 1: Heraldic Window at Undershaw
© Lynn Gale

What followed were ten of Doyle's most productive years. While residing at Undershaw, he was knighted and his personal investigation and defence of George Edalji in 1907 led to the establishment of the Court of Appeal. It was also from Undershaw that Conan Doyle thrust himself into politics and stood for Parliament as a Conservative candidate. He became a Deputy Lieutenant of Surrey, as well as a member of the local Chiddingfield Hunting Club (McKay) and founded a golf club in Hindhead (Lycett 307). It was also from Undershaw that he entered the Boer War as a volunteer army surgeon.

Several famous guests visited Undershaw, including Virginia Woolf, who took pictures of the family on the lawn in front of the house. E. W. Hornung, J. M. Barrie and Bram Stoker, who admired both the house and its surroundings greatly, were also regular guests. William Gilette, who played the famous detective in Doyle's play *Sherlock Holmes* in New York, also spent a weekend at Undershaw. The guest book is still in existence and proves that Doyle was able to be host to quite a few visitors in his home, whose dining room could seat up to thirty guests.

One of the more regular visitors was Jean Leckie, who would, after Touie's death, become Arthur's second wife (Barnes 248). However, despite his love affair with Jean, Doyle remained faithful to his wife and stayed by her side until her death. Touie died of consumption in 1906, thirteen years after she fell ill, and nine years after Arthur met Jean (Barnes 277). Arthur and Jean, who had spent a lot of time together and were quite obviously in love, got married a year later, both Barrie and Stoker being guests at their wedding. Not wanting to live at Undershaw because of the memories of Touie, they moved away to Crowsburough. Doyle kept the house, as he wanted Kingsley to inherit it after his death, but when his son died shortly after the first World War, Doyle sold the house in 1921 and used the money to fund his research in spiritualism.

After 1921 the house was used as a hotel and restaurant, turning into a place of pilgrimage for Doyle enthusiasts, one of them being Julian Barnes, who visited Undershaw when he wrote *Arthur and George* in 2004 (Barwood). In 2005, the owners of the house decided that the tenants who kept the hotel were not paying enough rent and were unable to grant the necessary repairs to the house. The tenants had to leave Undershaw and it has been unoccupied since. Until 2005, all interior and exterior elements of the house had been kept in their original state, offering guests an opportunity to travel back to the turn of the century and experience the house in the exact shape in which Sir Arhur had built it. (Fig.2)

Fig. 2: Undershaw Today
© Kim Pifer

After being oyle left unoccupied with no security to speak off, Doyle's antlers were stolen from the side of the house, lead was stripped from the roof, windows were broken (including the heraldic window with the family crests), rainwater was pouring straight through the roof and into the rooms below, walls crumbling and mould spreading everywhere (Barwood). (Fig. 3)

When the writer and Doyle enthusiast John Gibson visited Undershaw in 2006, he found the house in a very sorry state. He ultimately called on the Waverly Borough Council to report the damage and state of the building and was told that the owners would be notified. When he returned two weeks later, he found that nothing had changed at all (Barwood).

In early 2006, the owners applied for the building to be divided into three separate residential units and for permission to build fur-

Fig. 3: Undershaw Bedroom
© Lynn Gale

ther units next to the house itself. Undershaw received a Grade II listing on the Statutory List of Buildings of Special Architectural or Historic Interest in 1970, which means that at least the facade and exterior of the house has to be restored and kept in its original shape. However, the plan of the owners would have entailed a complete transformation of the interior, removing all original elements and sealing off the connecting doors between rooms to create three separate units.

The architectural historians of English Heritage decided that Grade II was sufficient, comparing Doyle unfavorably to the merits of Jane Austen and Charles Dickens (Hardman). Unsatisfied with this grading, the Victorian Society argued that even Tennyson's grandmother's house was listed Grade I because of its connection with the great poet. There is certainly no question that Doyle is one of the most famous British writers, and that his Sherlock Holmes is recognised all over the world. Another clear sign for the significance of the author for the British literary heritage is the fact that there are more than 400 Sherlock Holmes societies worldwide. In addition to not only being a house which the author had owned and spent ten of his most productive years in, it had also been constructed by him, and apart from Thomas Hardy's home it is the only example of a house which was built from scratch with the complete architectural control by the author who also lived in it.

The Victorian Society objected to the application of the owners and requested that English Heritage raise the listing from Grade II to Grade I or at least Grade 2*, which would mean that the interior would have to be kept in its original state as well (Hardman). In December 2006, the application for the alterations of the house was rejected, but the owners resubmitted it in early 2009. In 2007, Waverly Council ruled for the owners to erect scaffolding and a temporary roof protection; however, no repairs were executed.

After one potential purchaser reviewed the damages in 2008, he was advised that the restoration cost would amount to over one million pound sterling. Merely a year later, this sum has increased to £ 1,5 million; demonstrating the neglect of the property by the owners and the damage which these five years had done.

When the application was resubmitted, John Gibson and Lynn Gale founded the Undershaw Preservation Trust in 2009, hoping to be able to achieve a Grade I listing as well as the preservation of the house as one single entity. Lynn Gale formulates the present goal of the Undershaw Preservation Trust as follows: "At the moment the main focus of the UPT is to get a judicial review into the decision to award planning consent to the present owners of Undershaw". But Gale and Gibson were not the only ones concerned with the fate of Doyle's former home. As soon as the news of the state of the building spread, voices from all over the world spoke up in favour of saving Undershaw and restoring it to its original shape.

The UPT is under the patronage of Mark Gatiss (co-writer of the BBC series *Sherlock*, who also plays Mycroft Holmes in the TV show) and strongly supported by other rather famous Doyle enthusiasts such as Stephen Fry, Julian Barnes, Ian Ranking and Uri Geller – among many others. Stephen Fry has commented on the cause, saying that "there has never been a time when Conan Doyle has gone out of fashion". He points out that yet another Sherlock Holmes Hollywood blockbuster has just hit the screen. "Undershaw is 'Underthreat'," he declares. "Surely we can all see that this is a disastrous mistake?" (Hardman).

John Gibson explains the importance of the preservation of Undershaw: "Undershaw is our last proper link to an author who helped to define his age. Aside from the make-believe Sherlock Holmes Museum and gift shop in London's Baker Street, there really is nowhere else" (Hardman).

Kimberly Pifer, one of the international representatives for the Undershaw Preservation Trust from North Carolina, USA, explains: "The house is a connection to one of the most enduring literary figures in the last 120 years. Yet the British government has basically said the house was not of equal value to the homes of Jane Austen and Charles Dickens, which mystifies me. Conan Doyle basically created the modern detective story. He's the one who brought science into the realm of the mystery and made it the basis of how the crime was solved. I'd say there are few literary exports from England more globally known and loved than Sherlock Holmes" (Indyweek.com).

What will happen to the former home of one of the most beloved and widely read authors of the last 150 years? Only time can tell, but the UPT will keep on fighting for the preservation of this unique witness of literary history. Any further information on Undershaw and the Undershaw Preservation Trust, including a number of historical and modern photographs of the house can be found under <www.saveundershaw.com>.

Works Cited

(If not noted otherwise, the information on Undershaw was sent to me in an E-mail by the Co-Founder and Assistant Director of the Undershaw Preservation Trust, Lynn Gale.)

"A Scandal in Bohemia". *Independent Weekly*. 28 May 2011. <http://www.indyweek.com/indyweek/a-scandal-in-bohemia/Event?oid=2415958>.

Barnes, Julian. *Arthur & George*. London: Vintage Books, 2006.

Barwood, Lee. "The Case of the Derelict Estate-Saving the Arthur Conan Doyle Home". *Kings River Life Magazine*. 25 June 2011. <http://kingsriverlife.com/06/25/saving-the-arthur-conan-doyle-home/>.

Doyle, Arthur Conan. *Sir Arthur Conan Doyle: Memories and Adventures*. Ware: Wordsworth, 2007.

Gale, Lynn. "Notes on Undershaw". E-mail to Maria Fleischhack. 15 March 2011.

Hardman, Robert. "It's a mystery that would stump even Sherlock Holmes: Why on earth are we letting Conan Doyle's home fall into ruin?" *The Daily Mail*. 12 March 2010. <http://www.dailymail.co.uk/news/article-1257565/Its-mystery-stump-Sherlock-Holmes-Why-earth-letting-Conan-Doyles-home-fall-ruin.html#ixzz1QVTgtUDT>.

Indyweek. com. "A Scandal in Bohemia". 28 May 2011. <http://www.indyweek.com/indyweek/a-scandal-in-bohemia/Event?oid=2490063>.

Lellenberg, Jon, et al. *Arthur Conan Doyle: A Life in Letters*. New York: Penguin, 2007.

Lycett, Andrew. *Conan Doyle:The Man Who Created Sherlock Holmes*. London: Phoenix, 2008.

McKay, Sinclair. "Undershaw: What's to become of it, Watson?" *The Telegraph*. 20 Oct 2007. <http://www.telegraph.co.uk/property/3359609/Undershaw-Whats-to-become-of-it-Watson.html>.

Karl Hepfer

SIR GAWAIN AND THE GREEN KNIGHT
Ein Ritter auf der Suche nach sich selbst

Sir Gawain and the Green Knight ist eines der herausragenden Meisterwerke der mittelenglischen Literatur. Angesichts der sprachlichen Form, in der das Gedicht verfasst ist – in einem nördlichen Dialekt, der von der Sprache des Dreiecks Oxford – Cambridge – London völlig verdrängt wurde – ist es freilich kaum verwunderlich, dass es einem größeren Leserpublikum unbekannt ist. Ein Blick auf den Originaltext lässt sofort deutlich werden, dass die Lektüre intensive Kenntnisse des Altenglischen voraussetzt. Diese sehr sperrige sprachliche Form erklärt in mehrfacher Hinsicht die vielen Übersetzungen ins moderne Englisch. Die Botschaft, die das Gedicht vermittelt, ist jedoch außerordentlich modern: der Held, Gawain, gelangt durch eine Reihe von Prüfungen zur Selbsterkenntnis und erfährt, was es heißt, Mensch zu sein. Y. R. Ponsors Prosaversion des Gedichts scheint durch diese Einsicht motiviert. Im übrigen ist das Gedicht vielfach für Kinder nacherzählt worden im Zusammenhang mit all den Geschichten um König Artus und seine Tafelrunde. Die wenigen Versuche, den Stoff in der modernen Literatur heimisch zu machen, gipfeln in dem Roman von Iris Murdoch *The Green Knight*, der in diesem Essay ausführlich gewürdigt werden soll.

Sir Gawain and the Green Knight *"is the finest of all the romances in Middle English" (Spearing). But it cannot be thought surprising that such a work, written in a language as remote from Chaucer's as Chaucer's is from ours, is not well known to the general public. A glance at the original would tell a reader immediately how much of a student he would have to become to be able to read that text. Its northern dialect is still deeply rooted in Old English, a fact that accounts for the many translations into modern English which the poem has called forth. Apart from its poetic beauty it has, however, a message that must be called very modern: in the course of the various tests which the hero is subjected to, he is led towards self-knowledge and learns how to live as a human being. Y. R. Ponsor's prose adaptation is motivated by this insight. Otherwise the story of the poem has been retold for children in innumerable prose fairy-tale versions included in collections of Arthurian romances, but a serious re-handling of the subject matter is to be found only in one modern novel, namely in Iris Murdoch's* The Green Knight, *which will be discussed in detail in this essay.*

◊

Sir Gawain and the Green Knight ist ein Meisterwerk mittelalterlicher alliterierender Dichtung und neben dem Werk Chaucers das beste mittelenglische Gedicht des Zeitalters. Es unterscheidet sich von Chaucers Schriften so grundsätzlich, dass jeder Vergleich unmöglich ist. Neben der raffinierten Einfachheit von Chaucers Sprache nehmen sich die Verse des anonymen Dichters aus dem Nordwesten Englands wuchtig und fremd aus, was einmal zusammenhängt mit der altertümlichen Sprachform und zum anderen mit der Tatsache, dass sich darin eine frühmittelalterliche Kultur ausdrückt, die sich im Nordwesten des Landes, vermutlich in Lancashire, bis Ende des 14. Jahrhunderts erhalten hat und schließlich von der rivalisierenden Kultur des Südens (im Dreieck Oxford-Cambridge-London) verdrängt wurde. Der Lancashire-Dialekt, in dem das Gedicht verfasst ist, ist noch so stark im Altenglischen verwurzelt, dass er, im Gegensatz zu Chaucers Sprache, dem modernen Leser die allergrößten Schwierigkeiten bereitet. Nicht von ungefähr gibt es daher unzählige Übersetzungen, die heutigen Lesern den Text nahebringen.[1] In das Altenglische zurück geht zum Beispiel die Alliteration, ebenso wie die Schriftzeichen þ ('thorn') und ȝ ('yoke'), die bei Chaucer nicht mehr zu finden sind. Von dem Dichter weiß man nur, dass er aus dem Nordwesten Englands stammt. Er wird wohl für immer anonym bleiben, obgleich unzählige Vermutungen über seine Identität im Umlauf sind. Sein Gedicht umfasst 2530 Verse und ist damit sehr kurz; zum Vergleich: *Le Roman de Perceval* von Chrétien de Troyes hat 9232, der *Tristan* von Gottfried von Straßburg gar 19548 Verse.

---

[1] U. a. von Gollancz, Tolkien, Stone und Vantuano (vgl. Literaturverzeichnis).

Worum geht es in dem Gedicht? König Artus feiert in Camelot das Weihnachts- und Neujahrsfest. Er erklärt, sich nicht an die Tafel setzen zu wollen, ehe er nicht ein wunderbares Abenteuer erlebt habe. Da sprengt ein ganz in Grün gekleideter riesengroßer Ritter auf einem grünen Ross in die Halle. Er fordert die Kühnsten der Tafelrunde heraus, ihm mit der gewaltigen Axt, die er bei sich führt, einen Schlag zu versetzen. Die Artus-Ritter zögern und werden dafür von dem grünen Riesen verhöhnt, bis sich der junge Gawain zu dem Streich bereit erklärt. An Arthurs Stelle schlägt er dem Ritter den Kopf ab, der auf dem Boden fortrollt. Der Grüne Ritter ergreift ihn jedoch bei den Haaren und reitet damit davon, nachdem er Gawain ermahnt hat, sich in einem Jahr dem Gegenschlag bei der Grünen Kapelle zu stellen. Nach Ablauf eines Jahres macht sich Gawain also auf den Weg zur Grünen Kapelle. Auf seinem Ritt durch eine düstere, zerklüftete Winterlandschaft kommt er zu einem einsamen Schloss, in dem er freundlich empfangen wird. Der Schlossherr schlägt dem Gast vor, die Weihnachtstage auf dem Schloss zu verbringen. Er selbst wolle die folgenden drei Tage auf die Jagd gehen und am Abend mit ihm die Gewinne des Tages tauschen. Während der Abwesenheit ihres Mannes kommt die Dame des Hauses in Gawains Schlafzimmer und bietet ihm ihre Liebe an. Da Gawain nicht auf ihr Angebot eingeht, verlässt sie ihn, nicht ohne ihn vorher zu küssen. Die Szene wiederholt sich an den nächsten zwei Tagen, und Gawain kann seinem Gastgeber am ersten Tag einen, am zweiten zwei und am dritten drei Küsse im Austausch gegen dessen Jagdbeute geben. Am dritten Tag überredet die Dame Gawain, als Geschenk von ihr einen grünen Gürtel anzunehmen, der nach ihrer Aussage die Eigenschaft hat, seinen Träger unverwundbar zu machen. Diese Gabe verschweigt Gawain seinem Gastgeber. Am folgenden Tag trifft Gawain bei einem hohlen Hügel, der die Grüne Kapelle genannt wird, auf den Grünen Ritter. Dieser führt drei Schläge gegen Gawain, von denen ihn die ersten beiden nicht verletzen. Nur der dritte Schlag ritzt ihn leicht am Hals. Der Grüne Ritter verwandelt sich vor Gawains Augen in den Schlossherrn und gibt sich als Bercilak von Hautdesert zu erkennen. Er erklärt Gawain, dass ihn die ersten beiden Schläge nicht verletzt hätten, da er an den ersten beiden Tagen sein Versprechen treu eingehalten habe und nur, weil er den Gürtel verschwiegen und zurückbehalten habe – allerdings, um sein Leben zu retten, was ein verzeihlicher Fehltritt sei –, habe ihn der dritte Schlag leicht verletzt. Bercilak lässt Gawain auch wissen, dass hinter dem Abenteuer mit dem Grünen Ritter Morgan le Fay steckte. Sie habe sich an Artus und Guinever rächen und den Tod der Königin provozieren wollen. Gawain reißt sich den grünen Gürtel vom Leib und kehrt zerknirscht und niedergeschlagen nach Camelot zurück, wo ihn seine Gefährten lachend und vergnügt empfangen.

Im wesentlichen sind es drei Hauptelemente, die der Dichter in seinem Epos zusammengeführt hat: das Enthauptungsspiel, das Thema der Versuchung des Helden durch die Frau seines Gastgebers und der Austausch der Gewinne. Vermutlich gibt es keine einzelne Quelle, die alle drei Elemente bereits vereint. Die erste größere Untersuchung der Quellenlage stammt von George L. Kittredge (1916), der davon überzeugt war, dass dem englischen Dichter ein französisches Epos im Stil der Romane von Chrétien de Troyes vorgelegen haben müsse. Wie in der Tradition der Zeit üblich, machte sich Kittredge daran, dieses bis heute nicht aufgefundene Epos zu rekonstruieren. Etwa zwanzig Jahre später machte sich Otto Löhmann mit demselben Ansatz wie Kittredge auf die Spurensuche und kam dabei zu dem Ergebnis, dass die Sage von Gawain und dem Grünen Ritter ursprünglich eine Feenliebesgeschichte gewesen sein muss, die später zu einer Probe ritterlicher Tugenden umgestaltet wurde. Löhmann vermutete für *Sir Gawain and the Green Knight* und das fünfhundert Verse umfassende Gedicht *The Green Knight*, das im Percy Manuskript erhalten ist, eine gemeinsame Quelle, die *englisch* gewesen sein müsse. Auch diese Quelle ist bis heute unauffindbar geblieben (32).

Mit Sicherheit ist das *Beheading Game* keltischen Ursprungs und geht zurück auf das irische *Fled Bricrend*, in dem zwei Versionen der Episode enthalten sind. In der ersten nimmt Cuchulainn die Herausforderung des *shape-shifters* Uath mac Imomain (Terror, Son of Great Fear) an und enthauptet ihn. Der riesenhafte Uath hebt danach seinen Kopf vom Boden auf und geht, indem er verspricht, wiederzukommen und seinerseits Cuchulainn den Kopf abzuschlagen. Am nächsten Tag löst Cuchulainn sein Versprechen ein und bietet sich für den Gegenschlag an. Der Riese gibt ihm drei Schläge mit der flachen Klinge des Schwertes, verschont Cuchulainn und preist ihn als den besten Krieger der Iren. In der zweiten Version fordert Curoi in der Gestalt eines Riesen die anwesenden Krieger auf, ihn mit einer Axt zu enthaupten. Die Männer schlagen ihm mehrfach den Kopf ab (der ihm aber immer wieder auf die Schulter zurückspringt – er ist schließlich ein Gott), erscheinen aber nicht zum Gegenschlag. Cuchulainn ist der einzige, der zu seinem Wort steht. Der Riese verschont ihn auch diesmal und erkennt ihm die *champion's portion* zu, das heißt, er anerkennt ihn als den besten Krieger.

Das Thema 'Versuchung' hat keine direkte Originalquelle, ist aber in der arthurischen Literatur häufig vertreten. Elizabeth Brewer erwähnt in ihrem Artikel über die Quellen des Gedichts eine lange Reihe altfranzösischer und mittelhochdeutscher Romane, die das Motiv der Versucherin enthalten, angefangen bei *Le Chevalier à l'Epée*, über *Perceval, Yder, Lancelet del Lac, Lanzelet;* das Motiv erscheint sogar im *Roman de Troie* und in *Jason und Medea*. Uneinigkeit herrscht in der Beurteilung dieser Versucherszenen. Geht es um eine Keuschheitsprobe? Ist Liebe von Seiten der Dame im Spiel? Für Kittredge ist die Versuchung "a trial of Gawain's fidelity to his host and his loyalty to the chivalric ideal of truth" (76). Kittredges Bewertung ist sicher in beiden Punkten richtig, er fügt allerdings hinzu: "In our Temptation, the wife loves her husband alone, and it is in obedience to his instructions that she tempts the hero" (79). Die stürmische Direktheit der Dame bei ihren Verführungsversuchen lassen einen jedoch daran zweifeln. Sie sagt bereits bei ihrem ersten Besuch in Gawains Kammer: "Ye ar welcum to my cors/ yowre awen won to wale (you are welcome to my body/ to choose your own way)" (Verse 1236–37).[2] Nach Löhmanns Vorstellung lockt die

---

[2] Alle Zitate aus: *Sir Gawain and the Green Knight: A Dual Language Version*. Transl. William Vantuano.

Fee durch einen Boten (hier: den Grünen Ritter) den Mann, nach dem sie sich sehnt, in ihr Reich, und das heißt natürlich, dass sie ihn liebt. Spearing sieht die drei Szenen, in denen die Dame den Helden versucht, etwas differenzierter. Für ihn besteht zunächst kein Zweifel, dass hier Gawains Keuschheit auf die Probe gestellt wird (194). "The test Gawain undergoes at the hands of the Lady is one of sexual temptation. [...] The temptation would not work at all if it were not for its fundamental sexual content" (191). Und: "There is a persistent contrast between the outward *clannesse* of their conversation and the actual suggestiveness of the lady's behaviour, a contrast which offers a far more seductive temptation than greater openness and outspokenness could do" (192). Selbst das Geschenk des grünen Gürtels, das ihm die Dame macht, hat eine sexuelle Komponente. Und indem Gawain dieses "luf-lace" (love band) (Vers 1874) annimmt, begeht er symbolisch einen Verstoß gegen die 'clannesse' (Enthaltsamkeit).

Allerdings ist Gawain bemüht, nicht gegen 'cortaysye' (Höflichkeit und Höfischkeit) oder 'clannesse' zu verstoßen und keinen Verrat an seinem Gastgeber zu begehen. Im Sinne des Pentagramms auf seinem Schild mit den fünf Tugenden 'franchyse' (Großmut), 'fellawship' (Nächstenliebe), 'clannesse', 'cortaysye' und 'pité' (Mitleid und Frömmigkeit) will er nicht gegen die 'fellawship' verstoßen, indem er mit der Frau seines Gastgebers schläft. Er tut dies jedoch symbolisch dennoch dadurch, dass er den schützenden Gürtel annimmt und verbirgt, statt ihn seinem Gastgeber auszuhändigen, und verstößt auf diese Weise gegen die 'franchyse', die "liberality and loyalty that belong to knights" (Vers 2381) einschließt. So sind mindestens vier der fünf Tugenden, die das Pentagramm symbolisiert, durch den Verführungsversuch der Dame einem Test unterworfen. Spearing schließt seine Überlegungen mit dem Verdikt: "The Temptation brings out the complexity and internal interdependence of Gawain's value-system as this is symbolized in the pentangle. His virtues are so closely interlocked that a test of any one of them cannot help being also a failure in others" (209).

Parallel zu den Szenen in Gawains Schlafzimmer verlaufen die drei Jagdszenen, die zu den ersteren einen Kontrast bilden. So wie im Schlafzimmer vollkommene Sicherheit herrscht, so begleiten Gefahr und Tod die Jagd. Aber "it is well known that hunting is used in literature as a metaphor for sexual pursuit" (Spearing, 215) und "the game of love is as deadly as hunting or as the beheading game" (219). Im Mittelalter ist die Jagd zuvörderst eine Metapher für weltliches Vergnügen. In *Sir Gawain and the Green Knight* bilden die Jagdszenen zusammen mit den Szenen im Schlafzimmer Gawains einen markanten Gegensatz zu der grimmigen Verabredung bei der Grünen Kapelle. Die Schlafzimmerszenen sind eine andere Facette weltlichen Vergnügens, in dem die Lust des Fleisches im Vordergrund steht, und diese wird gemeinhin verdammt, denn sie ist ein *memento mori* (vgl. Roonby). Gawain ist daher von dem Besuch der Dame nicht überrascht. Er ist sich seiner Sterblichkeit bereits bewusst bei dem Gedanken an seinen Auftrag an der Grünen Kapelle.

Eine andere Interpretation der Jagdszenen findet sich bei H. L. Savage, der die kennzeichnenden Eigenschaften der gejagten Tiere in Gawains Verhalten wiederfindet. So ist er am ersten Tag schüchtern wie das Reh, am zweiten kühn wie der Eber, und am dritten schlau wie der Fuchs, (zitiert nach Roonby 159). Ähnlich argumentiert Peter McClure, der Reh (am ersten Tag) und Eber (am zweiten) als emblematisch für Gawains Verhalten an den entsprechenden Tagen ansieht und den Kontrast zwischen der Niedertracht des Fuchses am dritten Tag und der edlen Haltung von Reh und Eber als symbolisch für Gawains Verhalten an den drei Tagen betrachtet.

Das Motiv vom Austausch der Gewinne (Exchange of Winnings) ist in keiner der von E. Brewer aufgespürten Erzählungen, die das *Beheading Game* enthalten, vorhanden, obwohl es als Topos dem Volksmärchen durchaus vertraut ist. In *Sir Gawain and the Green Knight* tauschen der Schlossherr und sein Gast am Abend ihre Gewinne: Gawain erhält jeweils die Jagdbeute des Tages (obgleich nie klar wird, was er mit einer derartigen Menge Wildbret anfangen soll), und er gibt seinem Gastgeber die Küsse, die er von dessen Frau bekommen hat. Das hat für Gawain schlimme Folgen. Bercilak erklärt ihm, der Gürtel sei sein Eigentum, und die Versuche seiner Frau, ihn zu verführen, seien sein Werk. Aber da er den

Gürtel nur aus Liebe zum Leben angenommen habe, sei sein Vergehen weniger tadelnswert. Gawains Streben nach Vollkommenheit, wie in dem "endlosen Knoten" des Pentagramms symbolisiert, bekommt hier also einen Riss. Gawain reißt sich den Gürtel vom Leib und gibt ihn dem Ritter mit den Worten:

> There is the false favor; may misfortune befall it!
> Because of concern for your clout, cowardice taught me
> To reconcile myself with covetousness, to go against my
>   nature,
> Which is liberality and loyalty that belong to knights.
> (Verse 2378–81)

Und da er nicht der perfekte Ritter sein kann, ist er entschlossen, der erbärmlichste Sünder zu sein. Der große Sünder ist wenigstens eine heroische Gestalt von Statur, und so kann er sich mit den alttestamentarischen Helden wie Adam, Salomon, Samson oder David vergleichen.

Das Pentagramm, der fünfzackige Stern, den man, ohne abzusetzen, zeichnen kann (daher die Bezeichnung "Endless Knot"), der bei Goethe als Drudenfuß erscheint, wird nur in *Sir Gawain and the Green Knight* Gawain zugeschrieben. Es ziert seinen Schild und wird in den Versen 619–669 detailliert beschrieben. Es ist charakteristisch für des Dichters gelehrten und idealistischen Stil, Gawain mit diesem geheimnisvollen Pentagramm auszustatten. Das Pentagramm, die Quintessenz der Alchimisten, ist uralt. Es befindet sich bereits eingeritzt auf babylonischen Scherben von Ur und gilt in orientalischen Religionen als mystisches Symbol der Vollkommenheit. Den Pythagoräern war es ein Symbol der Gesundheit und den Gnostikern ein Schlüssel zum Reich des Lichts: die Jungfrau Sophia erlaubte nur den Trägern des Pentagrammsiegels den Zutritt zu ihrem Reich. In der christlichen Zahlenmystik ist fünf die Zahl des Menschen, der durch seine fünf Sinne sündigt und durch die fünf Wunden erlöst wird (vgl. E. Brewer 251). Auf diese Weise wird Gawain mit der christlichen Tradition in Verbindung gebracht. Auf der Innenseite seines Schildes trägt er im übrigen das Bild der Jungfrau Maria, so dass das Gedicht trotz seiner heidnischen Elemente als durchaus christlich gelten muss.

Sir Gawain and the Green Knight mit seinen 2531 Versen gehört zu den wohl am häufigsten kommentierten Werken der englischen Literatur. W. Vantuano fügt seiner Übersetzung des Gedichts eine Bibliographie an, die allein vierzig Seiten und um die 850 Titel umfasst. Die einhellige Meinung der Gelehrten drückt Spearing aus, der das Gedicht als "the finest of all the romances in Middle English" bezeichnet (172). Im Vorwort zu seiner Übersetzung gibt Vantuano einen Überblick über die bisherige Forschung. Darin fasst er unter anderem die Ausführungen von Rudnytsky, "Sir Gawain and the Green Knight: Oedipal Temptation"(1983) zusammen, wo Gawain mit dem griechischen Oedipus verglichen wird, der, ohne es zu wissen, auf der Suche nach seinem Ursprung ist. Demnach sind Bercilak und der Grüne Ritter identisch, weil sie für Gawain "twin faces of the father – his benign and his punitive aspects – initially perceived as separate but ultimately merged into one" (zit. nach Vantuano, xv) darstellen. Ebenso sind Bercilaks Frau und die Zauberin Morgan "two aspects of a single character, namely, the mother, the lovely lady, the 'good' mother, and Morgan, topos of the 'Loathly Lady', the 'bad' mother" (zit. nach Vantuano, xx). Für Rudnytsky sind Gawains zerstörerische Haltung dem Grünen Ritter, der Vater-Figur, und seine begehrliche Haltung Bercilaks Frau, der Mutter-Figur, gegenüber die dominierenden Faktoren des Gedichts und nicht das unloyale Versagen des Protagonisten aus Angst um sein Leben. Tiefenpsychologische Interpretationen dieser Art sind wenig ergiebig, obwohl moderne Kommentatoren mit einer gewissen Hartnäckigkeit darauf insistieren (vgl. Vantuano xxx–xxxiii). Das Gedicht selbst legt solche Interpretationen nicht nahe. Die Moral, die das Gedicht tatsächlich vermittelt, ist sehr modern: der Vollkommenheit anstrebende Held, der ein Modell der Ritterschaft ist, erweist sich am Ende als ein Mensch, der fehlbar ist wie wir alle. Sein Weg zur Grünen Kapelle ist der Weg zu sich selbst. Die Einsicht in seine Fehlbarkeit macht den Helden höchst betroffen. Den Grünen Gürtel wird er in Zukunft nicht als Schmuckstück, sondern als Erinnerung an sein Versagen tragen:

> But as a sign of my shame I shall see it often,
> When I ride in renown, to recall to myself
> The faultiness and frailty of the flesh so perverse,
> How it tends to be enticed to sinful transgressions.
> (Verse 2433–2436)

Erwähnung verdient noch die Farbe Grün, die zu vielen Kommentaren geführt hat. Zu Beginn des zwanzigsten Jahrhunderts, also zu der Zeit, als sich Kittredge mit dem Grünen Ritter beschäftigte, wurde der Grüne Ritter als Emanation eines Vegetationsgottes, eines Leben spendenden Geistes gesehen. Diese Sicht ergab sich aus dem zum Jahrhundertbeginn in den literarischen Zirkeln Englands weit verbreiteten Naturkult und Neopaganismus, deren Vertreter beispielsweise D. H. Lawrence, E. M. Forster oder Kenneth Grahame waren. Verbunden damit war eine Neigung zum Okkulten und eine Sucht, überall alte Mythen zu entdecken, die, wie man glaubte, durch das Heraufziehen des Christentums unterdrückt und schließlich vergessen wurden. Besonders trat Jessie Weston mit diese Haltung hervor, die in der gesamten arthurischen Geschichte den schäbigen Rest einer viel bedeutenderen heidnischen Literatur, die leider verschollen ist, sehen wollte. Löhmann, für den der Grüne Mann ein Feenwesen ist, sieht in der Farbe Grün eine ausgesprochene Feenfarbe. Auch er greift schließlich auf Weston zurück. Nun wäre es allerdings auch denkbar, dass die Farbe Grün im Mittelalter nur eine unter vielen war und Grün einer Laune des Dichters entsprang, um den unheimlichen Auftritt des riesenhaften Ritters am Hof Arthurs zu steigern.

Das Thema vom Grünen Ritter hat in der vorwiegend englischen Literatur wenig Nachhall gefunden, obwohl "prose fairy-tale versions, duly bowdlerized, do exist in collections of Arthurian romances for children", wie Stone in seinem Vowort schreibt (7). Der *Celtic heritage* angenommen hat sich W. B. Yeats mit der "Heroic Farce" *The Green Helmet* von 1910, die auf dem Fled Bricrend in Lady Gregorys *Cuchulainn of Muirthemne* fußt und als Einleitung zu *On Baile's Strand* gedacht ist. Die Anlehnung an die Quelle ist eher oberflächlich. Yeats benutzt nur Grundgegebenheiten: die Rivalität von Laegaire, Conall und Cuchulainn, ebenso die Rivalität ihrer Frauen, das Enthauptungsspiel mit dem Feendämon aus dem Wasser, die Auszeichnung Cuchulainns als dem besten aller Helden. Das Drama lässt in einem gedrängten, sehr lebendigen Ablauf ein Stück altirischer Sage auf der Bühne abrollen, wobei die Enthauptung des Dämon natürlich nicht auf der Bühne dargestellt werden kann.

Zu etwa derselben Zeit verfasste der Wagnerepigone Eduard Stucken das Bühnenstück *Gawan*, das auf dem Stoff des *Green Knight* basiert. Bei Stucken sind die drei Verführungsszenen zu einer zusammengezogen, und außerdem erweitert er die Probe von Gawains Rittertugenden zu einer Probe, bei der es um die Gewinnung des Grals geht. Die Begründung der Handlung durch die Feindschaft Morgans reicht Stucken nicht; er deutet den Grünen Ritter um zum Todesengel aus der Hölle. Der Autor hält sich im Ganzen sehr eng, um nicht zu sagen sklavisch, an seine mittelenglische Quelle und übernimmt daraus ganze Wortpassagen. Seinen Versen fehlt die frische Originalität, der schöpferische Schwung. Sie sind im übrigen voller Plattheiten, seltsamen Gesuchtheiten und hohlem Pathos – weshalb sein Bühnenstück heute mit Recht vergessen ist.

Eine Version für jugendliche Leser mit dem Titel *The Green Knight* von Vera Chapman kam 1975 auf den Markt. Bei dieser Erzählung von immerhin fast 200 Seiten geht es nicht um Selbstfindung und Selbsterkenntnis des Helden. Die Grundzüge der Erzählung sind zwar im wesentlichen erhalten: das Enthauptungsspiel, der Aufenthalt des Helden auf der Burg Hautdesert, die drei Verführungsversuche der jungen Frau samt den drei Jagdszenen und dem Treffen an der Grünen Kapelle. Im Mittelpunkt der Geschichte steht jedoch Morgan mit ihren Zauberkunststücken, die allerdings auch im Original die Drahtzieherin der Geschehnisse ist, wie Bercilak am Ende gesteht. Sie wird in Chapmans Geschichte zur bösen Teufelin, die auf den Untergang Arthurs sinnt. Der Held ist nicht Gawain, sondern sein Neffe, der denselben Namen trägt, und die junge Frau, die von Morgan zu einer Zwangsheirat mit Bercilak gezwungen wird, ist die Klosterschülerin Vivian, die Enkelin Merlins. Beide, Gawain und Vivian, werden von Morgan am Stonehenge ermordet und durch eine übermenschliche Anstrengung Merlins, der darüber sein Leben lässt, wieder erweckt. Eindrucksvoll in der Erzählung sind die Landschaftsbeschreibungen, die bereits im Original zu den schönsten Stellen des Gedichts gehören. Nicht überzeugend ist der erzählerische Kunstgriff der Autorin, die Ereignisse abwechselnd von Gawain und Vivian, jeweils bis zu ihrem Tod, erzählen zu lassen. Das Finale, die Wiedererweckung Vivians und Gawains, muss daher von einem dritten Erzähler, einem Schüler Merlins, wiedergegeben werden.

Bemerkenswert ist die Bearbeitung des mittelalterlichen Gedichts in der Oper *Gawain* von Harrison Birtwistle nach einem Libretto von David Harsent, die 1991 im Royal Opera House, Covent Garden, aufgeführt wurde. Die Oper dramatisiert die mittelalterliche Erzählung von Gawains Versuchung. Harsents Libretto benutzt den Originaltext nur spärlich, Struktur und Handlung entsprechen jedoch dem mittelalterlichen Gedicht. In der Oper steht allerdings Morgan ganz im Mittelpunkt. Sie ist Dreh- und Angelpunkt und setzt das Geschehen in Gang.

Die Prosaversion von Y. R. Ponsor, *Gawain and the Green Knight*, die 1979 in einer sehr schönen bibliophilen Ausgabe bei Macmillan in New York erschienen ist, ist ganz und gar durchdrungen von der moralischen Botschaft des mittelalterlichen Gedichts. Ponsor nennt ihre Übersetzung eine "prose adaptation" (IX), die versucht, den alliterierenden Rhythmus der Sprache beizubehalten. Im Vorwort schreibt sie: "I have attempted to keep the flavor of the poem by the rhythm of language, most apparent when read aloud, and by the occasional specific, if strange, word" (IX). Und die Begründung für ihre Übersetzung: "Man as a symbol is no more human than man as a machine, and his problem is a modern problem: how to live in this world as a human being. Although he 'falls', it is a fortunate fall indeed, for it is into something greater. He is human: that is the necessary lesson of his quest. As a human being, Gawain knows his own nature, and the court heals his scars with love and sharing" (IX).

Nun zu dem Roman von Iris Murdoch, *The Green Knight* (1993). In ihm werden Motive aus dem mittelalterlichen Gedicht mit modernem Geschehen verwoben. Der Roman spielt im London des zwanzigsten Jahrhunderts. Der Geschichtsprofessor Lucas Graffe verteidigt sich mit seinem Regenschirm gegen einen nächtlichen Räuber und tötet ihn. Ein Gerichtsverfahren spricht ihn frei. Graffe verschwindet daraufhin für längere Zeit aus der Stadt. Seine Freunde, Louise Anderson und ihre drei Töcher Aleph, Sefton und Moy, beobachten während seiner Abwesenheit einen hochgewachsenen Mann mit seinem grünen Regenschirm, der sich für ihr Haus zu interessieren scheint, und dabei stellt sich heraus, dass dieser Mann genau derjenige ist, den Lucas Graffe angeblich getötet hat. Dieser Mann stellt sich Louise als Peter Mir vor. Mir, der als Beruf Psychoanalytiker angibt, wird in dem Roman mit der Farbe Grün in Verbindung gebracht: seine Kleidung, Tasche und Schirm sind grün. Er erklärt, er sei Vegetarier, ökologisch orientiert und Mitglied der Partei der Grünen. Aleph, die älteste und hübscheste der drei Schwestern, bemerkt: "That's why you dress is green [...] you've got a green tie and a green umbrella and your suit is a sort of green, too" (194). Und wenig später, als die Damen im Spiel versuchen, ihm einen literarischen Charakter zuzuordnen, sagt Aleph: "I think he's the Green Knight" (195).

Als Lucas Graffe wieder auftaucht, gibt Mir seine Version der nächtlichen Begegnung mit ihm. Bei dem fatalen Zusammentreffen mit Graffe war auch dessen Bruder Clement anwesend. Mir sagt, Graffe habe in der Dunkelheit versucht, seinen Bruder Clement, der als Kind stets von seiner Mutter bevorzugt worden war, mit einem Baseballschläger zu töten. Er, Mir, habe sich zwischen die Brüder gestellt und den Schlag auf den Kopf abbekommen. Als Folge des Schlages habe er daraufhin seinen Beruf als Psychoanalytiker nicht mehr ausüben können. Er verlangt jetzt von Graffe Gerechtigkeit und Vergeltung. Genaugenommen verlangt er von Lucas – Geld hat er selbst genug – , er solle sich einem Gegenschlag auf den Kopf mit derselben Wucht unterziehen. Da Lucas nur wenig Entgegenkommen zeigt, gibt sich Mir, der als russischer Jude ohne Familie und Freunde in London lebt, zunächst damit zufrieden, in das soziale

Umfeld Graffes, die Familie der Andersons und deren Freunde aufgenommen zu werden.

Mir schwankt in seinen Verhandlungen mit Graffe, bei denen der liebenswerte Bruder Clement den Vermittler spielt, zwischen Rache und Bestrafung einerseits und der Bereitschaft zur Versöhnung. Schließlich einigen sich die Beteiligten auf eine Art Wiederholung des Schlages an demselben Ort. Mir hält den Akt für eine Art psychoanalytischer Therapie und glaubt hinterher in der Tat, dadurch wieder zu Gott und zu sich selbst gefunden zu haben. Auf dem Höhepunkt der Begegnung im Park zieht Mir aus seinem grünen Schirm ein Messer, mit dem er Graffe ein kleine Wunde am Hals beibringt. Clement wird bei der Szene ohnmächtig, so dass an dieser Stelle das Geschehen ausgeblendet wird. Wenig später gibt Mir für seine Freunde ein Fest, auf dem der Arzt Dr. Fonsett erscheint, um Mir wieder in die Klinik zurückzuholen, in der er wegen seines Schlages auf den Kopf in Behandlung war. Kurze Zeit darauf erfahren seine Freunde, dass er gestorben ist.

Clement, der die Ereignisse reflektiert, erinnert sich, wie sie alle nach Peters Weggang überlegten, wem er ähnlich war: "Aleph had said 'the Green Knight'. At the time Clement had vaguely assumed that she was referring to the green umbrella with which he had first appeared to them. But was there perhaps a deeper meaning, was there not some Middle English poem about a Green Knight?" (431). Irgendwie erinnerte er sich, während seines Studiums in Cambridge eine Übersetzung der Geschichte gelesen zu haben:

> Pieces of the story are there, but aren't they somehow jumbled up and all the wrong way round: Lucas cut off Peter's head, and Peter might have cut off his, but because he was noble and forgiving he only drew a little of Lucas's blood. It isn't really like the poem, yet it is, too, and it is something much more terrible. Lucas was brave and Peter was merciful. Or would Peter have killed Lucas if he hadn't been there? So am *I* also in the story. And Aleph, wasn't she the temptress, wasn't she what they both wanted? But that isn't quite right, the

> Lady was the wife of the Green Knight, and the Green Knight was good, though he was also a magician. Now, Lucas is a magician too, and Lucas is not good, but Aleph is Lucas's wife. Yes it's all mixed up [...] What has Aleph meant when she called him the Green Knight? She may have intuitively seen farther, seen him as an instrument of justice, a kind of errant ambiguous moral force, like some unofficial wandering angel [...] *There* the first blow was struck as a provocation to a mysterious adventure, *here* the first blow was struck by an evil magician, whose victim reappeared as another, ultimately good, magician [...] And what about the temptress who in the story was the good magician's wife? [...] Now the good magician was gone, receding into his mystery, and the beautiful maiden has been awarded to the evil one. (431–2)

Aleph, die in dem Roman die beiden Männer allenfalls durch ihre Schönheit versucht, verschwindet lautlos, indem sie Lucas Graffe heiratet, nach Amerika. Clement, dessen persönliches Scheitern am Ende aufgehoben wird durch seine Heirat mit Louise, kehrt in Gedanken zurück zu der Bedeutung, die das Auftauchen dieses modernen Grünen Ritters für das Leben aller Beteiligten hatte. Seine Interpretation der Rolle Mirs scheint übereinzustimmen mit der modernen Bewertung der Rolle des Grünen Ritters in dem mittelalterlichen Gedicht: er sieht ihn als eine jenseits unserer Erfahrung liegende fremde und von daher auch erschreckende Erscheinung, die jedoch vornehm und edel ist und als Instrument der Gerechtigkeit wirkt, durch die wir zur Selbsterkenntnis gelangen.

Zusammenfassend lässt sich sagen, dass Iris Murdoch an der Geschichte des Grünen Ritters das fasziniert hat, was auch bis heute die mittelalterliche Erzählung so frisch und aktuell erhalten hat: einmal die facettenhaften Bezüge der Personen unter- und zueinander, und zum anderen die Bewertung der Rolle des Grünen Ritters selbst, wie sie die Dichterin Clement in den Mund legt: "After all, the Green Knight came out from some other form of being, weird and un-Christian, not like Arthur's knight. But he was noble and he knew what justice was – and perhaps justice is greater than the Grail" (456). Diese moderne Dimension der Erzählung macht sowohl den Roman von Iris Murdoch zur spannenden Lektüre für den modernen Leser, wie sie auch das mittelalterliche Epos neu in den Blickpunkt seines Interesses und seiner Neugier zu rücken vermag.

Legouis und Cazamian, die *Sir Gawain and the Green Knight* immerhin zweieinhalb Seiten in ihrer Literaturgeschichte widmen, heben auf die Naturbeschreibungen in dem Gedicht ab: "Love of the open air and a feeling for nature are perhaps the most distinctive characteristics of this poem" (109). Eine Bewertung der moralischen Dimension der Erzählung ist erst in jüngster Zeit erfolgt. Sie steht hinter Y. R. Ponsors Prosa-Übersetzung und wird von Iris Murdoch in ihrem Roman ausgiebig interpretiert, der, wie die Rezensentin laut Klappentext im *Independent* schreibt, "rich and full and strange as one of Shakespeare's late comedies" ist.

Literaturverzeichnis

Aertsen, Henk. "Game and Earnest in *Sir Gawain and the Green Knight*". *Companion to Middle English Romance*. Ed. H. Aertsen and A. Mac Donald. Amsterdam: VU University Press, 1990. 83–100.
Brewer, Derek. "The Colour Green". *A Companion to the Gawain Poet*. Ed. D. Brewer and J. Gibson. Cambridge: D. S. Brewer, 1999. 181–190.
Brewer, Elizabeth. "The Sources of *Sir Gawain and the Green Knight*". *A Companion to the Gawain Poet*. Ed. D. Brewer and J. Gibson. Cambridge: D. S. Brewer, 1999. 243–255.
Chapman, Vera. *The Green Knight*. London: Rex Collins, 1975.
Christmas, Peter. "A Reading of *Sir Gawain and the Green Knight*". *Neophilologus* 58 (1974): 238–247.
Diekstra, Frans. "Narrative Mode and Interpretation of *Sir Gawain and the Green Knight*". *Companion to Middle English Romance*. Ed. H. Aertsen and A Mac Donald. Amsterdam: VU University Press, 1990. 57–82.
Legouis, Emile, and Louis Cazamian. *History of English Literature*. London: J. M. Dent, 1960.

Löhmann, Otto. *Die Sage von Gawain und dem Grünen Ritter*. Königsberg und Berlin: Ost-Europa-Verlag, 1938.
Kittredge, George L. *A Study of Gawain and the Green Knight*. Cambridge, Mass.: Harvard University Press, 1916.
McClure, Peter. "Gawain's Mesure and the Significance of the three Hunts". *Neophilologus*, 57 (1973): 375–387.
Murdoch, Iris. *The Green Knight*. Harmondsworth: Penguin, 1994.
Putter, Ad. *Sir Gawain and the Green Knight and French Romance*. Oxford: Clarendon, 1995.
Ponsor, Y. R. *Gawain and the Green Knight*. New York: Macmillan, 1979.
Roonby, Anne. "The Hunts in *Gawain and the Green Knight*". *A Companion to the Gawain Poet*. Ed. D. Brewer and J. Gibson. Cambridge: D. S. Brewer, 1999. 157–163.
Spearing, A. C. *The Gawain Poet: A Critical Study*. Cambridge: Cambridge University Press, 1970.
Sir Gawain and the Green Knight. Ed. and transl. Israel Gollancz. London: Oxford University Press, 1966.
Sir Gawain and the Green Knight. Transl. Brian Stone. Harmondsworth: Penguin, 1959.
Sir Gawain and the Green Knight. Ed. and transl. J. R. R. Tolkien. Oxford: Claredon, 1967.
Sir Gawain and the Green Knight: A Dual Language Version. Ed. and transl. William Vantuano. New York: Garland, 1991.
Stucken, Eduard. *Gawan*. Berlin: Deutsche Nationalbibliothek, 1911.
Vantuano, William. "Preface". *Gawain and the Green Knight: A Dual Language Version*. Ed. and transl. William Vantuano. New York: Garland, 1991. xiii–xxxviii.
Windeatt, Barry. "Sir Gawain at the Fin de Siècle: Novel and Opera". *A Companion to the Gawain Poet*. Ed. D. Brewer and J. Gibson. Cambridge: D. S. Brewer, 1999. 374–383.
Yeats, W. B. *The Green Helmet. Collected Plays*. London: Macmillan, 1953. 223–243.

Rudolf Drux

ZWISCHEN WERKSTATT UND LABOR

Zur poetologischen Paradigmatik des Menschenbildners Prometheus in der Goethezeit

Seit der Aufklärung wird der Demiurg Prometheus gerne als Vorbild für den Künstler in Anspruch genommen: Der Sohn des Japetos aus dem vorolympischen Geschlecht der Titanen formte Menschen aus Lehm, belebte sie und verhalf ihnen durch die Gabe des Feuers, unabdingbare Voraussetzung für ihre kulturelle Entfaltung, zu einem würdigen Leben; die gleiche Lebendigkeit sollte auch den Menschen zukommen, die auf dem Papier, der Bühne oder der Leinwand entstehen. Mit Beginn des 19. Jahrhunderts ist der poetologische Bezug auf die Prometheus-Gestalt jedoch nicht mehr auf den Künstler beschränkt; mit den Handwerkern und später den Arbeitern in den Fabriken, aber auch den Wissenschaftlern in den Laboratorien treten andere Berufe und gesellschaftliche Gruppen in Erscheinung, die sozialrelevante produktive Tätigkeiten verrichten und denen deshalb der Titan Prometheus als mythologisches Paradigma zugeordnet wird.

Since the Age of Enlightenment the demiurge Prometheus has often been regarded as the prototype of the artist: The son of Japetos, a member of the pre-olympic dynasty of the Titans, shaped men out of clay, animated them, and helped them to gain the dignity of human life through his gift of fire, the indispensable prerequisite of any cultural development; men created by the artist, whether on paper, stage or screen, were to be entitled to the same vitality. Since the early 19th century, however, the poetic reference to the figure of Prometheus has no longer been restricted to the artist; craftsmen, and later workers in factories, as well as scientists in laboratories have moved into the focus of writers who associate them with Prometheus as a mythological paradigm because of the socially significant productivity of these groups.

◇

In einem seiner *Beiträge zur Geschichte der neuesten Literatur* nimmt 1836 der Vormärz-Autor, Hegel-Schüler, Kulturredakteur und Büchner-Förderer Karl Gutzkow kritisch Stellung zur künstlerischen Produktion der romantischen Schriftsteller des Uhland-Kreises und verspottet die mit biedermeierlicher Behaglichkeit auf ihre enge Welt beschränkten Vertreter der Schwäbischen Schule als die "Gutherzigen, welche in ihrem Gott vergnügt sind, wenn sie einen Maikäfer, ein Bienchen, die Fliege an der Wand und sich besungen haben"; angesichts ihrer Werke drängt sich ihm gleich zweimal die Frage auf: "Wo ist Prometheus?" Den Sohn des Titanen Japetos, der hier als Prototyp des wahrhaft schöpferischen Künstlers von universeller Bedeutsamkeit erscheint, vermisst Gutzkow schmerzlich; mit Goethes Tod 1832 sei er aus deutschen Landen endgültig verschwunden.

Der poetologischen Berufung auf die mythologische Figur des Demiurgen Prometheus, d. h. ihrer Inanspruchnahme als Vorbildgestalt für den schaffenden Menschen in seinen verschiedenen sozialen Erscheinungsformen möchte ich im Folgenden an einigen literarischen Beispielen nachgehen, die aus der Goethezeit bzw. – epochengeschichtlich betrachtet – dem Zeitraum zwischen Sturm und Drang und Vormärz stammen.

Im Atelier des Künstlers

In der Aufklärung setzt der Rekurs auf den Mythos verstärkt ein: Der englische Philosoph und Essayist Anthony A. C. Earl of Shaftesbury prägt in seiner literaturtheoretischen Abhandlung "Soliloquy or Advice to an Author" (1710) die epochemachende Formel, der echte Poet sei "indeed a second maker: a just Prometheus, under Jove". Obwohl im Deutschen das Wort Dichter den 'eigentlichen Sinn' von *poet* (aus dem Griech. von *poein*, 'machen', 'schaffen') nicht wiedergibt, wird die Wendung, die an den *alter deus* der Renaissance anknüpft, auch in deutschen Landen gängige Prägung für den Künstler. Dabei kommt es zur Gleichsetzung von Prometheus als dem 'obersten Künstler' mit der wirkenden Natur, die alle Geschöpfe perfekt hervorgebracht hat. Diese Auffassung vertritt u. a. Johann Gottfried Herder, wenn er sich im *Ersten Kritischen Wäldchen* von 1769 scharf gegen die "Herren Allegoristen" wendet, die nur Maschinen mit Namen versähen und Statuen aus Begriffen herstellten; sie seien keine wahren Dichter, er sehe sie "nicht als zweite Prometheus, nicht als Schöpfer unsterblicher Götter und sterblicher Menschen" an (160). Dass die Lebendigkeit eines Werkes noch 1809 für August Wilhelm Schlegel als höchstes Kriterium in Sachen Kunst gilt, machen seine euphorischen Ausführungen über Skakespeares dramatisches Personal in seinen Wiener *Vorlesungen über dramatische Kunst und Literatur* deutlich;

> dieser Prometheus bildet nicht blos Menschen, er öffnet die Pforten der magischen Geisterwelt, läßt Gespenster heraufsteigen, Hexen ihren wüsten Unfug treiben, bevölkert die Luft mit scherzenden Elfen oder Sylphen, und diese nur in der Einbildung lebenden Wesen haben eine solche Wahrheit, daß, wären sie auch misgebohrne Ungeheuer wie Caliban, er uns dennoch die bestimmende Ueberzeugung abnöthigt: gäbe es dergleichen, so würden sie sich so benehmen. Mit einem Worte, so wie er die fruchtbarste kühnste Fantasie in das Reich der Natur hineinträgt, so trägt er auf der anderen Seite die Natur in die jenseits des Wirklichen liegenden Regionen der Fantasie hinüber. Wir erstaunen über die vertrauliche Nähe des Außerordentlichen, Wunderbaren, ja Unerhörten. (134f.)

Auf eben dieser Fähigkeit, Lebendiges von natürlich wirkender Art hervorzubringen, beruht auch im Wesentlichen die selbstbewusste Haltung des Prometheus in Goethes gleichnamiger Hymne (1774). Diese ist zum großen Teil aus Elementen des Dramenfragments (1773) zusammengesetzt, in dessen Eingangsszene Prometheus in seiner Werkstatt unter den von ihm gebildeten, noch unbelebten Menschenstatuen zu sehen ist. Und wie im Drama sucht er auch im lyrischen Monolog die Konfrontation mit dem Herrscher im Olymp. Der Gegensatz Zeus – Prometheus, der in der Antithese von Tatenlosigkeit der Götter und Schaffenskraft des Titanen gipfelt, wird gleich in der Gewitterszene der ersten Strophe umfassend markiert:

> Bedecke deinen Himmel, Zeus
> Mit Wolkendunst!
> Und übe, dem Knaben gleich,
> Der Disteln köpft,
> An Eichen dich und Bergeshöhn!
> Mußt mir meine Erde
> Doch lassen stehn,
> Und meine Hütte,
> Die du nicht gebaut,
> Und meinen Herd,
> Um dessen Glut
> Du mich beneidest.
> ("Prometheus" 44f.)

Die Gebiete sind deutlich getrennt. Die Eingrenzung des prometheischen Wirkungsfeldes (Erde – Hütte – Herd) geht dabei einher mit einer abgestuften Annäherung an den Kern titanischen Tuns: Vom Lebensraum der Erde wird der Blick über die Hütte hin zum Herd gelenkt, der das Feuer bewahrt. Wie das Nomen "Glut" (metonymisch) auf das zum Wohle der Menschen domestizierte Element verweist, so drückt das Verbum "glühen" (metaphorisch) die leidenschaftliche Bewegtheit, die psychische Kraft aus, die dem Herzen eigen ist, das, mit den Eigenschaften "heilig, jung und gut" belegt, als biologisches und religiöses Zentrum erscheint; "innre Wärme, Seelenwärme, Mittelpunkt" lauten seine Attribute in "Wandrers Sturmlied" (41). Mit der Formung von Menschen, die empfinden und den "Schlafenden dadroben [...] nicht achten", wird der grundlegende Dualismus aufgehoben in der freien Tätigkeit und absoluten Vorbildhaftigkeit des von angemaßter Herrschaft unberührten Ichs, das den markanten Schlusspunkt des Gedichtes bildet.

Die literarischen Fassungen des Prometheus-Mythos sind von der Forschung gründlich recherchiert und ausgiebig erörtert worden. Zwei Bände füllt z. B. der Komparatist Raymond Trousson mit Materialien aus verschiedenen Gattungen, Epochen und Nationalliteraturen, um *La thème de Prométhée dans la littérature européenne* als Muster eines heroischen Stoffes darzustellen. Und Hans Blumenberg geht bei seiner intensiven *Arbeit am Mythos* dessen kulturgeschichtlicher Biographie nach, wobei er sich in mehreren aufschlussreichen Kapiteln besonders mit Texten der Goethezeit von Wieland bis Heine auseinandersetzt. Aber selbst in derart kenntnis- und umfangreichen Untersuchungen findet E. T. A. Hoffmanns Version des Mythos – oder der "Fabel", wie der Autor mit dem damals gebräuchlichen Synonym sagt, – keine Erwähnung. Hoffmanns Interesse an der Geschichte des Japetiden, die seit den 1770er Jahren in allen Künsten aufgegriffen wurde, ist maßgeblich durch Beethovens Ballettmusik *Die Geschöpfe des Prometheus* (1800/01) angeregt, auch wenn in seiner Erzählung "Die Jesuiterkirche in G." aus den *Nachtstücken* (1816/17) nicht die Musik, sondern die Malerei als das prometheische Betätigungsfeld erscheint.

Ein "reisender Enthusiast", der sich als "Kenner und Ausüber der edlen Malerkunst" versteht, begegnet bei seinem Aufenthalt in G. dem Maler Berthold, dem er bei nächtlichen Marmorierungsarbeiten in der dortigen Kirche der Jesuiten behilflich ist. Seinen Einwand, dass dieser eigentlich "zu etwas Besserem taugt" als der Architekturmalerei, bei der "Geist und Fantasie in die engen Schranken geometrischer Linien gebannt" würden, während die Wiedergabe von Historien und Landschaften "unbedingt höher" zu veranschlagen sei, wehrt Berthold entschieden ab; "frevelhaft" sei es, "die verschiedenen Zweige der Kunst" in eine gleichsam feudalistische "Rangordnung" zu zwingen, "frevelhafter" noch, nur denen Achtung zu zollen, die sich von den Ketten des Irdischen frei fühlen und

> "[...] selbst sich Gott wähnen und schaffen und herrschen wollen über Licht und Leben. – Kennst du die Fabel von dem Prometheus, der Schöpfer sein wollte, und das Feuer vom Himmel stahl, um seine toten Figuren zu beleben? – Es gelang ihm, lebendig schritten

> die Gestalten daher, und aus ihren Augen strahlte jenes himmlische Feuer, das in ihrem Innern brannte; aber rettungslos wurde der Frevler, der sich angemaßt Göttliches zu fahen, verdammt zu ewiger fürchterlicher Qual. Die Brust, die das Göttliche geahnt, in der die Sehnsucht nach dem Überirdischen aufgegangen, zerfleischte der Geier, den die Rache geboren und der sich nun nährte von dem eignen Innern des Vermessenen. Der das Himmlische gewollt, fühlte ewig den irdischen Schmerz." (112f.)

Der Enthusiast ist von der Applikation des Mythos überrascht, glaubt er doch nicht, dass sich die Sage und – vor allem – das ihr inhärente harte moralische Urteil auf den bildenden Künstler, überhaupt auf eine mimetische Tätigkeit beziehen lasse. Er übersieht dabei, dass sich Berthold im Einklang mit der poetologischen Tradition befindet, und zwar in doppelter Hinsicht: Neben der erwähnten Gleichsetzung des künstlerischen Produktionsprozesses mit dem Schöpfertum des Demiurgen war auch die Kritik am Feuerdiebstahl des Prometheus (bzw. seine symbolische Bedeutung) prominent zu belegen, und zwar wiederum mit Goethe. Schon früh hatte dieser sich vom aufbegehrenden Titanen seiner Frankfurter Zeit, der sich einzig auf sein "produktives Talent" und damit auf die Natur verlässt, abgewendet; der Geburtstag von Herzog Carl August 1783 gibt ihm Gelegenheit, im Rückblick auf eine längst vergangene Epoche, das titanische Schöpfertum abzuweisen. "Die reine Himmelsglut", mit der Prometheus seine Lehmfiguren zum Leben erweckte, lässt sich, so lautet die Botschaft des Kasualpoems "Ilmenau", in der Geschichte nicht bewahren; diese schmerzliche Einsicht löst eine scharfe Selbstanklage aus, die auf die Unverantwortlichkeit absoluten Hervorbringens abhebt:

> Ich brachte reines Feuer vom Altar –
> Was ich entzündet, ist nicht reine Flamme,
> Der Sturm vermehrt die Glut und die Gefahr.
> Ich schwanke nicht, indem ich mich verdamme. (110)

Die harte Kritik am genialischen Kunstwerk, dessen lautere Absicht sich im Laufe seiner Rezeption verliert – Blumenberg spricht von der "Verselbständigung der Wirkung gegenüber dem Werk" (545) –, übt Berthold zwar nicht – immerhin wurden seiner Version nach die prometheischen Gestalten lebendig ("aus ihren Augen strahlte jenes himmlische Feuer, das in ihrem Innern brannte"); aber ihr Schöpfer muss seine frevelhafte Tat teuer bezahlen. Die "Sehnsucht nach dem Überirdischen" zehrt ihn auf – so deutet Berthold/Hoffmann das Mythem vom Leber fressenden Adler um, "den die Rache geboren und der sich nun nährte von dem eignen Innern des Vermessenen". André Gide wird später, am Ende des titanischen Jahrhunderts, 1899, in seiner Prosa-Farce (sotie) Le Prométhée mal enchaîné den olympischen Vogel gleichfalls endogen verstehen, d. h. als wahrlich beißendes Gewissen (und gemäß der Doppelbedeutung des franz. conscience zugleich als Bewusstsein, das, sich mästend mit den Innereien – "mit meinem Blut, meiner Seele", sagt Prometheus an einer Stelle seiner Adler-Rede (145) – "sehr schön werden kann"). Zuletzt wird es gebraten und verspeist; das ist gewiss eine groteske Befreiung vom Über-Ich, aber wenigstens eine nahrhafte.

Auf derart sensualistische Weise lässt sich der "ewige Schmerz" eines Künstlers vom Schlage Bertholds jedoch nicht überwinden. Das macht ja gerade sein tragisches Leid aus: Die sinnliche Vergegenständlichung des "himmlischen Funkens" verlangt Erdennähe; kaum hat er sich aber darauf eingelassen, verlischt das göttliche Feuer. Konkret: Berthold versucht lange Zeit vergeblich, die Bilder, die er "in seinem Innern geschaut", künstlerisch zu verwirklichen; ihm fehlt der Ansatz zur Materialisierung seiner Traumgestalten. Erst als er eines Tages ganz flüchtig der "Gestalt eines hochherrlichen Weibes" begegnet (129), erwacht seine Produktivität: "Wie von göttlicher Kraft beseelt, zauberte er mit der vollen Glut des Lebens das überirdische Weib, wie es ihm erschienen, hervor". Seitdem erstrahlt in seinen Werken, vornehmlich Altarbildern, "die wunderherrliche Gestalt seines Ideals" (130).

Verhängnisvollerweise tritt dieses als real existierende Frau in sein Leben, und da er, statt sie als Künstler zu verklären, als Mann begehrt, ja sie sogar heiratet, versiegt seine Kunst: Statt totem Material Leben einzuhauchen, verwandelt Berthold medusengleich das lebendige Wesen in ein totes Gebilde. "Die herrliche Himmelsgestalt, die den Götterfunken in seiner Brust entzündet" (132), lässt sich, da sie ihm als Gattin leiblich angehört und, sichtbarstes Zeichen ihrer Körperlichkeit, sogar einen Sohn gebiert, nicht mehr auf die Leinwand bannen. Es ist eben ein "teuflischer Trug", verurteilt er sich selbst, wenn der Künstler das seinem irdischen Dasein einpassen zu können vermeint, "was er über den Sternen erschauen wollte"; "der heilige Zweck aller Kunst" sei es vielmehr, eine Ahnung von einem höheren Sein zu vermitteln. Dass er das Ideal ins Irdische herabzog, musste Prometheus mit "ewiger fürchterlicher Qual" büßen. Und auch deshalb fühlt sich der gepeinigte Maler Berthold dem titanischen "Ahnherrn" der Künstler, wie ihn Heine bezeichnet (204), verwandt. An diese ergeht Hoffmanns Sublimationsgebot, der Frau zu entsagen, die als Muse "die innere Musik" anzustimmen wusste. Wird es missachtet, dann ist, konstatiert der Komponist Theodor in Hoffmanns Erzählung "Die Fermate", aller poetischer "Zauber vernichtet und die innere Melodie, sonst Herrliches verkündend, wird zur Klage über eine zerbrochene Suppenschüssel oder einen Tintenfleck in neuer Wäsche" (74).

Von der Werkstatt zur Werkhalle

Als sich 1807 zwei junge Männer, Leo von Seckendorf und Josef Ludwig Stoll, mit der Bitte an Goethe wandten, einen Beitrag für ihren neugegründeten Musenalmanach *Pandora* (eigentlich: *Prometheus*) zu verfassen, folgte er diesem Ansinnen nicht zuletzt deshalb, weil "der mythologische Punkt, wo Prometheus auftritt" (wie in der Geschichte von der künstlichen Frau Pandora), ihm "immer gegenwärtig und zur belebten Fixidee geworden" sei (*Werke* V, 661). Allerdings taucht dann im Festspiel *Pandoras Wiederkunft* (1807/08) ein veränderter Prometheus auf. Er ist ein 'Macher', der Schmiede, Hirten und Krieger befehligt, also auf handwerklichem, agrarischem und militärischem Sektor das Sagen hat. Ein szenisches Detail mag die Veränderung vom trotzigen Titanen der Sturm-und-Drang-Zeit zum klassischen Menschenlenker verdeutlichen:

Statt der Hütte, dem Symbol des einfachen naturnahen Lebens, ist als prometheische Wirkungsstätte die Höhle zu sehen, wo der Schmiede Schar "hartes Erz nach eurem Sinne zwingend formt" (*Pandora* 339). Wie später bei Wagner die proletarischen Nibelungen in Nibelhains Höhlen das Rheingold bearbeiten und so zum Tauschwert umgestalten werden, so bereiten hier die "Nützenden" sich die Utensilien der Macht: Ökonomische Stärke wird durch die Ausnutzung der Ressourcen gewonnen, politische aber ist allein mit Waffengewalt zu erhalten: "Drum, Schmiede! Freunde! Nur zu Waffen legt mir's an, / Das andre lassend, was der sinnig Ackernde, / Was sonst der Fischer von euch fordern möchte heut. / Nur Waffen schafft! Geschaffen habt ihr alles dann, / Auch derbster Söhne übermäß'gen Vollgenuß" (*Pandora* 341). Der Feuerraub hat jetzt seine sittliche Qualität endgültig verloren; der Kulturschaffende weicht dem Imperialisten, die Natur wird beherrscht, ausgebeutet, die Erde wird ausgeplündert. "Furchen und Striemen ziehn, / Ihr auf den Rücken hin / Knechte mit Schweißbemühn" (338). Prometheus ist jetzt solch "schwitzender Knechte" Chef, vom Schützer der Menschen hat er sich zu ihrem Zwingherrn gewandelt. Nachdem sich Goethe spätestens mit "Ilmenau" vom Titanen der Geniezeit losgesagt hat, radikalisiert er ihn im Festspiel zum skrupellosen Stoffverwerter, zum machtbewussten, arbeitssüchtigen Technokraten. Ironisch klingt die Anrede der versinkenden Eos: "Fahre wohl! du Menschenvater!" Und dem in dieser Funktion längst schon Abgedankten schiebt sie, die Göttin der Abendröte, noch einen Merkspruch nach, der den Titanismus völlig relativiert und die Götter, die dem Stürmer und Dränger als Schlafende auf Olympeshöhn erschienen, letztlich unangreifbar macht: "Merke: / Was zu wünschen ist, ihr unten fühlt es; / Was zu geben sei, die wissen's droben. / Groß beginnnet ihr Titanen; aber leiten / Zu dem ewig Guten, ewig Schönen, / Ist der Götter Werk; die laßt gewähren" (*Pandora* 365).

In dem Maße aber, in dem der bürgerliche Dichter aus den Spuren des Japetiden tritt, wird dieser für andere soziale Gruppen oder Berufe vorbildhaft. Öfter noch als der geschichtsmächtige Staatsmann, Napoleon z. B., der nach Blumenbergs Vermutung Goethes Prometheus-Vorstellung seit 1807 völlig okkupiert (577), – eher als der Monokrat wird im Titanen der Arbeiter als Vertreter einer neuen Klasse gesehen. Wenn Johannes R. Becher 1940 im Moskauer Exil seinen Prometheus den Sturz der "Götterfeste" verkünden lässt: "Es naht die Zeit / Der Menschenmacht! Der Herrschaft der Titanen" (615), so kann er sich bereits auf eine fast hundertjährige Tradition stützen. Sie reicht über die expressionistische Erhöhung des Arbeiters in Karl Ottens emphatischen Versen: "Dich an Rad, Drehbank, Hammer, Beil, Pflug geschmiedeten / lichtlosen Prometheus rufe ich auf!" (227), und über sozialkritische Gedichte der Gründerzeit, zu denen Eduard Fuchs' "Prometheus unserer Zeit" zählt, der sich "dem Gotte Kapital" widersetzt, zurück bis in den Vormärz: Ferdinand Freiligrath hat 1845 ein Gedicht mit dem Titel "Von unten auf!" geschrieben, in dem die Schiffsreise Friedrich Wilhelms IV. von Preußen nach der restaurierten Burg Stolzenfels dargestellt wird. Den Dampfer, der herkömmlicherweise zum Staatsschiff allegorisiert wird: "Wie mahnt das Boot mich an den Staat!" (360), setzt das Feuer in Bewegung, das der "Proletarier-Maschinist" im Kesselraum entfacht und kontrolliert, der erste Industrie-Arbeiter, der in der deutschen Lyrik zu Wort kommt. Er ist sich seiner Macht bewusst, weshalb er in einem stummen Zwiegespräch mit dem Herrscher die Feststellung treffen kann: "Du bist viel weniger ein Zeus als ich, o König, ein Titan!" Er versteht sich als Repräsentant des Standes, den er selbst "das Proletariat" nennt: "Wir sind die Kraft! Wir hämmern jung das alte morsche Ding, den Staat [...]!" (361).

Freilich, die Verwendung der gemischten Allegorie in der Rede des Heizers verwundert ebenso wie seine Berufung auf den Mythos vom "Feuerbringer" und Rebellen Prometheus. (Seine wohl prominenteste Repräsentation in diesem Kontext wird ihm auf dem berühmten Flugblatt zuteil, das am 10. Mai 1849, am Tag nach dem Verbot der von Karl Marx redigierten *Neuen Rheinischen Zeitung*, erschienen ist und diesen als den an eine Druckerpresse *gefesselten Prometheus* darstellt, dem der preußische Adler die Leber aus dem Leibe reißt.) Die geballte Bildung des Maschinisten entspricht natürlich nicht gesellschaftlicher Realität, sondern idealisiert das Proletariat in seinem neuen Klassenbewusstsein, das sich aus dem gesamten Erbe des Abendlandes einschließlich seiner Hochkultur speist. Allerdings ist der titanische Heizer realistisch genug zu erkennen – und in diesem Punkt zumindest stimmt Freiligrath mit seinem Freund Marx, den er seit ihrer gemeinsamen Exilzeit in Brüssel kennt, überein –, dass die Zeit zum Aufruhr, die Entmachtung der Unterdrücker bzw. die Enteignung der Ausbeuter (oder, wie es in der Marx'schen Terminologie heißt: die 'Expropriation der Expropriateurs'), noch nicht gekommen ist. Deshalb ruft er, "der grollende Zyklop" (dem Zeus – so Hesiod in der *Theogonie* – den Macht sichernden und erhaltenden Blitz verdankt), den im Kessel zischenden Flammen zu: "Heut, zornig Element, noch nicht!" (361). Doch angesichts der schön renovierten gotischen Restaurationsfeste entwirft er bei Kapellen mit anarchistischer Freude noch eine kleine revolutionäre Utopie:

Der bunte Dämpfer unterdes legt vor Kapellen zischend an;
Sechsspännig fährt die Majestät den jungen Stolzenfels hinan.
Der Heizer auch blickt auf zur Burg; von seinen Flammen nur behorcht,
Lacht er: "Ei, wie man immer doch für künftige Ruinen sorgt!"

(361)

Das Pathos der proletarischen Rede erinnert an den leidenschaftlichen Ton der Stürmer und Dränger; während aber diese sich systemkonform um eine Wandlung der Mentalitäten bemühten, zielt der Vormärz-Dichter mit seinem Dampfkessel-Prometheus auf die soziale Revolution, auf den Umsturz des Staatsgebäudes, dessen Spitze jetzt noch der König einnimmt. Das Feuer des Prometheus ist dabei im wörtlichen Sinn das Feuer, das der Proletarier im Ofen entfacht und kontrolliert, zugleich symbolisiert es jedoch die Flamme der Revolution, die dann 1848 tatsächlich auflodern sollte. Im selben Jahr erscheint das von Marx und Engels gemeinsam verfasste *Manifest der kommunistischen Partei*, in dem der 'unvermeidliche Untergang' der bürgerlichen Klasse durch den Sieg des Proletariats prognostiziert wird, aus deren Schoß dieses hervorgegangen ist. So wird der Mythos wieder in Kraft gesetzt: Der Titan, der die Titanen besiegt, steht nunmehr in den Fabriken, den Produktionsstätten des industriellen Zeitalters.

Im Labor des Lebens

Neben Atelier und Fabrik verfügt die Prometheus-Gestalt in der Goethezeit noch über einen weiteren Arbeitsplatz, nämlich das Labor. Mit großer Wirkung hat ihn die junge englische Autorin Mary Wollstonecraft Shelley in ihrem Roman *Frankenstein; or, The Modern Prometheus* (1818) dorthin versetzt. Ihr war der Prometheus-Mythos bestens vertraut, nicht zuletzt durch intensive Gespräche mit ihrem Mann Percy B. Shelley, der für sein lyrisches Drama *Prometheus Unbound* (1820) ebenfalls auf diesen Stoff zurückgriff, und dem gemeinsamen Freund Lord Byron in der am Genfer See gelegenen Villa Diodati, dem Geburtsort ihres *Frankenstein*. Unverkennbar weicht der Demiurg in der Version Mary Shelleys aber von seiner mythologischen Bezugsfigur in wesentlichen Zügen ab. Der auffälligste Unterschied besteht im Verhältnis des Schöpfers zu seinem Geschöpf: Während der antike Prometheus sich für seine Menschen verantwortlich fühlt und im Wissen, dass ihrer physischen Bildung die geistige Ausbildung folgen muss, für ihr Wohlergehen unermessliches Leid billigend in Kauf nimmt, verfolgt der moderne sein Ziel, Leben hervorzubringen, ohne Rücksicht auf die Befindlichkeit seiner Kreatur. Dass diese überhaupt menschlich empfinden könne, kommt Frankenstein gar nicht in den Sinn. Demgegenüber hat Goethes Prometheus noch das von ihm geformte Menschengeschlecht mit einer reichhaltigen Gefühlsskala ausgestaltet, und gerade im Vermögen, "zu leiden, zu weinen, / genießen und zu freuen sich", ist es ihm gleich, bezeugt es die Fähigkeit des 'Poietes', naturgleich zu schaffen.

Frankenstein dagegen ist ein fanatischer Wissenschaftler, der mit "unermüdlichem und atemlosem Eifer" und "von ständig zunehmender Besessenheit gehetzt" (70), eben jene natürlichen Gegebenheiten ignoriert. Gewiss, ihn treibt ein eigentlich hehrer Gedanke an; immerhin ist er, da ihm klar wird, "leblose Materie beleben" zu können, bestrebt, den Tod zu besiegen, d. h. einen toten Körper der Verwesung zu entreißen und mit neuem Leben zu erfüllen. Wird aber schon seine Absicht, die, wie er meint, "imaginären Grenzen" zwischen Leben und Tod zu überschreiten, durch die Aussicht, dabei grenzenlosen Ruhm zu erlangen und tiefe Dankbarkeit von denen zu empfangen, die ihm "ihr Leben verdanken", in ihrer idealistischen Ausrichtung erheblich relativiert, so entlarvt seine panische Reaktion beim "grauenhaften Anblick" seines missratenen Geschöpfes sein "lebenspendendes Unternehmen" als verantwortungslose Veranstaltung in narzisstischer Wissenserprobung: Nachdem er "die Ursachen aller Zeugung und allen Lebens entdeckt" und die Gültigkeit seiner grundlegenden Erkenntnisse – gleichsam in angewandter Forschung – mit der Belebung eines aus Leichenteilen zusammengeflickten Körpers bewiesen hat, überlässt er das "erbärmliche Monster" sich selbst. Er kommt also der sich angeblich selbst auferlegten "Verpflichtung", nach Kräften "für sein Glück und Wohlergehen zu sorgen" (278), nicht nach, weicht vielmehr den sittlichen und sozialen Konsequenzen aus, die die 'Geburt' eines "vernunftbegabten Wesens", und sei sie noch so künstlich, nun einmal nach sich zieht. So bleibt er, da er sich sowohl in der Euphorie des Entdeckens als auch im Schrecken des Betrachtens nur auf die leibliche Seite seiner Kreatur konzentriert und ihre seelische ignoriert, untrennbar mit ihr verbunden, bis zu seinem Ende in der unendlichen Weite und unerträglichen Kälte des ewigen Eises. Seine Maßlosigkeit im Bemühen, dem Geheimnis des Lebens auf die Spur zu kommen, spiegelt sich in der Ungeschlachtheit seiner Kreatur wider, und der Einsamkeit, die er in zwanghafter Verfolgung seines Ziels freiwillig auf sich genommen hat, entspricht die gesellschaftliche Isoliertheit seines Geschöpfes, die diesem allerdings seiner Schrecken einflößenden Erscheinung wegen aufgezwungen ist; sie erst verursacht seinen "gewaltsamen Wechsel" zum mörderischen "Dämon" (281), in dem sich das Böse verkörpert. Obwohl aus totem Menschenmaterial komponiert, verfügt das Monster doch über menschliche Empfindungen, sehnt sich nach Geborgenheit und Liebe, und da ihm die Erfüllung seiner Bedürfnisse verwehrt ist, rottet es alle, die seinem Schöpfer nahestehen, aus, um diesen leiden zu lassen, dabei aber selbst unermessliche Qualen erleidend, bevor es nach dessen Tod auch seinem traurigen Leben ein Ende setzt.

Solch offenkundige Parallelen im Leben und Sterben der beiden haben sicher einer der berühmtesten (metonymischen) Verschiebungen im allgemeinen Sprachgebrauch Vorschub geleistet: Mit dem Namen 'Frankenstein' pflegt ein unförmiges oder unfertiges, jedenfalls abstoßendes menschliches Wesen belegt zu werden. Andrerseits wird das Monster, und auch das indiziert der ihm vorenthaltene Eigenname, von Anfang an nicht als Individuum wahrgenommen, sondern auf seine Monstrosität reduziert. Zudem hat diese Metonymie (der Name des Schöpfers wird auf das Geschöpf übertragen) den schlichten rezeptionsgeschichtlichen Grund, dass der Shelley'sche Roman einer breiteren Öffentlichkeit weit weniger bekannt ist als die vielen Filme, die über seinen Stoff und unter seinem Titel gedreht worden sind – und mit seinem Personal, aus dem Frankensteins Kreatur eben als besonders markante Gestalt im wahrsten Sinne des Wortes herausragt.

Über den konkreten Prozess seiner Entstehung lässt Mary Shelley ihre Leser weitgehend im Unklaren – und auch ihr Titelheld hütet verständlicherweise sein Geheimnis lebenslang, gibt es selbst dem Polarforscher Walton nicht preis, der, wie sein "unglückseliger und bewundernswerter Freund" (280) die biologischen, seinerseits geographische Grenzen auf seiner Expedition in die Arktis überschreitet. Dass ein menschliches Wesen, aus Leichenteilen zusammengeflickt, lebendig wird und sofort über eine hohe Intelligenz und stupende Bildung verfügt, hat jedenfalls den Roman und seine zahlreichen intermedialen Variationen in den Bereich der Phantastik ('fantasy') gerückt und bisweilen vergessen gemacht, dass Mary Shelley bei der phantastischen Schilderung der monströsen Menschenproduktion durchaus auf wissenschaftliche Vorgänge und Erkenntnisse ihrer Zeit rekurriert und damit dem von Hans Richard Brittnacher veranschlagten "Paradigmenwechsel in der Phantastik" Rechnung trägt, der sich unter "den Verhältnissen der modernen Welt" ereignet: "Die Rituale von Geheimbündlern in Klöstern und Grabkammern ersetzt das Experimentieren von Chemikern und Ärzten in Labor und Sektionssälen" (269), die sich wie auch jene erfindungsreichen Konstrukteure, die an die Stelle obskurer Magier und mysteriöser Hierophanten rücken, zumeist als "besessene Wissenschaftler" (engl. *mad scientists*) erweisen.

Die Realitätsspur zieht sich sichtbar durch Frankensteins Studien an der Universität Ingolstadt, lassen sie doch die Techniken erkennen, die er zur Belebung des zusammengestückelten Leichnams anwendet. Dem "Wesen und Ursprung des Lebens" (66) nachforschend, wendet er sich vor allem der Physiologie und Anatomie zu, also den Disziplinen der Medizin, die für Bau und Funktion des menschlichen Körpers zuständig sind. Zuvor schon hat er sich mit der Chemie (dem "Zweig der Naturwissenschaften, in dem die größten Fortschritte gemacht worden sind und vielleicht noch gemacht werden" (63), wie Herr Waldmann, sein verehrter Professor, feststellt) so eifrig befasst, dass er "nach Ablauf von zwei Jahren" Wege zur "Verbesserung gewisser chemischer Apparate" aufzuzeigen vermochte. Dabei nimmt er die Mahnung seines Lehrers, nicht als "beschränkter Experimentierer" sein Talent an rein empirischen Untersuchungen und einer positiven Klassifizierung von Phänomenen zu vergeuden, durchaus ernst und huldigt den Geheimwissenschaften, die ihm schon in frühester Jugend in Werken von Heinrich Cornelius Agrippa und Paracelsus begegnet waren (d. h. Gelehrten, die Entwicklung und Existenz künstlicher Menschen beschrieben haben). Von ihren "längst überholten Systemen" (52) hatte er sich bereits distanziert, als er Augenzeuge der gewaltigen Macht eines Blitzschlags wurde; seitdem widmete er dem damals hochaktuellen "Thema Elektrizität und Galvanismus" seine ganze Aufmerksamkeit.

Dass nun Viktor Frankenstein in jener "trüben Novembernacht", deren Schilderung im fünften Kapitel des Romans dessen Keimzelle bildet (74ff.), die, wie Mary Shelley in ihrer "Einführung" von 1831 selbst dargelegt hat, auf eine alptraumhafte Vision im Dämmerzustand zurückgeht (10f.), dass also Frankenstein an der "reglosen Masse" um "ein Uhr morgens" unübersehbare Anzeichen von Leben wahrnehmen kann, das spricht für die erfolgreiche Kombination der für seinen Zweck herangezogenen Fächer, oder anders gesagt: Erzeugung und Belebung seiner nach (al)chemischen Studien, anatomischen Kenntnissen und galvanischen Vorstellungen entwickelten Kreatur reflektieren den naturwissenschaftlichen Standard ihrer Entstehungszeit.

Das entspricht durchaus literarischer Tradition; denn seit der Antike prägen naturwissenschaftliche Entdeckungen und technische Entwicklungen das poetische Erscheinungsbild des künstlich hergestellten Menschen: Die beweglichen Statuen des sagenhaften Baumeisters Dädalus, die, wie der sizilianische Geschichtsschreiber Diodor berichtet, so lebensecht wirkten, daß "das Bild für ein beseeltes Geschöpf" gehalten wurde, fanden ihre handfeste Bestätigung in den Automaten der Mechanikerschule von Alexandrien im 1. Jh. n. Chr., die auf pneumatischer und hydraulischer Basis funktionierten. Die Übereinstimmung mit ihren natürlichen Vorbildern, Bedingung für die in der Literatur der Romantik so oft geschilderte Verwechselbarkeit von Mensch und Automat, war das Gütesiegel für die Androiden (aus dem Griech. von *anér, andrós* = Mann, Mensch), die, angetrieben von komplizierten Uhrwerken, im Zeitalter der Aufklärung entstanden. Die Mechanik lieferte im 18. Jahrhundert aber nicht nur die theoretischen Grundlagen für den Bau solcher Figuren, die musizieren und schreiben konnten, sondern prägte das ganze Weltbild: Der Staat, ja die Natur und somit auch der Mensch, zumindest sein Körper, seien, so die Ansicht der rationalistischen Philosophie, mechanische Systeme, die ausschließlich den Gesetzen der Physik gehorchten. Der französische Arzt und Anatom Julien Offray de La Mettrie vermochte, weil er eben vom maschinellen Wesen des Menschen ausging, was der Titel seiner 1748 erschienenen Abhandlung *L'homme machine* bezeugt, die Androiden des genialen Automatenbauers Jacques de Vaucanson, insbesondere dessen von der Königlichen Akademie der Wissenschaften in Paris 1738 ausgezeichneten Flötenspieler, als Modelle für den Menschen heranzuziehen. Wenn der Ingenieur, so La Mettrie, etwas "mehr Kunst anwenden" würde, dann könne aus einem Androiden, der Flöte spielt, sogar ein "Sprecher" werden, womit selbst die Fähigkeit, die die Natur dem Menschen vorbehalten hat, die der Sprache nämlich, auf technische Weise beherrschbar sei. Von daher kann es nicht verwundern, daß La Mettrie den Automatenbauer Vaucanson in mythische Dimensionen rückt und in ihm einen "neuen Prometheus" sieht (83). Ihm folgt der "moderne" Prometheus der Mary Shelley namens Frankenstein, der von Maschinen- zu Körperteilen fortschreitet und sich nicht mehr mit menschenähnlichen Automaten zufrieden gibt, sondern bestrebt ist, der Natur ihr "größtes Geheimnis" zu entreißen und das Leben selbst künstlich herzustellen. Allerdings wird es noch bis zum Ende des 20. Jahrhunderts dauern, bis den Bemühungen, in den Entstehungsprozess des Menschen einzugreifen, durch die Versuche der Biotechnologien greifbare Ergebnisse beschieden sind.

So lässt sich zum Schluss die zitierte Ausgangsfrage "Wo ist Prometheus?" aus der Perspektive eines erweiterten Kulturbegriffs, der dem Literaturkritiker Gutzkow fremd sein musste, doch noch beantworten: Nicht in der Werkstatt des schreibenden oder bildenden Künstlers, nicht in den Werkhallen der Industriebetriebe ist Prometheus anzutreffen, sondern er dürfte, was Mary Shelley im *Frankenstein* (1818) und übrigens auch Goethe in der Homunculus-Szene aus *Faust II* (1832) literarisch antizipierten, wohl am ehesten in den Labors der Biotechnologen und Reproduktionsmediziner zu finden sein, die spezifisch menschliche Fähigkeiten technisch nachbilden und menschliches Leben manipulieren. Dabei besteht der entscheidende Unterschied zwischen dem "modernen Prometheus", dessen Geschöpfe bei allen Feinheiten ihrer materiellen Konkretion letztlich nie den Bereich der Fiktion und Phantasie verlassen haben, und dem postmodernen Demiurg im Wesentlichen darin, dass mit ihm der Mythos der künstlichen Menschenschöpfung den unaufhaltsamen Weg in die Wirklichkeit angetreten hat.

Literaturverzeichnis

Becher, Johannes R. "Prometheus". *Gesammelte Werke*. Bd. 4. *Gedichte 1936–1941*. Berlin und Weimar: Aufbau-Verlag, 1966. 612–615.
Blumenberg, Hans. *Arbeit am Mythos*. Frankfurt a. M.: Suhrkamp, 1979.
Brittnacher, Hans Richard. *Ästhetik des Horrors: Gespenster, Vampire, Monster, Teufel und künstliche Menschen in der phantastischen Literatur*. Frankfurt a. M.: Suhrkamp, 1994.

Drux, Rudolf. "Dichter und Titan: Der poetologische Bezug auf den Prometheus-Mythos in der Lyrik von Goethe bis Heine". *Heine-Jahrbuch* 1986. 11–26.
—. "E. T. A. Hoffmanns Version der 'Fabel von dem Prometheus'". *E. T. A. Hofmann Jahrbuch* 1 (1992–93). 80–89.
—. "Frankenstein oder der Mythos vom künstlichen Menschen und seinem Schöpfer". *Der Frankenstein-Komplex: Kulturgeschichtliche Aspekte des Traums vom künstlichen Menschen*. Hg. Rudolf Drux. Frankfurt: Suhrkamp, 1999. 26–47.
Freiligrath, Ferdinand. "Von unten auf!". *Freiligraths Werke*. Hg. Paul Zaunert. 1. Bd. Leipzig u. Wien: Bibliograph. Institut Meyer, [1912]. 358–361.
Fuchs, Eduard. "Prometheus". *Aus dem Klassenkampf. Soziale Gedichte*. Hg. Eduard Fuchs, Karl Kaiser, Ernst Klaar. München: M. Ernst, 1894. 3–4.
Gide, André. "Der schlechtgefesselte Prometheus" (1899). *Sämtliche Erzählungen*. Deutsch von Maria Schäfer-Rümelin. Stuttgart: Dt. Verlags-Anstalt, 1962. 121–159.
Gutzkow, Karl. "Göthe, Uhland und Prometheus". *Beiträge zur Geschichte der neuesten Literatur*. Bd. 1. Stuttgart 1836. 57–66.
Goethe, Johann Wolfgang. "Ilmenau, am 3. September 1783". *Goethes Werke in 14 Bänden*. Hg. Erich Trunz ("Hamburger Ausgabe"). Bd. 1. Hamburg: Wegner, 1969. 107–112.
—. "Pandora". *Goethes Werke in 14 Bänden*. Hg. Erich Trunz ("Hamburger Ausgabe"). Bd. 5. Hamburg: Wegner, 1969. 332–365.
—. "Prometheus" (Dramen-Fragment). *Goethes Werke in 14 Bänden*. Hg. Erich Trunz ("Hamburger Ausgabe"). Bd. 4. Hamburg: Wegner, 1969. 176–187.
—. "Prometheus". *Goethes Werke in 14 Bänden*. Hg. Erich Trunz ("Hamburger Ausgabe"). Bd. 1. Hamburg: Wegner, 1969. 44–46.
—. "Wandrers Sturmlied". *Goethes Werke in 14 Bänden*. Hg. Erich Trunz ("Hamburger Ausgabe"). Bd. 1. Hamburg: Wegner, 1969. 33–36.
Heine, Heinrich. "Der Gesang der Okeaniden". *Sämtliche Schriften*. Bd. 1. Hg. Klaus Briegleb. München: Hanser, 1976. 204.
Herder, Johann Gottfried. *Werke in zehn Bänden* (FA). Bd. 2. *Schriften zur Ästhetik und Literatur 1767–1781*. Hg. Gunter E. Grimm. Frankfurt a. M.. Dt. Klassiker Verlag, 1993.
Hoffmann, Ernst Theodor Amadeus. "Die Jesuiterkirche in G." *Nachtstücke* (1817). Hg. Gerhard R. Kaiser. Stuttgart: Reclam, 1990. 106–136.

—. "Die Fermate". *Die Serapions-Brüder*. Nach dem Text des Erstausgabe (1819–21). München: Winkler, 1976. 57–74.

La Mettrie, Julien Offray de. *Der Mensch eine Maschine*. Aus dem Franz. übers. v. Theodor Lücke. Nachwort von Holm Tetens. Stuttgart: Reclam, 2001.

Otten, Karl. "Arbeiter!" *Menschheitsdämmerung* (1929). Hg. Kurt Pinthus. Hamburg: Rowohlt, 1959. 227–230.

Schlegel, August Wilhelm. *A. W. v. Schlegel's Vorlesungen über dramatische Kunst und Literatur*. Krit. Ausg. Eingel. und mit Anm. vers. von Giovanni Vittorio Amoretti. Bd. II. Bonn und Leipzig: Schroeder, 1923. 123–135.

Shaftesbury, Anthony Earl of. "Soliloquy or Advice to an Author". *Characteristics of Men, Manners, Opinions, Times*. Vol. I. Ed. John M. Robertson. Gloucester, Mass. 1963. 135–36.

Shelley, Mary. *Frankenstein oder Der neue Prometheus. Roman* (1818). Aus dem Engl. übers. Ursula und Christian Grawe. Anmerkungen und Nachwort von Christian Grawe. Stuttgart: Reclam, 1986.

Storch, Wolfgang, und Burghard Damerau, Hg. *Mythos Prometheus: Texte von Hesiod bis René Char*. Leipzig: Reclam, 1995.

Trousson, Raymond. *Le thème de Prométhée dans la littérature européenne*. 2 Bde. Genf: Droz, 1964.

Adam Barkman

"NO DOUBT THEY ARE SUBSTANTIALLY RIGHT"

C. S. Lewis and the Calvinists

While C. S. Lewis and his theology are loved by Christians as diverse as Anglicans and Eastern Orthodox, Pentacostals and Catholics, he remains unread, and at times even reviled, by many Calvinists. This is partly due to Lewis's uncharacteristic hostility to the major figures in Calvinism, and partly due to the quick-to-judge spirit that has often characterized zealous Calvinists. In neither case, however, is Lewis's actual theology and Christian world view deeply antithetical to Calvinism. Emotion more than reason has caused this sad divide. Thus, this paper endeavors to show how Lewis is actually very close to Calvinism, and why both need to pay more attention to this.

Während so unterschiedliche Christen wie Anglikaner, Orthodoxe, Anhänger der Pfingstbewegung und Katholiken C. S. Lewis und seine Theologie schätzen, wird er von vielen Kalvinisten nicht gelesen, ja manchmal sogar geschmäht. Zum Teil ist das zurückzuführen auf Lewis' untypische Feindseligkeit gegenüber herausragenden Vertretern des Kalvinismus, zum Teil auch auf die Neigung zu vorschnellen Verurteilungen, die einige eifrige Kalvinisten an den Tag gelegt haben. Auf keinen Fall aber stehen Lewis' tatsächliche Theologie und sein christliches Weltbild in einem tiefen Gegensatz zum Kalvinismus. Der Antagonismus gründet eher auf Gefühlen als auf rationalen Urteilen. Dieser Aufsatz versucht daher zu zeigen, dass Lewis eigentlich dem Kalvinismus sehr nahe steht, und weshalb beide Seiten stärker auf diese Gemeinsamkeiten achten sollten.

◊

Few would disagree with philosopher Peter Kreeft when he declares C. S. Lewis "the best apologist for the Christian faith in the twentieth century" (210). Indeed, according to some figures, the Oxford Don is "the best-selling […] and the most quoted Christian author of all time" (56). Evangelicals, Anglicans, Lutherans, Catholics and even Eastern Orthodox Christians have found Lewis, an Anglican "mere" Christian, to be an invaluable mentor and interlocutor.

However, there is one branch of Christianity – Calvinism – that has had little to say, or at least little positive to say, about Lewis's theological writings.[1] As a Lewis scholar writing from within a Calvinist community, I find this troubling, for though there are differences between Lewis and Calvinists, these differences have been exaggerated partly by Calvinists who have misunderstood Lewis, such as Cornelius Van Til, and partly by a few misleading things Lewis believed true of, and thus said about, certain Calvinist or broadly Calvinist thinkers, such as Karl Barth, John Knox and even John Calvin himself.

Consequently, I want to compare and contrast Lewis and Calvinist thinkers – not just theologians but philosophers and others as well – on general issues related to the three basic features of the Christian world view: creation, fall and redemption. Of course, since Calvinist thinkers (be they Reformed, Presbyterians, Reformed Baptists or others) differ from each other as much as any particular thinker in any particular group, my selection of thinkers will appear a bit arbitrary. Nevertheless, my goal is largely to select Calvinist thinkers who come closest to agreeing with Lewis, thus achieving an important Christian task: greater understanding and unity in the one, undivided body of Christ. Indeed, it is significant that Lewis himself admits that Calvinists are "no doubt [...] substantially right" (*Collected Letters* II, 352 [Feb. 18, 1940]).

Creation

Lewis and Calvinists agree that before we can talk about creation, we first need to talk about its *Creator*. Thus, Reformed theologian R. C. Sproul maintains, "Reformed theology is first and fore-

---

[1] You can, of course, be a Calvinist who is Anglican (the Puritans were such), but even then Calvinist Anglicans, with the exception of N. T. Wright, typically ignore Lewis.

most theocentric rather than anthropocentric" (25) and in nearly every story Lewis ever wrote, God the sovereign Creator and King receives powerful expression. When Dutch Reformed statesman Abraham Kuyper declares, "There is not one square inch of the entire creation about which Jesus Christ does not cry out, 'Mine!'" (488) he asserts precisely what Lewis proclaims at nearly the same time just across the Channel: "There is no neutral ground in the universe: every square inch, every split second, is claimed by God [its Rightful Lord] and counter-claimed by Satan" ("Christianity and Culture" 90).

Thus, Lewis and Calvinists agree that God is the transcendental cause and ground of all creation: without God, nothing in creation would be possible, for nothing created can literally do anything without the Creator's strength and permission (though not necessarily His *approval*). Hence, Lewis envisions Satan "sawing off the branch he is sitting on" (*Preface to Paradise Lost*, 96) and Reformed theologian Vern Poythress asserts the same thing somewhat crudely when he says, "*All* scientists – atheists and theists alike – believe in God. They have to to do their work" (13). Furthermore, because Lewis and Calvinists acknowledge God as the perfection of Power, Goodness and Rationality, all of creation – that is, all of God's kingdom – was declared *good*, and, in the language of Reformational philosophy, is "subject" to, and rationally ordered by, the Only Wise and Benevolent King's "creational laws". These laws are either norms, such as "don't murder", or the laws of nature, such as gravity, and these laws may be either general, such as "don't murder" or gravity, or particular, such as "sacrifice your son, Isaac" or "Jesus walked on water." Although Calvinists are (sometimes rightly, sometimes wrongly) distrustful of the language of Natural Law (often fearing that such implies an ethical absolute *separate* from God), the ethical norms of God's creational laws are precisely this provided that they are understood as Lewis understands them, namely, as being inextricably linked to God's nature, thus implying that these norms are in fact the voice of the Holy Spirit directly revealing something of Himself to us in our conscience: "Is not the [Natural Law] the Word Himself considered from a particular point of view?" (*Collected Letters* III, 1227 [Jan. 11, 1961]). And, of course, something similar is true of the laws of nature, "If God directs the course of events at all, then He directs the movement of every atom at every moment. [...] The 'naturalness' of natural events does not consist in being somehow outside God's providence" (*Miracles* 1232).

Furthermore, Lewis and Calvinists agree that the crown of earthly creation, man, was created in the image of God, meaning, among other things, that he was more loved by God than the rest of earthly creation. Being more loved by God, man was elected to a greater calling or destiny than the rest of earthly creation (we will discuss the precise meaning of election later). For Lewis, just as much as for Calvinists, this destiny is best expressed in the words of the Westminster Confession, namely, that man is "to glorify God and enjoy Him forever".[2] Of course in order to achieve this great calling, God had to give man the necessary equipment for the task – rational cognitive faculties and free will – for only if man has free will can man bless God in this special way (that is, the love of free creatures is more meaningful than that of coerced creatures), and man, in turn, being made by God, for God, was created such that he can only find real happiness in a (proper or just) covenantal relationship with God. Man, therefore, was created to *know* and *love* God. Of course, each person should love God in *all* that he or she does (Reformed Christianity's "cultural mandate" or Lewis's "We can play, as we can eat, to the glory of God" – "Christianity and Literature", 419); however, since all people have been designed differently (Christians are *unique* members in the one body of Christ), each person needs to love God according to what he or she is (as rational souls, of course, but also as men, as women, as elder, as younger, etc.) and also according to his or her fluctuating vocation in God's creation (as professors, as students, etc.).

---

[2] "Now the disquieting thing is not simply that we skimp and begrudge the duty of prayer. The real disquieting thing is that is should have to be numbered among duties at all. For we believe that we were created to 'glorify God and enjoy Him forever'" (C. S. Lewis, *Prayer: Letters to Malcolm*, 631).

Of course, God's knowledge of, and love for, man come *prior* to anything that man knows or does. However, regarding man, he must first know that God exists and something of the divine nature in order to love God: a person cannot love something he knows nothing about. In other words, some revelation of God to man (we will discuss the types of revelation later) is necessary in order for man to achieve his purpose. Thus in Romans 1, Paul tells us that knowledge of God's existence (in Calvin's phrase, a *sensus divinitatis*) can be known by *all* people. Moreover, because this knowledge makes people "without excuse" for failing to worship God, having a moral duty to worship God – that is, having general awareness of justice (the ethical norms of the creational law of which I spoke of earlier) – can also be known by *all* people.

However, when it comes to discerning the precise nature of the knowledge of God's existence and the ethical norms of God's creational laws, Calvinists differ amongst themselves. Some Calvinists, including Sproul, B. B. Warfield and Emil Brunner, endorse natural theology, wherein God's existence is inferred by way of argument (the cosmological argument, for instance), while others – indeed the majority of Calvinists these days, not the least of whom is Alvin Plantinga – think that God's existence is properly basic, meaning that people immediately – without inference or induction – just *see* that God exists on certain occasions, such as when one sees the beauty of the world from the top of a mountain, when one is in dire need or when things are going perfectly: we are designed by God such that on all of these occasions a properly functioning human being will be aware of the existence of God and something of His nature, namely, that God is the author of all creation (the Creator), the source of Happiness (the Father), and perfect Moral Goodness and Order (the King).

Although Lewis has often been included in the natural theology camp, this is not totally accurate. Yes, Lewis is famous for his formulations of the argument from morality, the argument from reason and the argument from joy. And yes, all of these arguments, in one form or another, helped Lewis in his conversion to Christianity. However, Lewis, just as much as Plantinga, found the ontological argument, among others, helpful but wanting, and, moreover, there is strong agreement between Lewis and Plantinga when we conjoin the two following quotes from the Oxford Don: "The *form* of the desired is in the desire" (*Surprised by Joy*, 1371) and, "If we are made for heaven, *the desire for our proper place will be already in us*" ("The Weight of Glory", 98).[3] Although many Calvinists will want more clarification about the "desire" in the latter quotation (again, we will pick this up later), what is crucial to notice here is that since one cannot desire something that one does not have *any* knowledge of, these sentences imply that Lewis believes all people to have some basic (innate, acquired or occasioned) knowledge of God. Perhaps, then, Lewis belongs more to the Plantinga camp (or better, both are of the Augustinian or Christian Platonist camp) in that they acknowledge God's existence (and the existence of God's moral law) as basic, yet at the same time endorse the use of natural theology not only to respond to challenges to Christianity ("negative apologetics") but also to point out problems with alternatives to Christianity ("positive apologetics").

Consequently, in regard to God (His existence and nature), His creational laws (which are inextricably linked to His very nature at every moment), and His creation (especially man: his destiny and means of achieving such) there is really no disagreement between Lewis and Calvinists as I have construed them. At this point in our discussion, both are merely orthodox in their Christianity.

Fall

Nevertheless, the Fall, true to its name, separates: man from God, of course, but also one theological interpretation from another. Yet even here Lewis is not nearly so far from Calvinist interpretations of the Fall as some – including Lewis himself – might think.

To begin with, since Lewis and Calvinists will generally agree that justice means loving each person or thing as he or it ought to be

---

[3] We should note that when Lewis says we were made for "Heaven", he is using Heaven as a synonym for "God".

loved (wherein the value of each thing or person is given by either God's free choice or flows from a necessary aspect of God's very nature), God, being the greatest person, ought to be loved above all else. However, since man loved himself (the inferior) more than God (the superior), man committed injustice or sin. As a result, God justly cursed man in kind in that *all* that is subordinate to man now rebels against him: his mind, will and emotions rebel within; his body, once immortal, now rebels against his immortal soul in that his body is now susceptible to diseases and death; animals and the entire natural world threaten man and make his life difficult; and man's children – who are rightly subordinate to him – properly inherit the curse called original sin.

Now those who are familiar with Lewis's writings will want to stop me here, demanding to see the evidence of Lewis's supposed agreement with Calvinists in regard to the scope of the Fall – after all, did Lewis not explicitly reject the doctrine of Total Depravity?

> The doctrine of Total Depravity – when the consequence is drawn that, since we are totally depraved, our idea of good is worth simply nothing – may thus turn Christianity into a form of devil-worship. [...] [Consequently] I disbelieve [in Total Depravity] partly on the logical ground that if our depravity were total we should not know ourselves to be depraved, and partly because experience shows us much goodness in human nature. (Lewis, *The Problem of Pain*, 487, 503)

Quite rightly, Calvinists will be upset with Lewis's understanding and rejection of the "T" in their theological TULIP since what Lewis has described is *not* Total Depravity at all but rather *utter depravity*, which Calvinists, just as much as Lewis, reject. That is, both Lewis and Calvinists agree that *all* that is below man was touched by the curse of the Fall,[4] yet both agree that in spite of this curse,

---

[4] "Since the Fall, no organization or way of life whatsoever has a natural tendency to go right" (C. S. Lewis, "The Sermon and the Lunch", 343).

fallen man and the rest of creation still bear the marks of their Creator.

Specifically in regard to man, Lewis believes that by God's common grace (he does not use this language but implies such), unregenerated man – *without* acknowledging God as the source of truth – can still discover truth:

> As regards the Fall, I submit that the general tenor of scripture does not encourage us to believe that our knowledge of the Law has been depraved in the same degree as our power to fulfill it. [...] Our righteousness may be filthy and ragged; but Christianity gives us no ground for holding that our perceptions of right are in the same condition. They may, no doubt, be impaired; but there is a difference between imperfect sight and blindness. A theology which goes about to represent our practical reason as radically unsound is heading for disaster. (Lewis, "The Poison of Subjectivism" 663)

Some Calvinists, particularly presuppositionalists of the Van Tillian sort, will challenge this, claiming that without acknowledging God as the source of truth, no one can say *anything* truthful. But surely this is a confusion between epistemology (believing that God exists) and metaphysics (God being the ground of all rationality). Alvin Plantinga comments,

> According to John Calvin, 'As soon as ever we depart from Christ, there is nothing, be it ever so gross or insignificant in itself, respecting which we are not necessarily deceived.' Perhaps Calvin means only what we have already noted: one who doesn't know God fails to know the most important truth about anything else. He may mean to go even further, however: perhaps he means to say that those who don't know God suffer much wider ranging cognitive deprivation and, in fact, don't really have any knowledge at all. [...] That seems a shade harsh, particularly because many who don't be-

> lieve in God seem to know a great deal more about some topics than most believers do. (Could I sensibly claim, for example, that I know more logic than, say, Willard van Orman Quine, even if I can't do any but the simplest logic exercises, on the grounds that at any rate I know *something* about logic and he, being an unbeliever, knows nothing at all about that subject or indeed anything else?) As it stands, this suggestion is desperately wide of the mark. (Plantinga, *The Analytic Theist* 217)

Thus, presumably what Van Tillians *want to say* is precisely what Lewis says: that God's existence is the necessary condition for human thought to be possible, but if one wants to grow in rationality, one needs to know that God exists, for knowledge without knowledge of God is always knowledge, in the ultimate sense, out of context and hence misleading in ultimate matters.

That is the *mind* of fallen or unregenerated man, but what about his *will*? Lewis clearly believed that even fallen man has some small desire for God, though this desire is usually *qua* the desire for Happiness, the desire for Truth or even the desire for Justice. For instance, in *The Last Battle*, a pagan named Emeth, who, at least some of the time, *really* loved Justice, was shown to have really loved Aslan/Christ indirectly. And in essay after essay, Lewis wrote much the same thing:

> The Christian doctrine that there is no 'salvation' by works done according to the moral law is a fact of daily experience. […] If the new Self, the new Will, does not come at His own good pleasure to be born in us, we cannot produce Him synthetically. The price of Christ is something, in a way, much easier than moral effort – it is to want Him. *It is true that the wanting itself would be beyond our power but for one fact.* The world is so built that, to help us desert our own satisfactions, they desert us. War and trouble and finally old age take from us one

by one all those things that the natural Self hoped for at its setting out. Begging is our only wisdom, and want in the end makes it easier for us to be beggars. Even on those terms the Mercy will receive us. (Lewis, "Three Kinds of Men" 316; emphasis mine)

Now here many Calvinists (following the later Augustine) will probably disagree with Lewis, insisting that while fallen man still has free will, such a man can never actually choose God since fallen man's desire is *utterly depraved* in that fallen man *utterly* loves injustice or himself over and against God, either directly or indirectly conceived of. Moreover, because man always chooses according to his strongest desire, fallen man always chooses evil. Typically such Calvinists quote something like this from Calvin to support their idea: "In this way, then, man is said to have free will, not because he has a free choice of good and evil, but because he acts voluntarily, and not by compulsion" (Calvin 1331). The conclusion then appears to be that all acts of justice and mercy that a fallen man performs are not, in fact, acts of justice and mercy at all: these acts appear to be acts of justice and mercy but since the desire or intention behind them is aimed purely at an *unjust* or *inordinate* love of self, such acts are not real acts of justice and mercy. They are acts of "civic virtue", not real virtue.

Nevertheless, a minority of prominent Calvinists such as Alvin Plantinga (again), hesitate over this interpretation since Total Depravity, *not* utter depravity, appears to be the biblical and most correct Calvinist position. Seeing a legitimate analogy between the mind's fallen, but not utterly fallen, state, and the will's fallen, but not utter fallen, state, Plantinga says of unregenerated man, "We are prone to hate God but, confusingly, in some way also inclined to love and seek him; we are prone to hate our neighbour, to see her as a competitor for scarce goods, but also, paradoxically, to prize her and love her" (*Warranted Christian Belief* 210).

As regards the Fall, then, there is not much disagreement between Lewis and Calvinists. Yes, there is some disagreement between Lewis and a minority of Calvinists over unregenerated man's ability to know things, and it is true that there is also some disagreement between Lewis and many Calvinists – though certainly not *all* Calvinists – over unregenerated man's ability to desire God and Justice, but overall, the conflict between Lewis and Calvinists, particularly Lewis and a Calvinist like Plantinga, is minor at best.

Redemption

All orthodox Christians, including Lewis and Calvinists, insist that the chief blueprint for determining how to live our lives is the Bible, the God-inspired text of special revelation. Nevertheless, all orthodox Christians, Lewis and Calvinists alike, will reject the "narrow scripturalism" that denies that God also reveals a lot of Himself and His creational laws through general revelation.

Based on both special and general revelation, orthodox Christians agree *that* man cannot save himself. More specifically (and now based solely on special revelation), all orthodox Christians believe *that* God the Son became a man, died, rose, and offers, out of pure grace and mercy, forgiveness of sins to all who, out of faith, submit to Him. Genuine belief in this is what makes a Christian a Christian – regardless of whether a person is Anglican, Catholic, Eastern Orthodox, Reformed or whatever. Moreover, it is generally agreed that when the Holy Spirit gives Christians saving faith in terms of knowledge, it is knowledge of these, and usually just these, *basic beliefs*. Thus, keeping a clear distinction between the biblical *that* (the God-revealed fact) and the theological *how* (the manmade explanation) is vital.

Now Calvinist theology is extremely systematic, which is what we should expect since its theological founder, John Calvin, was trained as a lawyer. Calvinist theology, therefore, prides itself "on understanding a doctrine in a coherent and unified matter [...] in discerning the interrelatedness of the teachings of Scripture itself" (Sproul 23). Consequently, the *how* of saving faith is confidently extrapolated in Calvinism's TULIP, especially the U, L, I, and P of it. The idea is roughly this:

Before the creation of the world – before anyone was created, and *not* based on any foreknowledge He had about the *merit* or *desire* of future individuals – God elected, out of special grace, to save some, but not all, people from their sins: this is the "U" in TULIP – Unconditional Election. Connected to this, is the flipside of the same coin: the doctrine of double predestination, wherein God simply chooses to pass over – not to extend a saving hand to – the rest of the sinful humanity: these, so the logic goes, receive justice, while the elect receive mercy. Consequently, Christ did not die for *all* people, but only for those He elected to save: this is the "L" in TULIP – Limited Atonement. Moreover, the Holy Spirit inwardly testifies to the elect, giving them faith in terms of both saving knowledge of what Christ has done (namely, helping them to believe the most vital statements in the Bible) and a softened will such that they can – indeed, cannot do anything but – believe this testimony and knowledge: this is the "I" in TULIP – Irresistible Grace. And if the elect cannot – if it is beyond their free will to – resist God's grace, then it makes sense that the elect can never lose their salvation; they are eternally secure: this, of course, is the "P" in TULIP – the Perseverance of the Saints. Finally God's saints are those who enter into a covenant with God – a covenant or agreement to be God's people and to continue the restorative work – the kingdom-building work, the work of regaining and healing *every aspect* of creation – which Christ began on the cross and will finish when He returns again.

What would Lewis say to all this, particularly the U, L, I and P of TULIP? On the surface, some might see him as a typical Arminian, believing that God wants to save all sinners but is frustrated in this because some sinners do not want to be saved; thus, Lewis writes things like, "I willingly believe that the damned are, *in one sense*, successful, rebels to the end; the doors of hell are locked on the inside" (*The Problem of Pain* 583). However, those who have read the Oxford Don in more detail will soon see that this is not always clear.

To begin, Lewis rarely used the biblical word "election", and when he did use it, it is not clear from his writings what he meant by it. Nevertheless, Lewis had no trouble admitting that God, being the perfection of Freedom, has the sovereign ability to assign greater or lesser value, or a greater or lesser destiny, to things He creates (cf. Lewis, "Membership" 338). In keeping with this emphasis on God's sovereign choice, when a member of the Billy Graham Evangelistic Association asked Lewis, in true Arminian fashion, if he had "made a decision" to follow Jesus at the time of his conversion, Lewis replied in a Calvinistic manner, "I would not put it that way. What I wrote in *Surprised by Joy* was that 'before God closed in on me, I was in fact offered what now appears a moment of wholly free choice'. But I feel my decision was not so important. I was the object rather than the subject in this affair. *I was decided upon*" ("Cross-Examination" 553). Clearly, Lewis perceived the Holy Spirit, through special grace (yes, he used the word[5]), making efforts to save him and having gone about doing so using whatever means – though particularly using his desire for Happiness (the argument from joy), Truth (the argument from reason) and Justice (the argument from morality) – to get him to the point of saving faith. However, this is not Unconditional Election, for nowhere does Lewis say that merit or desire played *no* role in God's decision to set out to save him. Nevertheless, this silence on Lewis's part did *not* imply the Arminian opposite. It is significant that, true to "mere Christianity", Lewis intentionally tried not to take a strong position on this theological *how*, writing:

> What I *think* is this. Everyone looking back on *his own* conversion must feel – and I am sure the feeling is in some sense true – 'It is not *I* who have done this. I did not choose Christ: He chose me. It is all free grace, which I have done nothing to earn.' That is the Pauline account: and I am sure it is the only true account of every conversion *from the inside*. Very well. It then seems to us logical & natural to turn this personal experience

---

[5] "The operation of Faith is to retain, so far as the will and intellect are concerned, what is irresistible and obvious during the moments of special grace" (C. S. Lewis, "Is Theism Important?" 57).

into a general rule 'All conversions depend on God's choice.'
But this I believe is exactly what we must not do: for generalizations are legitimate only when we are dealing with matters to which our faculties are adequate. Here, we are not. How our individual experiences are in reality consistent with (a) Our idea of Divine justice, (b) The parable [of the sheep and goats: Matt. 25:30–46, in which "all depends on works"]. What is clear is that we can't find a consistent formula. I think we must take a leaf out of the scientists' book. They are quite familiar with the fact that, for example, Light has to be regarded both as a wave in the ether and as a stream of particles. No one can make these two views consistent. Of course reality must be self-consistent: but till (if ever) we can see the consistency it is better to hold two inconsistent views than to ignore one side of the evidence.
The real inter-relation between God's omnipotence and Man's freedom is something we can't find out. Looking at the Sheep & the Goats every man can be quite sure that every kind act he does will be accepted by Christ. Yet, equally we all do feel sure that all the good in us comes from Grace. We have to leave it at that. I find the best plan is to take the Calvinist view of my own virtues and other people's vices: and the other view of my own vices and other people's virtues. But though there is much to be *puzzled* about, there is nothing to be *worried* about. It is plain from Scripture that, in whatever sense the Pauline doctrine is true, it is not true in any sense that *excludes* its (apparent) opposite. (*Collected Letters* III, 354–5 [August 3, 1953])

Writing as a literary historian, Lewis went further, insisting that the problem with Calvinism's Unconditional Election and subsequent Limited Atonement is that these doctrines are indicative of overconfidence in man's ability to discern theological truths from particular biblical statements. Thus, for example, Lewis speaks of "straw-splitting dialogues in Calvinist theology" (*Collected Letters* III, 1265 [May 9, 1961]) and considers the puritan Thomas Cartwright "twisted by dangerous certitude" (*Poetry and Prose* 446), for even though the Holy Spirit gives us faith in terms of deeper knowledge of Himself, this does not mean that every biblical statement will be equally apparent to the elect. Calvinists are right in asserting that God's creation is rationally ordered and that the elect will see more of this rational order than others (hence they are right in emphasizing *some* systematization), but they – or at least some, including Cartwright and even Calvin himself – are mistaken in thinking that the elect will therefore have knowledge – as opposed to mere opinion – of the true meaning of obscure biblical passages dealing with election and the scope of the atonement. Speaking of the early Reformers, Lewis remarks,

> Propositions originally framed with the sole purpose of praising the Divine compassion as boundless, hardly credible, and utterly gratuitous, build up, when extrapolated and systematized, into something that sounds not unlike devil-worship. [...] In it Calvin goes on from the original Protestant experience to build a system, to extrapolate, to raise all the dark questions and *give without flinching* the dark answers. (*Poetry and Prose* 33, 43; emphasis mine).

Thus, in regards to election and the scope of the atonement, we should say that Lewis took the middle ground between Calvinists and Arminians – the ground of temporary agnosticism in respect to the precise state of affairs between God's and man's actions.

Unsurprisingly, therefore, Lewis was similarly agnostic in respect to the doctrine of Irresistible Grace. On the one hand, he does speak of God's "irresistible [...] grace" in certain respects ("Is Theism Important?" 57), but on the other hand, because he appears to have been libertarian in respect to man's free will,[6] it seems more likely than not that he would have rejected the doctrine of Irresistible Grace (since a consistent libertarian would probably say that God can only *woo* the elect to saving faith, rather than *drag* them to it). However, since there are Calvinists who are libertarians (Plantinga is one of them), *perhaps* one could say that man has libertarian freedom in all matters but that of salvation. Whatever the case, Lewis is not perfectly clear on this doctrine (or at least no clearer than Plantinga).

In regards to the doctrine of the Perseverance of the Saints, Lewis, on the one hand, seems to deny it, saying things like

> The world does not consist of 100 percent Christians or a 100 percent non-Christians. There are people [...] who are slowly ceasing to be Christians but who still call themselves by that name. [...] There are other people who are slowly becoming Christians though they do not yet call themselves so. There are people who do not accept the full Christian doctrine about Christ but who are so strongly attracted by Him that they are His in a much deeper sense than they themselves understand. There are people in other religions who are being led *by God's secret influence* to concentrate on those parts of their religion which are in agreement with Christianity, and who thus belong to Christ without knowing it. (*Mere Christianity* 455)

This said, on the other hand, there is nothing in this quotation at odds with the doctrine of the Perseverance of Saints *provided that* Lewis's "Christians" are only Christians so-called from man's perspective and not from God's. However, if Lewis means something stronger than this – that a man who at one point in his life was given

---

[6] "If what our will does [is] not 'voluntary', and if 'voluntary' does not mean 'free', what are we talking about?" (Lewis, *Collected Letters* III, 237–238 [October 20, 1952])

saving faith but that he has now lost it – then this quotation would be incompatible with the doctrine. As it stands, however, Lewis's precise meaning is ambiguous, though I think it can easily be read alongside the following words of a Calvinist like Plantinga:

> Those who don't share our commitment to the Lord are in transition, just as we are. As Calvin says, there is unbelief within the breast of every Christian; but isn't there also belief within the breast of every non-Christian? The antithesis is of course real; but at any time in history it is also less than fully articulated and developed. The City of God stands opposed to the City of the World: sure enough; but we all live in God's world, and those in the City of the World are subject to the promptings and blandishments of our God-given natures, of the *Sensus Divinitatis*, and of the Holy Spirit. Were the two cities completely formed and articulated, they could have little intellectual commerce or contact with each other. The believer would see the world a certain way, or perhaps in one of a certain range of ways; the unbeliever would see it quite differently, and feel no unease or discomfort in seeing it his way [...]. *But the cities, and the citizens therein, are not completely formed and developed.* (*The Analytic Theist* 346–7; emphasis mine)

Now although Lewis is temporarily agnostic toward the U, L, I and P of TULIP, he is not so toward the subsequent Calvinist or better, Neocalvinist, emphasis on furthering the kingdom of God and restoring creation to its former splendour.

True, Lewis's conception of the New Earth may be more Lutheran than Calvinist (in that the Old Earth is destroyed and rebuilt, rather than being healed per se); and true, Lewis, as a Christian Platonist, had a slightly distorted idea of the afterlife, often speaking of Christians "going to Heaven" rather than peopling the New Earth. Nevertheless, on the whole, Lewis and Calvinists agree that when the Holy Spirit gives the elect faith, they become creatures infused with new life and understanding with which they can act as God's agents in creational transformation.

This new knowledge or understanding – Herman Dooyeweerd's "the religious fullness of meaning", Dirk Vollenhoven's "Christian logic", or Lewis's "the correction of reason" – needs to be applied to kingdom-building – to acting Christianly toward *all* aspects of creation. Thus, Lewis said things like, "What we want is not more little books on Christianity, but more little books by Christians on other subjects – with their Christianity *latent*" ("Christian Apologetics" 150) and,

> The work of a Beethoven, and the work of a charwoman, become spiritual on precisely the same condition, that of being offered to God, of being done humbly 'as to the Lord'. This does not, of course, mean that it is for anyone a mere toss-up whether he should sweep rooms or compose symphonies. A mole must dig to the glory of God and a cock must crow. We are members of one body, but differentiated members, each with his own vocation. ("Learning in Wartime" 583)

In this way, Lewis and Calvinists oppose "a moderated religion" that falsely separates the world into realms where Christianity is appropriate and where it is inappropriate. Since God is sovereign over all, all aspects of creation need to be subjugated to Him. Although Lewis and most Calvinists believe that Christians and non-Christians can find common ground (since both are made in the image of God and both retain something of that image and its ability to hear God's general revelation), Lewis and Calvinists vehemently reject the notion that Christianity is only for Sundays or only for priests: "The application of Christian principles, say, to trade unionism or education, must come from Christian trade unionists and Christian schoolmasters: just as Christian literature comes from Christian novelists and dramatists – not from the bench of bishops getting together and trying to write plays and novels in their spare time"

(*Mere Christianity* 374). Both Lewis and Calvinists seek to be in the world but not of the world and in all things to glorify God.

So in respect to redemption, Lewis agrees with Calvinists on the centrality of Scripture and the kingdom-building task. As for the U, L, I and P of TULIP, Lewis neither agrees nor disagrees with these, preferring – because he separates biblical *thats* from theological *hows* – to remain temporarily agnostic about these doctrines. On the whole, then, there is not a lot of major disagreement between Lewis and Calvinists.

Conclusion

Is C. S. Lewis, as he self-confesses, Calvinist "slush", (*Collected Letters* II, 351 [Feb. 18, 1940]) or is he, as he says of Shakespeare in contrast to the Calvinists of his day, "gloriously anomalous"?[7] That is for the reader to decide. For my part, I have tried to emphasize ecumenism – to set aside misunderstandings and exaggerations in order to show that Lewis and Calvinists belong to the same family, and, what is more, that their theological disagreements are not, or do not have to be, as large as Lewis and many Calvinists think. If we can get past both Lewis's uncharacteristic malice (saying that certain Calvinists are comparable to "devil worshippers" or "magicians"[8]),

---

[7] "Of course not all Calvinists were puritans. Nor am I suggesting that the great fighting puritans who risked ruin and torture in their attack on the bishops were merely conforming to a fashion. We must distinguish a hard core of puritans and a much wider circle of those who were, at varying levels, affected by Calvinism. But a certain severity [...] was diffused even through the wider circle, in the sense that denunciation of vice became part of the stock-in-trade of fashionable and even frivolous writers [...]. The gentleness and candour of Shakespeare's mind has impressed all his readers. But it impresses us still more the more we study the general tone of sixteenth-century literature. He is gloriously anomalous" (Lewis, *Poetry and Prose in the Sixteenth Century*, 43).

[8] "In the magician and the astrologer we saw a readiness either to exaggerate or to minimize the power and dignity of Man. Calvinism perhaps satisfies both inclinations by plunging the unregenerate man as deep as the astrologers and exalting the elect as highly as the magicians" (Lewis, *Poetry and Prose in the Sixteenth Century*, 49–50).

and certain Calvinist tendencies to promote utter depravity or to exalt manmade theological formulae to the same level as clear biblical statements, then this paper will have served its purpose.

Works Cited

Calvin, John. *Institutes of the Christian Religion*. Transl. Ford Lewis Battles. Philadelphia: Westminster Press, 1960.
Kreeft, Peter. *Heaven: The Heart's Deepest Longing*. San Francisco: Ignatius Press, 1989.
Kuyper, Abraham. "Sphere Sovereignty". *Abraham Kuyper: A Centennial Reader*. Ed. James Bratt. Grand Rapids, MI: Eerdmans, 1998. 50–78.
Lewis, C. S. "Christian Apologetics". *C. S. Lewis: Essay Collection & Other Short Pieces*. Ed. Lesley Walmsley. London: HarperCollins, 2000. 147–159.
—. "Christianity and Culture". *C. S. Lewis: Essay Collection & Other Short Pieces*. Ed. Lesley Walmsley. London: HarperCollins, 2000. 71–92.
—. "Christianity and Literature". *C. S. Lewis: Essay Collection & Other Short Pieces*. Ed. Lesley Walmsley. London: HarperCollins, 2000. 411–420.
—. *The Collected Letters of C. S. Lewis. Volume II: Books, Broadcasts, and the War 1931–1949*. Ed. Walter Hooper. San Francisco: HarperSanFrancisco, 2004.
—. *The Collected Letters of C. S. Lewis. Volume III: Narnia, Cambridge, and Joy 1950–1963*. Ed. Walter Hooper. San Francisco: HarperSanFrancisco, 2007.
—. "Cross-Examination". *C. S. Lewis: Essay Collection & Other Short Pieces*. Ed. Lesley Walmsley. London: HarperCollins, 2000. 551–557.
—. "Is Theism Important?". *C. S. Lewis: Essay Collection & Other Short Pieces*. Ed. Lesley Walmsley. London: HarperCollins, 2000. 54–57.
—. "Learning in Wartime". *C. S. Lewis: Essay Collection & Other Short Pieces*. Ed. Lesley Walmsley. London: HarperCollins, 2000. 579–586.
—. "Membership". *C. S. Lewis: Essay Collection & Other Short Pieces*. Ed. Lesley Walmsley. London: HarperCollins, 2000. 332–340.
—. *Mere Christianity. C. S. Lewis: Selected Books* [Long Edition]. London: HarperCollins, 1999. 3111–466.
—. *Miracles. C. S. Lewis: Selected Books* [Long Edition]. London: HarperCollins, 1999. 1095–1238.

—. *Poetry and Prose in the Sixteenth Century*. The Oxford History of English Literature, vol. 4. Oxford: Clarendon Press, 1997.
—. "The Poison of Subjectivism". *C. S. Lewis: Essay Collection & Other Short Pieces*. Ed. Lesley Walmsley. London: HarperCollins, 2000. 657–665.
—. *Prayer: Letters to Malcolm. C. S. Lewis: Selected Books* [Short Edition]. London: HarperCollins, 2002. 223–304.
—. *A Preface to Paradise Lost*. Oxford: Oxford University Press, 1969.
—. *The Problem of Pain. C. S. Lewis: Selected Books* [Long Edition]. London: HarperCollins, 1999. 467–556.
—. "The Sermon and the Lunch". *C. S. Lewis: Essay Collection & Other Short Pieces*. Ed. Lesley Walmsley. London: HarperCollins, 2000. 341–345.
—. *Surprised by Joy. C. S. Lewis: Selected Books* [Long Edition]. London: HarperColllins, 1999. 1239–1382.
—. "Three Kinds of Men". *C. S. Lewis: Essay Collection & Other Short Pieces*. Ed. Lesley Walmsley. London: HarperCollins, 2000. 315–316.
—. "The Weight of Glory". *C. S. Lewis: Essay Collection & Other Short Pieces*. Ed. Lesley Walmsley. London: HarperCollins, 2000. 96–106.
Plantinga, Alvin. *The Analytic Theist: An Alvin Plantinga Reader*. Ed. James Sennett. Grand Rapids, MI: Eerdmans, 1998.
—. *Warranted Christian Belief*. Oxford: Oxford University Press, 2000.
Poythress, Vern. *Redeeming Science: A God-Centered Approach*. Wheaton, IL: Crossway Books, 2006.
Ryken, Philip. "Winsome Evangelist: The Influence of C. S. Lewis". *C. S. Lewis: Lightbearer in the Shadowlands* Ed. Angus Menuge. Wheaton, IL: Crossway Books, 1997. 55–78.
Sproul, R. C. *What Is Reformed Theology?* Grand Rapids, MI: Baker Books, 2005.

Christian Schneider

DISREPUTABLE HEROES

A Re-examination of Robert E. Howard and His Literature

Robert E. Howard's literature has been subject to various criticisms, including reproaches of racism, misogyny, the glorification of violence, and fascism. The following essay takes a closer look at the author and his writing in an attempt to assert to what extent these criticisms are justified. Since there has been much speculation about Howard's alleged mental disturbances, his psychological condition will also be addressed.

Die von Robert E. Howard verfasste Literatur sah sich im Laufe der Zeit verschiedensten Vorwürfen ausgesetzt und wurde mit Rassismus, Frauenfeindlichkeit, Gewaltverherrlichung und Faschismus in Verbindung gebracht. Der folgende Artikel versucht herauszufinden, inwiefern diese Vorwürfe gerechtfertigt sind. Da über Howards (vermeintlichen) Geisteszustand viele Spekulationen angestellt wurden und immer noch werden, wird auch dieses Thema behandelt.

1. Robert E. Howard's Work as a Subject of Academic Study

Throughout much of the 20th century, fantasy literature experienced a hard time gaining acceptance as a serious field of literary study. It was only after the enormous success of J. R. R. Tolkien's *The Lord of the Rings* and the erosion of the traditional literary canon that courses dealing with fantasy fiction started appearing in certain universities. By the early 21st century, the situation had changed a great deal. Today, one only has to skim through a list of recently (or soon-to-be) published academic papers to find dissertations dealing with J. R. R. Tolkien, C. S. Lewis, J. K. Rowling, Stephenie Meyer and other well-known fantasy authors. Upon closer examination, however, it becomes clear that those works generally deemed worthy of scholarly research, either because of a certain literary value (in case of Tolkien) or their status as a pop-cultural phenomenon (in case of Meyer), comprise only a part of the fantasy genre. One subgenre remarkably absent from the aforementioned lists of academic papers, as well as from university classrooms, is one that dominated the American pulp magazines of the 30s: *Sword and Sorcery* (S & S). According to *The Encyclopedia of Fantasy*, the term *S & S* itself was coined by Fritz Leiber in order "to describe the fantasy subgenre featuring muscular HEROES in conflict with a variety of VILLAINS, chiefly WIZARDS, WITCHES, evil SPIRITS and other creatures whose powers are – unlike the hero's – supernatural in origin" (915).

The undisputed master, and arguably even father (McCullough), of this genre was the Texan author Robert E. Howard. His stories, the most famous of which center around the barbarian hero Conan, paved the way for countless imitators, but also inspired well-known authors such as Fritz Leiber and Michael Moorcock. In fact, the influence Howard had on the development of 20th century fantasy literature is – according to some critics – second only to Tolkien's (Finn 18; De Camp 135). Today, Robert E. Howard's popularity not only remains unflagging, but given the fact that various publishers reprint his most popular fiction in new editions and considering the great number of Howard adaptations (or pastiches) that are finding their way into comic stores, cinemas, and onto computer screens, we might even speak of a "second Howard Boom" (Finn 245). Despite their huge success, Howard's writings were, for a long time, widely ignored by literary scholars. Those few who commented on his works generally frowned upon them as boyish fantasies at best, and despised them as racist, misogynist and fascist at worst – notions that have ever since been associated with the S & S genre in general and Robert E. Howard in particular.

It is my opinion that the lack of academic studies on Robert E. Howard and his work, especially in the German-speaking world, does not do justice to his immense influence on both fantasy literature and popular culture. I will therefore attempt a re-examination of Robert E. Howard and his fiction, analyzing various criticisms aimed at Howard's writings and asserting to what extent they are justified. To achieve this, I will examine selected articles on Howard familiar to German readers that have shaped the academic public's view of the Texan author, such as "The Miscast Barbarian" by L. Sprague de Camp and "Loincloth, Double Ax, and Magic: 'Heroic Fantasy' and related Genres" by German author Hans Joachim Alpers. Although it is always necessary to draw a line between the author and his writings, this essay will also examine Robert E. Howard's (supposed) psychological condition, a subject which is frequently brought up by critics. While German academics have left Howard's fiction virtually untouched since the appearance of "Loincloth, Double Ax, and Magic" in the 1970s, his works have lately sparked the interest of several American and French scholars such as Mark Finn, Don Herron, Steve Tompkins and Patrice Louinet, who have tried to rehabilitate Howard and his fiction. I will keep a certain critical distance when dealing with these Howard scholars, as they usually do not hide that they are fans of Howard's writing and try to portray the author in a more positive light than earlier critics do. Whether – or to what extent – such a rehabilitation of Howard and his literature is possible, is the focus of this essay.

2. The Life and Work of Robert E. Howard

2.1. A Short Biography

Robert Ervin Howard, born in Peaster, Texas, in 1906, spent most of his childhood moving from town to town until his father, a doctor, settled down in Cross Plains in 1919. Robert proved an intelligent and bookish youngster, but also showed great interest in physical activities such as boxing and weightlifting. An avid reader and writer, he opted for a professional writing career after he graduated from high school. In 1924, he sold his first story to the pulp magazine *Weird Tales*. Many more followed, and by the end of the decade, he sold stories to several pulp magazines on a regular basis, which provided him with a reasonable income. His first S & S story, and arguably the first S & S story ever published, was "The Shadow Kingdom" (1929), which introduced the muscle-bound barbarian hero Kull. After writing several more Kull yarns (as he liked to call his stories), he developed a new barbarian hero whose adventures took place in the *Hyborian Age*, a fictional prehistoric time period between Kull's *Thurian Age* and the beginnings of known history. This hero – Conan the Cimmerian – would become Howard's most famous and successful creation, featuring in 23 stories of various length, including one novel, as well as in several unfinished fragments and synopses. Conan can be considered the epitome of the S & S hero, and stories featuring him are among the main targets of the criticism this sub-genre has had to face. Nevertheless, we must always keep in mind that Howard wrote hundreds of other short stories, novelettes, novellas and novels, most of which were not fantasy. Actually, the greater part of his yarns were either boxing or western stories, many of them humorous. Furthermore, Howard also wrote a vast amount of poetry that never reached the popularity of his fiction.

Despite his relatively successful writing career – according to L. Sprague de Camp, he was the person with the highest income in town for a while (170) – Howard was never satisfied with his life, and numerous conversations and correspondences he had with his friends and acquaintances make it clear that he must have suffered from depression. When his mother, terminally ill for many years, fell into a coma in 1936, Howard committed suicide. The circumstances of his suicide as well as certain forms of behavior that he displayed in his lifetime led to wild speculations about possible mental illnesses or disturbances, including an Oedipal relationship with his mother, paranoia and an inability to distinguish between reality and fiction. I will return to these speculations later in this essay.

2.2. *Howard's Heritage*

The popularity of his Conan stories, as well as the demand for S & S in general, endured after Howard's death despite the decline of the pulps. Robert E. Howard's estate passed to Dr. Pere M. Kuykendall, who commissioned science fiction author L. Sprague de Camp to write more Conan stories. From the late 50s to the early 80s, de Camp, together with Lin Carter and Björn Nyberg, subsequently wrote a number of Conan stories usually referred to as Conan *pastiches*. De Camp further completed several unfinished Conan stories as so-called *posthumous collaborations* and even turned some of Howard's unpublished non-Conan stories into Conan yarns. He also created an official time line of Conan's adventures, which included both Howard's original tales and the new pastiches. From a legal point of view, "de Camp had assumed full control over anything related to Conan" (Finn 242) by the mid–1970s. De Camp's work may have helped make the character of Conan more popular, but his practice of re-writing Howard's stories and mixing them with his own pastiches earned him a somewhat dubious reputation among Howard fans (Finn 241ff.). While the 80s and 90s saw dozens of further Conan pastiches from various authors such as Robert Jordan, Andrew J. Offut and John Maddox Roberts, it was not until the first decade of the new millennium – and after de Camp's death – that all of Howard's original and unrevised Conan stories were, for the very first time, published in complete editions that did not include any pastiche material.

Besides pastiche novels and short stories, Howard's work also formed the basis for various comic book series, most of which center around Conan. Moreover, there have been various films based on Howard's work, such as *Conan the Barbarian*, *Conan the Destroyer* or *Kull the Conqueror*, as well as an animated Conan cartoon and a live-action television show. However, all of these films and shows are based so loosely on Howard's characters that it is arguable whether we can even call them adaptations. In recent years, the gaming industry has also shown strong interest in Howard's most famous character. Conan has found his way into several pen-and-paper or tabletop role-playing games, as well as a number of computer and video games, including the massively multiplayer online role-playing game *Age of Conan*, which again spawned a board game and several novel spin-offs.

Of course, Howard not only inspired other authors to write Conan pastiches, but also had a strong impact on the development of the whole S & S genre. There are numerous S & S writers who modeled their heroes on Howard's Cimmerian. From Jake Jones (*Brak the Barbarian*) to Lin Carter (*Thongor of Lemuria*), these writers have tried to emulate Howard's characters, style, and success, and have usually failed. Others were influenced by Howard without merely copying him, such as Fritz Leiber, Karl Edward Wagner (the Kane series), Charles Saunders (*Imaro*) or David Gemmell (*Legend*, among others). In fact, there is hardly any author writing under the label of S & S who could claim that Howard did not exert a certain influence on him or her. Howard's Conan did not only serve as an inspiration for other writers, however. His influence extends to fantasy art (e. g. that of Frank Frazetta), music (in particular heavy metal), film (countless S & S movies of the 1980s), games (the *barbarian* class in *Dungeons & Dragons* and other role-playing games), and other aspects of popular culture.

3. Critical Reception

3.1. Summary

The judgment passed on Howard and his fiction by literary critics has, for the most part, been overwhelmingly negative. While quite a number of reviews and articles on Howard exist, I will focus on three texts that I believe were the most influential, and most representative. The first major critique of Howard's work was a review of *Skull-Face and Others* (a collection of various horror and fantasy tales) by Hoffman Reynold Hays for the *New York Times Book Review* from 1946. "Superman on a Psychotic Bender" is chiefly concerned with the psyche of Howard and his readers and was possibly the first article that tried to establish a link between Howard's writing and his alleged mental disturbances. The most influential writing on Howard, however, was done by L. Sprague de Camp, who, according to Mark Finn, "began the first attempts at serious criticism" (243). De Camp did so in 1975 by writing "The Miscast Barbarian", an extensive historical article on Robert E. Howard which he later expanded into a full biography called *Dark Valley Destiny*. Since no other Howard biography was widely available until Finn's *Blood & Thunder*, and since de Camp appeared to be the most knowledgeable Howard scholar at the time, his statements from "The Miscast

Barbarian" and *Dark Valley Destiny* clearly shaped the perception of Howard by the literary world. The final text I will examine is particularly interesting, as it is one of the few articles on Howard's fiction written by a German critic. Hans Joachim Alpers' "Lendenschurz, Doppelaxt, und Magie: Heroic Fantasy und verwandte Gattungen" was published in 1976 and spawned enough interest to be translated into English and published in the March 1978 issue of *Science Fiction Studies* as "Loincloth, Double Ax, and Magic: 'Heroic Fantasy' and Related Genres", albeit slightly abridged. For the sake of consistency, and with regard to readers not versed in German, this essay deals with the English version of the article. While Alpers discusses S & S in general, he spends a significant amount of time on Howard's Conan, whom he calls the "king of the genre". Considering that no German scholar has written a major article on Howard's literature ever since, it is likely that "Loincloth, Double Ax, and Magic" has significantly influenced the image of Howard's writing among academics in this country. I will closely examine the assertions Hays, de Camp, Alpers and certain others have made about Robert E. Howard and the literature he produced in the following section of this essay.

3.2. Howard's Psyche

Several critics and authors, including Hays and de Camp, suggested that Howard suffered from multiple mental illnesses or at least disturbances, the most frequently mentioned of which are "an Oedipean devotion to his mother" (de Camp, *The Science Fiction Handbook*, quoted in Finn 239) and "paranoid delusions of persecution" (de Camp 169) as a result of childhood bullying (de Camp 136). Science fiction critic Damon Knight further maintained that Howard had "the madman's advantage of believing whatever he wrote" (quoted in Finn 240), implying an inability to distinguish between fiction and reality.

Unfortunately, the length of this essay does not allow a detailed analysis of these claims, but even a short look at the facts shows that they are mere speculation. While Howard's relationship to his mother was a close one, and while there are hints at certain dysfunctions within the Howard family (Finn 218ff.), the use of terms like *Oedipean* or *Oedipal* for a person who was never examined by a psychologist seems pseudo-scholarly at best. As for Howard's alleged paranoia and inability to distinguish between reality and fiction, we must not forget how deeply the author was rooted in what Mark Finn calls the "Texan tall tale tradition" (58). Howard frequently employed hyperbole, both in his correspondence and in his stories. Thus, exaggerated statements about possible enemies or claims about past lives as a barbaric warrior may in fact be the product of a vivid imagination rather than a maladjusted mind. On a side note, in a close examination of *The Collected Letters of Robert E. Howard*, I did not find any hints for regular bullying during Howard's childhood, the alleged reason for his supposed paranoia. Neither did Finn, who affirms, "there's no evidence of ritual torture by sadistic bullies" (129).

When it comes to Howard's psyche, the only thing we can be relatively sure about is that he suffered from clinical depression. Hints for this can be found in Howard's constant harsh criticism of his own writing abilities, in spite of his success, as well as in his suicidal thoughts, which he first uttered in a letter to Tevis Clyde Smith from 1925 (Finn 221f.). Mark Finn provides further evidence of Howard's depression by mentioning the author's visit to a hospital in 1930, where he complained about symptoms which, according to Finn, "modern-day medical thinking links [...] to neurotic depressive disorder" (222). Keeping in mind how many things about Howard's life we simply do not know – as Mark Finn admits (249) – we should view any further speculation about Howard's psychological makeup made by critics and writers such as de Camp and Hays with a healthy degree of skepticism.

3.3. Morally Questionable Aspects of Howard's Work

3.3.1. Racism

Robert E. Howard's fiction has often been accused of racism, for example by Hans Joachim Alpers, who maintains that in the Conan stories, "men and women worth their salt are, like Conan himself, white", whereas "[b]lacks are cannibals and/or oversexed. The Rest of the scoundrels have crooked noses, a stealthy step, or yellow skin."

The *Britannia Online Encyclopedia* defines racism as

> any action, practice, or belief that reflects the racial world view – the ideology that humans are divided into separate and exclusive biological entities called 'races,' that there is a causal link between inherited physical traits and traits of personality, intellect, morality, and other cultural behavioral features, and that some races are innately superior to others.

There can be absolutely no doubt that according to this definition, Robert E. Howard's fiction contains racist ideas. There are Conan stories such as "The Man-Eaters of Zamboula" or "The Vale of Lost Women" in which black people are partially portrayed as described by Alpers. In the latter, Conan rescues a white girl from a tribal village, telling her he is "not such a dog as to leave a white woman in the clutches of a black man" (308). Similar statements can be found in some non-Conan stories, for example in "Marchers of Valhalla", where James Allison claims that "[a] man is no better and no worse than his feelings regarding the women of his blood, which is the true and only test of racial consciousness" (95). The most blatant example of racism in Howard's work can probably be found in "The Last White Man" (1923), which takes place in a fictitious future in which the black population has overthrown the complacent, decadent whites (Finn 84f.). This story, which has not seen large-scale publishing for obvious reasons, was meant to be "a warning to the white races" (Finn 79) and probably marks the apex of Howard's racism.

However, there are other stories in which the Texan author seems to take a different stance towards non-whites. In some of his later adventures on the African continent, Howard's Puritan hero Solomon Kane receives help from his black blood brother and mentor N'Longa and makes friends among the local population, whom he assists against slavers and flying monsters. In the Conan story "Beyond the Black River", Howard's Picts resemble stereotypical *red devils*. Yet Howard also wrote "The Thunder-Rider", a story from the perspective of a reincarnated Comanche warrior that is very similar to his James Allison yarns – only this time, it is Native American warriors that fight their way through "an age of racial drift" as a "nation of invincible warriors, sweeping a red trail of conquest" (327).

These examples show that Howard's views on people of other races were highly ambiguous. Given that his most obviously racist story, "The Last White Man", was written early in his career, while most of the positive examples mentioned above stem from the 1930s, it is likely that "as Robert matured, his viewpoint on other cultures matured, as well." This process may have been influenced by Howard's "love for the underdog of any nation or race, his admiration of black boxer Jack Johnson, and his early exposure to black storytellers in East Texas", which "all softened the hard-nosed sentiments of his youth" (Finn 80). Despite this maturation process, and despite the fact that most Texans in Howard's days might have been significantly more intolerant than he, the portrayal of non-whites, in particular blacks, in some of his stories leaves a bitter aftertaste, and we cannot completely dismiss the reproach of racism by Howard's critics.

3.3.2. *Misogyny*

Howard's writing is often associated with an objectification of women, and Alpers accordingly lists "oppression of women" as one of the characteristics of S & S. Yet, not unlike his portrayal of non-whites, Howard's treatment of women in his fiction is somewhat ambiguous and underwent several changes during his career. In his Kull stories, which were written between 1927 and 1930, there are few significant female characters, and Kull, who "was not interested in women" ("The Cat and the Skull" 89) and "had never been a lover" ("By this Axe I Rule!" 164), never develops a love interest. If we consider the Atlantean barbarian to be Howard's "attitudinal doppelgänger" (xxiii), as Steve Tompkins does, Kull's situation is highly reminiscent of young Howard's, which he described in a letter to Tevis Clyde Smith: "No, I'm not a girl-hater. I have the highest respect for the feminine sex. I just prefer other amusements as a general rule. I'm no lady's man" (quoted in Finn 85).

As a character, Kull was superseded by Conan, whose adventures Howard wrote between 1932 and 1936. While the first Conan yarns, with the notable exception of "The Frost-Giant's Daughter" and "Queen of the Black Coast", did not feature many female characters, "Black Colossus" began a trend towards scantily clad damsels in distress who have to be rescued by the barbarian, either from a supernatural menace or from the clutches of a villain. This pattern kept occurring in several of the following Conan stories and may be responsible for much of the criticism Howard's fiction has faced. Mark Finn explains this sudden trend when he notes, "Robert had a good idea of what was selling, and he tailored the Conan stories to fit the market. [...] Robert [...] went where the sales were, and Conan began rescuing the damsel *du jour* in each story, albeit with much grumbling and grousing" (173). Considering the fact that the cover of *Weird Tales* usually featured a half-naked woman and that "Black Colossus" was, unsurprisingly, the first Conan story featured on a cover, Finn's explanation seems likely.

Nonetheless, the portrayal of women in Howard's fiction has apparently evolved towards the end of his career. His last Conan story, "Red Nails", features a female protagonist named Valeria, who is not weak and in constant need of help, like many of her predecessors, but almost as proficient in battle as the Cimmerian. Other strong female heroes include Red Sonya from "The Shadow of the Vulture" and Dark Agnes, who first saw action in "The Sword Woman". Suggestions that Dark Agnes or Valeria were influenced by Howard's girlfriend Novalyne Price, whom he first met in 1933, are mere speculation, but there can be no doubt that women in Howard's fiction, against wide-spread belief, were often more than objectified damsels in distress.

In his article "The Dark Barbarian" from the anthology of the same title, Don Herron arrives at a similar conclusion pertaining to the question of misogyny in Howard's literature. Herron, who admits that "Sword-and-Sorcery deservedly has drawn critical abuse by offering a ready market for schoolboyish sexism and 'humour'" and that Howard "contributed his share of objectionable material", also believes that "[Howard] *did* transcend his worst level *frequently*" (173). Herron names one factor that may have influenced Howard's poor reputation when it comes to the portrayal of women: after examining several of the Conan pastiches written by L. Sprague de Camp and Lin Carter, he suggests that "the imitators [...] have followed the more pathetic female characterizations that may be found in Howard, rather than creating more women along the lines of Valeria or Belít" (*sic*, 173). As he notes, "Howard cannot be faulted for the 'Conan' stories he never wrote" (173f.). A closer examination of the pastiches would exceed the scope of this essay, but it is possible that criticism regarding the objectification of women – as well as repetitive plot structures – may indeed have been fueled by Howard's Conan stories, often in revised form, being marketed as a single saga together with pastiche material written by L. Sprague de Camp or Lin Carter.

3.3.3. Glorification of Violence
Many critics have taken offence at the depiction of violence in S & S fiction. Much of this criticism has been directed at the Conan stories, which are usually considered the prime example of the genre, since "what elsewhere dribbles, flows here" (Alpers). While Hays' description of Conan as "a sadistic conqueror who, when cracking heads did not solve his difficulties, had recourse to magic and the aid of Lovecraft's Elder Gods" (quoted in Finn 233) can quickly be dismissed, as Conan never shows signs of sadism (and of course, has no magical abilities), Alpers' points are more elaborate. In section 3.3 of his article, which deals with what he calls "hardcore HF [Heroic Fantasy]", he lists a number of quotes from Conan stories that describe violent acts of killing and sums up several other parts of Conan stories that he considers particularly distasteful. He continues by listing several characteristics of S & S, one of which is "a specific attitude to violence, i.e. to oppressing and killing human beings:

it is practiced not only by villains, but primarily by the heroes." According to Alpers, most S & S heroes "have scarcely any inhibitions; they kill for trivial reasons, indiscriminately and wholesale". He later concludes that one of the ideologies propagated by S & S is thus "glorification of violence, particularly killing".

Compared to Hays, Alpers seems rather more knowledgeable about the Conan stories. Still, some of his assertions indicate that he may not have studied them in great detail. For example, he does not delineate a difference between the Conan yarns written by Howard and those by de Camp or Carter. Some of the examples he gives to emphasize his point must be taken from pastiches, since Conan never "rams his spear into [an enemy's] body" in any of the original stories. Neither does Conan ever get "fixed to a magnetic column while from its top a clump of protoplasm slowly lowers itself." This event takes place in "The Curse of the Monolith" – a short story written by L. Sprague de Camp and Lin Carter. Of course, this confusion might have to do with the way the Conan stories were marketed at the time, but it still makes Alpers appear a sloppy researcher, given that he specifically referred to Conan as "Howard's Conan" at the beginning of the paragraph, only a few lines earlier.

Alpers' claims that S & S heroes "oppress human beings" and kill "indiscriminately" are highly questionable. Although many of these heroes have certain amoral traits – for example, Conan, just like Leiber's Fafhrd and Grey Mouser, lived as a thief for some time – they generally follow certain moral standards that make them easy to root for and identify with. Even though we learn that Conan plundered ships and coastal villages as a pirate, the plot of the actual Conan stories clearly establishes him as a "good guy", whereas "oppression" and "indiscriminate killing" is left to his civilized enemies. As Mark Finn puts it in reference to the Conan yarn "The God in the Bowl", "Conan is far more decent a person than the rest of the civilized men who sit in judgment of his abject barbarism" (170). In fact, we never see Conan harm a truly innocent person in any of the stories, with the possible exception of a man whom he catches in bed with his (Conan's) lover in "Rogues in the House". However, even this killing is not exactly "indiscriminate", and the man he kills is not necessarily innocent, since Howard describes him as a thug and a thief (285).

Of course, there is no denying the fact that Howard's Conan stories are full of violent, gory fight scenes, such as the following from "The Pool of the Black One", in which a female character watches a fight between pirates and giant black creatures:

> Details stood out briefly, like black etchings on a background of blood. She saw a Zingaran sailor, blinded by a great flap of scalp torn loose and hanging over his eyes, brace his straddling legs and drive his sword to the hilt in a black belly. She distinctly heard the buccaneer grunt as he struck, and saw the victim's tawny eyes roll up in sudden agony; blood and entrails gushed out over the driven blade. The dying black caught the blade with his naked hands, and the sailor tugged blindly and stupidly; then a black arm hooked about the Zingaran's head, a black knee was planted with cruel force in the middle of his back. His head was jerked back at a terrible angle, and something cracked above the noise of the fray, like the breaking of a thick branch. (270)

It is obvious that S & S depicts violence in a much more graphic and realistic fashion than most other works of fantasy. It is also apparent that fights like this tend to occur more often in S & S, simply because short stories, which are the common form for S & S, do not leave much room for padding out the plot. Nevertheless, the fact that S & S stories, especially those by Howard, contain more violence (or more graphic descriptions thereof), does not necessarily mean that they glorify it. The reader of such a passage might not feel "elevated" by the description of blood and gore, but disgusted.

S & S characters like Conan surely *do* use violence as a means to solve their conflicts, but in this respect, they are not significantly different from the protagonists of more well-established works of fantasy such as *The Lord of the Rings* or *The Chronicles of Narnia*, who also need to defeat their enemies on the battlefield. The main difference between these two types of fantasy literature lies in the heroes' motivation to fight. In his article "The Demarcation of Sword an Sorcery", Joseph A. McCullough V states that typical S & S heroes are self-motivated and serve their own agenda, whereas the protagonists of other heroic fantasy stories are usually forced into their adventures by circumstances or destiny and serve a higher cause.[1] In short, Conan fights because he chooses to do so in order to achieve his own goals, Aragorn *has to* fight in order to save Middle-earth. One might thus argue that S & S offers worse "role-models", since its heroes are chiefly concerned with their own well-being, while the protagonists of what McCullough calls "the rest of heroic fantasy" tend to use violence as a necessary means to serve a greater cause. On the other hand, we may counter this argument by adding that many atrocities have historically been committed in the name of so-called "greater causes".

Although Robert E. Howard' S & S stories do not propagate indiscriminate killing the way Alpers describes it, one could argue that they still endorse violence to a certain degree. If they glorify violence, however, they do not glorify it significantly more than other, well-established works of fantasy literature.

3.3.4. *Fascism*

Towards the end of "Loincloth, Double Ax, and Magic", Hans Joachim Alpers lists what he considers major shortcomings of the S & S genre, some of which I have already discussed. He then proceeds to tell us what his line of argumentation finally boils down to: "[t]here is but one word that sufficiently sums up all these ideological elements: fascism."

It is worth noting that the first individual to liken S & S (or heroic fantasy in general) to fascism was not Alpers, but probably Norman Spinrad, author of *The Iron Dream* (1972). This book contains the fictitious novel *The Lord of the Swastika*, written by an al-

---

[1] While many authors use the terms *S & S* and *heroic fantasy* synonymously, McCullough considers S & S to be one of two subgenres of heroic fantasy (the second subgenre being novels in the mold of *The Lord of the Rings*).

ternate-history Adolf Hitler who emigrated to the US and became a successful author of heroic fantasy and science fiction. By creating a tale that is blatantly racist, fascist and full of repressed homoeroticism, while following the plot of a supposedly typical heroic fantasy or science fiction novel, Spinrad tried to demonstrate how close these genres are linked to the prevalent ideologies of Nazi Germany. Spinrad's novel found considerable critical acclaim, including a Nebula award nomination. Ursula Le Guin praised it in her article "On Norman Spinrad's *The Iron Dream*", which appeared in the Spring 1973 issue of *Science Fiction Studies*. Le Guin writes that "taken as a parody of S & S, the book hits all its targets". She identifies S & S as "Moorcock's [...] Runestaff saga, and [...] Conan the Barbarian, and Brak the Barbarian, and those Gor books, and so on". After the publishing of "Loincloth, Double Ax, and Magic" in *Science Fiction Studies* in March 1978, Spinrad himself wrote a letter published in the next issue. Spinrad sides with Alpers, writing that the German author, except for one minor statement, "is pretty dead on" with his analysis. By the end of the 70s, it seems to have become rather fashionable to draw parallels between certain authors' works and fascism. On an ironic side note, Michael Moorcock, whose S & S tales were criticized in both Alpers' and Le Guin's articles, in his turn likened *The Lord of the Rings* to fascism in his 1978 essay "Epic Pooh". LeGuin notes that Moorcock also provided a quote for the back cover of *The Iron Dream*, in which he compared *The Lord of the Swastika* to the works of J. R. R. Tolkien, C. S. Lewis, G. K. Chesterton, and Sir Oswald Mosley.

The most reasonable way to begin our examination of Howard's work pertaining to fascism is by giving a definition of the very term itself – something most critics have failed to do. According to the *Britannica Online Encyclopedia*, fascism is a "political ideology and mass movement" that is marked by characteristics such as "extreme militaristic nationalism, contempt for electoral democracy and political and cultural liberalism, a belief in natural social hierarchy and the rule of elites, and the desire to create a *Volksgemeinschaft* (German: 'people's community'), in which individual interests would be subordinated to the good of the nation".

As this definition and the subsequent elucidations in the *Britannica* article show, fascism is a very complex concept that is not easy to define, since it incorporates ideas stemming from various schools of thought. In fact, it may be the heterogeneous nature of fascism that makes it so easy to label all sorts of works as "fascist".

There are no direct references to European fascism in Howard's S & S fiction, but his letters give us a clear idea of what Howard himself thought of it. The following letter to H. P. Lovecraft from December 1934 is only one of many:

> I do not condemn the reforms you say would be possible under Fascism. I simply do not believe they would exist under a Fascist government. Of course you can draw glowing pictures of a Fascist Utopia. But you can not prove that Fascism is anything but a sordid, retrogressive despotism, which crushes the individual liberty and strangles the intellectual life of every country it inflicts with its slimy presence ... I know it is the fad now to sneer at Democracy; but Democracy is not to blame for the troubles of the world. The men who are most to blame are the very men who now would 'save' the country under the new name of Nazis, or Fascists ... (quoted in Finn 174)

In "Twilight of the Gods: Howard and the 'Völkstumbewegung'" (*sic*), Scott Connors notes:

> Howard personally despised Mussolini and Hitler and fascism of all varieties, noting to Lovecraft in a December 1934 letter that 'outrages committed on women by the Fascists of Germany and Austria [were] characteristic, both of the Fascist movement and of the European character.' In the same letter he said that he regarded both these sprouting dictators as 'figure-heads and tools for international capitalism'. (106)

De Camp arrives at a similar conclusion, stating that "Lovecraft praised Mussolini and Fascism, Howard, to whom personal liberty was the prime political principle, denounced Mussolini as a butcher and racketeer and Fascism as despotism, enslavement, and a front for the financial oligarchy" (de Camp 148). De Camp defines Howard's political position – "racial questions aside" – as that of a "vigorously anti-authoritarian liberal" (150).

We can also find anti-authoritarian notions in Howard's fiction, especially when it comes to the Conan stories. Time and again, e. g. in "The God in the Bowl" or in "Queen of the Black Coast", Conan defies civilized authorities. Even when Howard's heroes Conan and Kull become kings, they continue to treat their subjects with respect and are bored or even frustrated by civilized customs and power structures. In "By this Axe I Rule!", Kull wants to allow the marriage between a nobleman and a slave girl, but for most of the story, his hands are tied because ancient law forbids such a marriage. The story ends with Kull shattering the law tablet, finally enabling the couple to marry (179). The predominance of individuality and liberty as major values in Howard's correspondence as well as his fiction speak of a world-picture that contradicts our definition of fascism – "in which individual interests would be subordinated to the good of the nation" – in almost every conceivable way. It is therefore safe to say that Robert E. Howard was no friend of fascism and did not consciously incorporate fascist ideology in his fiction.

The only link that might be established between Howard's work and fascism lies in notions such as Social Darwinism, certain racist beliefs, the glorification of Nordic mythology, and an interest in occult theories (e. g. those revolving around Thule and Atlantis), which were entertained by both Howard and fascist circles in Nazi Germany. There is no doubt that the inclusion of these ideas in Howard's writing may make some of his stories hard to digest for modern readers. Nonetheless, considering how wide-spread these beliefs were in Howard's days, and bearing in mind Howard's emphasis on personal liberty, it seems far-fetched to label his works as "fascist", and outright ridiculous to claim that they, or any other S & S stories, "might have the task of providing ideological preparation for the road to a new fascism" (Alpers).

4. Robert E. Howard – Rehabilitated?

After examining a number of critical reproaches that have been voiced against Howard and his work, and that seem to have somewhat shaped the public opinion of Howard, we can safely say that many of them need to be relativized. There is little factual evidence for de Camp's assertions on Howard's alleged mental disturbances, and apart from Howard's depression, we can only consider any claims about his psychological makeup as wild speculation. While we cannot deny that Howard's writings contain racist elements, the objectification of women often associated with Howard is limited to a certain number of stories. Interestingly, Howard also created several strong, self-reliant heroines that are often overlooked when discussing his fiction. Whether Howard's literature, in particular his S & S fiction, glorifies violence, is most likely a matter of definition. In any case, it does not glorify violence significantly more than other works of heroic fantasy, and when compared to today's horror films and first-person shooter games, it might actually seem quite tame. Schools of thought that also found their adherents among fascists, in particular German National Socialists, shaped the world view that shines through Howard's S & S stories. Nonetheless, an examination of Howard's correspondence shows that he was in strong opposition to European fascism. At the very core of his writing also lies a firm belief in freedom and individual liberty, which disproves most of Hans Joachim Alpers' claims pertaining to the Conan stories.

Many of the pre-conceived notions regarding the character of Conan may be the result of the vast amount of non-Howard Conan material published since his death. When we compare the sheer mass of pastiches and adaptations (including films, comics and games) to the relatively small number of actual Conan stories written by Howard, it becomes clear that the picture of Conan most people have in their minds is not necessarily that of Howard's Conan (who, for example, prefers to wear armor instead of a loincloth, and who is highly intelligent, defying the cliché of the dumb barbarian). In fact, to some degree, Conan has shared the fate of Sherlock Holmes,

Tarzan, or James Bond, whose filmic (mis-) representations are better known than the original literary characters.

As for the original Conan stories, whatever faults they may have, virtually no critic – not even Hays – denies that they are written at a competent level. Perhaps today, with Howard's work widely accessible without any additions or alterations by de Camp, interested fantasy readers can give the Conan stories, and Howard's other writings, a chance, and decide for themselves whether their merits outweigh their shortcomings.

Works Cited

Alpers, Hans Joachim. "Loincloth, Double Ax, and Magic: 'Heroic Fantasy' and Related Genres." Trans. Robert Plank. *Science Fiction Studies* 14 (1978). 28 June 2011. <http://www.depauw.edu/sfs/backissues/14/alpers14art.htm>.

Connors, Scott. "Twilight of the Gods: Howard and the 'Völkstumbewegung'". *The Barbaric Triumph*. Ed. Don Herron. Berkeley Heights: Wildside Press, 2004. 95–110.

De Camp, L. Sprague. "The Miscast Barbarian". *Literary Swordsmen and Sorcerers: The Makers of Heroic Fantasy*. Ed. L. Sprague de Camp. Sauk City: Arkham House Publishers, 1976. 135–177.

"fascism". *Britannica Online Encyclopedia*. 28 June 2011. <http://www.britannica.com/EBchecked/topic/202210/fascism>.

Finn, Mark. *Blood & Thunder: The Life and Art of Robert E. Howard*. Austin: MonkeyBrain Books, 2006.

Herron, Don. "The Dark Barbarian". *The Dark Barbarian*. Ed. Don Herron. Berkeley Heights: Wildside Press, 1984. 149–181.

Howard, Robert E. "By This Axe I Rule!" *Kull: Exile of Atlantis*. Ed. Patrice Louinet. New York: Random House, 2006. 157–180.

—. "The Cat and the Skull". *Kull: Exile of Atlantis*. Ed. Patrice Louinet. New York: Random House, 2006. 89–116.

—. "Marchers of Valhalla". *The Black Stranger and Other American Tales*. Ed. Steven Tompkins. Lincoln: University of Nebraska Press, 2005. 77–109.

—. "The Pool of the Black One". *The Coming of Conan the Cimmerian*. Ed. Patrice Louinet. New York: Random House, 2003. 251–276.

—. "Rogues in the House". *The Coming of Conan the Cimmerian*. Ed. Patrice Louinet. New York: Random House, 2003. 279–300.

—. "The Thunder-Rider". *The Black Stranger and Other American Tales*. Ed. Steven Tompkins. Lincoln: University of Nebraska Press, 2005. 320–340.

LeGuin, Ursula K. "On Norman Spinrad's *The Iron Dream*". *Science Fiction Studies* 1 (1973). 28 June 2011. <http://www.depauw.edu/sfs/backissues/1/leguin1art.htm>.

McCullough, Joseph A. V. "The Demarcation of Sword and Sorcery". *www.swordandsorcery.org*. 28 June 2011. <http://www.swordandsorcery.org/demarcation-of-sword-and-sorcery.htm>.

"racism". *Britannica Online Encyclopedia*. 28 June 2011. <http://www.britannica.com/EBchecked/topic/488187/racism>.

Spinrad, Norman. "On Alpers on Heroic Fantasy and Nazism". *Science Fiction Studies* 15 (1978). 28 June 2011. <http://www.depauw.edu/sfs/backissues/15/notes15.htm>.

"Sword and Sorcery". *The Encyclopedia of Fantasy*. Ed. John Clute and John Grant. London: Orbit, 1997.

Tompkins, Steven. "Introduction". *Kull: Exile of Atlantis*. Ed. Patrice Louinet. New York: Random House, 2006. xix–xxix.

Juliane Kreppel

RESIGNATION ODER WIDERSPRUCH?

Christoph Meckels
"Gedicht in Ermangelung eines Besseren"

Er ist angekommen. So, er ist angekommen.
Im Glück? Im Spital? Im Computer? In der eigenen Tasche?
Bei den Weisen der Vorzeit? Unsterblich im Finanzamt
    oder per Nachnahme bei den Toten?
Er ist angekommen im Gedächtnis seiner Mitwelt   5
endlich angekommen im offenen Kleid seiner Geliebten?
Auf alle Fälle: einer ist angekommen.

Das Gedicht handelt nicht von ihm.
    Es handelt von dem, der nicht ankommt.
Es sucht den Mann, der nicht auf der Party erscheint,   10
und den Namen dessen, der ohne Nachruf verschwindet
    in jeder Gesellschaftsordnung, im letzten Loch –
der nicht einverstandene Peter, der unversöhnliche Klaus,
der aussortierte, mehrmals gehäutete Hans.

Es handelt von dem, der rumläuft, allein   15
durch Babylons Städte
zwischen unversenkbaren Särgen, gescheucht durch den
    Limbo
ausgebrannt von Neinsein, Schwarzpulvergesicht,
ungerecht verteilt auf den Zorn und die Zukunft   20
heulend nach einem Wort, das ihn kennt und auslöst,
und wer vor ihm zurückweicht, wird wohl ein Mensch sein
und noch ein Mensch, zurück ins Feuilleton,
und noch ein Seelversorger in sein rechtmäßiges Amt,

und er kann sein Gesicht wieder einpacken, kann er, 25
und den Tag zurückgeben, unverbraucht an jede Musikbox,
    an nichts und niemand.

Das Gedicht und was von ihm übrig bleibt in der
    gesammelten Zukunft
handelt vom Gegensatz und von dem, der drin lebt 30
heillos, in Ermangelung eines Besseren.
In Ermangelung eines Besseren. Ja, in Ermangelung eines
    Besseren.
In Ermangelung einer zweiten Welt, einer süßen Revolution
in Ermangelung eines Gedichts oder eines Lebens 35
und in Ermangelung eines Schlafs, der die Umarmung
    entwaffnet.
Auf den Tod genau vorhanden
handelt es von der Hoffnung ohne erkennbaren Anlaß
und von dem, was ist und sein wird: leibhaftiges Nein, 40
unwiderlegbar, von keiner Antwort gewürdigt, in der
    Geschichte ohne Vernunft und Freude –
der nicht einverstandene Peter, der unversöhnliche Klaus
und die fällige Anzahlung auf ein Glas Wasser.

Das Gedicht handelt unerbittlich von jedem Dasein. 45
Seine Handlung setzt sich fort an der nächsten Ecke
    und zu jedem Zeitpunkt, in jeder Sprache,
sie sickert durch jeden Knochen ohne Anlaß.
Und was es zu tun hat und wo es hinkommt mit niemandes
    Hilfe 50
in Ermangelung eines Besseren – ja wo es hinkommt!
ja was es zu tun hat!

Christoph Meckel, geboren 1935, gilt als Verfasser von Texten (Gedichten, Erzählungen, Romanen, Essays, Kinderbüchern und Hörspielen), die sich durch eine "teils der Fantastik, teils der Realistik verpflichtete [...] Schreibweise" (Launer 89) auszeichnen. Daneben liegt von ihm ein entsprechend beschreibbares grafisches Werk vor. Als besonders kennzeichnend gilt für das Œuvre Meckels außerdem die Bedeutung autobiografischer Elemente (vgl. ebd.). Die Thematisierung persönlicher Erlebnisse geht dabei vielfach mit einer Auseinandersetzung mit gesellschaftlich relevanten Themen und Entwicklungen einher, die ihrerseits immer wieder in Verbindung mit poeotologischen Überlegungen geführt wird. Als eine der bekanntesten Arbeiten von Meckel lässt sich hierfür *Suchbild. Über meinen Vater* (1980) anführen, ein Prosawerk, in dem der Autor das Versagen seines Vaters, des Schriftstellers Eberhard Meckel (1907–1969), gegenüber dem Nationalsozialismus aufdeckt. Durchgehend begleitet von grundlegenden Reflexionen über den Akt des Erzählens und über verschiedene Ansätze des Schreibens kombiniert der Text dabei Kindheitserinnerungen des Autors, Tagebuchnotizen des Vaters und eine märchenhaft fantasievolle "Nachgeschichte". Als Frontispiz ist dem Buch schließlich eine ebenfalls Reales und Fantastisches integrierende Grafik beigefügt.

Selbstverständlich eröffnet die Kombination von Fantastik und Autobiografie (bzw. 'Realistik') in Meckels Werk im Einzelnen verschiedene und differenziert zu betrachtende Deutungsmöglichkeiten. Grundlegend lässt sich mit Uwe-Michael Gutzschhahn aber feststellen, dass Meckel die Fantasie niemals willkürlich gestaltet, sondern sie stets bewusst in ein oppositionelles Verhältnis zur Realität setzt, um damit der Gefahr zu entgehen, eine "bodenlose Phantasie" (Gutzschhahn 41) zu produzieren. Gutzschhahn erläutert dies ausführlich unter Betonung von Meckels literarischem Verantwortungsbewusstsein und unter Hervorhebung seines dichterischen Selbstverständnisses als eines an gesellschaftlichen Zusammenhängen interessierten Autors (vgl. Gutzschhahn 41–62, 154–164, 334–340).

In Christoph Meckels "Gedicht in Ermangelung eines Besseren" findet dieses Selbstverständnis exemplarisch seinen Ausdruck. Dass der Text als ein poetologischer angelegt ist, deutet schon die Platzierung der beiden existierenden Fassungen an, von der sich die erste im 1978 erschienenen *Lyrik-Katalog Bundesrepublik* findet, die zweite im 2000 veröffentlichten Gedichtband

Zähne.¹ So wird dem Text in beiden (übrigens nur marginal voneinander abweichenden) Publikationen durch sie eine programmatische Bedeutung zugesprochen: im *Lyrik-Katalog* explizit vermittels der Präsentation als "poetologisches Statement", in *Zähne* dagegen implizit durch seine Stellung am Anfang des Bandes. Offenkundig verweist darüber hinaus auch der Titel des Gedichts auf dessen poetologische Ausrichtung, denn schließlich liefert er an prominenter Stelle einen Hinweis auf die Hintergründe der Entstehung des Textes.

Die durch den Titel besonders herausgestellte Behauptung vom Verfassen eines Gedichts "in Ermangelung eines Besseren" soll als Ausgangspunkt des folgenden Interpretationsansatzes dienen. Sie ist dabei zuallererst vor dem kultur- und mentalitätsgeschichtlichen Hintergrund der ursprünglich veröffentlichten Fassung zu betrachten. Es handelt sich hierbei um die Zeit nach der radikalen Politisierung aller Lebensbereiche in den ausgehenden 1960er Jahren. Im zeitgenössischen Kontext wurde für diese eine zunehmende politische Ernüchterung festgestellt und von einer die gesamte Gesellschaft prägenden 'Tendenzwende der 1970er Jahre' gesprochen. Für die Literaturproduktion jener Zeit stellte die Literaturkritik demnach auch eine 'Tendenzwende der Literatur' fest und legte das Schreiben pauschal darauf fest, nunmehr Ausdruck von politischer Resignation statt des fortgesetzten Bestrebens zu sein, politisch Position zu beziehen. Den zeitgenössischen AutorInnen wurde dementsprechend eine Tendenz zum frustrierten Rückzug aus der Öffentlichkeit ins Private attestiert.²

Der Titel "Gedicht in Ermangelung eines Besseren" scheint dieser Zuschreibung auf den ersten Blick Recht zu geben, sieht es doch so aus, als wolle er den nachstehenden Text als Eingeständnis jeder fehlenden Alternative kennzeichnen, zum Beispiel also auch als Eingeständnis der fehlenden Möglichkeit einer öffentlich-politi-

---

¹ Vgl. Hans et al. 409–410 und Meckel, *Zähne*, 7f. Der oben abgedruckte Text folgt der Erstfassung aus dem *Lyrik-Katalog Bundesrepublik*.
² Vgl. zu diesen Zusammenhängen ausführlich Kreppel 28–46.

schen Stellungnahme. Wenngleich dies ohne eine konkrete Bezugnahme auf den vorliegenden Text geschieht, ist Meckels Lyrik der 1970er Jahre am Ende des Jahrzehnts dann tatsächlich auch entsprechend eingeschätzt worden. Beispielhaft lässt sich dafür Uwe-Michael Gutzschhahns Resümee anführen, das die Texte jener Zeit als Ausdruck der "enttäuschte[n] Hoffnung" des Autors und als Hinweis auf dessen Kapitulation vor den "Verhältnisse[n] in unserer Wirklichkeit" (164) versteht.

Zieht man demgegenüber Beurteilungen aus jüngerer Zeit hinzu, etwa Rezensionen zu dem vom *Gedicht* eingeleiteten Band *Zähne*, zeichnet sich dagegen ein anderes Verständnis ab. So verweist z. B. Christoph Bartmann in der *Frankfurter Allgemeinen Zeitung* darauf, dass viele Gedichte des Bandes – und insbesondere das Eingangsgedicht – deutlich in der "'Mein-Gedicht-ist-mein-Messer'-Tradition" stünden und sich damit bewusst "quer zum Weltlauf" stellten.[3] Besonders hebt Bartmann auf diese Weise Meckels Ansatz der poetologischen Reflexion auf die Bedeutung der Poesie im gesellschaftlichen Kontext hervor, wobei er betont, dass sich der Autor damit seit den Anfängen seines lyrischen Schaffens in den ausgehenden 1950er Jahren treu geblieben sei. Neben Bartmann stellt diesen Aspekt schließlich auch Thomas Betz in seiner Besprechung für das Forum *literaturkritik.de* heraus und verweist damit seinerseits auf Meckels fortgesetztes und kontinuierlich reflektiertes Interesse am Gesellschaftsbezug seiner Lyrik. Mit Blick auf das *Gedicht* heben beide Rezensenten in diesem Zusammenhang die von Meckel vermittelte Ansicht hervor, dass Lyrik – letztlich unabhängig vom zeitgeschichtlichen Kontext ihrer Entstehung – dazu in der Lage sei, sich zu behaupten und eine gesellschaftliche Bedeutung zu entfalten. Bezug genommen wird damit vor allem auf die entsprechend aussagekräftigen Verse "Das Gedicht und was von ihm übrig bleibt in der / gesammelten

---

[3] Bartmann. Der Ausdruck 'Mein-Gedicht-ist-mein-Messer' rekurriert auf die 1955 von Hans Bender herausgegebene Anthologie *Das Gedicht ist mein Messer*, welche poetologische Stellungnahmen politischer Lyriker versammelt.

Zukunft / handelt vom Gegensatz und von dem, der drin lebt / heillos, in Ermangelung eines Besseren" (Vs. 28–31).

Vor diesem Hintergrund ist nun noch einmal zum historischen Kontext der Erstfassung des Gedichts zurückzukehren und anzumerken, dass die meisten zeitgenössischen AutorInnen der durch die Literaturkritik beförderten Feststellung von einer Tendenzwende der Literatur in den 1970er Jahren vehement widersprochen haben. Deutlich wird dies in individuellen poetologischen Stellungnahmen sowie – stellvertretend vorgetragen von Jürgen Theobaldy – in der so genannten 'Lyrik-Diskussion 77'. Dabei handelt es sich um einen 1977 in fünf Ausgaben der Literaturzeitschrift *Akzente* geführten Streit um das eng mit dem Begriff der 'Tendenzwende' verbundene Schlagwort der 'Neuen Subjektivität'.[4] Dieses war von Seiten der Literaturkritik angesichts der deutlichen Hinwendung der zeitgenössischen Lyrik zur individuellen, persönlichen Mitteilung eingeführt und als Merkmal des nun vermeintlich unpolitischen Dichtens bestimmt worden. Als Ausgangspunkt diente dabei das durch die idealistische Ästhetik (d. h. insbesondere durch G. W. F. Hegel) geprägte Verständnis von Lyrik als der subjektiven Gattung, die wesentlich durch den poetischen Prozess der Verinnerlichung gekennzeichnet sei und die sich damit jeglichem zeitkritischen Impetus verweigere.[5]

Eine tiefer gehende Erläuterung dieses Lyrikverständnisses ist im gegebenen Zusammenhang nicht notwendig. Entscheidend ist hier lediglich der Hinweis, dass dieses grundlegend mit der Vorstellung von der Autonomie der Kunst einhergeht und dass sich die AutorInnen der 1970er Jahre von eben dieser Vorstellung ausdrücklich abgegrenzt haben. Jürgen Theobaldy stellt diesen Aspekt deutlich heraus, wenn er im Rahmen der 'Lyrik-Diskussion 77' die "alte bürgerliche Auffassung" verwirft, nach der das schreibende Ich "als ein autonomer Körper in welchen Stürmen auch immer erscheint, als ein monolithischer Block mit 'Klüften und Brüchen', angesie-

---

[4] Die 'Lyrik-Diskussion 77' ist dokumentiert in Hans 453–512.
[5] Vgl. dazu ausführlich Kreppel 47–68.

delt oder so dahintreibend auf der geschichtsabgewandten Seite der Erde" (465).

Der Rekurs auf das idealistische Subjektivitäts-Kriterium wird dem programmatischen Anspruch der 1970er-Jahre-Lyrik damit offensichtlich nicht gerecht.[6] Hervorzuheben ist aber, dass die zeitgenössischen AutorInnen die Relevanz des Subjektiven für ihre Lyrik gleichwohl betont haben. Wie es Theobaldy zusammenfasst, manifestiert sich dies in dem Versuch, die Texte durch eine Subjektivität zu kennzeichnen, die als "durchdrungen von gesellschaftlichen Widersprüchen" (Theobaldy 464) verstanden und die im Akt der Rezeption entsprechend nachvollzogen werden soll. Das Schlagwort von der 'Neuen Subjektivität' wurde in diesem Sinne als Bezeichnung für eine neue Form von lyrischer Subjektivität aufgegriffen, die sich von der traditionellen Bestimmung durch einen impliziten, von Seiten der Leserschaft nachzuempfindenden Gesellschaftsbezug abgrenzen sollte.

Jener Gesellschaftsbezug ist – wie hier zu betonen ist – keinesfalls mit der in den ausgehenden 1950er und den beginnenden 1960er Jahren verbreiteten Vorstellung von einer immanenten Gesellschaftlichkeit der Lyrik gemäß dem Verständnis von Th. W. Adorno gleichzusetzen. Diese basiert ihrerseits nämlich auf der Gültigkeit der in den 1970er Jahren verworfenen traditionellen Vorstellung von lyrischer Subjektivität.[7] Demgegenüber lässt sich der von den zeitgenössischen AutorInnen anstrebte Gesellschaftsbezug als begründet durch die Vorstellung von einer lyrischen *Intersubjektivität* begreifen. Der Begriff der 'Intersubjektivität' fokussiert dabei insbesondere auf die rezeptionsästhetische Ausrichtung der 1970er-Jahre-Lyrik. Das heißt, er betont den Anspruch, die von ihren VerfasserInnen verteidigte kritische Auseinandersetzung mit Fragen der eigenen Zeit innerhalb der Texte durch eine spezifische Textgestaltung auch bei der Leserschaft anzuregen.

---

[6] Zu der daraus resultierenden Problematik der Adaption des idealistischen Lyrik-Verständnisses durch die Literaturkritik der 1970er Jahre vgl. Gnüg.
[7] Zu Adornos Verständnis von der immanenten Gesellschaftlichkeit der Lyrik vgl. seine "Rede über Lyrik und Gesellschaft".

Für das Konzept der lyrischen Intersubjektivität ist angesichts dessen vor allem festzuhalten, dass es für die lyrische Mitteilung das sprachlich erzeugbare Potenzial einer (relativen) Deutungsoffenheit herausstellt. Dieser rezeptionsästhetisch relevante Aspekt lässt sich mit Hubert Zapf durch den Hinweis darauf erklären, dass die

> Intersubjektivität der Sprache und des Verstehens [...] niemals garantiert oder vollständig, sondern mit dem geschichtlichen, kulturellen und persönlichen Horizont der Subjekte vermittelt [ist]. Sie ist daher [...] eine 'gebrochene Intersubjektivität', die durch das kommunikative Handeln der konkreten Subjekte stets neu realisierbar ist, aber gleichwohl eine unhintergehbare normative Implikation von Sprache selbst darstellt. (Zapf 241)

Legt man den hier skizzierten und durch den Begriff der 'Intersubjektivität' theoretisch untermauerten Ansatz der 1970er-Jahre-Lyrik einer Interpretation von Meckels "Gedicht in Ermangelung eines Besseren" zugrunde, lässt sich zeigen, dass der Text ihn – ganz gemäß seiner ursprünglichen Veröffentlichung als poetologisches Statement – selbst vermittelt. Als erstes ist dabei auf die Tendenz zu einer gewissen Widerspruchs-Haltung zu verweisen. Sie zeigt sich beispielhaft direkt im Eingangsvers, der mit dem einleitenden Satz "Er ist angekommen" zunächst die Vorstellung von Ruhe und Geborgenheit hervorruft, der diese durch die spöttische Repetition der Aussage im Folgesatz "So, er ist angekommen" sogleich aber wieder in Frage stellt. Auf den ersten Vers des Gedichts folgen dazu passend eine Reihe von Fragen, die den Zustand des Angekommenseins nachdrücklich ironisieren. Es sind dies Fragen nach dem Ort der vermeintlichen Ankunft, die als mögliche, zum Teil aber auch als absurde Antworten konzipiert sind:

> Im Glück? Im Spital? Im Computer? In der eigenen Tasche?
> Bei den Weisen der Vorzeit? unsterblich im Finanzamt
> oder per Nachnahme bei den Toten?

Er ist angekommen im Gedächtnis seiner Mitwelt
endlich angekommen im offenen Kleid seiner Geliebten?
(Vs. 2–6).

Indem diese Fragen sowohl nachvollziehbare als auch absurde Alternativen formulieren, vermitteln sie nicht nur eine ironische Haltung, sondern erinnern auch ganz allgemein an das, was Meckels Lyrik schon in den 1950er und 1960er Jahren geprägt hat: an die "charakteristische Verschmelzung surrealer Einfälle mit herkömmlichen Denkgewohnheiten" (Brackert-Rausch 223). Eine zentrale Rolle spielt im Text demnach die Fantasiewelt bzw. die Einbringung fantastischer Elemente. Der Begriff des 'Fantastischen' ist in diesem Zusammenhang zwar relativ weit zu fassen, angesichts der prägenden Tendenz zum Widerspruch ist gleichwohl aber davon auszugehen, dass das Fantastische hier ebenso wie in einem engeren Sinne dazu dient, der im Text vorgestellten Realität eine Gegenwelt entgegenzusetzen. Im Rekurs auf die gängige Bestimmung der literarischen Fantastik ist dabei hervorzuheben, dass jene Gegenwelt, damit sie "einen Freiraum der Imagination eröffnen" kann, grundsätzlich "eine 'Deutungsoffenheit'" (Krah 68f.) aufweisen muss.

Die fantastischen Elemente in Meckels *Gedicht* sind demnach geradezu dazu prädestiniert, dem Ansatz der Intersubjektivität gerecht zu werden. Ihr Einsatz sollte, auch wenn zu konstatieren ist, dass er in Meckels Werk der 1970er Jahre weit weniger dominant ist als in früheren Texten (Gutzschhahn 164), deshalb nicht übersehen und weiterhin als Ausdruck einer grundlegend oppositionellen Haltung gegenüber der Realität gedeutet werden.

Diese Haltung wird in Meckels *Gedicht in Ermangelung eines Besseren* im Folgenden schließlich auch explizit poetologisch erklärt. Dazu erläutert der Text im Anschluss an die einleitenden Verse in vier weiteren Abschnitten die Verweigerung des Gedichts gegenüber der Rede vom 'Angekommen-Sein'. Emphatisch heißt es dabei direkt zu Beginn des zweiten Abschnitts: "Das Gedicht handelt nicht von ihm [dem, der angekommen ist]. / Es handelt von dem, der nicht ankommt" (Vs. 8f.). Die folgenden Verse schildern kontrastiv zum Eingangsvers dementsprechend Momente der Einsamkeit, der Fremdheit und der Rastlosigkeit, d. h. sie handeln "von dem, der rumläuft, allein / durch Babylons Städte / zwischen unversenkbaren Särgen, gescheucht durch den / Limbo" (Vs. 15–18). Darüber hinaus verweisen sie auf die Unterprivilegierten "jeder Gesellschaftsordnung", auf den "nicht einverstandene[n] Peter", den "unversöhnliche[n] Klaus," und den "aussortierte[n], mehrmals gehäutete[n] Hans" (Vs. 12–14). Im Wesentlichen artikuliert sich die Opposition gegenüber der Realität hier also im Fokus auf lyrische Handlungselemente, die exemplarisch auf Mängel und Probleme des gesellschaftlichen Lebens verweisen. Der Widerspruch zu der scheinbaren Ruhe und Geborgenheit, die der erste Satz des Gedichts "Er ist angekommen" konnotiert, wird damit konsequent fortgesetzt, und zwar als Widerspruch gegen eine Lyrik, in der beides widerspruchsfrei in Erscheinung tritt.

Weiterhin spielt auch hierbei die dichterische Fantasie eine Rolle. So wird an ihrer Relevanz nun vor allem dadurch festgehalten, dass die im Anschluss an den ersten Abschnitt vorgestellten Handlungselemente frei assoziiert aneinander gereiht, statt in der logischen Folge eines nachvollziehbaren Handlungszusammenhangs entwickelt werden. Obwohl sich der lyrische Sachverhalt offenkundig auf Aspekte des gesellschaftlichen Lebens bezieht, verunsichert dies den Realitätsbezug des Gedichts und die Zusammenhänge des dargestellten Inhalts merklich. Der Bezug auf die Realität wird demnach immer wieder durch die Einbringung von Elementen gestört, die nicht in den Kontext dieser Realität zu passen scheinen.

Diese Beobachtungen sind für die Auslegung des Gedichts als eines poetologischen Statements noch weiterreichend von Bedeutung. So präzisiert der Text, indem er einerseits die Erwartung einer konsistenten, an der gesellschaftlichen Realität orientierten Bestimmung von lyrischen Handlungselementen aufbaut, sich ihr andererseits durch die Verwirrung einzelner Zusammenhänge aber zugleich verweigert, nun nämlich auch implizit poetologisch sein offensives Konzept des Widerspruchs. Die Präzisierung macht dabei deutlich, dass jenes Konzept in der Auseinandersetzung mit realen Verhältnissen grundlegend gegen alles eindeutig Erklärbare und eindeutig Festgelegte im Kontext von Dichtung opponiert.

Das Potenzial, das der Text damit zu entfalten vermag, zeigt sich besonders eindrücklich im mittleren Abschnitt des Gedichts, in dem "von dem, der rumläuft, allein / durch Babylons Städte" (Vs. 15) berichtet wird, er sei

> ausgebrannt von Neinsein, Schwarzpulvergesicht,
> ungerecht verteilt auf den Zorn und die Zukunft
> heulend nach einem Wort, das ihn kennt und auslöst,
> und wer vor ihm zurückweicht, wird wohl ein Mensch sein
> und noch ein Mensch, zurück ins Feuilleton,
> und noch ein Seelversorger in sein rechtmäßiges Amt,
> und er kann sein Gesicht wieder einpacken, kann er,
> und den Tag zurückgeben, unverbraucht an jede Musikbox,
> an nichts und niemand. (Vs. 19–27)

Zunächst einmal kann anhand dieser Verszeilen die Feststellung verifiziert werden, dass es sich bei den angeführten lyrischen Inhaltselementen um frei assoziierte Vorstellungen handelt. Dabei ist anzumerken, dass dieser Eindruck nicht zuletzt auch durch die sprachliche Gestaltung des Textabschnitts entsteht, d. h. durch den eigentümlichen Sprachgebrauch, der den zitierten Absatz prägt. Dieser tritt beispielhaft in Gestalt der Wortschöpfungen "Neinsein" und "Schwarzpulvergesicht" hervor (Vs. 19) und macht sich zudem in der Verwendung des veralteten Begriffs vom "Seelversorger" bemerkbar (Vs. 24).[8] Darüber hinaus ist die Sprache der angeführten Textpassage durch verschiedene grammatikalische Besonderheiten gekennzeichnet: so etwa durch die im Plural stehende Genitivkonstruktion "Babylons Städte" (Vs. 16), durch den Gebrauch des amerikanischen Ausdrucks "Limbo" für 'Limbus' (V. 18)[9] sowie durch

---

[8] Nachweise für die Verwendung des Begriffs vom 'Seelversorger' (für 'Seelsorger') finden sich im Grimmschen Wörterbuch (vgl. Grimm 55).
[9] Die Rückführung des Ausdrucks 'Limbo' auf 'Limbus' ergibt sich aus Meckels Erläuterungen zu dem in seinem Werk wiederholt verwendeten Begriff 'Limbo' in der Vorbemerkung zu seinem Grafikzyklus *Limbo, ein Zyklus*. Der Rückgriff auf den amerikanischen Wortgebrauch wird hier ausdrücklich vermerkt (vgl. Meckel, *Limbo* 3).

den Verzicht auf sinnstiftende Verben in den Verszeilen "und noch ein Mensch, zurück ins Feuilleton, / und noch ein Seelvorsorger in sein rechtmäßiges Amt" (Vs. 23f.). Sprachlich auffällig ist zuletzt außerdem der Wechsel von der asyndetischen zur syndetischen Reihung der Verseinheiten, der durch die rhythmische Segmentierung der Verszeilen und den Übergang zur anaphorischen Versgestaltung noch besonders hervorgehoben wird.

In Bezug auf die hier beschriebenen sprachlichen Eigenheiten ist hervorzuheben, dass sie die lyrische Mitteilung als dichterisch gestaltet und als betont subjektiv kennzeichnen. Für die damit herausgestellte poetische Form der Sprachverwendung ist allerdings auch festzustellen, dass sie keineswegs rein subjektiv und damit 'einsinnig' bleibt, sondern dass sie – ganz im Sinne des Anspruchs der Erzeugung einer (lyrischen) Intersubjektivität – Deutungsoffenheit produziert. Dies lässt sich vor allem angesichts der Tatsache behaupten, dass einzelne der sprachlich verschlüsselten Handlungselemente bei genauerer Betrachtung als Motive bzw. als Teile eines Motivzusammenhangs rekonstruierbar sind, sich dabei als solche aber keineswegs widerspruchslos in die mögliche Rekonstruktion einfügen. Sie bieten sich also einer bestimmten 'traditionellen' Deutung an, weisen diese aber zugleich als nicht festgelegt aus.

Nachvollziehbar wird diese Lesart, wenn man den Ausdruck "Babylons Städte" mit der Kritik an "jeder Gesellschaftsordnung" (Vs. 12) in Verbindung bringt und als Hinweis auf die zunehmende Verbreitung 'babylonischer Zustände' in der Gesellschaft versteht. Babylon symbolisiert danach die "verruchte Stadt" (Daemmrich 333) im Sinne der christlichen Tradition, d. h. die "große Hure Babylon" (*Bibel* Offb. 17–19), die schließlich an ihrer Dekadenz zugrunde geht. "Babylon-City",[10] das in Meckels Werk wiederholt als "Vorhölle und [...] Moloch unter allen modernen Metropolen" (Glossner 16) gestaltet wird, lässt sich gemäß dieser Verbindung als

---

[10] Dieser Ausdruck findet sich anstelle der im Plural gehaltenen Genitivkonstruktion "Babylons Städte" in der späteren Fassung vom "Gedicht in Ermangelung eines Besseren", die in dem Band *Zähne* abgedruckt ist (vgl. Meckel, *Zähne* 7).

ein Element intertextueller Zusammenhänge deuten. In erster Linie scheint es dabei allerdings nicht auf den Nachweis einer spezifischen Einzeltextreferenz anzukommen, sondern vielmehr auf das allgemeine Faktum einer offenen, vom Leser erst zu rekonstruierenden Bezugnahme auf den Mythos Babylon.[11]

Für diese Deutung spricht insbesondere die sprachliche Verfremdung des Motivs ("Babylons Städte"), die in der Pluralform gleichsam auf eine unüberschaubare Potenzierung dessen verweist, was traditionell mit der 'verruchten Stadt' verbunden ist. Darüber hinaus wird sie aber auch durch die Möglichkeit bestätigt, die Anspielung auf Babylon mit anderen Handlungselementen des Textes zu verbinden und auf diese Weise sinngenerierende Bezüge zwischen Kontexten herzustellen, die von ihrer Tradition her ursprünglich zu unterscheiden sind. Exemplarisch ist dafür die Verknüpfung von Babylon mit dem "Limbo" als "Aufenthaltsort der Gerechten vor der Erlösung, oder: Zwischenwelt, Vorhölle" (Meckel, *Limbo* 3), die sich – ganz unabhängig von einer traditionellen Begründung – aus der syntaktischen Struktur von Meckels Versen ergibt.[12] Und beispielhaft ist im gegebenen Textzusammenhang außerdem die Vergegenwärtigung der 'babylonischen Sprachverwirrung', die der Vers "heulend nach einem Wort, das ihn kennt und auslöst" (Vs. 21) evoziert. – Denn der Turmbau zu Babel, der damit in Erinnerung gerufen wird, steht schließlich in einem anderen biblischen Kontext als der Niedergang der 'großen Hure Babylon'.[13]

---

[11] Demnach ist der oben verwendete Begriff der 'Intertextualität' hier nicht im engen Sinne einer markierten Intertextualität gemeint, sondern in einem erweiterten Sinne, der gleichwohl aber auch von den antihermeneutischen, subjektlosen Intertextualitätskonzepten des Poststrukturalismus abzugrenzen ist.

[12] Der Begriff des 'Limbus', auf den Meckel hier rekurriert, geht zurück auf die katholische Lehre von der Vorhölle als Aufenthaltsort der vorchristlichen Gerechten und der ungetauft gestorbenen Kinder (vgl. Höfer und Rahner). Entscheidend ist dabei im gegebenen Zusammenhang, dass diese Lehre (anders als der Mythos Babylon) nicht aus der Bibel begründet werden kann.

[13] Zum Turmbau zu Babel vgl. *Die Bibel*. 1. Mose 11; zum Niedergang der 'großen Hure Babylon' vgl. *Die Bibel*. Offb. 17–19.

Der Ausdruck "Babylons Städte" lässt sich durch die entsprechend neu gestifteten Zusammenhänge schließlich spezifizieren. Im erneuerten Sinn fasst er Orte zusammen, in denen nicht nur Dekadenz herrscht, sondern auch menschliche Überheblichkeit und gesellschaftliche Verblendung.[14] Es sind dies Orte, die durch menschliches Verschulden zu einem nahezu unbewohnbaren Gebiet geworden sind,[15] und die – wie Herbert Glossner es in einem Überblick über Meckels "babylonische Metaphern" konstatiert – das Bild einer Welt hervorrufen, in der "nur noch Profit und Effizienz gewertet werden" (18). – So etwa Profit und Effizienz vom Zustand Angekommen-Seins, wie ihn der Anfang des *Gedichts* gemäß den obigen Ausführungen anführt und sogleich offensiv in Frage stellt.

Vor dem Hintergrund der hier angestellten Überlegungen lässt sich für Meckels *Gedicht in Ermangelung eines Besseren* somit auch unabhängig von dem von Bartmann und Betz in ihren Rezensionen herausgestellten Zitat ein kritischer Gesellschaftsbezug nachweisen. Von Bedeutung ist, dass der Text damit seinem eigenen Titel, das heißt der Rede von der Produktion des *Gedichts* "in Ermangelung eines Besseren", widerspricht. Die Formulierung des Titels kann demnach nämlich selbst als Konsequenz der poetologischen Forderung nach einer Dichtung aufgefasst werden, die gegen alles Eindeutige opponiert, und dies schließt es letztlich aus, den Titel, wie eingangs skizziert, als eindeutigen Ausdruck der Rekapitulation vor den gesellschaftlichen Verhältnissen bzw. als Eingeständnis jeder fehlenden öffentlichen Handlungsalternative zu verstehen.

Zu dieser Auslegung passt weiterhin, wie die Rede von der "Ermangelung eines Besseren" schließlich im vierten Abschnitt des

---

[14] Diese Konnotation ergibt sich aus der Evokation der Geschichte vom Turmbau zu Babel, deren traditionelle Bedeutung Meckel zuvor schon in seinem Grafikzyklus *Der Turm* aktualisiert hat (vgl. dazu auch Gutzschhahn 349).

[15] Vgl. dazu Meckels Erläuterung zu der spezifischen Verwendung des Begriffs 'Limbo' im Amerikanischen. Danach bezeichnet 'limbo' "ein Gebiet (häufig am Rand großer Städte), das als nicht bewohnbar gilt. In ihm vermischen sich Müllhalden, Rohbauten, Slums, Abstellgleise, Ödgelände, Fabriken, Trampelpfade, Höhlen, Ruinen und Wracks etc." (Meckel, *Limbo* 3).

Gedichts (das heißt in dem von Bartmann und Betz herausgehobenen Zitat) aufgegriffen wird. So geschieht dies, indem ihr Bezug nun bewusst offen gehalten wird. Diese Beobachtung ergibt sich aus der Möglichkeit, den Vers "heillos, in Ermangelung eines Besseren" (Vs. 31) entweder auf das Subjekt und das dazugehörige Prädikat des Satzzusammenhangs zu beziehen, in dem er steht – also auf "Das Gedicht [...] handelt [...]" (Vs. 28–30) –, oder aber auf das Objekt, das heißt auf den "Gegensatz", in dem, wie es heißt, einer "lebt" (Vs. 30). Im ersten Fall wäre dies so zu verstehen, dass das Gedicht "heillos, in Ermangelung eines Besseren" vom Leben im Gegensatz "handelt", im zweiten Fall dagegen so, dass der, der "im Gegensatz [...] lebt", dies "heillos, in Ermangelung eines Besseren" tut. Bemerkenswerter Weise erscheint es gar nicht vorrangig von Bedeutung, für welche Lesart man sich schließlich entscheidet. Viel relevanter ist nämlich, dass das *Gedicht* durch die erneute und nun fast trotzig wirkende Wiederholung der Rede von der "Ermangelung eines Besseren" im Folgenden selbst als oppositionelle Reaktion auf jenen Umstand der "Ermangelung" ausgewiesen wird und somit nicht nur als Thematisierung des 'Lebens im Gegensatz' zu lesen ist, sondern zugleich als dessen Repräsentation. Das Schreiben des *Gedichts* kann in Anbetracht dessen auch als mögliche Alternative zu den exemplarisch angeführten fehlenden Alternativen "einer zweiten Welt, einer süßen Revolution [...] eines Lebens / und [...] eines Schlafs, der die Umarmung entwaffnet" (Vs. 34–36), begriffen werden.

Abschließend ist damit zu konstatieren, dass Meckels "Gedicht in Ermangelung eines Besseren" als poetologisches Gedicht die Überzeugung des Autors von und sein Interesse an der kontinuierlichen Bedeutung der Poesie im gesellschaftlichen Kontext vermittelt. Dafür spricht im letzten Abschnitt auch noch einmal der Hinweis darauf, dass vom "Gedicht" etwas "übrig bleibt in der gesammelten Zukunft" und dass sich "seine Handlung [...] fort[setzt] an der nächsten Ecke" (Vs. 46). Der Text ist demnach offenkundig nicht als Ausdruck von Resignation zu verstehen, sondern vielmehr als Widerspruch gegen Resignation. Wie gezeigt werden konnte, macht er dabei sowohl explizit als auch implizit poeotologisch deutlich, auf welche Weise sich ein solcher Widerspruch seinem Autor nach dichterisch umsetzen lässt: in Form einer Poesie nämlich, die durch einen intersubjektiv wirksamen Sprachgebrauch gekennzeichnet ist, bei dem nicht zuletzt auch die Einbringung fantastischer Elemente eine Rolle spielt.

Literaturverzeichnis

Adorno, Theodor W. "Rede über Lyrik und Gesellschaft". *Noten zur Literatur I*. Frankfurt a. M.: Suhrkamp, 1958. 73–104.

Bartmann, Christoph. "Nuß und Motte: Christoph Meckels neue Verse". *Frankfurter Allgemeine Zeitung* v. 17. 01. 2001.

Bender, Hans, Hg. *Mein Gedicht ist mein Messer: Lyriker zu ihren Gedichten.* Heidelberg: Rothe, 1955.

Betz, Thomas. *Das Gedicht und was von ihm übrig bleibt: Fragen zu Christoph Meckels Gedichtband "Zähne"*. 30. Juni 2011. <http://www.literaturkritik.de/public/rezension.php?rez_id=4975>.

Brackert-Rausch, Gisela. "Christoph Meckel". *Schriftsteller der Gegenwart. Deutsche Literatur.* Ed. Klaus Nonnenmann. Olten/Freiburg i. Br.: Walter, 1963. 221–227.

Daemmrich, Horst S., und Ingrid G. Daemmrich. "Stadt". *Themen und Motive in der Literatur. Ein Handbuch.* Ed. Horst S. und Ingrid G. Daemmrich. Zweite überarbeitete und erweiterte Auflage. Tübingen/Basel: Francke Verlag, 1995. 332–37.

Die Bibel. Nach der Übersetzung Martin Luthers. Mit Apokryphen und Wortkonkordanz. Stuttgart: Deutsche Bibelgesellschaft, ²1994.

Glossner, Herbert. "Christoph Meckel. Essay". *Das KLG auf CD-ROM. Kritisches Lexikon zur deutschsprachigen Gegenwartsliteratur.* Ed. Heinz L. Arnold. München: edition text + kritik, 1999. 3–19.

Gnüg, Hiltrud. "Was heißt 'Neue Subjektivität'?" *Merkur* 356 (1978): 60–75.

Grimm, Jacob, und Wilhelm Grimm. *Deutsches Wörterbuch. Zehnten Bandes erste Abteilung* [Bd. 10, I]. Leipzig: Verlag von S. Hirzel, 1905.

Gutzschhahn, Uwe-Michael. *Prosa und Lyrik Christoph Meckels.* Mit einem vollständigen bibliographischen Verzeichnis von Uwe-Michael Gutzschhahn und Wulf Segebrecht. Köln: Literarischer Verlag Braun, 1979.

Hans, Jan, Uwe Herms und Ralf Thenior, Hg. *Lyrik-Katalog Bundesrepublik. Gedichte. Biographien. Statements.* München: Goldmann, 1978.

Höfer, Josef, und Karl Rahner, Hg. *Lexikon für Theologie und Kirche.* Begründet von Dr. Michael Buchberger. Zweite, völlig neu bearbeitete Auflage. Bd. 6. Freiburg: Herder, 1961. 1057–1059 [Eintrag: "Limbus"].

Krah, Hans. "Phantastisch". *Reallexikon der deutschen Literaturwissenschaft, Bd. III.* Ed. Jan-Dirk Müller. Berlin/New York: Walter de Gruyter, 2003. 68–71.

Kreppel, Juliane: *"In Ermangelung eines Besseren"? Poetik und Politik in bundesrepublikanischen Gedichten der 1970er Jahre.* Köln/Weimar/Wien: Böhlau Verlag, 2009.

Launer, Christoph: "Meckel, Christoph". *Killy Literaturlexikon. Autoren und Werke des deutschsprachigen Kulturraumes.* 2., vollständig überarbeitete Auflage, Bd. 8. Ed. Wilhelm Kühlmann. Berlin/New York: de Gruyter, 2010. 88–90.

Meckel, Christoph. "Gedicht in Ermangelung eines Besseren". *Lyrik-Katalog Bundesrepublik. Gedichte. Biographien. Statements.* Hg. Jan Hans, Uwe Herms und Ralf Thenior. München: Goldmann, 1978. 408–10.

—. *Limbo, ein Zyklus.* Stuttgart: Steiner, 1987.

—. *Suchbild: Über meinen Vater.* Mit einer Grafik des Autors. Düsseldorf: Claassen, 1980.

—. *Der Turm. Radierungen.* München: Ellermann, 1961.

—. *Zähne: Gedichte.* München: Hanser, 2000.

Theobaldy, Jürgen. "Literaturkritik, astrologisch: Zu Jörg Drews' Aufsatz über Selbsterfahrung und Neue Subjektivität in der Lyrik." *Lyrik-Katalog Bundesrepublik. Gedichte. Biographien. Statements.* Ed. Jan Hans [u. a.]. München: Goldmann, 1978. 463–467.

Zapf, Hubert. "Intersubjektivität". *Metzler Lexikon Literatur- und Kulturtheorie.* Ed. Ansgar Nünning. Stuttgart/Weimar: Metzler, 1998. 240–41.

Dominik Becher

EDWIN MORGANS PANOPTIKUM

Stimmen aus dem Werk eines Whittrick

Ein Mann, in seinem Werk so vielfältig wie Schottland. Dies ist der Konsens vieler Kritiker, Biographen und Journalisten über den 2010 Verstorbenen, der als erster das 2004 eingeführte Amt des *Scots Makar* bekleidete, des Schottischen Nationaldichters. Ihn hier als einen Dichter der Phantastik zu präsentieren, wäre durchaus möglich, denn Science Fiction, Folklore und Mythos sind häufig anzutreffende Elemente seiner Arbeit. Jedoch, so paradox es klingen mag, würde eine klassische Genredefinition diesem Mann nicht gerecht werden, den man vielleicht besser mit seiner eigenen Metapher als *whittrick* (Scots: "Wiesel") bezeichnen könnte. Um Edwin Morgans Œuvre zu charakterisieren, muss man tiefer gehen, hin zur der Phantastik und aller Fiktion zugrunde liegenden Schöpferkraft der Imagination, welche sich frei bei allen Genres und Schreibmodi bedienen darf. So zum Beispiel haftet dem Schottischen Titel *Makar* noch deutlich sichtbar der germanische "Macher" an, der originär Herstellende, und genau dies war Edwin Morgan. Der Wiesel hingegen ist eine von ihm erfundene tricksterhafte Persona,[1] welche das Scharfsinnige, Schelmische, Verspielte, und auch Bissige des Autors manifestiert – vergleichbar vielleicht mit Ted Hughes' "Thought-Fox" (vgl. Jackaman 177).

In "Dialogue II: Hieronymos Bosch and Johann Faust" legte Edwin Morgan eine Beschreibung des *whittrick* in den Mund von Hieronymus Bosch:

---

[1] Namensgebend für seinen Gedichtband *The Whittrick: a Poem in Eight Dialogues*.

> I once had a whittrick, now painted over,
> A tiny whittrick, very lithe and smiling.
> No, you won't find him anywhere now, he's gone.
> Yet he became the focus of this picture,
> I built the turbulence round his irony,
> I saw the monstrous place fixed by his bright eye.
> And then my brush had covered him up as if
> He had played his part only to disappear.
> The painting was complete. And now fantasy
> And reality, the energies of work
> And the energies of imagination
> Swirl in me so hauntingly, so mockingly
> That I wonder, was the whittrick ever there?
> (*Collected Poems* 85)

Der Wiesel ist ironisch-inspirierend am Werk an der Grenze zwischen Phantasie und Realität, hält beides im Gleichgewicht und verschwindet letztlich hinter der künstlerischen Gestaltgebung. Eine treffende Metapher für Edwin Morgan selbst, der im Versuch, sich ihm über sein Werk zu nähern, eine ähnlich facettenreiche und flüchtige Gestalt annimmt.

Im Folgenden sollen, zwangsläufig auszugshaft, einige der Stimmen präsentiert werden, welche Morgan erschuf und die im konkreten motivischen oder figurativen Bezug zu gängigen Themen der Phantastik stehen, am ehesten im Gewande des Mythos oder der Science Fiction. Weil Edwin Morgan hierzulande wenig bekannt ist, möchte ich mit einer biographischen Notiz beginnen.

Stimme Schottlands

Als zurückhaltend und freundlich beschrieben, mit einem ausgeprägten Sinn für das Private, wirkte Edwin Morgan bis zu seiner Berufung zum Nationalpoeten durch das schottische Parlament eher über sein Werk und seine persönliche Erscheinung als durch die Medien, die viele seiner Gedichte inspirierten. In Schottland, wo eine im Vergleich zu Deutschland lebendigere poetische Tradition wirkt, wurde Edwin Morgan als Stimme von Glasgow und schließlich der Nation hochgeschätzt. Seine Werke hatten große Präsenz im öffentlichen Raum.[2] Zur Eröffnung des Parlamentsgebäudes in Holyrood (Edinburgh) 2004 schrieb er die vielzitierten Zeilen:

> What do the people want of the place? They want it to be filled with thinking persons as open and adventurous as its architecture.
> A nest of fearties is what they do not want.
> A symposium of procrastinators is what they do not want.
> A phalanx of forelock-tuggers is what they do not want.
> And perhaps above all the droopy mantra of 'it wizny me' is what they do not want.
>
> (Scottish Parliament)

Ein Bekenntnis des Dichters zum neuen, selbstbewussten und zunehmend von London unabhängigen Schottland – und auch ein frischer Glaube an die Demokratie und das Mandat des Volkes. Noch vor kurzem, beinahe ein Jahr nach seinem Tod, sorgte sein Testament für Aufsehen, denn es beinhaltet die mit 1 Million Pfund bisher größte Zuwendung an die SNP, die Schottische Nationalpartei, welche mit dem Geld wohl einen Teil ihrer Kampagne für das geplante Unabhängigkeitsreferendum finanzieren will (Carrell). Morgans Lebenszeit und Werk spiegelt die wichtigen Etappen des Devolutionsprozesses im 20. Jahrhundert. Gleichzeitig wird er auch als Letzter der *Schottischen Renaissance* gesehen, einer Dichterbewegung um Hugh MacDiarmid (1892–1978), die man vielleicht als die schottische Version der "klassischen Moderne"

---

[2] Vor allem seine Liebesgedichte erfreuen sich großer Popularität. Ein schönes Zeugnis dafür liefert die bei YouTube eingestellte Sendung der *BBC Culture Show* ("Edwin Morgan Poems on BBC Culture Show"). Auch die dort erwähnte Tatsache, dass 15 000 Kopien einer neuen Edwin-Morgan-Anthologie kostenlos verteilt wurden, veranschaulicht seinen Bekanntheitsgrad und Stellenwert. Ein anderes Beispiel wären die *Subway Poems*, welche eine Zeit lang in der Glasgower U-Bahn auf Werbeschildern allgegenwärtig waren.

beschreiben könnte. Aus diesem Zusammenhang rührt auch seine transformatorische Rückbesinnung auf die frühe, spezifisch schottische literarische Tradition und die Aufwertung der schottischen (Alltags-)Sprache. Vor allem seit *The Second Life* (1968) war Morgans Grundton optimistisch und fortschrittlich-schöpferisch. Er gehörte zu jenen seltenen Erscheinungen, welche dazu imstande sind, die moderne *conditio humana* kritisch und dennoch positiv zu repräsentieren (Watson 203).

Edwin Morgan stammte aus Glasgow, wie Liz Lochhead, die Nachfolgerin seines Amtes, und Carol Ann Duffy, die gegenwärtige *poet laureate* des Vereinigten Königreiches. Dort wurde er 1920 geboren, besuchte Schule, Universität, lehnte später eine Stipendium für Oxford ab, um der Stadt treu zu bleiben, wurde selbst Dozent, setzte sich (zeitig) 1980 zur Ruhe, um sich ganz der Dichtung zu widmen. Seine Homosexualität ist auf subtile Weise in den Gedichten präsent; auch anhand dieses Topos bildet sein Gesamtwerk die Geschichte eines gesellschaftlichen Wandels ab. Erst mit 70 Jahren war die Zeit für ihn reif für ein öffentliches Bekenntnis, 1990, in dem Jahr als seine Heimatstadt Glasgow "European capital of culture" wurde.

Edwin Morgans Tätigkeitsfeld war das des Dichters, Dozenten, Kritikers und Übersetzers. Mit einer *Beowulf*-Übersetzung begründet er 1952 seinen Ruhm auf diesem Feld. Er übersetzte aus acht Sprachen ins Englische und Schottische, darunter Mayakovski, Brecht, Neruda. Ab den 90er Jahren war er Teil einer Welle von Adaptionen klassischer Theaterstücke in die schottische Umgangssprache, unter seinen letzten Übersetzungen findet sich auch eine Adaption des *Gilgamesh* (2005).

Insgesamt veröffentlichte er mehr als 20 Gedichtbände und zahlreiche kleinere Schriften, die bedeutendsten Anthologien sind *The Second Life* (1968), *From Glasgow to Saturn* (1973), *The New Divan* (1977), *Sonnets from Scotland* (1984), *Themes on a Variation* (1988), *Collected Poems* (2. Auflage, 1996) und *Cathures: News Poems 1997–2001* (2002). Zu seinen Auszeichnungen gehören die *Queens Medal for Poetry* im Jahr 2000 und der *Weidenfeld Prize for Translation* im darauffolgenden Jahr (Walker 204).

Stimmen von anderswo

"Nichts, das keine Botschaften enthält" (*Nothing Not Giving Messages*), so lautet der Titel einer Sammlung von Aufsätzen, Vorlesungen und Interviews, welcher Edwin Morgans poetische Experimente charakterisiert: Er war ein Meister darin, den alten und neuen Dingen Stimmen zu geben, eine Strategie, die unweigerlich über das Bekannte hinaus in den Bereich des Phantastischen führt. So lernt etwa in *The Second Life* (1968) der Computer sprechen.

Noch vor der Ära allgegenwärtiger Heimelektronik begegnet dieser uns mit einem frohen, nicht ganz den Erwartungen entsprechenden, aber doch sehr liebenswertem Weihnachtsgruß in "The Computer's First Christmas Card":

j	o	l	l	y	m	e	r	r	y
m	e	r	r	y	m	e	r	r	y
m	e	r	r	y	C	h	r	i	s
a	m	m	e	r	r	y	a	s	a
C	h	r	i	s	m	e	r	r	y
a	s	M	E	R	R	Y	C	H	R
Y	S	A	N	T	H	E	M	U	M

(*Collected Poems* 177)

Immer wieder verlieh Morgan dem Computer Sprache und Wesen, eine ganze Reihe von Gedichten mit Titeln wie "The Computer's First Code Poem" zieht sich durch sein Werk, bald spricht der Computer auch fließend Schottisch, mit Glasgower Akzent, und hat sich zu einer ausgewachsenen Künstlichen Intelligenz entwickelt, in "The Computer's First Dialect Poem" etwa.

MacGillivray und Gifford vergleichen Edwin Morgans Science-Fiction-Gedichte mit Edwin Muirs Remythifizierung Schottlands – während letzterer archaisierend in die Vergangenheit blickt, richtet Edwin Morgan seine Aufmerksamkeit auf die Zukunft:

> In his poetry, science fiction has come to serve the same purpose as myth does in the poetry of Edwin Muir. Action occurs on the kind of epic scale which allows it comfortably to carry the weight of symbolic significance [...] producing with natural ease [...] large resonances [...] and raising in a spacious context the questions about identity and stature of humanity that clearly concern Morgan. (Gifford 775)

Das phantastische Genre ist für Morgan also ein Vehikel zu den großen Menschheitsfragen, der Entwurf einer zeitgemäßen Sprache, die nicht auf den tiefen Sinn verzichtet. Im Ungesehenen, aber auch dem Unbeachteten, sucht er nach neuen Formen der Erfahrung, wie Hamish Whyte bestätigt:

> He has always seen poetry itself as an instrument of exploration, like a spaceship, navigating new fields of feeling and experience. He has also said that 'it requires a peculiar kind of imagination that is willing to bend itself to meet a world which is lying there in the rain like an old shoe.' (Whyte, "The Milk of Space")

Dabei ist die Gestalt des Vehikels nicht auf das "Raumschiff" Science Fiction beschränkt, und die Matrize "Edwin Muir: Fantasy, Mythos, Vergangenheit" vs. "Edwin Morgan: Science Fiction, Moderne, Zukunft" ist ein sehr grobes, aber doch irgendwie zutreffendes Raster – denn Morgan sieht auch im Alten beständig das Neue. So kommen zum Beispiel in in "The Horseman's Word" (1970) Pferde zu Wort,[3] und man findet die Stimmen mythischer, historischer und alltäglicher Pferdewesen verschiedener Kulturkreise nebeneinander: Zentaur, Hrimfaxi, Kelpie uvm. Der Zentaur meditiert in konkreter Poesie: "I am, horse/unhorse, me ... I am horse: unhorse me!" (*Collected Poems* 210).

---

[3] Vgl Edwin Muirs dystopisches Gedicht "The Horses".

Die Sammlung *From Glasgow to Saturn* (1973), welche bereits im Titel die thematische Bandbreite Morgans gut veranschaulicht, enthält neben *space poems* auch die dadaistische Stimme des Monsters Nessie.

The Loch Ness Monster's Song

Sssnnnwhuffffll? Hnwhufflhhnnwflhnflhfl?
Gdroblboblhobngblgblgl g ggglbgl.
Drublhaflablhaflubhafgabhaflhaflflfl –
gmgrawwwwwgrfgrawfawfgmgraw gm.
Hovoplodok – doplodovok – plovodokot – doplodokosh?
Splgrawfokfoksplgrafhatchgabrlgabrlfoksplfok!
Zgrakragkafok!
Grofgrawffgahf?
Gomblmblbl –
blmplm,
blmplm,
blmplm,
blp.

(*Collected Poems* 248)

Das Lautgedicht[4] fällt im Vergleich mit Hugo Ball oder Kurt Schwitters durch die ausführliche Punktuation auf, welche nicht nur im Sinne einer Regieanweisung der Performanz der Sprachmelodie dient, sondern eine dramaturgische Funktion hat: Das Loch Ness Monster erhebt sich aus dem See, erblickt und kommentiert die moderne Welt, und versinkt wieder in der Tiefe – so zumindest verstand Morgan selbst seinen Text – ohne auf diese Sichtweise zu drängen, natürlich (Morgan, *Nothing* 255).

Ebenfalls in *From Glasgow to Saturn* erhalten wir Einblick in die Gedanken eines zurückgelassenen Moduls einer Raumlandefähre, "Thoughts of A Module" (1973). Später, in *Star Gate: Science Fic-*

---

[4] Zu hören unter: <http://www.poetryarchive.org/poetryarchive/singlePoem.do?poemId=1683>, vorgetragen vom Autor selbst.

tion Poems (1979), kam Morgan dem vermittelndem Auftrag der Science Fiction nach, und widmete sich dem Problem, dass viel zu wenige Erkenntnisse der modernen Wissenschaft Eingang in die Kunst gefunden haben. Augenzwinkernd stellt er uns Elementarteilchen in den "Particle Poems 1" vor:

> The old old old particle
> smiled. 'I grant you I'm not beautiful,'
> he said, 'but I've got charm.
> It's charm that's led me where I am.'
> Opened up his bosom, showed me a quark.
> (*Collected Poems* 384)

Hier wird mit dem Poetischen der Sprache der Quantenphysik ("Charm" ist eine der abstrakten Eigenschaften von Quarks) gespielt, und mit den endlosen Entdeckungen, die im kleinsten Raum zu erwarten sind – das Gedicht setzt sich mit vielen Fragmenten aus dem Munde der kaum greifbaren Teilchen fort, die trotz ihrer Flüchtigkeit allesamt sehr auf ihre Individualität bedacht sind.

Dass Morgan bei allem Humor und Fortschrittsoptimismus den Konsequenzen der modernen Wissenschaft keineswegs unkritisch gegenüberstand, zeigt er zum Beispiel im "Clone Poem" aus demselben Band, welches iterativ aus Redewendungen konstruiert ist, und das geklonte Neue, als eine multiplizierende Variation des Alten entlarvt, mit der man es nicht übertreiben sollte:

> [...] you can have too much of a good too much of a good too
>   much you can have too much you can you can too much of
>   a good thing you can have too much too much of a good
>   thing
> (*Collected Poems* 390)

Nicht nur den 'Fabelwesen' der Science Fiction legt Morgan gern Worte in den Mund, sondern auch den klassischen, mythischen Wesen und Göttern – oder den Stereotypen der Fantasy. Diese Stimmen entwickeln fragmentarische Perspektiven einer medial vermittelten Wirklichkeit, welche in ihrer Gesamtheit jedoch, als Panoptikum, ein kohärentes Bild zeigen. Einzeln gesehen, dienen die figürlichen Perspektiven als entfremdende oder zueignende Teleskope, die wie in einer Presseschau wichtige Koordinaten der Gegenwart beleuchten. Manchmal kommt dabei eine Kritik der Gehörlosigkeit der Medien oder unseres arroganten Umganges mit der Vergangenheit zum Vorschein, wie etwa in "The Mummy" (1976).

Wie bei vielen Gedichten Morgans stammt die Anregung dazu aus einer Nachrichtenmeldung: "The Mummy [of Rameses II] was met at Orly airport by Mme Saunier-Seïté. News item, Sept. 1976" (*Collected Poems* 397). Die Reporterin interviewt die Mumie, welche aus offensichtlichen Gründen nur "Mmmmm" antworten kann. Als sich die Mumie aufzuregen beginnt, weil sie gegen ihren Willen gegen einen Pilzbefall behandelt werden soll, droht sie zu zerbrechen und wird kurzerhand mit einem Betäubungsmittel ruhig gestellt:

> – I really hate to have to use
> a hypodermic on a mummy.
> But we cannot have you strain yourself.
> Remember your fungus, Your Majesty.
> – Fng. Zzzzzzz.- That's right.
> – Aaaaaaaah.
> (*Collected Poems* 399)

Die Underdogs, Außenseiter und Vergessenen mit den großen Träumen haben es Morgan im Modus des Phantastischen besonders angetan – von der Peripherie aus sah er das Ganze deutlicher. So endet etwa der "Archeopteryx's Song" mit derselben Sehnsucht nach den Sternen, welche die zweite Hälfte des 20. Jahrhunderts beflügelte: "I will teach my sons and daughters to live / on mist and fire and fly to the stars" (*Collected Poems* 403). Edwin Morgan fand im Traum des Fliegens ein Kontinuum über die Grenzen von Zeit und Spezies hinweg – sind die modernen Raumfahrer Nachkommen des Archeopterix, oder werden sich eines Tages doch die Nachfahren der Vögel ins All erheben? Der Traum jedenfalls bleibt derselbe.

"Grendel" (aus *Themes on a Variation*, 1988) zieht aus der exzentrischen, halbmenschlichen Perspektive seine Spezifik und philosophiert: "It is being nearly human / gives me that spectacular darkness" (*Collected Poems* 428). Nur durch diesen 'Blick aus dem Dunkel' kann Grendel in herrlich neo-angelsächsischer, epischer Diktion – man hat ganz offensichtlich einen bedeutenden Beowulf-Übersetzer vor sich! – dem Anthropozentrismus einen Schlag versetzen:

> Who would be a man? Who would be the winter sparrow
> that flies at night by mistake into a lighted hall
> and flutters the length of it in zigzag panic,
> dazed and terrified by the heat and noise and smoke,
> the drink-fumes and the oaths, the guttering flames,
> feast-bones thrown to a snarl of wolfhounds,
> flash of swords in sodden sorry quarrels,
> till at last he sees the other door
> and skims out in relief and joy
> into the stormy black?
>
> (*Collected Poems* 428)

Betrachtet man das Weltgeschehen durch Grendels Augen, so muss man zugeben, dass sich seit dem "finsteren" Mittelalter an den wesentlichen Dingen nicht wirklich viel geändert hat – diese Form der Wiederkehr des Immergleichen macht Beowulf zu einem aktuellen Text, besonders in Morgans Version "Grendel".

Auch "Merlin" aus *Nine in Glasgow* (2002) ist ein Außenseiter, der in besonderem Sinne die Gegenwart der Vergangenheit hervorhebt: "What time, what year, what universe, all's one" (*Cathures* 12) beginnt der Barde sein Lied, das aus der Zeit König Rodericks (670 A.D.) bis ins heutige Cathures (d.i. Glasgow) reicht. Absichtlich vermengt Morgan die Arthurische Tradition mit dem "Merlin Caledonius"[5], einem Propheten und "Wilden Mann" aus der Gegend des heutigen Glasgow. Dieser Merlin flieht in Mor-

---

[5] Vgl. "History of the Town and Castle of Dumbarton".

gans Version in die Wälder, als er über die siegreichen Schlachten des Königs singen soll, denn alles, was er zum Krieg zu verewigen hat, ist das beständig gleiche Leid, welches dieser verursacht: "War wins wounds, widows, it eclipses the sun / For many. I could only run" (*Cathures* 12). In den Wäldern überdauert Merlin die Zeiten, bis er von den sanften Melodien der Moderne zurück zur Zivilisation gelockt wird. Nun haust er gemeinsam mit seiner Tochter, die er mit Ada Byron vergleicht, in einem extradimensionalen Observatorium, als alchimisierende Geister der Stadt:

> … We donate our spirit
> To that gallus city. We are quicksilver
> With no mould to run into. Watch us change.
> This glass house which is not made of glass
> Is Merlin's esplumoir, his moulting-cage
> Where high above the rambling Molendinar[6]
> He waits until the new enchanter
> Flashes a more formidable feather
> And that, too, not for ever.
>
> (*Cathures* 13)

Mit diesem Gedicht schuf Morgan einen Geist von Glasgow, welcher vielleicht das 1999 eingeführte Amt des Stadtpoeten beschreibt: beständig im Fluss, stellt der jeweilige "Verzauberer" schöpferisch die Kontinuität zwischen den ältesten Legenden der Stadt und ihrer Zukunft her.

Der Rubrik "Favourite Authors" angemessen, möchte ich den Blick in Edwin Morgans Panoptikum mit der mir liebsten phantastischen Persona abschließen, welche der Dichter in 20 Gedichten entworfen hat, dem *Demon* (1999). Auch dieser steht im Zeichen des ständigen Wandels, aktiver und energischer vielleicht, als der Chronist "Merlin".

---

[6] "A stream in Glasgow, passing the 6th century settlement that has evolved into the city" ("Molendinar_Burn").

Demon ist der anarchische und aggressive Bruder des eingangs beschriebenen *whittrick*, ein Außenseiter *par excellence*, vielleicht sogar Manifestation des Fremden in uns. Colin Nicholson analysiert den *Demon* ausführlich als "agency of dissent" (188ff.), auch kann die Persona erneut als Metapher für einen Dichtertyp herhalten, der diesmal die Gestalt eines ruhelosen, politisch aktiven Humanisten trüge, eines Anti-Mephistopheles, der das gute Potential im Bösen aktiviert. In "A Demon" stellt dieser sich als Provokateur vor, der den Sänger (Orpheus in diesem Fall) so lange reizt, bis dieser aus Wut und Angst über sich selbst hinauswächst und lernend beginnt, sich aus seiner Unmündigkeit zu erheben:

> My job is to rattle the bars. It's a battle [...]
> I am not trying
> to get out; nor am I trying to get in ... My rod [...] has
>   made the singer devilish angry
> devilish fearful, and at last devilish strong.
>   (*Cathures* 93)

Das Motto des Tricksters, abgelesen aus "The Demon Sings", ist eine Hymne an das Konträre, an die Chance in der Katastrophe: "Against is not for nothing" (*Cathures*, 100). Freudig lobt der Dämon Hochwasser, Malstrom und Abgrund, jedoch niemals sinkt er auf das bloß Grausame und Unmenschliche herab. Deutlich wird dies in "Another Demon", welches die Begegnung mit einem stereotypischen Vertreter seiner Art schildert, der ihm zu den traditionellen Tätigkeiten einlädt: Ernten verderben, Lahme die Klippen herabstürzen, deren Blut saufen ... *Demon* antwortet:

> Well that was that. There are demons and demons.
> [...]
> The last thing I would drink was human blood,
> I had not come from beyond the grave
> And had no grave to go to, a zombie
> Could never fathom me in a century of years
>   (*Cathures* 111)

Nein, die 'Bosheit' Demons liegt auf anderen Gebieten. In "The Demon in the Whiteout" macht er sich zum Beispiel auf den Weg zum Nordpol, um Frankensteins Monster zu verspotten, welches dort noch immer vergeblich den Tod sucht. Er gibt der verzweifelten Kreatur ein Paradox auf, aus dem letztlich dessen Wille zum Leben entspringt:

> It may be a human thought to want to die,
> But it is more human not to.
> (*Cathures* 103)

So wird *Demon* zum Lebensretter der Kreatur, zum schalkhaften, ja vielleicht sogar zum heroischen Genius des Lebens:

> He would live to trouble both gods and men.
> I leapt from floe to floe, south now, south,
> Whistling my hearty, unsafe amen.
> (*Cathures* 103)

Eine Stimme, überaus liebenswert

Nach solchen Zeilen und Stoffen, und dem Versuch darzustellen, wie Edwin Morgan den Entfremdungen der Moderne durch die Kunst eine Kontinuität zu verleihen sucht, könnte man ihn durchaus auch als Romantiker im Gewand der Moderne bezeichnen. Dies wäre ein weiterer Versuch, den *whittrick* zu fangen. Unter gewissen Gesichtspunkten wäre diese Bezeichnung treffend, denn mit den Romantikern hatte Morgan nicht nur thematische Schnittpunkte. Auch bei Morgan war 'Natur' universell und beseelt, sogar groß genug, auch das Künstliche der Moderne in sich aufzunehmen – so sind seine Landschaften zumeist urban. Der Mensch kann sich der Natur als einer Einheit jedoch nur durch die Kunst bewusst werden, und deshalb betrachtet man in Morgans Panoptikum zuerst das Menschliche, um dann durch dieses hindurch auch das Natürliche zu erblicken. Obwohl viele seiner Werke fragmentarischer und experimenteller nicht sein könnten, schreibt Roderick Watson über Morgans Science Fiction: "Where other writers see only confusion, decay, or empty technology, Morgan discovers growth, change, flux, and delight" (Watson 203).

Diese Aussage kann man bedenkenlos auf Morgans ganzes Œuvre ausweiten. Ich möchte mich hier vor allem auf den letzten Aspekt besonders stützen, das Vergnügen an der Moderne im besten Sinne. Denn das Besondere an Edwin Morgans Stimmen ist für mich, dass sie der Gegenwart mit all ihrem Häßlichen ins Auge sehen, ja die Sinne dafür noch schärfen, und dennoch niemals abgründig werden.

"Deplore what is to be deplored, / and then find out the rest" (*Collected Poems* 167) beendet er ein Gedicht über King Billy, einen Glasgower Bandenführer, welches seit Jahren an vielen schottischen Schulen fester Bestandteil des Lehrplans ist. Genau diese schonungslose Einstellung eines hart erarbeiteten Optimismus machte Edwin Morgan zu einer Ausnahmeerscheinung: Seine Stimmen sind immer, vor allem, und *trotz allem*, liebenswert.

Carol Ann Duffy sagte anläßlich seines Todes: "A great, generous, gentle genius has gone" (Scottish Poetry Library) Das ist unbestreitbar, doch – der Dichtkunst sei Dank! – wird den *whittrick* das nicht daran hindern, auch in Zukunft noch zu den "Favourite Authors" von vielen zu gehören.

Literaturverzeichnis

Carrell, Severin. "Scotland's national poet Edwin Morgan leaves SNP £ 1 m in will". *Guardian*, 20. 6. 11. 17. 8. 2011. <http://www.guardian.co.uk/politics/2011/jun/20/edwin-morgan-leaves-snp-1m-in-will>.
"Edwin Morgan Poems on BBC Culture Show". 24. Aug. 2011. <http://www.youtube.com/watch?v=NhUI2BmHB08>
Gifford, Douglas, Sarah Dunnigan, and Alan MacGillivray, eds. *Scottish Literature*. Edinburgh: Edinburgh University Press, 2002.
"History of the Town and Castle of Dumbarton". 17. 8. 2011. <http://www.electricscotland.com/history/dumbarton/dumbarton3.htm>.
Jackaman, Rob. *Broken English/breaking English: A Study of Contemporary Poetries in English*, Madison: Fairleigh Dickinson Univ. Press, 2003.

"Molendinar Burn". 17. 8. 2011. <http://en.wikipedia.org/wiki/Molendinar_Burn>.
Morgan, Edwin. *Collected Poems*. Manchester: Carcanet, 1990.
—. *Cathures*. Manchester : Carcanet, 2002.
—. "The Loch Ness Monster's Song". 17. 8. 2011. <http://www.poetryarchive.org/poetryarchive/singlePoem.do?poemId=1683>.
—. *Nothing Not Giving Messages: Reflections on Work and Life*. Ed. Hamish Whyte. Edinburgh: Polygon, 1990.
—. "Opening of the Scottish Parliament, 9. 10. 2004". 17. 8. 2011. <http://www.scottish.parliament.uk/nmcentre/events/holyroodOpening/edwinMorgan.htm>.
—. *The Whittrick: a Poem in Eight Dialogues*. Penwortham: Akros, 1973.
Nicholson, Colin. *Edwin Morgan: Inventions of Modernity*. Manchester: Manchester University Press, 2002.
Duffy, Carol Ann "Tribute to Edwin Morgan's Death". *Scottish Poetry Library*. 17. 8. 2011. <http://scottishpoetrylibrary.wordpress.com/2010/08/19/edwin-morgan-1920-2010/>.
Walker, Marshall. "The Voyage Out and the Favoured Place: Edwin Morgan's Science Fiction Poems". *About Edwin Morgan*. Ed. Robert Crawford and Hamish Whyte. Edinburgh: Edinburgh University Press, 1990. 54–64.
Whyte, Hamish. "The Milk of Space". *Bottle Imp* 8 (November 2010). 17. 8. 2011. <http://www.arts.gla.ac.uk/ScotLit/ASLS/SWE/TBI/TBI-Issue8/Whyte2.html>.

Besprechungen

ZU FANTASY FICTION UND VERWANDTEN GATTUNGEN

Neues von der Fantastikfront
Zeitschrift für Fantastikforschung 1/2011. Hg. Daniel Illger, Jacek Rzeszotnik und Lars Schmeink im Auftrag der Gesellschaft für Fantastikforschung e.V. (GFF). Berlin: Lit-Verlag, 2011. 146 S., € 14,90.

Fantastik hat Konjunktur: Wenn es noch eines Beweises für das Offensichtliche bedurft hätte, die enorme Resonanz auf den von Mitgliedern der Universität Hamburg ausgegangenen Aufruf zur Gründung einer "Gesellschaft für Fantastikforschung" (GFF) hätte ihn geliefert, belegt sie doch, dass die nicht-mimetische Literatur endlich auch im deutschsprachigen akademischen Establishment angekommen ist. Gleichsam als Siegel ihrer akademischen Respektabilität hat die im Oktober 2010 gegründete GFF nun auch eine eigene Zeitschrift etabliert, die fortan zweimal im Jahr erscheinen soll und deren erste Nummer im Sommer 2011 herausgekommen ist.

"Die *ZFF* ist das erste deutschsprachige Periodikum, das gezielt der strikt-wissenschaftlichen Auseinandersetzung mit fantastischen Stoffen im deutschsprachigen Raum ein Forum bieten will", schreiben die Herausgeber in ihrem Grußwort. "Sie ist interdisziplinär angelegt, versteht den Begriff "Fantastik" in seiner umfassenden Definition, und zielt somit auf wissenschaftliche Auseinandersetzungen mit dem Fantastischen in sämtlichen Genres, Modi und zeitlichen Perioden ab" (2). Diese Positionierung innerhalb des Spektrums ähnlicher Periodika ist zugleich weit und eng: weder auf einen einzelnen Autor konzentriert (wie *Hither Shore*, das Jahrbuch der Deutschen Tolkien Gesellschaft) noch auf eine Autorengruppe (wie das *Inklings-Jahrbuch*, das allerdings immer den Spagat zwischen den Oxforder Inklings und einem sehr weit verstandenen Umfeld geübt hat), noch auf eine einzelne Gattung wie Science

Fiction, Fantasy Fiction oder Gothic Fiction – aber unter strikter Abgrenzung von stärker marktorientierten Organen wie *Magira* oder diversen Internet-Plattformen, sowie unter bewusstem Verzicht auf fremdsprachliche Beiträge, wodurch die ZFF sich auch von dem sich dezidiert international gebärdenden *Fastitocalon* unterscheidet.[1]

Die interdisziplinäre Ausrichtung der ZFF demonstriert bereits das vorliegende erste Heft. Drei der vier Artikel – allesamt lesenswert und auf tadellosem wissenschaftlichem Niveau – beschäftigen sich nicht primär mit Literatur, sondern mit Formen des zeitgenössischen fantastischen Films. Vera Cuntz-Leng untersucht in "Frodo auf Abwegen" – differenziert und stets auf der Hut vor allzu kühnen Spekulationen – "das queere Potenzial des aktuellen Fantasykinos", also unterschwellige (homo)erotische Bedeutungsebenen in Fantasy-Stoffen von Tolkien und Rowling, die in den Filmversionen deutlicher spürbar sind als in den Originaltexten und, nebenbei bemerkt, auch von zahllosen Verfasser(inne)n von *slash fan fiction* fleißig ausgebeutet werden, was in dem Aufsatz ebenfalls Berücksichtigung findet. Um Gespenster in Christian Petzolds im allgemeinen als 'realistisch' geltenden Filmen geht es in dem Beitrag von Matthias Grotkopp, und Steffen Hantke unterzieht die dystopische Mini-Fernsehserie *2030 – Aufstand der Alten*, die im Januar 2007 im ZDF ausgestrahlt wurde, einer filmkritisch-soziologischen Analyse.

Um "die Anbindung der deutschsprachigen Forschung an internationale Diskurse [zu] fördern", soll in der ZFF "in jeder Ausgabe [...] ein internationaler Beitrag erstmalig auf Deutsch zur Verfügung gestellt werden, der innerhalb der entsprechenden Genre- oder Fachdiskurse als besonders wichtig und produktiv angesehen wird" (3). Auch dieser Aufsatz fällt in der vorliegenden Nummer in das filmwissenschaftliche Ressort. Robin Woods "Der amerikanische Albtraum" ist eine für die 1980er Jahre typische, auf Marx,

---

[1] Zu den namentlich genannten Periodika vgl. die Besprechungen in den Inklings-Jahrbüchern 23 (231–34) und 28 (240–43).

Freud und Marcuse aufbauende kultursoziologische Analyse des amerikanischen Horrorfilms der 1970er Jahre. Der ursprünglich als Kapitel eines Buches 1983 veröffentlichte Text (überarbeitete und erweiterte Neuauflage 2003) hat kein bisschen Staub angesetzt und ist als Lehrbeispiel für die Wechselbeziehung zwischen der geistigen Befindlichkeit einer Gesellschaft und ihren kulturellen Produkten nach wie vor lesenswert. Ob es einer Übersetzung bedurfte, um ihn hierzulande dem filmwissenschaftlich interessierten Publikum zugänglich zu machen, sei allerdings dahingestellt: Lässt das nicht die deutschsprachige Fantastikforschung provinzieller erscheinen als sie (hoffentlich) ist?

Lediglich der erste Artikel des Heftes beschäftigt sich nicht mit Filmen, sondern mit Literatur. Hans-Heino Ewers unternimmt den "Versuch einer Gattungsdifferenzierung" (so der Untertitel), indem er die Gattung 'Fantasy' als "Heldendichtung unserer Zeit" deutet und so in einen größeren literarhistorischen Zusammenhang stellt. Der Essay reizt an einzelnen Stellen zum Widerspruch (etwa wenn er behauptet, im englischen Sprachgebrauch entspreche *fantasy* der deutschen 'Phantastik' im weiten Sinne, was nur bei einzelnen Forschern, aber keineswegs generell zutrifft), aber er bietet doch eine differenzierte, insgesamt überzeugende Charakterisierung des Kernbereichs der Fantasy Fiction, die in der Tat eine "vormoderne Thematik – Heldentum, Weltrettung, Erlösungstat des Heroen etc. [...] aus der Sicht der und in Relation zur modernen Gegenwart [zeigt]" (12): überzeugend nicht zuletzt deshalb, weil Ewers sehr wohl auch die Tendenz der modernen Fantasy Fiction sieht, sich von diesen historischen Eierschalen zu befreien, was er abschließend anhand der All-Age-Romane der deutschen Autorin Kirsten Boje demonstriert.

Bleiben noch die Rezensionen zu erwähnen, bei denen ebenfalls Filme eine herausragende Rolle spielen. Alles in allem ist diese erste Nummer ein verheißungsvoller Auftakt zu einer Unternehmung, der man nur Glück und Erfolg wünschen kann: Schließlich belebt bekanntlich Konkurrenz das Geschäft, und damit die Konjunktur.

DIETER PETZOLD

Einführung in die Einführung

Spiegel, Simon. *Theoretisch phantastisch: Eine Einführung in Tzvetan Todorovs Theorie der phantastischen Literatur*. Norderstedt: Books on Demand, 2010. 202 S., €13,90.

Der Verfasser hat sich ein ehrenwertes Ziel gesetzt: Er will dem literaturwissenschaftlichen Laien das Verständnis des Todorovschen Texts erleichtern. Tatsächlich scheint er aber v. a. darum bemüht, Todorovs Theorie, die "oft falsch verstanden wurde" (14), auf absurde Weise zu vereinfachen, ihre Thesen in ihr Gegenteil zu verkehren und sie mit eigenen theoretischen Bastelarbeiten zu vermengen. So behauptet Spiegel beispielsweise, die Markierung des nicht-realitätskompatiblen Ereignisses müsse durch eine glaubwürdige Instanz erfolgen: Wenn der Held Drogen genommen habe, sei dies nicht der Fall (76f.). Diese Auffassung ist der Todorovs konträr, nach dessen Theorie die Unschlüssigkeit gerade dadurch entsteht, dass die Zuverlässigkeit der Instanz, die das wunderbare Ereignis schildert, durch Hinweise auf Wahn, Drogenrausch und dergleichen destabilisiert wird.[1]

Dass Roger Caillois und Louis Vax einen "ähnlichen Phantastik-Begriff" (33) wie Todorov vertreten, ist gleichfalls eine erstaunliche Behauptung, zumal für diese Autoren das für Todorovs Phantastikbegriff entscheidende Merkmal der Unschlüssigkeit des implizierten Lesers gar kein Genrekriterium darstellt. Zudem definieren sie das Genre – was Todorov scharf kritisiert – über die Motivik und die Angst des realen Lesers. Das Chaos wird noch vermehrt, als Spiegel erklärt, dass "Todorovs Phantastik ungefähr der *Gothic Novel* respektive dem deutschen Begriff des *Schauerromans*" (41) entspreche, wohingegen Todorov sehr deutlich feststellt, dass es in der Gothic Novel "das Fantastische im eigentlichen Sinne nicht [gibt], nur Gattungen, die ihm benachbart sind" (Todorov 40).

Ebenso hat Spiegel die Todorovsche Unterscheidung zwischen *historischen* und *systematischen* Gattungen (Genres) missverstan-

---

[1] Vgl. Tzvetan Todorov. *Einführung in die fantastische Literatur*. Frankfurt a. M.: Fischer, 1992, S. 44.

den. Er erklärt: "Was zu einem bestimmten Zeitpunkt als (historische) Gattung wahrgenommen wird [...], lässt sich [...] jeweils auf eine abstrakte Struktur zurückführen. Die tatsächlich existierenden Gattungen sind somit nur die 'oberflächlichen' Erscheinungsformen eines theoretischen Idealtyps – der systematischen Gattung" (36). Diese Darstellung ist falsch. Todorov unterscheidet mit den genannten Begriffen zwischen historisch *realisierten* Genres und solchen, die zwar aus einer Systematik bzw. einer Theorie der Literatur als *möglich* erschließbar sind, aber nicht historisch (als konkrete Erzählung) manifestiert sein müssen (vgl. Todorov 16f.). Mit Idealtypen hat dies nichts zu tun. Vielmehr liegt eine Analogie etwa zur Linguistik vor, die eine Theorie der Wortbildung entwirft und auf dieser Grundlage systematisch bildbare, aber historisch nicht realisierte Wörter erschließen kann. Spiegels Kritik, die er an Todorovs vermeintlicher Differenzierung auf den folgenden Seiten vornimmt und an zahlreichen Stellen seines Buchs wiederholt, basiert auf einer Fehlinterpretation.

Dem intendierten Laien-Leser dürfte es nicht wenige Probleme bereiten, aus den widersprüchlichen Aussagen des Verfassers schlau zu werden. "In einer Welt", behauptet Spiegel, "in der ohnehin alles unklar und rätselhaft ist, sind übernatürliche [wunderbare] Phänomene nicht mehr als solche auszumachen" (87). Diese allgemeine Behauptung unterschätzt die Möglichkeiten des Systems Literatur. Sind die Vorkommnisse in H. P. Lovecrafts *The Music of Erich Zann* etwa nicht als wunderbar zu bestimmen? Der Verfasser bezieht sich indes auf Montage-Techniken und vielstimmige Erzählweisen, die einen Eindruck von Undurchschaubarkeit erzeugen, und kommt zu dem Schluss: "Die Phantastik benötigt somit, was man eine *klassische Erzählweise* nennt. Bei dieser Erzählweise ist der Erzähler allwissend, stehen die Figuren im Vordergrund und wird eine eindeutige Auflösung angestrebt" (90). Das ist falsch und das Gegenteil richtig, das Spiegel an einer anderen Stelle selbst vertritt: "Eine allwissende Erzählinstanz, die [...] in alle Figuren 'hineinsieht' und das Geschehen überblickt, ist [... für das Phantastische] ungeeignet" (59).

Wenig erhellend sind desgleichen die Versuche, die der Verfasser unternimmt, das Realismusproblem zu lösen. Bekanntlich stellt das plötzlich auftauchende Wunderbare in der Phantastik (in den meisten historischen Fällen) die Ordnung einer realistischen Welt in Frage. Was aber ist nun unter Realismus zu verstehen? Spiegel kritisiert (die Argumente ungenannter Forscher gebrauchend) zwar Todorovs empirischen Realismusbegriff, vertritt ihn aber zugleich selbst (65). Unter Herbeiziehung einer seltsamen Vorstellung von "Inhalt" (= Ontologie der erzählten Welt (78)) müht er sich sodann, einen innerfiktionalen, d. h. konventionsorientierten Realismusbegriff um das Verhältnis der Literatur zur Wirklichkeit zu ergänzen. Indes ist der Begriff der "wirklichen Welt" so problematisch, dass die wissenschaftlich überholte Untergliederung des Texts in eine "inhaltlich-fiktionale" Ebene, eine "stilistische" (= "formale" (70)) und eine "Wirkungsebene" (74) keinen Schritt weiterführt.

Da Todorovs Untersuchung auf einem strukturalistischen Konzept beruht, geht Spiegel zu Recht davon aus, dass einige Erläuterungen über den Strukturalismus für seine Leser hilfreich sein könnten. Dabei vertritt er die simplistische These, der Strukturalismus sehe die Literatur als "ein eigenständiges System" an, das mit der Wirklichkeit "nicht [...] in Verbindung" stehe. Offensichtlich ist Spiegel das grundlegende Modell eines Systems von Systemen, wie es im strukturalistischen Manifest vertreten wird, unbekannt.[2] Nur so lässt sich seine Klage über das angebliche "Ausblenden von jeglichem Kontext" verstehen: "Warum sollen wir uns überhaupt mit Literatur beschäftigen, wenn sie nichts über die Welt aussagt [...]?" (25f.). Noch bezeichnender wird es, als Spiegel einwendet, der Strukturalismus habe "etwas Lustloses, höchst Unsinniges an sich" (27). Es scheint, als seien dem Autor die Unterschiede zwischen Wissenschaft und Erotik nicht geläufig. Aber schon Lotman hat sich mit derlei 'Argumenten' herumärgern müssen: "Was würde man von einem Witzbold denken", schrieb er 1971, "der behauptet,

---

[2] Vgl. Roman Jakobson/Jurij Tynjanov. "Probleme der Literatur- und Sprachforschung". 1928. In: Roman Jakobson. *Poetik: Ausgewählte Aufsätze 1921-1971*. Hg. Elmar Holenstein und Tarcisius Schelbert. Frankfurt a. M.: Suhrkamp, 1989. 63–66.

Genetik sei sinnlos, weil sie die Freuden der Liebe nicht ersetzen und kein lebendiges Kind zur Welt bringen könnte?"[3]

Eigenartigerweise sind Spiegels angeführte Beispiele mehrheitlich filmischer Natur, und zwar selbst dann, wenn der Film auf einer Romanvorlage beruht.[4] Dabei schiebt der Verfasser Todorov gern allerlei Aussagen über diese Kunstform unter, etwa in der Art: "Die unproblematischste Gattung ist wohl das *unvermischt Wunderbare*. Es handelt sich hierbei um Erzählungen und Filme, in denen Dinge möglich sind, die es in unserer Welt (noch) nicht gibt" (44.) Todorov äußert sich jedoch ausschließlich über literarische Texte. Abgesehen von Spiegels Vorliebe für den Film gibt es für die Einbeziehung dieses Mediums keine erkennbaren Gründe. Dass ein solches Vorgehen nicht unproblematisch ist, liegt auf der Hand, sogar Spiegel selbst weist darauf hin, dass Realismuskonventionen durchaus nicht nur genre-, sondern auch mediengebunden sein können. Diese Einsicht hält ihn aber nicht davon ab, seine Kritik an Todorovs Unschlüssigkeitskriterium an filmischen Beispielen festzumachen. Eine konkrete Bezugnahme auf die von Todorov angeführten Beispiele wäre hier sicher zielführender gewesen.

Gibt es gar nichts Freundliches zu sagen? Immerhin scheint das Kapitel zur "Pseudophantastik" ein interessantes theoretisches Problem aufzuwerfen: Kann es noch eine Unschlüssigkeit geben, wenn schon der Titel (z. B. "Invasion vom Mars") die Wunderbarkeit verrät (82–84)? Wir fragen: Warum nicht? Da ja nur das thematische Material, nicht aber dessen Inszenierungsweise vorab offenbart wird, sind weiterhin alle Möglichkeiten offen; wir weisen jedoch darauf hin, dass der Begriff der Pseudophantastik schon anderweitig vergeben ist. Und ansonsten? Erfreulicherweise ist in Spiegels Buch das Problem der poetischen und allegorischen

---

[3] Jurij M. Lotman. "Bemerkungen zur Struktur des künstlerischen Textes". 1971. In: Jurij M. Lotman. *Aufsätze zur Theorie und Methodologie der Literatur und Kultur.* Hg. Karl Eimermacher. Kronberg: Scriptor, 1974. 9–20, hier S. 9.
[4] Z. B. *Invasion of the Body Snatchers* (Don Siegel, USA 1956) nach dem Roman von Jack Finney, *The Body Snatchers* (45), oder *Rosemary's Baby* (Roman Polanski, USA 1968) nach dem gleichnamigen Roman von Ira Levin (50).

Erzählweise sauber erläutert. Auch die Todorovsche Thementheorie wird gut dargestellt und plausibel kritisiert. Der Begriff des implizierten Lesers erfährt eine mustergültige Bestimmung. Desgleichen lässt sich nichts gegen die Aufarbeitung der Todorovschen Thesen zum angeblichen Tod der Phantastik sagen. Aber diese wenigen Seiten wiegen die oben dargestellten Mängel auf vielen anderen keineswegs auf.

So ist Spiegels Buch keine Einführung in Todorovs Untersuchung, sondern in ein Sammelsurium von Missverständnissen, das auf den letzten Seiten (nach einer kritischen Würdigung anderer Arbeiten) auch noch in eine Lobpreisung der Dissertation des Verfassers zum Science-Fiction-Film mündet. Diese, so lesen wir, "ist ein filmwissenschaftliches Buch mit allem was dazugehört [...]. Und als Bonus liegt dem Buch eine DVD mit Filmausschnitten bei!" (185).

Bleibt zu hoffen, dass endlich ein deutscher Verlag Todorovs Untersuchung wieder auf den Markt bringt. Da dieser Text keineswegs so unverständlich ist, wie man ob Spiegels Buch glauben könnte, sondern klar und nachvollziehbar argumentiert, dürfte sich damit der Bedarf an 'Erläuterungen' erübrigen.

MAIKE VAN DELDEN/UWE DURST

Summa phantastica: Darko Suvin und die Science Fiction

Suvin, Darko. *Defined by a Hollow: Essays on Utopia, Science Fiction and Political Epistemology*. Oxford etc.: Peter Lang, 2010. 582 pp., $70,95/€ 50,00.

Ohne jede Übertreibung kann man sagen: Will man phantastische Literatur betrachten, kommt man an Darko Suvin nicht vorbei. Spätestens seit der großen Aufsatzsammlung, die 1979 als *Metamorphoses of Science Fiction* erschien, ist er einer der, wenn nicht sogar *der* Genretheoretiker, die die Science Fiction akademisch fassbar und damit hoffähig gemacht haben. Doch er ist mehr als das. Suvin, auch das wird in der vorliegenden Summa seiner Forschung deutlich, ist ein Solitär voller augenscheinlicher Paradoxien: Ein systematischer Analyst – und Lyriker. Ein marxistischer Exeget – und Romantiker. Ein klarer Denker – mit Hang zu barockem Schreibstil.

Und so typisch es für den ewigjungen Nestor der SF-Theorie ist, im eigenen Werk hinter den Subjekten, denen er seine kognitive Radikalkur angedeihen lässt, zurückzutreten, so passt es zu ihm, als Alterswerk eine selbst edierte und voluminöse Anthologie vorzulegen. In dieser brennt er ein Feuerwerk an Texten und Gedichten, Polemiken und Traktaten ab – und widmet den Band den Partisanenkämpfern des 2. Weltkrieges, ohne die, so die Paraphrase, erst die Nazis sein Leben beendet hätten und danach das politischsoziale Klima seines heimatlichen Jugoslawiens ein anderes gewesen wäre.

Nach diesem Auftakt folgt der Band einer prinzipiell chronologischen Struktur: Insgesamt 14 Aufsätze der Jahre 1973 bis 2007 zeichnen die wissenschaftliche und ideologische Entwicklung Suvins vom literaturtheoretischen *firebrand* zum zornig mahnenden *elder statesman* nach, wobei die eingeschobenen vier Gedichtzyklen Brüche in ebendieser Entwicklung markieren, Wegweiser in Suvins gelegentlich an der Grenze zur Hermetik operierende Texte.

Der erste dieser Blöcke ist wenig überraschend von seinem Hauptwerk, den oben erwähnten *Metamorphoses* geprägt; mit Schwerpunkt auf seiner zentralen Innovation, der Lektüre von SF durch die Brille Brecht'scher Verfremdung. In seiner Theorie vom Novum als der SF analog zur Satire innewohnendem kritischem Potenzial zeigt sich schon der thematische Kern, der Suvins Schaffen bis heute prägt: Ein sehr sensibles Gespür für globale Ungerechtigkeiten, politische Verwerfungen und ökonomische Unmenschlichkeiten.

Gleich einer Welles'schen Montage tragen uns die *Poems of Hope and Doubt* in die Achtziger Jahre, in denen sich Suvin unter anderem originell mit dem aktuellen Subgenre des Cyberpunk auseinandersetzt, bevor die *Eight Nasty Poems* einen ersten deutlichen Paradigmenwechsel hin zu einer Literaturkritik einläuten, die noch stärker als zuvor von politischen Parametern beeinflusst ist. In den

Neunzigern, als Geiz und Gier begannen, geil zu werden, bürstet Suvin mithilfe seines zuvor entwickelten, von Brecht, Benjamin und Bloch geprägten Instrumentariums den Zeitgeist gegen den Strich, indem er im Zeichen der SF die richtigen Fragen an die Kultur stellt. Was sollen (wir) Intellektuellen im Post-Fordismus tun? (Kapitel 9); Must Collectivism be against people? (Kapitel 11). Aber dieser wohlgewählte Ausschnitt zeigt auch erste Resignation, etwa wenn er in "A Tractate on Dystopia 2001" (Kapitel 13) die dystopische Qualität der Gegenwart herausarbeitet.

Auch in den poetischen Interludien reflektiert sich diese Entwicklung, wenn auf die "Poems from the Utopian Hollow" die "Farewell Fantasies" folgen. Gerahmt von beiden sind zwei weitere vornehmlich politisch-dialektische Texte, bevor der letzte Aufsatz in einer des Abschlusses würdigen Synthese noch einmal in Suvins unnachahmlicher Weise Literatur- und Gegenwartskritik in einer Analyse von LeGuins *The Disposessed* zusammenbringt.

Der Band trägt auch editorisch unverkennbar Darko Suvins Handschrift: Von der bewusst eklektischen Textauswahl über die fast barock anmutenden Epigraphen und Titel bis hin zum umfänglichen Apparat. Und damit beweist er auch, dass er noch viel zu sagen hat – gerade im letzten, 2007 entstandenen Text erweist er sich als nach wie vor scharfsinniger Interpret von Text und Wirklichkeit. Dass er die Verwerfungslinie zwischen beiden erst sichtbar und in jahrzehntelanger Akribie fassbar gemacht hat, ist sicherlich Suvins größter Verdienst. Davon gibt der Band beredt Auskunft, ohne museal zu wirken: Die Arbeit geht weiter. Auf, Brüder, zur Sonne!

JOHANNES RÜSTER

Besprechungen: Fantasy Fiction und verwandte Gattungen

Märchen: Verzauberung und Entzauberung

McAra, Catriona, and David Calvin, eds. *Anti-Tales: The Uses of Disenchantment*. Newcastle upon Tyne: Cambridge Scholars Publishing, 2011. 299 pp., £ 44,99.

Märchen und phantastische Literatur weisen fließende Grenzen auf; wer dort als Zollbeamter tätig wäre, hätte es schwer. Eine Übergangsform ist das Anti-Märchen oder das umgeschriebene Märchen. Bekannte Muster wie die vom Rotkäppchen werden aktualisiert, auf den Kopf gestellt oder verfremdet. Eine Meisterin in dieser parodistischen Form, die allerdings auch Botschaften wie die des Feminismus enthält, war etwa Angela Carter. Die hier vorgelegten Aufsätze gehen jedoch weit über das Revidieren von Märchen hinaus. Texte wie *Alice in Wonderland* oder Bruno Schulz' *Strasse der Krokodile* werden ebenso in ihren Transformationen vorgestellt wie die visuellen Beispiele von Blake und Goya. Schwarzer Humor spielt eine große Rolle bei diesen Verwandlungen, und so sind denn auch Roald Dahl und James Thurber eigene Artikel gewidmet. Ein großer Urwald an Erzählungen und deren subversiven Gegenspielern tut sich auf, ein wahres Ökosystem der Fiktionen, denn ohne Antagonismus und Subversion könnte die Literatur gar nicht leben. Claire Massey hat recht, wenn sie sagt: "Where the fairy tale leaves us with answers, the anti-tale leaves us with questions." Oder nicht ganz, denn wir kehren zu den Märchen zurück und stellen fest, dass sie aus vielen Fragen bestehen oder sie aufwerfen, was schon mit der Frage der Versionen beginnt. Nur haben uns die Anti-Märchen diese Fragen erst bewusst gemacht.

ELMAR SCHENKEL

ZU EINZELNEN AUTOREN

Johann Wolfgang von Goethe

Skorniakova, Kristina. *Moderne Transzendenz: Wie Goethes Wilhelm-Meister-Romane Sinn machen.* Leipzig: Leipziger Universitätsverlag, 2010. 423 S., € 29,90.

In Goethes "Prometheus" hat der Dichter die Bewusstseinslage der Moderne in der Bildlichkeit von Licht und Finsternis eindrucksvoll umrissen. Während das Feuer auf Prometheus' Erde, in seiner selbstgebauten Hütte und auf seinem Herd sich gegenüber Zeus' Gewitterblitzen und Stürmen behauptet und zunehmend manifestiert, kündigt sich bereits eine weitere und dramatischere Wende an: die unpersönlichen Mächte Zeit und Schicksal ziehen als düsteres Doppelgestirn herauf und lassen nicht nur das Tageslicht des Zeus, sondern auch das Feuer der Technik, das Prometheus entzündet hat, zu Bedeutungslosigkeit und Ohnmacht verblassen. Hütte, Herd und Glut bieten in einer fremd werdenden Welt weder Heimat noch Zuflucht. In den letzten Worten des Prometheus klingt das "Lieber noch das Nichts wollen als nicht wollen" Nietzsches bereits an. Nicht nur der "neue Mensch" wird von Prometheus erschaffen werden, sondern auch ein Sinn, der selbstverständlich nicht gefunden, sondern "gemacht", produziert wird.

Andererseits finden sich im späteren und Spätwerk Goethes explizite Bezüge zur traditionalen Philosophie, besonders zum Neuplatonismus:

> Das Ew'ge regt sich fort in Allem
> Denn Alles muß in Nichts zerfallen
> Wenn es im Sein beharren will.
> ("Eins und Alles")

Bis in Bildlichkeit und Begrifflichkeit finden sich plotinische Gedankengänge in

> Wär' nicht das Auge sonnenhaft
> Die Sonne könnt' es nie erblicken.
> Läg' nicht in uns des Gottes eig'ne Kraft,
> Wie könnt' uns Göttliches entzücken?

oder in den Zeilen aus den "Zahmen Xenien":

> Angedenken an das Gute
> Hält uns immer frisch bei Mute.
>
> Angedenken an das Schöne
> Ist das Heil der Erdensöhne.
>
> Angedenken an das Liebe –
> Glücklich, wenn's lebendig bliebe!
>
> Angedenken an das Eine
> Bleibt das Beste, was ich meine.

Goethes Interesse an Hegels Philosophie, deren Beziehung zum spätantiken Neuplatonismus durch rezente Studien umfassend belegt ist,[1] zeigt sich auch in seinem Briefwechsel mit Hegel.

In ihrer Studie zu Goethes Wilhelm-Meister-Romanen stellt Kristina Skorniakowa diese als Werke dar, die exemplarisch für die Moderne seien, eine These, die sich auch im scheinbar lässig-umgangssprachlich formulierten Untertitel "Wie Goethes Wilhelm-Meister-Romane Sinn machen" sprachlich niederschlägt.

Trotz des seit den 1990er Jahren zunehmenden wissenschaftlichen Interesses an den Wilhelm-Meister-Romanen ist Skorniakowas Arbeit die bisher einzige, die sich der Untersuchung des gesamten Romankomplexes widmet, einmal abgesehen von einer Monographie Max Wundts aus dem Jahr 1913.

---

[1] Vgl. *Hegel und der spätantike Neuplatonismus: Untersuchungen zur Metaphysik des Einen und des Nous in Hegels spekulativer und geschichtlicher Deutung.* Bonn: Bouvier, 1999; sowie Halfwassen, Jens. *Geist und Selbstbewusstsein: Studien zu Plotin und Numenios.* Stuttgart: Franz Steiner Verlag, 1994.

Die Verfasserin sieht den Schlüssel zum Verständnis der Romane in der Vorstellung von "moderner Transzendenz"; der Transzendenzbegriff sollte also klar definiert und präzise formuliert im Zentrum der Studie stehen. Diesem Thema widmen sich das Einleitungskapitel und das Schlusswort der Studie. Der Transzendenzbegriff und die Thematisierung von möglichen Transzendenzerfahrungen erscheinen jedoch eigentümlich vage; das mag daran liegen, dass die Autoritäten, die Skorniakova hierfür heranführt (mehrheitlich N. Luhmann und K. Eibl) nicht Philosophen im Fachsinn sind.

Zur Verdeutlichung der Begrifflichkeit verwendet die Autorin zum einen das Bild der Jakobsleiter (Genesis 28,12ff.), zum anderen umreißt sie die Thesen Luhmanns und Eibls, deren Terminologie sie für ihre Interpretation der Genesis-Erzählung unhinterfragt verwendet. Die Vision Jakobs versteht sie als Erfahrung einer "Totalitätskorrespondenz" (17), die die immanente Erde mit dem transzendenten Himmel verbinde. Die Thesen von Luhmann und Eibl verorten die Bedeutung transzendenter Vorstellungen in der Absicht, "Unbestimmbares bestimmbar" zu machen (22), also Macht auszuüben, wobei nach Eibl in der Moderne "die Poesie die Funktion der Religion" übernehme (22), sowie in der Intention, "Immanenz und Transzendenz [...] rein formal ohne metaphysische Implikationen" (25) zu interpretieren.

Dieser Formalismus führt bereits in der Interpretation von Genesis 28,12ff. zu einem recht undifferenzierten Ergebnis, da weder die hochkomplexe Bildlichkeit der Episode noch deren relevanter Erzählkontext einbezogen werden.[2] Von einem solchen eher aussagelosen Formalismus heben sich die in der philosophischen Tradition erfahrenen und reflektierten Zugänge zum Wesen der Transzendenz durch gedankliche Präzision, umfassenden Diskurs und tiefreichende Erkenntnisse eindrucksvoll ab. Das plotinische Eine ist "jenseits des Seins [...], auch jenseits der Energeia und jenseits des Geistes und Denkens" (Enneade VI, 8, 16, 34)

---

[2] Vgl. Ch. 1 ("The Stolen Birthright") in: Prickett, Stephen. *Origins of Narrative: The Romantic Appropriation of the Bible*. Cambridge: Cambridge UP, 1996.

und demnach auch jenseits einer irgendwie vorgestellten Totalitätserfahrung eines Individuums. Durch die Dialektik eines Denkens, das seine eigene Intention negiert, ist die Transzendenzerfahrung als "Lücke" (408) keineswegs der Moderne vorbehalten, sondern wesentliches Charakteristikum jedes klar reflektierten Transzendenzbegriffs, wie Gedankengänge von beispielsweise Plotin, Anselm von Canterbury, Meister Eckhart, Hadewijch bis hin zu Kierkegaard hinlänglich belegen.

Skorniakovas Studie widmet sich der Untersuchung von Transzendenz-Konzeptionen im Sinne von Eibls "Totalitätskorrespondenzen" (27), die Thema der drei Wilhelm-Meister-Romane seien. Aufgrund der unterschiedlichen Entstehungszeiten der Romane unterscheiden sich die jeweiligen Schwerpunkte ebenfalls. In *Wilhelm Meisters Theatralische Sendung* (also dem Teil des Werkes, das dem "Prometheus" am nächsten ist) liege der Nachdruck auf dem "Transzendenzkonzept Genie", während für *Wilhelm Meisters Lehrjahre* und *Wilhelm Meisters Wanderjahre oder Die Entsagenden* jeweils das der Bildung bzw. das der Tätigkeit im Mittelpunkt stünden.

Skorniakova geht methodisch "textnah" (27), also eher paraphrasierend vor, eine Untersuchungsmethode, die auch dem mit Goethes Werk weniger vertrauten Leser ermöglicht, die Handlung der Romane nachzuvollziehen und sich mit der Analyse der Verfasserin konkret auseinanderzusetzen; dies wird durch die jedem Abschnitt vorangestellte Frage und nachfolgende Schlussfolgerung erleichtert. Im Lauf der Untersuchung legt Skorniakova nahe, dass die drei genannten Transzendenzkonzepte nicht "greifen": weder das Konzept des Genies, noch das der Bildung, noch das der Tätigkeit führten zu einer "Totalitätserfahrung" im Sinne Eibls.

Transzendenz werde im Kontext der Moderne nicht mehr von der Religion als Garanten eines "Sinnganzen" (408) vermittelt. Die moderne Poesie als Religionsersatz "kann und will Sinn" jedoch ebensowenig "garantieren" (408); allerdings vermöge sie auf die "Lücke", das Fehlen eines übergeordneten Kontextes im modernen Weltbild hinzuweisen: auf die "Schwebe von Sinn zwischen dem

Wunsch nach Transzendenz und dem immer wieder vorgeführten Scheitern desselben" (410) als Charakteristikum der Moderne.

In ihrem Schlusswort "Moderne Transzendenz" (408) skizziert Skorniakova die Erzähltheorie, die sie als Basis ihrer Wilhelm-Meister-These ansieht. Erzählen sieht sie als Ausdruck des Bedürfnisses nach Sinn, einer "anthropologischen Grundkonstante" (409). Ohne die Orientierungshilfe einer erzählten Weltordnung sei auch, so insbesondere Eibl (409), ein Überleben des Menschen im biologischen Sinne nicht möglich, denn "Wer erzählt, schafft Ordnung in der Welt" (408).

Trifft das überhaupt grundsätzlich zu, wenn man sich beispielsweise Erzählbotschaften wie die von Mörikes Maler Nolten, Büchners Woyzeck, Jean Pauls Rede des toten Christus herab vom Weltgebäude, Kafkas Strafkolonie vor Augen führt? Diese Werke könnten allerdings als charakteristisch für die Moderne verstanden werden, für die nach Skorniakova die "Dialektik [...] der Sehnsucht nach einem [...] übergeordneten Sinn und der gleichzeitigen Erfahrung von dessen Verweigerung" (409) charakteristisch sei.

Überblickt man jedoch Zeiträume, die außerhalb der Moderne liegen, so wird diese "Lücke" zwischen dem Sinnpostulat und dessen Verweigerung immer wieder thematisiert. Es ist nämlich nicht nur ein Charakteristikum der Moderne, Sinnkrisen und Transzendenzverlust zu erfahren. Auch in Zeiträumen, von denen ein expliziter Transzendenzbezug angenommen wird, ist der Bruch zwischen dem Transzendenzverlangen und dem Transzendenzverlust ein zentrales Erzählthema. Eines der ältesten Erzählmuster, das der schamanischen Reise, hat als zentrales Motiv die Krise, die tödliche Verwundung des Heilers, seine Skelettierung in der Unterwelt; auf die Dialektik des Aufstiegs zum Einen im Platonismus wurde bereits weiter oben hingewiesen. Ein tieferer Pessimismus als der, den die Schlussstrophe des Nibelungenliedes zum Ausdruck bringt, lässt sich kaum vorstellen. Solche Beispiele lassen sich beliebig vermehren.

"Where has gone the steed? Where has gone the man? Where has gone the giver of treasure? [...] Truly, that time has passed away, has grown dark under the helm of night as though it had never been" heißt es in der altenglischen Elegie "The Wanderer".[3] Verglichen mit einem solchen Statement sieht die "Moderne Transzendenz" der Wilhelm-Meister-Romane doch sehr zahm aus.

ADELHEID KEGLER

Lewis Carroll

Davis, Richard Brian, ed. *Alice in Wonderland and Philosophy: Curiouser and Curiouser.* Hoboken: Wiley, 2010. 227 pp., € 14,99.

Philosophie scheint (wieder) schwer angesagt zu sein – dieser Eindruck muss sich einem aufdrängen, wenn man die vielen Neuerscheinungen und auch Verkaufserfolge entsprechender populärwissenschaftlicher Bücher betrachtet. Besonders im anglo-amerikanischen Bereich gibt es dabei eine Tendenz, bekannte Filme, Serien oder andere Fiktionen als Aufhänger für eine *tour de force* durch die philosophische Ideengeschichte zu nehmen. Seit dem großen Erfolg von *Philosophy in the Simpsons*, das es in mehreren Ländern auf die Bestsellerlisten schaffte, erscheinen mittlerweile in schneller Folge ähnliche Werke, wobei die Qualität zwischen diesen Büchern und den enthaltenen Aufsätzen stark schwanken kann und die Beziehung zum populären Aufhänger mitunter etwas bemüht wirkt. Mit Lewis Carrolls *Alice in Wonderland* haben sich die Herausgeber der 'Philosophy and Pop Culture Series' jedoch ein Werk ausgesucht, das in seiner komplexen Absurdität regelrecht nach einer philosophischen Betrachtung verlangt. In der Literaturwissenschaft wird Carrolls Meisterwerk schon lange nicht mehr als Kinderbuch abgetan, und auch die Linguistik hat ihre Freude an diesem Klassiker der viktorianischen Literatur, sodass vor allem in der Anglistik eine ganze Reihe von Studien zu *Alice in Wonderland* vorliegen, die teilweise auch philosophische Konzepte beleuchten. Blackwells 'Philosophy and Pop Culture'-Serie möchte jedoch weniger ein Fach-

---

[3] "The Wanderer", Exeter Book fol. 76^b–78^a. In: *Everyman Anglo-Saxon Poetry.* London: Dent, 1995. 324–325.

publikum als eher den an Philosophie interessierten Alltagsleser ansprechen, was zu einer interessanten Gratwanderung zwischen Anspruch und allgemeiner Verständlichkeit führt. Mit ironischem Unterton verspricht die Einführung des Bandes: "The Alice-addicted philosophers in this book will clear the air of the hookah smoke [...] You can put it all together for the first time" (2–3).

Die vierzehn Aufsätze von *Philosophy in Alice in Wonderland* sind in vier thematische Gruppen eingeordnet, wobei sich der erste Teil vornehmlich sozialen Beziehungen widmet, Teil zwei das Problem der Logik ergründet, der dritte Abschnitt verschiedene Realitätsbegriffe beleuchtet und der Schlussteil die Frage der persönlichen Identität in den Vordergrund rückt. Viele philosophische Aspekte in Carrolls Roman wurden schon in Martin Gardners Erläuterungen in *The Annotated Alice* angesprochen, allerdings ermöglicht der vorliegende Sammelband eine weit tiefergehende und modernere Betrachtung als die mittlerweile fünfzig Jahre alte Luxusausgabe des Werkes – eine Chance, die manche beteiligte Autoren leider nur teilweise nutzen. Schon der erste Aufsatz "Unruly Alice: A Feminist View of Some Adventures in Wonderland" zeigt die Vor- und Nachteile einiger Beiträge dieses Bandes auf. Zum einen ist für das Verständnis der meisten Essays keinerlei philosophische Vorbildung notwendig, zum anderen darf man allerdings auch nicht erwarten, immer Einblick in eine philosophischen Denkrichtung zu bekommen. Mit dem angekündigten "feminist view" bekommt der Leser nicht etwa eine kurze Einführung in feministische Ansätze in der Philosophie, die mit Carrolls Werk in Beziehung gesetzt werden, sondern die Hauptfigur Alice wird auf unterhaltsame Weise im Kontext von weiblichen Rollenbildern betrachtet. Dabei werden zwar z. B. aktuelle Vergleiche zu Hillary Clinton, Sarah Palin und der amerikanischen Abtreibungsdebatte gezogen, aber keine Verbindungen zu philosophischen Strömungen oder zur Philosophiegeschichte hergestellt, und entsprechend wird auch fast keine Sekundärliteratur bemüht.

Man sollte den Sammelband aber nicht an den ersten drei Aufsätzen messen, die vielleicht bewusst seicht daherkommen, um den Leser nicht mit zu viel Philosophie gleich wieder zu vergraulen. Die

Aufsätze haben oft eine persönliche, humorvolle Note und werden mit Anekdoten aus dem Alltagsleben der Beitragenden verknüpft, was sicherlich die Anschaulichkeit und den Unterhaltungswert erhöht; andererseits wird der didaktische Plauderton in vielen Beiträgen auch manche Leser stören, besonders wenn sie schon ein gewisses Vorwissen haben. Vermutlich wird mit dem Buch eine recht junge Zielgruppe ins Auge gefasst, die nicht mit einem akademischen Schreibstil verschreckt werden soll; glücklicherweise muten etliche der Autoren den Lesern aber inhaltlich etwas mehr zu und gehen mit ihren Aufsätzen auf die philosophische Ideengeschichte ein. So zeigt zum Beispiel der vierte Aufsatz, "'You're Nothing but a Pack of Cards!': Alice Doesn't Have a Social Contract", dass man auch auf eine spielerisch-anekdotische Weise wichtige Konzepte von Sokrates/Platon, Hobbes, Locke und Rawls zu Rechtsordnung und Ethik vermitteln kann. Fast alle Beiträge weisen einen deutlichen Bezug zur Popkultur und der amerikanischen Politik auf, mitunter mit sehr kritischen Untertönen, wie zum Beispiel im Beitrag "Nuclear Strategists in Wonderland", der Begebenheiten und Metaphern aus *Alice in Wonderland* als Aufhänger nimmt, um amerikanische Militär- und Propagandastrategien als eine politische "MAD Tea Party" (37) zu geißeln.

In circa der Hälfte der Aufsätze wird Philosophie in *Alice in Wonderland* vornehmlich als kritisches Denken über die Gegenwart verstanden, für das Carrolls Roman passende Stichworte und Bilder als Ausgangspunkt liefert. Die andere Hälfte der Beiträge widmet sich jedoch wirklich einer Analyse des Textes aus einer bestimmten philosophischen Perspektive, wie z. B. der Exkurs in Logik in "Six Impossible Things before Breakfast", der die nur scheinbare Unlogik im Roman geschickt aufdröselt, u. a. mit Rückgriff auf Platon, Hume und Chesterton. Ein anderes spannendes Beispiel ist eine Nietzscheanische Interpretation von *Alice in Wonderland* als Tragödie, auf Grundlage der Philosophie von Carrolls umstrittenem Zeitgenossen. Eine ganze Reihe von Essays beschäftigen sich erwartungsgemäß mit Nonsens als tiefergehendem Konzept, u. a. in Verbindung mit den Philosophien von Platon, Hume, Chesterton und Wittgenstein, wobei die philosophische Sprengkraft scheinbaren Unsinns und die ironische Tiefgründigkeit von Lewis Carroll deutlich wird.

Insgesamt sind fast alle wichtigen Philosophen in *Philosophy in Alice in Wonderland* vertreten, angefangen bei den antiken Klassikern bis hin zu (post-)modernen Vertretern wie Donald Davidson und Richard Rorty, wobei der Fokus wie üblich auf dem westlichen Kanon liegt, mit wenigen Ausnahmen wie dem daoistischen Philosophen Zhuangzi, der in einem Aufsatz zu Träumen, Drogen und Realitätsbestimmung in Carrolls Meisterwerk herangezogen wird. Dabei wird teilweise auch deutlich, dass die Geschichte von Alice wichtige philosophische Ideen des 20. Jahrhunderts vorweggenommen hat, die z. B. im Werk von Franz Kafka oder Aldous Huxley hervortreten. *Philosophy in Alice in Wonderland* zeigt nicht nur die Vielschichtigkeit von Carrolls Roman als "treasure of philosophical puzzles" (183), sondern auch die Aktualität von Philosophie für das Verständnis literarischer Werke und die Verwirrungen der Gegenwart. Der Leser spürt, dass die Autoren des Bandes nicht in einem akademischen Elfenbeinturm sitzen, sondern sich wie Alice auf einer abenteuerlichen Reise durch das Reich des menschlichen Geistes befinden. Wer Carrolls Roman mag und sich auf einen unterhaltsamen Exkurs in die philosophischen Aspekte von Lewis Carrolls Erwachsenen-Kinderbuch begeben möchte, dem sei *Philosophy in Alice in Wonderland* ans Herz gelegt.

STEFAN LAMPADIUS

Winchester, Simon. *The Alice Behind Wonderland*. Oxford: Oxford UP, 2011. 110 pp., £ 9,99.

The dust jacket of this handsomely printed little book is full of "Praise for Simon Winchester", OBE (Officer of the Order of the British Empire) and author of five *New York Times* non-fiction best-sellers. But, as Alice (in Lewis Carroll's *Alice in Wonderland*) famously pointed out, "what is the use of a book without pictures or conversations?" Being no children's fiction, *The Alice Behind Wonderland* may be excused for having neither, but since – its title notwithstanding – it is only marginally about the 'real' Alice (i. e., Charles Lutwidge Dodgson's child friend and recipient of his handwritten book *Alice's Adventures Underground*) but mostly about Dodgson (a. k. a. Lewis Carroll) the photographer, and about the pictures he produced, a few illustrations would not have been superfluous. Winchester is marvellously skilled in bringing Dodgson's biography to life – his childhood at Daresbury and Croft-on-Tees, the young student, and later instructor of mathematics, at Christ Church College, Oxford, his relationship with the family of Henry George Liddell, Dean of Christ Church College and father of Alice (as well as of many more sisters and sons). He is very knowledgeable when it comes to the technical details, and the cultural role, of photography in middle-class Victorian England, and he is particularly good at describing the pictures Carroll made – so much so that we can almost – but not quite – forgive the publishers for withholding practically all illustrations. (Buyers should make sure they preserve the dusk jacket since it is only there that they are treated to a small print of the picture Winchester rhapsodizes, and fantasizes, about over several pages (cf. 5–10, 83–87): Carroll's most famous photograph, featuring Alice dressed as a beggar child.)

And, since the book is so entertainingly written, we may also forgive the author for having little new to say, especially since he does make shrewd use of the vast Carrollian scholarship and, in his appended "Suggestions for Further Reading", warmly recommends a much more thorough biography. And we may, finally, forgive the publishers for choosing (or allowing the author to choose?) a rather misleading title. After all, Carroll himself has provided an illustration of the unreliability of titles in his *Through the Looking Glass And What Alice Found There* where the White Knight (generally regarded as the author's self-portrait) explains that the *name* of the song he is going to sing is *called* "Haddock's Eyes" while the name itself *is* "The Aged Aged Man", whereas the song itself *is called* "Ways and Means" but really *is* "A-sitting On A Gate". Likewise, while the *name* of the book is *The Alice Behind Wonderland*, it really *is* "About Lewis Carroll and the Photographs He Made".

And what would I call it? – Perhaps "Charming But Not As Illuminating As it Might Have Been"?

DIETER PETZOLD

Arthur Conan Doyle und H. G. Wells

Batory, Dana Martin. *Dreams of Future Past: The Science Fiction Worlds of Arthur Conan Doyle & H. G. Wells*. Indianapolis: Wessex Press, 2010. viii + 141 pp., $ 13,95.

Dreams of Future Past is Dana Martin Batory's collection of fifteen self-penned essays originally published in "small, sometimes obscure literary journals directed at a niche audience" (2) between 1980 and 1998. The volume focuses on the science fiction of H. G. Wells and Arthur Conan Doyle though, rather than being a comparative study, the collection consists of 9 essays on Doyle and 6 on Wells. Given the amateur nature of these essays, it is unsurprising to find them uneven in quality. I will therefore focus only on those which may be of interest for further academic research.

Batory is not a literary academic, being a geologist turned cabinetmaker, but he clearly enjoys his subject, and offers a number of thoughtful observations about the stories he considers. In "'The Terror of Blue John Gap': A Geological and Literary Study", co-authored with William A. S. Sarjeant, the authors take clues from Doyle's narrative to determine the location of Blue John Gap (Treak Cliff, Derbyshire), the nature of the "terror" (a scimitar cat) and to critically appraise Doyle's geological knowledge of the region and its natural make up. The authors close the essay by considering possible sources of Doyle's geological knowledge, and while much of this is speculation (assuming Doyle walked in Derbyshire during a short stint as a doctor in Sheffield, and suggesting certain museums he may have visited in Sheffield, Plymouth and Exeter, e. g.), there are clearly clues for future researchers to consider when exploring the sources for Doyle's ideas.

In "The Biblical *War of the Worlds*", Batory argues that "Wells reworked the raw material of old religious symbols and mythological images into extraterrestrial forces of evil" and suggests that *The War of the Worlds* (1897–98) is "an allegory by which Wells meant to expound his social ideas" (25). Rather than pursue this line of thought, however, Batory limits this brief essay to reproducing extracts from the story alongside quotations from the Old and New Testaments to demonstrate Wells's Biblical knowledge and his debt to those abundant sources. While this results in a mere *Notes and Queries*-type product, Batory nonetheless produces a useful series of observations from which future research can pursue the Biblical *War of the Worlds* in greater detail. A similar approach is taken in "The Other *War of the Worlds*", where Batory considers the *Pearson's Magazine* serialisation of the story. He calls it "a more raw, exciting, and gripping account of the merciless devastation of the Martian invasion – more ambitious and absorbing" (50) and, despite his enthusiasm for it, he does not take a critical approach to the differences between it and the Heinemann book version. Instead he reprints a number of the differences "To stir the interest of Wells scholars" (51).

In "Dating *The War of the Worlds*", Batory uses astronomical data to determine that the Martian invasion occurred in June 1901, "early in the twentieth century" (72) as Wells's narrator alerts, and just a few months after that year's Earth-Mars opposition. Based on incidental remarks made by the narrator in *The War of the Worlds*, Batory uses this starting point to date many significant events of the story. Thus the first Martian cylinder is launched on 12 June, landing on 21 June (followed by nine further cylinders at 24-hour intervals), and the tale ends with the narrator's return to Leatherhead on 16 July, three days after the death of the last Martian invader. Despite a number of dating inconsistencies by the narrator, Batory presents a convincing chronology of the events of the war of the worlds.

Perhaps the most important essay in the collection is "H. G. Wells' *Island of Dr Moreau*". In it, Batory analyses Wells's story to determine literary influences behind it, and the moral of the story. Batory sees the Bible and Shakespeare's *The Tempest* (1610–11) as the chief literary influences on Wells during the writing of *The*

Island of Doctor Moreau (1896). Prospero's educating of Caliban and his use as a slave offer a model for Moreau's Beast Folk (90) while, "Though Wells was an atheist he did not reject the traditions of the Bible or its legends, he skillfully grafted them onto all his stories" (89). In considering the Law which Moreau uses to control the Beast Folk, Batory claims that "The major impulse and purpose behind Wells' story was to show organized religion as an opiate used to control man and keep him down" (91). Generally, when attacking religion in his writings, "Wells usually emphasized science's achievements and the omnipotence of matter and order" (92). *The Island of Doctor Moreau* treats science and religion differently, however. Whilst no apologist for religious indoctrination, Wells was also warning against deifying science: "Wells […] was *not* saying that creation is God's right and to create new lives ourselves is blasphemy. More likely he was stating that when one plays God, he ends up being as savage as God" (96). Batory convincingly demonstrates that Wells rejects religious control in *The Island of Doctor Moreau*, but nonetheless advocates an ethical basis for scientific research which Moreau clearly lacks.

In *"When the World Screamed*: Literary Echoes", Batory traces the influences Doyle absorbed when penning his fourth Professor Challenger story. For the construction of the research station at which the excavation is prepared, Doyle relied on imagery present in Jules Verne's *From the Earth to the Moon* (1865) (103–04), while Verne's blast off anticipates the vomiting of Challenger's experimental apparatus from the earth when his drill pierces below the crust (105). Another influence is identified as Francis Richard Stockton's *The Great Stone of Sardis* (1897), where the earth's core is penetrated by an endowed scientist working in secret with highly paid, discrete staff (107). In Doyle's, Verne's and Stockton's stories, "we find the common features of a scientist, his wealthy patron, isolated building sites, the select workers, the sophisticated equipment, the great shaft, and with the exception of Verne, the destruction of said shaft" (108). Batory also points out Doyle's likely familiarity with Camille Flammarion's "A Hole Through the Earth", published in the same September 1909 issue of *The Strand Magazine* in which Doyle himself published "Some Recollections of Sport", in which Flammarion advocates the "sinking [of] a shaft into the earth for the express purpose of scientific exploration, descending as far below the surface as the utmost resources of modern science would permit" (109). Thus reliant on previous literary efforts, "From this mixture of creativity and borrowing came a truly unique fantasy tale of science" (110).

In "Sussex Iguanodon Footprints and the Writing of *The Lost World*", co-authored with William A. S. Sarjeant, the authors tell of Conan Doyle's firsthand experience of discovering and investigating Iguanodon prints in a quarry near his Crowborough home in Sussex. While visits by British Museum (Natural History) palaeontologists resulted in no published research, Doyle had casts made of the prints, and was inspired by the rich prehistoric heritage around him to pen *The Lost World* (1912). Also of influence was E. Ray Lankester's *Extinct Animals* (1905), especially the illustrations which aided Doyle in his descriptions of the dinosaurs discovered by Professor Challenger and his expedition.

In "Conan Doyle Shows His Hand", Batory demonstrates Doyle's debt to Mary Shelley's *Frankenstein* (1818) in the writing of his short story, "The Brown Hand" (1899), while "Genesis of *The War of the Worlds*" considers the scientific developments and contemporary geopolitical events which might have contributed to the ideas behind the Martian invasion of the story. In "The Climax of *When The World Screamed*", Batory catalogues the linguistic evidence for Doyle's story paralleling an incestuous rape, with Professor Challenger drilling to the jelly below the earth's crust for no apparent reason (scientific or otherwise), and causing an orgasmic scream and a liquid gush from the vaginal cavern! In "The Rime of *The Polestar*", Batory identifies the autobiographical aspects of the story, including Doyle's time as a ship's surgeon and his early knowledge of spiritualism, as well as the influence of *Frankenstein* and Samuel Taylor Coleridge's "Rime of the Ancient Mariner" (1798) on it. In "The Frankenstein Motif and Sir Arthur Conan Doyle", Batory catalogues textual similarities between *Frankenstein* and Conan Doyle's "Lot No. 249" (1892).

As mentioned at the outset, Batory's essays are not literary scholarship, and yet he uses his enthusiast's eye to identify influences and connections which have not been made before concerning some of the science fiction stories of Doyle and Wells. While Batory's collection asks more questions than it answers, it will prove, for that reason, a useful reference for future researchers, especially given his many intertextual observations.

JOHN S. PARTINGTON

J. R. R. Tolkien

Dubs, Kathleen, and Janka Kaščáková, eds. *Middle-earth and Beyond: Essays on the World of J. R. R. Tolkien.* Newcastle: Cambridge Scholars Publishing, 2010. 145 pp., £ 34,99.

Das Anliegen der Herausgeberinnen des vorliegenden Bandes ist es, neue Zugänge zu Tolkien oder andere als die üblichen Texte zu berücksichtigen sowie überkommene Meinungen zu korrigieren. Wenngleich dieser auch im Titel ausgedrückte Anspruch hinsichtlich der untersuchten Texte nicht ganz eingehalten wird, da sich die meisten Beiträge auf *The Lord of the Rings* bzw. das Mittelerde-Legendarium beziehen, betreten die Artikel in der Tat nicht nur ausgetretene Pfade – im Gegenteil.

Dies zeigt sich schon im ersten Beitrag, in dem Jason Fisher einer in der Tolkienforschung beliebten Tätigkeit nachgeht und sich auf Quellensuche begibt. Denn das Objekt seiner Suche – der Ausdruck "Circles of the World" – blieb bislang in dieser Hinsicht unbeachtet. Fisher zeigt hier überzeugende Verbindungen zur *Heimkringsla*, der *Vulgata* (besonders dem Buch Weisheit) und (wie er selbst betont: spekulativer) zur *Hereford Mappa Mundi* auf und äußert die Vermutung, "that they may very well have fertilized the leaf-mould of Tolkien's mind, out of which grew the seed of this beautiful and moving metaphor for mortality, for the passing of time, for change, and for nostalgia and loss" (15).

Eine ganze Reihe von Texten Tolkiens nimmt Sue Bridgwater in den Blick, wenn sie sich der Frage nach Stasis versus Bewegung bzw. Zuhausebleiben oder Reisen sowohl in geographischer als auch metaphysischer Hinsicht zuwendet. Im Zentrum ihrer Untersuchung stehen die Entscheidungen, zu gehen oder zu bleiben sowie über die zu wählende Richtung. Sie deutet dabei Beziehungen zu anderen Themenfeldern wie Ungehorsam, Schicksal und Willensfreiheit oder Begrenztheit an und sieht einen "discernible bias in Tolkien's stories in favour of the notion that the foolhardy, those who seem to be taking the *wrong* road in terms of common sense, perhaps going against the advice of a more experienced guide or blindly committing themselves to the demands of fate, are the ones taking the *right* road in moral terms" (37), wobei Tolkien dies nicht verabsolutiere.

Es folgen zwei Beiträge – von Liam Campbell und Kingan Jenike –, die sich mit Tom Bombadil und besonders der Frage nach seinem Wesen auseinandersetzen. Während Jenike in ihrem kurzen Beitrag den rätselhaften Charakter Bombadils betont, indem sie darlegt, dass er zu keinem Volk und keiner Rasse Mittelerdes gehört, argumentiert Campbell sehr ausführlich dafür, ihn in der Tradition des *Green Man* als "spirit of nature under threat" zu verstehen. Er beginnt dazu mit einer detaillierten Diskussion verschiedener Forschungsmeinungen und zeigt gerade an seinem Umgang mit dem Ring seinen Nichtwillen zur Macht auf. Besonderes Gewicht verleiht er den Aussagen in Tolkiens Werk, die sich auf Bombadils bedrohte Existenz beziehen, und verbindet diese mit der Tradition des *Green Man*. Tolkiens Porträt "sets Tom up against forces whose assault on the landscapes and ecology of Middle-earth becomes a vivid evocation of everything Tolkien feared was threatening the pastoral lands he knew well" (62f.).

Anschließend behandeln Silvia Pokrivčakova und Anton Pokrivčak die Rolle des Grotesken in *The Hobbit* und *The Lord of the Rings*, wozu sie zunächst das Groteske und Groteskheit theoretisch diskutieren und auf dieser Basis Trolle und Orks als Materialisierungen des Bösen und moralischer Verderbtheit, Gollum als Monster kontinuierlicher Transformation, die Zwerge als grotesk in ihrer Doppeldeutigkeit, die Hobbits als groteske Genießer und schließlich die Elben als groteske Feier des Lebens und der Natur vorstellen.

Der nächste Beitrag von Janka Kaščáková widmet sich der Bedeutung des Essens und Trinkens in *The Lord of the Rings*. Sie argumentiert dafür, Essen als Hauptunterschied zwischen Hobbits und anderen Völkern Mittelerdes (und besonders zu den Elben) zu verstehen, zeigt auf, wie es als Quelle von Humor fungiert, und betont die große Bedeutung für die persönliche Entwicklung der Hobbits, was gerade bei Sam und seinem Verzicht auf das Kochgeschirr exemplarisch deutlich wird.

Kathleen Dubs behandelt in ihrem Artikel den Humor in *The Lord of the Rings* und widerspricht der weit verbreiteten Annahme, dieser komme nur sporadisch vor. Sie gibt nicht nur zahlreiche Beispiele für schlagfertige Antworten oder humorvolle Szenen auf, sondern auch, wie Humor als strukturelles Werkzeug und zur Charakterisierung eingesetzt wird. Wie in der damit verbundenen Analyse, wer weswegen, wann und wie lacht, deutlich wird, ist Lachen nicht immer mit Humor verbunden und wird sowohl für positive wie negative Zwecke eingesetzt – z. B. als psychologisches Mittel zur Stärkung oder um andere lächerlich zu machen oder zu entmutigen.

Im letzten Beitrag widmet sich Roberto di Scala der Frage nach dem Verhältnis von "Lit.", "Lang." und "Ling.", das er auf der Basis der Kommunikationstheorie Paul Grices an der "Lay of the Children of Húrin" bespricht. Indem er nachzuweisen sucht, "that Tolkien's poetic fragment acts as an intentional, rational, and transparent token of communication" (138), plädiert er dafür, "linguistics" und nicht "philology" als geeignete Betrachtungsweise der Verbindung linguistischer und literarischer Aspekte anzusehen.

Zusammenfassend kann die Lektüre dieses Bandes empfohlen werden, da die Beiträge nicht nur unübliche oder (weitgehend) unbehandelte Fragestellungen in den Blick nehmen, sondern dies auch auf lesenswerte und durchaus überzeugende Weise tun. Einzig der eher essayistische Beitrag von Jenike fällt im Vergleich zu den gehaltvolleren anderen etwas ab, ohne damit den Gesamteindruck nennenswert zu schmälern.

THOMAS FORNET-PONSE

Kehr, Eike. *Natur und Kultur in J. R. R. Tolkiens* The Lord of the Rings. SALS: Studien zur anglistischen Literatur- und Sprachwissenschaft 35. Trier: wvt, 2011. 198 S., € 21,50.

Über Klassiker etwas Neues zu sagen, ist schwer. Gegen dieses Handicap hat auch Eike Kehr zu kämpfen, denn es geht ihm in seiner Dissertation um nichts Geringeres als "um die [dem Roman] implizit zu Grunde gelegten Ideen und Werte – und damit letztlich auch um die ethisch-moralischen Implikationen, die sich aus der Lektüre von Tolkiens Roman für den Leser ergeben" (3). Er bewegt sich damit im Kernbereich der klassischen Textinterpretation, in dem sich naturgemäß vor ihm schon etliche andere Forscher getummelt haben – nicht zuletzt er selbst, wie ein Blick in sein 2003 erschienenes, über weite Passagen mit der Dissertation identisches Buch *Die wiederbezauberte Welt: Natur und Ökologie in Tolkiens "The Lord of the Rings"* (Wetzlar: Förderkreis Phantastik in Wetzlar) erkennen lässt.

Kehr hält sich nicht lange mit der Definition oder gar Problematisierung seiner Schlüsselbegriffe auf. Kultur sieht er (in Anlehnung an Nünning) als "das 'mentale Gesamtprogramm' einer Gesellschaft" (2), Natur "einerseits als Bezeichnung für die außermenschliche, nicht-kulturelle Welt […] und andererseits als Bezeichnung für ein kosmologisches Ordnungssystem, das der Welt unterliegt" (3) – wodurch 'Natur' paradoxerweise, aber zu Recht, selbst als ein Kulturprodukt aufgefasst wird. Er verzichtet auch auf eine systematische Darstellung der Forschungslage und begnügt sich mit einem Minimum an theoretischer Reflexion. Für seinen Ansatz schlägt er die Bezeichnung "eine aufgeklärte Form des *New Criticism* oder des *New Historicism*" vor (4). Der aufgeklärte Leser, auf solche Weise vor die Wahl gestellt, wird sich wohl für eine moderate Form des *New Criticism* entscheiden, denn: "Im Zentrum des Interesses steht hauptsächlich das Bedeutungspotential des Textes; darüber hinausgehende Untersuchungen – etwa zum historischen Kontext oder zur Rezeption des Werkes – werden nachrangig behandelt und erfolgen stets auf der Basis eines *close reading*" (4).

Die positive Seite dieses Theorieminimalismus ist der Verzicht auf terminologische Hochstapelei. Kehrs Argumentation ist umsichtig, vernünftig, klar formuliert und nachvollziehbar; sie stützt sich in der Tat in erster Linie auf den Text, setzt sich aber auch mit (ausgewählten Teilen) der bisherigen Forschung auseinander. Ausgehend von der richtigen Erkenntnis, dass die Darstellung von Natur und Kultur in einem literarischen Werk kein 'grünes' Spezialthema ist, sondern grundlegende philosophische, theologische und literaturtheoretische Fragen impliziert, holt Kehr weit aus und beschäftigt sich in seinem 2. Kapitel erst einmal mit dem Verhältnis von Tolkiens Fantasiewelt zur außerliterarischen Realität. Wie etliche seiner Vorgänger stellt er fest, dass dieses nicht mit dem (von Tolkien verworfenen) Begriff *allegory* zu beschreiben ist, sondern eher mit dem (von Tolkien vorgeschlagenen) Begriff *applicability*. Interessanter ist seine Beobachtung, dass die Hobbits (obwohl sie 'eigentlich' keine Menschen sind) "als Mediatoren zwischen Mittelerde und der Welt des Lesers gelten können" (16) – nicht nur, weil sie so 'menschlich' erscheinen, sondern auch, weil sie "des Öfteren einen leserähnlichen Standpunkt" (16) einnehmen.

Mit Kapitel 3, "Mensch und Natur in *The Lord of the Rings*", dringt Kehr ins Zentrum seines Themas vor. Er untersucht das Verhältnis zur Natur bei den verschiedenen 'Völkern' sowie einigen Einzelwesen von Mittelerde und beschreibt die rhetorischen Mittel, mit deren Hilfe die Natur als menschlich-belebt, ja sogar als mit einem eigenen Willen ausgestattet dargestellt wird. Und natürlich geht es um die Nutzung der Natur durch die agrarischen Hobbits einerseits und ihre Ausbeutung durch Sauron, Saruman und Konsorten andererseits. Tolkiens Naturbild wird zu Recht als ein romantisches identifiziert; dass Tolkien damit die Erschütterung des abendländischen Denkens weitgehend (aber nicht vollständig, wie z. B. die Figur der Spinne Shelob zeigt) ignoriert, welches im 19. Jahrhundert durch die Erkenntnis der Amoralität der natürlichen Ordnung (vgl. Tennysons "nature red in tooth and claw") und die Darwinsche Evolutionstheorie ausgelöst wurde, wäre zumindest eine Erwähnung wert gewesen.

Mit dem folgenden, um die Hälfte längeren Kapitel über "Religion und Theologie in *The Lord of the Rings*" leuchtet Kehr eines der Randgebiete seines Themas aus. Es geht um die göttliche Ordnung (angelehnt an der mittelalterlichen *Chain of Being*), die Rolle des freien Willens (essentiell und doch dem Prinzip der Vorsehung untergeordnet), das Wesen des Bösen (im Kern im augustinischen Sinn verstanden als *privatio boni*). Die Befunde sind differenziert und überzeugend, einschließlich der Feststellung, dass sich der Katholik Tolkien "über die christliche Dogmatik seiner Zeit" (76) erhebt, indem er gegen die im christlichen Denken jahrhundertelang dominierende Naturfeindlichkeit Front macht: "In diesem Sinne ist es Tolkiens Verdienst – wenn auch nur auf literarischer Ebene –, ökologische Konzepte in einem christlichen Kontext zu etablieren – eine Leistung, die den führenden Theologen erst Jahrzehnte später gelingt" (77).

Ähnlich überzeugend sind Kehrs Ausführungen zu den sozialen Werten, die Tolkiens Buch unaufdringlich propagiert. Im Einklang mit der konservativen Grundausrichtung stehen die von den Helden verkörperten Tugenden "Treue und Pflichtbewusstsein, Ehrlichkeit und Verlässlichkeit, Demut und Bescheidenheit oder [sic] Mitleid und Barmherzigkeit" (176). Macht ist nicht per se schlecht, aber es kommt auf das rechte Maß an: "Nicht ein Maximum an Macht und Größe kann das Ideal sein, sondern die Besinnung auf den eigenen Platz im Universum und die Rückkehr zu einem 'menschlichen Maß'" (84–5). Allerdings könnte man einwenden, dass dieser "plain hobbit sense" (84), der noch bei dem "Scouring of the Shire" die Oberhand über Polizeistaat und Manchesterkapitalismus erringt, nicht an allen Stellen des Romans dominiert. Über die enthusiastische Darstellung einer idealisierten mittelalterlich geprägten Monarchie in *The Return of the King* zum Beispiel verliert Kehr kein Wort. Der dort (besonders im 5. Kapitel) zutage tretende rhapsodische Führerkult ist ein Indiz für ideologische Brüche und Widersprüche in *The Lord of the Rings*, die Kehr entweder nicht sieht oder nicht sehen will.

Entsprechend schwer tut er sich mit der Erklärung der Inanspruchnahme Tolkiens durch die verschiedensten gesellschaftlichen

Gruppen, die er im 8. Kapitel erfreulich ausführlich dokumentiert. Friedliche und militante Umweltschutzbewegungen, der 68er Studentenprotest, die Verteidiger der russischen Perestroika, Links- und Rechtsradikale, Katholiken, Protestanten, Neo-Pagane – alle haben Tolkien als Apostel benutzt und missbraucht. Dass dies mit der Widersprüchlichkeit von Tolkiens Text zusammenhängen könnte, deutet Kehr immerhin an ("Anzumerken bleibt, dass die meisten der hier vorgestellten politischen Deutungen nicht grundsätzlich falsch oder absurd sind, sondern in ihren Ansätzen durchaus begründet" – S. 164), aber er verfolgt den Gedanken leider nicht systematisch. Spätestens hier (aber auch schon bei der Darlegung der hierarchischen Ordnung von Mittelerde in Kapitel 3) wäre auch eine Auseinandersetzung mit dem unter Tolkienforschern und -fans eifrig diskutierten Vorwurf des Rassismus angebracht gewesen: schließlich befindet sich dieses Thema genau an der Schnittstelle von 'Natur' und 'Kultur'. (Als Ideologie ist der Rassismus offensichtlich ein kulturelles Phänomen, aber Rassisten rechtfertigen sich gerne mit der Behauptung, die Existenz und Hierarchie der Rassen seien 'natürliche' Phänomene.)

Auch zu den beiden vorhergehenden Kapiteln seien einige kritische Anmerkungen erlaubt. In "*The Lord of the Rings* als Kritik und Alternativkonzept zur Ideologie der Moderne" zeigt Kehr durchaus überzeugend, dass der Konservatismus Tolkiens, wie er sich in seinem Roman manifestiert, gegen die mit der Moderne assoziierte "Entmystifizierung der Welt, [...] den Herrschafts- und Besitzanspruch des Menschen gegenüber der Natur, die Technologisierung und Industrialisierung, das Ideal vom Fortschritt und [...] die Hoffnungs- und Orientierungslosigkeit" (101) eine "optimistische Weltsicht" (127) setzt. Mit Blick auf die Rezeption könnte man hier fragen, ob dieser Optimismus (auch wenn er bei Tolkien religiös begründet ist) nicht doch *auch* auf einen Eskapismus hindeutet, welcher der Gattung Fantasy Fiction inhärent ist, da diese zwar nicht ohne Bezüge zur außerliterarischen Realität auskommt, aber doch so viel Freiheit besitzt, dass sie sich leisten kann, ein verfremdetes, vereinfachtes und/oder geschöntes (Gegen-)Bild der Wirklichkeit zu präsentieren.

Und natürlich steht die Fantasy Fiction in dieser Funktion nicht allein. Insofern ist es sinnvoll, wenn Kehr im 7. Kapitel sich dem "literarischen Kontext" des Romans zuwendet. Seine Vergleiche des Romans mit anderen Gattungen fallen allerdings unterschiedlich erhellend aus. Die Ausführungen zum Märchen und zum Epos gehen kaum über Offensichtliches hinaus – interessanter wären die Bezüge zum Mythos gewesen –, und die Betrachtung des Romans "als Fantasyliteratur" (144) beschränkt sich im Wesentlichen auf eine kritiklose Wiedergabe der sattsam bekannten Theorien, die Tolkien in "On Fairy Stories" entwickelt hat. Interessanter ist dagegen die Feststellung, dass *The Lord of the Rings* tragische und komische Element in sich vereint, und dass letzten Endes "vor allem die komische, ökologische Perspektive affirmiert" wird (144). Dazwischen (und in gewisser Weise quer dazu) liegt ein Teilkapitel, welches den Roman in "die Tradition der Romantik" stellt (137). Es hebt auf das Naturbild der englischen Romantiker ab und auf deren Kritik an der Technisierung, erwähnt aber nicht deren Verklärung des Mittelalters, die mit dieser Fortschritts-Skepsis eng zusammenhängt, was am deutlichsten an dem Spätromantiker William Morris, einen der wichtigsten Anreger Tolkiens, zu beobachten ist.

Vielleicht hätte der Verfasser doch gut daran getan, seinen Blick nicht nur "nachrangig" über den Tellerrand des *close reading* zu erheben, aber innerhalb der gesteckten Grenzen bietet die Arbeit durchaus detaillierte Einblicke in die Art und Weise, wie Tolkien mit seiner Sekundärwelt Kritik an seiner – und unserer – Primärwelt übt.

DIETER PETZOLD

Campbell, Liam. *The Ecological Augury in the Works of JRR Tolkien*. Zurich and Jena: Walking Tree Publishers, 2011. 305 pp., CHF 20,00.

Wenngleich zum Thema der vorliegenden Studie – eine "grüne" Lektüre Tolkiens – vor allem mit den Untersuchungen Patrick Currys und Matthew Dickersons & Jonathan Evans schon bedeutende Arbeiten vorliegen, hat es seitdem eher an Aktualität gewonnen.

Wie Campbell zeigt, ist auch noch nicht alles gesagt worden. In von einer ausführlichen Einleitung und einer Zusammenfassung (nebst einem längeren Nachwort) gerahmten fünf Kapiteln votiert Campbell auf der Basis vor allem von *The Lord of the Rings*, aber auch Tolkiens weiteren narrativen wie wissenschaftlichen Werken und seiner privaten Korrespondenz, dafür, Tolkien als einen visionären Verteidiger der Natur zu verstehen, der die Umweltbewegung schon vor ihrem Auftreten hätte antizipieren können. Auf diese Weise zeigt Campbell auch sehr deutlich auf, wie aktuell Tolkiens Werke sind – und wie Tolkien auch als zeitgenössischer Autor zu verstehen ist.

Hierzu ordnet er in der Einleitung seine Untersuchung zunächst in den Kontext "grüner" Lesarten ein, wobei er mit Blick auf frühe Reaktionen und diverse Umfragen gegen Ende des 20. Jahrhunderts ausführlich für die Modernität und Aktualität seines Werkes plädiert – und sich damit vehement gegen den Eskapismus-Vorwurf an Tolkien wendet.

Auf dieser Basis widmet der Verfasser sich im ersten Kapitel Tolkiens kritischer Einstellung gegenüber Maschinen und Industrialisierung, die er zunächst autobiographisch in dessen Kindheit in Sarehole verortet, und anschließend seine Liebe zu Bäumen vorstellt, die mit den von Tolkien gesehenen und beschriebenen Gefahren konfrontiert werden. In diesem Kontext unterstreicht er auch die herausragende Bedeutung von "The Scouring of the Shire", worin die Gefahren einer Industrialisierung sehr deutlich werden, die hier sogar die Form einer Umweltzerstörung ohne Vorgabe eines höheren Zweckes annehmen. Des Weiteren zeigt Campbell den Zusammenhang von Tolkiens ökologischen Anliegen und seinen christlichen Überzeugungen auf, ohne damit Tolkien als Pantheisten zu bezeichnen; vielmehr betont er dessen Verständnis der Natur als Schöpfung Gottes.

In den nächsten beiden Kapiteln werden die beiden für die Fragestellungen der Arbeit bedeutendsten Figurenpaare besprochen – Tom Bombadil und Saruman sowie Gandalf und Sauron, wobei er dafür votiert, "that there are clearly discernible cultures of opposition represented not only in the battle lines drawn up between the agents of evil and those who resist but also, and perhaps more vitally, in his individual character portrayals" (71). Die auffälligste Gegenüberstellung von Personen sieht er bei Saruman und Tom, dessen jeweilige Einstellung zur Natur auch ein Schlüssel zum Verständnis ihres Charakters sei. Tom wird in einer ausführlichen Diskussion als "Green Man" und bedrohte Natur verstanden, während Saruman etwas knapper diskutiert wird. Der Kontrast zwischen beiden besteht vor allem in ihrer Einstellung zur Macht (die auch ihren Umgang mit dem Ring und der Natur prägt), die für Tom bedeutungslos ist, während Saruman seinem Machtstreben alles unterzuordnen bereit ist. Sein Handeln und seine Unterwerfung der Natur kann nach Campbell auch als Verrat an seiner ursprünglichen Aufgabe verstanden werden.

Das dritte Kapitel beginnt mit einer Charakterisierung Gandalfs als Gesandten der Valar und Truchsess Mittelerdes, was zu einer Diskussion seiner Rolle in Mittelerde (gerade auch im Vergleich mit den anderen Istari) führt, die Campbell als diejenige eines Führers und Aktivisten benennt. Nach Überlegungen zu seiner Indienstnahme anderer Mächte für den Kampf gegen Sauron werden dieser und das Wesen des Bösen besprochen, wobei auch hier sein Bezug zur Maschine herausgestellt wird. Wie beim vorigen Figurenpaar können die Unterschiede zwischen Gandalf und Sauron als konfligierende Weltanschauungen zusammengefasst werden: Gandalf bewahrend und dienend, Sauron zerstörend und beherrschend.

Das vierte Kapitel widmet sich der Stellung des Menschlichen und Nicht-Menschlichen in Tolkiens Werk und berücksichtigt dabei vor allem die Bedeutung der Elben und ihrer metaphysischen Beziehung zur Erde und zu den Kräften der Natur. Diese seien aber "but one example of how Tolkien elevates the non-human to present his own ecosphere of interconnections in which the fate of races such as elves, men and hobbits is intrinsically tied to the fate of all other life forms in Middle-earth and the Undying Lands" (153). Aufgrund ihrer besonderen Beziehung zur Natur leiden sie aber stärker als Menschen unter Schädigungen der Umwelt und der Natur, was Campbell als Indiz dafür wertet, wie bedeutend Umweltfragen für Tolkien waren – zumal Tolkien im Unterschied zu einem breiten Strang der christlichen Tradition auch nicht von einer menschlichen Herrschaft über die Natur ausgehe.

Nachdem Campbell somit wesentliche Themen seiner "grünen" Lektüre behandelt hat, wendet er sich im fünften Kapitel der Frage zu, wie sich Tolkien als Schriftsteller und als Literaturtheoretiker zu den Grundideen dessen verhält, was man heutzutage als "Ecocriticism" versteht. Hierzu zeigt er die Parallelen zwischen *The Lord of the Rings* und Rachel Carsons *A Fable for Tomorrow* auf, um weiterhin Tolkiens Beschreibung der Hobbits und des Auenlands als die pastorale Tradition in der englischen Literatur repräsentierend zu skizzieren. Schließlich behandelt er Tolkiens Auffassung des schöpferischen (und damit auch literarischen) Prozesses hinsichtlich der Frage einer impliziten Verbindung von Literatur und Natur und bemüht sich auf dieser Grundlage auch darum, diese Überzeugungen als mit seinen religiösen vereinbar seiend auszuweisen.

Nachdem er in einer Zusammenfassung die Ergebnisse noch einmal gebündelt hat, setzt sich Campbell in einem Nachwort noch mit der Kritik Fliegers auseinander, Tolkiens Behandlung von Umweltfragen sei nicht konsistent, wie sich am Umgang der Hobbits mit dem Alten Wald zeige. Mit Curry hält Campbell diese Analyse für unzureichend und verteidigt die Konsistenz des Tolkien'schen Ansatzes. Wenn zuweilen auch Bäume und die Natur leiden müssten, sei dies ein Ausdruck dafür, dass "the tree here, like Frodo, Treebeard, Boromir, Théoden, the elves and even Gandalf himself, must, in a land where nature is at once so vibrantly alive and so under threat, play their part and carry some of the burden that comes with a unified resistance against the forces of darkness" (272).

Mit dieser Studie ist Liam Campbell eine überzeugende und vielschichtige Analyse ökologischer Themen in Tolkiens Werk gelungen, der gerade auch mit ihren Überlegungen zu den behandelten Charakteren oder den Elben eine Rezeption auch über "grüne" Lesarten hinaus zu wünschen ist.

THOMAS FORNET-PONSE

Besprechungen: Zu einzelnen Autoren

C. S. Lewis

Barkman, Adam. *C. S. Lewis & Philosophy as a Way of Life: A Comprehensive Historical Examination of His Philosophical Thoughts.* Allentown, PA: Zossima Press, 2009. 611 pp., € 38,99.

Adam Barkman ist als Beiträger in vielen Inklings-Jahrbüchern gut bekannt. Das hier vorliegende umfangreiche Buch zu C. S. Lewis nimmt auch einige Themen der Jahrbuch-Artikel wieder auf, geht aber weit darüber hinaus und stellt ein wahres Kompendium zur philosophischen Entwicklung und – wenn man so will – 'Lehre' von C. S. Lewis dar. Neben den Originalschriften von Lewis – auch den unveröffentlichen aus dem Nachlass im Wade Center – wird vieles aus dem reichen (englischsprachigen) Sekundärschrifttum zitiert. Letzteres wird überhaupt umfassend bibliographisch dokumentiert und legt so dem Lewis-Leser ein 'weites Feld' offen, das hierzulande wohl noch weitgehend eine *terra incognita* ist. (Selbst das große Lewis-Buch von Norbert Feinendegen von 2008 hat diese Literatur nur teilweise rezipiert; dass sie sich "nicht ernsthaft auf das Denken Lewis' ein[ließe]", wie Thomas Fornet-Ponse in seiner betreffenden Rezension im Inklings-Jahrbuch 28, S. 273, sagt, oder sich gar nur "vor allem an das Kinopublikum" richte, scheint mir eine unverständliche Behauptung.)

Barkman breitet vor dem Leser eine solche Fülle an Material aus, dass es auch dem gegenwärtigen Rezensenten nicht gelingen kann, einen genügenden Eindruck davon zu vermitteln. Gelegentlich kommt ihm (dem Rezensenten) allerdings das Bedenken, ob nicht der Autor dasjenige – vielleicht sogar im Übermaß – produziert, was C. S. Lewis selbst einmal im Vorwort seiner MacDonald-Anthologie als "pigeonholing" abwehrend ironisiert – eine Kategorisierung also, die auch hier manchmal beinahe als freischwebender Selbstzweck erscheint. Freilich sind Absicht und Ziel beider Veröffentlichungen grundverschieden. So bleibt dem Leser im vorliegenden Fall nichts als ehrliches Staunen und Dankbarkeit ob des zur Verfügung gestellten und übersichtlich geordneten Materials, das demjenigen, der es durcharbeitet (das ist freilich notwendig), ein umfassendes Bild von Entwicklung und Lehre des "Philosophen" C. S. Lewis vermittelt.

Nicht so sehr allerdings eine "Lehre" als vielmehr eine – wie der Titel verheißt – philosophische Lebensform will Lewis – nach Barkmans Deutung – in seinen diskursiven, ebenso sehr aber auch in seinen poetischen Schriften darbringen. Dabei ist zunächst zu notieren, dass Lewis als "Philosophen" zu verstehen, vielleicht schon eine Kühnheit an sich ist, denn als solcher wird er in den *pigeonholes* der Philosophiegeschichte bisher nicht verzeichnet. Aber Lewis' Philosophie ist eben auch eine besondere.

Barkman tut sich anfangs etwas schwer damit, genau zu bezeichnen, was gemeint ist, wenn er Lewis' Philosophie als "a way of life" beschreibt. Dass er es mit Hinweis auf ein Werk des französischen Philosophiehistorikers Pierre Hadot versucht, hat in der Tat etwas Zufälliges. Wahrscheinlich hat er sich dazu von der englischen Übersetzung dieses Werkes (*Philosophy as a Way of Life*) anregen lassen, denn das französische Original, das die eher historische Absicht des Werks beschreibt (*Exercices spirituels et philosophie antique*), hätte das sicher nicht unmittelbar nahegelegt. Aber immerhin: in Anlehnung an Hadot kann er ein paar Kriterien formulieren, die ein solches, gewissermaßen praxisnahes Philosophieren zu kennzeichnen vermögen. Stichworte sind – wenn man es noch einmal konzentriert – "choice", "training", und "change" bzw. "conversion". Oder im wörtlichen Zitat: "philosophy is the transformation of life and not merely an academic exercise" (5). Es handelt sich also um eine initiierende philosophische Erfahrung, die aufgrund einer intensiven Einübung in eine vollständige Umkehrung oder Neustrukturierung der eigenen Lebensführung einmündet. Spontan hat der Leser das Gefühl, dass dies eine gewisse Nähe zu dem anzeigen müsste, was man "Existenzphilosophie" genannt hat. Überrascht stellt man aber fest, dass zu einem solchen eventuellen Bezug in dem reichhaltigen Buch fast keine Anhaltspunkte zu finden sind. Barkman listet einige Autoren auf, die er "theistic existentialists" (207) nennt und die Lewis allenfalls mit Zustimmung registriert habe. (Allerdings wird man – vom 'kontinentalen' Gesichtspunkt aus – Denker wie Martin Buber und Helmut

Kuhn nur mit Mühe in diesen Kontext bringen.) Darüber hinaus aber scheinen einige wenige Hinweise grundsätzlich darauf hinauszulaufen, dass "existentialism [...] was something that Lewis felt was deeply opposed" (206) – nämlich "opposed" zu derjenigen Philosophie, die Lewis selber für maßgeblich hielt.

Und dies sei eben die "klassische". Überrascht ist der Leser, Informationen zu erhalten über die ausgiebige Rezeption Lewis' von Philosophen, die man bisher kaum mit ihm in Verbindung bringen konnte. Im ersten Teil seines Buches schlüsselt Barkman den philosophischen Lebenslauf von Lewis anhand von sieben Phasen auf. Der junge Lewis geht von einem materialistischen und pessimistischen Grunderlebnis aus, das mit den Namen Lukrez und Schopenhauer belegt ist. Die zweite Periode ist geprägt von Namen wie Platon, Berkeley und William Morris. Erstaunlicherweise ist es aber in dieser Zeit Henri Bergson, der die entscheidenden Weichen zu einer Transformation des Lewis'schen Denkens stellt zu etwas, was Barkman "Pseudo-Manichean dualism" nennt. Bemerkenswert ist, dass es William Morris war, der Lewis erstmals Klarheit im ethischen Feld verschaffte. Moral hat demnach nicht unbedingt etwas mit Satzungen oder Vereinbarungen zu tun, sondern ist "a kind of art, an object to be pursued for its own beauty" (Lewis, zit. 34). Die Überwindung seines jugendlichen Pessimismus – "(thanks to Bergson)"; 35 – führt Lewis in seiner dritten Phase zu einem "stoical materialism" und schließlich zu einem "idealistischen" Denken in zwei Varianten: einem "subjective idealism" und einem "absolute idealism". In diesen Perioden ist die Freundschaft mit Owen Barfield auch philosophisch entscheidend. Sie brachte die Wendung zur nächsten Stufe des philosophischen Wegs, insofern gerade von Barfield der wichtige Hinweis kommt, dass Philosophie "wasn't a subject [...] it is a way" (Lewis, zit. 51). Barkman fasst von daher Lewis' Rückwendung zum Christentum als die letzte Phase eines aber gerade *philosophisch* gewürdigten Weges auf. Die Erkenntnis, dass Philosophie etwas mit einem konkreten Lebensweg zu tun hat, bringt zwingend auch die umgekehrte Konsequenz mit sich, dass eine Lebensentscheidung – wie diejenige Lewis' zum Christentum – im Horizont des bisherigen Lewis'schen Denkens nur eine solche zur Wahrheit selber sein kann: "Lewis only endorsed Christianity because he thought it *true* " (53). Die Namen, die im Hintergrund von Lewis' Wendung zu einem – wie Barkman definiert – "neuplatonischen Christentum" stehen, sind neben Chesterton (als Katalysator, gewissermaßen) vor allem Augustinus, Boethius und Dante.

Nach dieser chronologischen Erforschung von Lewis' "philosophical journey", die nach Barkman mehr von "rational discourse" bestimmt gewesen sei, geht es nun in den nächsten drei Kapiteln darum, den "non-rational and supra-rational part of Lewis's philosophical formation" (67) zu diskutieren. Auch wenn eine solche Entgegensetzung einer letzten Überzeugungskraft entbehrt und der Sache nach zu hinterfragen ist, wird doch unter den Titeln "Heavenly Desire" (67ff.), "Myth" (101ff.) und "Culture" (155ff.) wiederum eine Menge aufschlussreichen Materials dem Leser dargeboten. Vor allem das Kapitel über "heavenly desire" interessiert und lässt auch intensiv nach einer möglichen deutschen Entsprechung dieses Begriffes suchen, mit dem Barkman Phänomene wie Eros, Numinoses, Sehnsucht, Hoffnung, *joy* oder *romanticism* zusammengreifen möchte. In diesem Kapitel kommen auch noch einige Referenzautoren zu Sprache, die im "historischen" Teil noch fehlten, so etwa Rudolf Otto oder die Romantiker. Allerdings fällt gerade in diesen Seiten auf, dass der Einfluss von George MacDonald, immerhin von Lewis selber unbezweifelbar dokumentiert, von Barkman offenbar deutlich geringer eingeschätzt wird als es gewöhnlich der Fall ist.

Am Beginn des Kapitels "Myth" stellt sich heraus, dass auch der Mythos noch eine Modifikation des "heavenly desire" darstellt. Und gerade der Mythos ist das Element, das in zielgenauer Weise auf den Schlusspunkt von "Lewis's philosophical journey" hinweist: das Christentum. Die besondere Wichtigkeit des Mythos für Lewis wird von Barkman dadurch unterstrichen, dass er die Verwendung des Begriffes wiederum für alle sieben Phasen des historischen Teils durchdekliniert. In der letzten Phase, in der Lewis' "neuplatonisches Christentum" hervortritt, gipfelt das Mythosverständnis in der Erkenntnis, dass "Christ as the True Myth" (133) zu verstehen sei. Inwieweit diese These nachträglich zu einer Abwertung des Mythos und zu einer "konservativen" Färbung von Lewis' eigenem Verständnis des Christentums führt, hat Rez. im Inklings-Jahrbuch 28, S. 200ff., in einigen Andeutungen zu reflektieren versucht.

Diese "konservative" Charakteristik – wenn nicht von Lewis' Denken selbst, so doch von gewissen Konsequenzen, die er daraus zieht –, wird deutlich im Kapitel "Culture". Barkman hat das Thema dieses Kapitels bereits im Inklings-Jahrbuch 25, S. 254ff. abgehandelt und dort Lewis' Selbstbezeichnung als eines "Old Western Man" vorgestellt. Im vorliegenden Buch wird auf S. 168 eine Liste von 8 Kennzeichen eines solchen "Old Western Man" resp. seines Denkens aufgestellt, deren markantestes vielleicht in der Zurückweisung des "grand evolutionary myth of progress" und der Betonung der "hierarchical, not [...] egalitarian, conception of existence" bestehen. Barkman, der ansonsten kaum einmal auf kritische Distanz zu seinem Gegenstand geht, spricht an einer anderen Stelle davon, dass an einem gewissen Punkt Lewis' Denken "is plagued with difficulties" und dass er, der Interpret, "will not try to help Lewis out of these problems" (434f.). Dem Rezensenten lagen die gleichen Worte auf der Zunge, als er beispielsweise die Ausführungen Barkmans über die von Lewis behauptete hierarchische Struktur der Beziehung zwischen den Geschlechtern las. Die Schwierigkeiten liegen nicht so sehr darin, dass Lewis etwa zur Sache unmittelbar eine falsche Einsicht hätte, sondern darin, dass es Elemente in seiner Doktrin gibt, die mit anderen Elementen – oder sogar mit einer dem Leser, wie dieser glaubt, durchaus zugänglichen und ersichtlichen Grundintuition – nicht in Einklang zu bringen ist.

Bevor dem noch ein wenig nachzugehen ist, sei erwähnt, dass der gesamte zweite – größere – Teil des Barkmanschen Buches, ab S. 215, nicht mehr seinem eigentlichen Thema folgt, sondern in fünf weiteren Kapiteln Essays über den jeweiligen Beitrag von Lewis zu den unterschiedlichen Zweigen der Philosophie enthält. Die Kapitel heißen "Metaphysics", "Psychology, Logic and Epistemology", "Ethics", "Socio-Political Philosophy" und "Aesthetics". Diese Kapitel sind in sich abgeschlossen und können durchaus für sich gelesen werden. Sie sind hochinteressant und in jeder

Weise empfehlenswert; es finden sich allerdings Wiederholungen der Themen des ersten Teils. Insbesondere das Thema der gesellschaftlichen, genauer der geschlechtlichen Hierarchie kommt – der Sache nach vollkommen verständlich – im Kapitel über die sozialpolitische Philosophie wieder zum Vorschein. Hier findet sich vor allem auch die Diskussion mit Mary Stewart Van Leeuwen wieder (436ff.), die Barkman bereits im Inklings-Jahrbuch 26, S. 158ff. geführt hatte. Es ist natürlich nicht möglich, diese Debatte hier in voller Breite aufzunehmen. Auffällig ist nur, dass Lewis, ebenso wie Barkman selbst, mit "biblical arguments" (439) im Zusammenhang dieses Themas auf eine Weise umgeht, die von der heutigen exegetischen Erkenntnis aus als naiv zu bezeichnen ist. Ein anderer Punkt ist aber vielleicht noch wichtiger. Im Kapitel "Culture", wo auf S. 195f. das Thema Hierarchie bereits besprochen wird, kommt Barkman zur Begründung der Hierarchie – offenbar in Anspielung auf die Leib-Analogie aus dem ersten Korintherbrief (1 Kor 12,12) – auf das Bild des "himmlischen Tanzes", wie Lewis es von Chalcidius übernommen und von Charles Williams bestätigt erhalten hätte. Dieser "celestial dance" freilich, wie er in der Schlussapotheose von *Perelandra* als "Great Dance" grandios inszeniert wird, hat aber im Grunde Implikationen, die über eine bloß "konservative" Deutung von Hierarchie weit hinaus geht. Auch dazu hat Rez. (im Inklings-Jahrbuch 26, S. 55) einige Andeutungen gemacht. Es scheint, dass Lewis gerade in diesem Text Erkenntnisse und Intuitionen aufgegriffen und realisiert hat, die seinen (und Barkmans) diskursiven (Klein-)Mut durchaus überragen.

Insgesamt bleibt die dankbare Empfehlung, dieses im wahrsten (und besten) Sinne viel-seitige, nicht so bald auszuschöpfende Buch in die Lewis-Rezeption auch im deutschsprachigen Raum aufzunehmen, umso mehr, als der Autor den Lesern des Inklings-Jahrbuchs schon lange kein Unbekannter mehr ist.

Josef Schreier

Michèle Roberts

Castagna, Valentina. *Shape-Shifting Tales: Michèle Roberts's Monstrous Women*. Bern: Peter Lang, 2010. 127 pp., € 32,10.

Valentina Castagna's *Shape-Shifting Tales: Michèle Roberts's Monstrous Women* could have been a much needed addition to the as yet small body of critical work on feminist author Michèle Roberts – a poet, essayist and author of fourteen works of fiction who has been marginalised by the academic marketplace so far. However, this volume does not do justice to Roberts's work. In a rather erratic manner, this very slender book (which comprises a mere hundred pages) focuses on four short stories by Michèle Roberts, "Anger" (1988), "The Life of Saint Christine" and "The Life of Saint Agnes" (both in Roberts's novel *Impossible Saints*, 1997), and "The Cookery Lesson" (2001). In the introduction, the author claims that her "analysis of these works is aimed at highlighting how monstrosity [...] becomes an instrument of subversion for the young heroines, who, inheriting monstrosity from their mothers, make use of it as a vehicle of agency" (12). As her text focuses on just four short narratives, her description of motherhood in Roberts's other texts is somewhat simplistic – as becomes clear later in the text, the author has decided to focus on short stories in which "a denunciation of the complicity of silent mothers with the patriarchal system" (38) forms a key aspect of the plot. This, however, is not necessarily representative of Roberts's *œuvre* as a whole, which can in many ways be described as a complex exploration of maternity and the mother-daughter relationship from diverse angles, a circumstance that should have been made clear in the introduction.

Chapter 1, "Fairy Tales and Contemporary Women's Short Stories", which takes up almost one half of the volume, forms the theoretical foundation of the subsequent analyses but is, in parts, unorganised and therefore not always easy to follow. Castagna takes her cue from Adrienne Rich's notion of 're-visioning' and then briefly explores feminist discussions of the fairy tale with a strong focus on Marina Warner's *From the Beast to the Blonde* (1994); this leads to the question of (oral) narration and storytelling in fairy tales.

In contrast to its title, the chapter does not focus exclusively on fairy tales, but also includes a short discussion of hagiography: in a subchapter called "Rewriting fairy tales and hagiography", the author moves from a very brief account of structuralist fairy tale analysis to feminist 're-visioning' of fairy tales to, surprisingly, an account of post-colonial criticism which is not used later on and could have been cut in order to make this chapter more focused and coherent. The author then points out parallels between hagiography, folklore and (literary) fairy tales, which she establishes in the genres' didactic purpose and use of 'miraculous' or supernatural elements. The next sub-chapter tackles motherhood and offers a brief (but superficial) account of motherhood in Roberts's novels. While Castagna's contention that "Roberts's mother figures are often not biological mothers" (42) might be true of the short stories under consideration, it is certainly not true of Roberts's work as a whole. The mother-daughter relationship is examined via brief depictions of theorists Nancy Chodorow, Jane Flax and Luce Irigaray, and the question of monstrosity as empowerment in contemporary feminist fairy tales is explored through the use of 'monstrosity' as defining new maternal functions. While women's bodies (and with them motherhood) have traditionally been linked to the monstrous or the Kristevan abject, Castagna points out that feminist writing has increasingly turned to a redefinition of the monstrous as "the mother's intellectual or artistic heirloom, which the daughter retrieves and uses to free herself from patriarchal dominion" (61) – female monstrosity enables daughters to re-examine their relationship with their mothers and to renegotiate their position within (patriarchal) society.

The second chapter, "Monstrous Inheritance: Animal Bodies", focuses on Michèle Roberts's "Anger", a short story based on the Melusine myth. The story is read in the context of the tradition of the *contes melusiniens* and the Greek myth of Thetis and Peleus (Achilles's parents), and Castagna convincingly demonstrates the complex intertextuality of Roberts's tale. While she shows in what way the theme of motherhood is central to the text, Castagna neglects the role of the father, whose eventual reconciliation with Melusine heals his daughter from wounds brought about by her mother Bertrande – the story's oedipal scenario includes both mother *and* father and thus allows for a re-evaluation of both parents' roles. Whereas the relation of Bertrande and Melusine is persuasively read as a positive reinterpretation of monstrosity which allows women to skirt the requirements of a patriarchal society, the analysis of Bertrande is in parts inconsistent. Castagna interprets her as eventually "yield[ing] to the rules of the patriarchal family" (69) while at the same time acknowledging that Bertrande's maiming of her daughter is "an extreme act of rebellion against expectations regarding maternal functions of nurture and care" (72), whereas in her short story, Roberts makes quite explicit that Bertrande is an outsider in the village because she does *not* stick to the established rules, and Melusine eventually inherits her mother's crayons and with them her gift for painting as a non-symbolic (i. e. non-patriarchal) form of communication and self-expression.

It is to hagiography that the next chapter, "Cutting the Body Free: Between Hagiography and Fairy Tales" turns in its interpretation of "The Life of Saint Christine" and "The Life of Saint Agnes", two of the short stories that Roberts weaves into the main narrative of her novel *Impossible Saints*, and the very detailed analysis of the monstrous aspects of Christine's and Agnes's bodies is one of the more convincing aspects of *Shape-Shifting Tales*. However, the author's decision to focus on mother-daughter relations exclusively, which has already limited the scope of her reading of "Anger", is even more problematic in this case, as father figures are as important as mothers in Roberts's novel, which draws on the Freudian family romance and both Roberts's own adolescent feelings for her father and the struggle with imaginary images of fatherhood, a focus that is explicitly omitted in Castagna's text (see 80–81). Additionally, the restriction of the analysis to a mere two short stories from *Impossible Saints* (instead of taking into account the novel as a whole, which features more than ten short stories) is never explained satisfactorily – on the contrary, the text repeatedly refers to "the broader scope and meaning of the novel" (94) and thus implies that the analysis of two stories might be reductive.

Finally, in chapter 4 ("Knowledge and Desire: Cannibal Appetites"), Roberts's short story "The Cookery Lesson" is read as a rewriting of "Hansel and Gretel" and "The Robber Bridegroom". As with the other texts, the intertextual references are pointed out in detail, but in this case, Castagna does not work with these intertexts in a productive manner – for example, she maintains that Roberts's story works through a reversal of gender roles and expectations as her protagonist, a cannibalistic stalker, is female and her victim, a celebrity cook, is male; that the protagonist might be read as an updated version of the witch in "Hansel and Gretel" is not explored fully, even though the similarities are remarked upon in passing. Her conclusion that this story "offers up an image of female monstrosity which is empowering" (108) is not as strong as it might sound: Roberts's heroine is clearly depicted as a vengeful psychopath whose first-person narrative is highly unreliable, and her plans to kill and eat her prey are, in their transgressive and abject potential, never represented as a model. While the empowering potential of the monstrous body is demonstrated as an element of Roberts's work in the two previous chapters, this story presents a woman whose monstrosity is one of mind, not body; that this is a different category of 'monstrosity' is not even mentioned. Castagna concludes with the insight that "[t]he notion of monstrosity is reshaped and linked to a new form of maternal function in which mothers refuse to apply their power over their daughters and, on the contrary, offer them strategies for empowerment" (111) – this, however, is not true of her analysis of "The Cookery Lesson", as the author can neither definitively demonstrate the presence of a mother figure in the tale nor that Roberts's deranged heroine is, in fact, empowered by her monstrosity.

The editing and overall presentation of the volume can only lead to the assumption that this is a piece of work that has been assembled hastily and with little care. The text suffers from a multitude of paragraphs, an overuse of signposting (such as "In the short stories that I shall be examining", 43), incomplete sentences (see 35), and mistakes in punctuation and grammar which clearly point to the lack of proof-reading by a qualified native speaker before publication. Slapdash editing – typos like "Daniel De Foe" (99) and inconsistent formatting (especially when it comes to quotations) – adds to this impression, as do the repetitive references to other feminist writers known for their rewritings (esp. Angela Carter, but also Margaret Atwood, A. S. Byatt or Marina Warner), which are never used productively (see 15, 28, 39, 97). While Michèle Roberts's work certainly merits academic attention, this book cannot be recommended to those who want to familiarise themselves with her work.

SUSANNE GRUSS

Joanne K. Rowling

Berndt, Katrin, and Lena Steveker, eds. *Heroism in the Harry Potter Series*. Farnham: Ashgate, 2011. 248 S., £ 55,00.

Das Harry-Potter-Phänomen ist seit der Publikation des ersten Bandes *Harry Potter and the Philosopher's Stone* (1997) nunmehr über zehn Jahre später nach Beendigung der Heptalogie und mittlerweile auch der Film-Adaptionen von Kritikern zerlegt, gepriesen und von seiner Anhängerschaft umjubelt worden. So entsteht auch leicht der Eindruck, dass eigentlich bereits alles darüber gesagt wäre. Während oftmals die abgedroschene Handlung und allzu klischeebehafteten Charaktere beklagt werden, die zumindest noch zu Beginn der Reihe stark von Schwarzweißmalerei geprägt zu sein scheinen, befürworten Verfechter der Romanreihe den Effekt, den es auf das Zielpublikum hatte, nämlich die zahlreichen widerwilligen Kinder wie durch Zauberhand über Nacht in Leseratten zu verwandeln. Ein weiterer Kritikpunkt, der sich zumeist auf die Popularität der Heptalogie bezieht, wird im Bezug zur literaturwissenschaftlichen Forschung von Mary Pharr im ersten Kapitel passend zusammengefasst: "Where readers go, scholars follow" (10).

Als weltweit gefeiertes wie auch geschmähtes Phänomen hat die Harry-Potter-Heptalogie nunmehr auch ihren festen Platz in der Forschung eingenommen und bietet gerade aufgrund der vielfältigen Themen und Motive die Möglichkeit zu immer neuen

Interpretations- und Analyseansätzen. Somit ist die Herausgabe einer weiteren Publikation zum Harry-Potter-Kult aber auch eine recht herausfordernde Aufgabe, besonders wenn man nicht nur Bezug auf vorhergehende Publikationen nehmen will. Der Sammelband *Heroism in the Harry Potter Series* scheint sich somit durch sein eher einschränkendes Thema zum Heldentum in der Heptalogie vorerst kaum von den übrigen Abhandlungen abzuheben. So versucht auch dieser Band, das Phänomen und seine Popularität zu ergründen, was trotz dieser vermeintlichen Einschränkung unter dem Titelbegriff Heroismus ein durchaus breites Spektrum innerhalb der einzelnen Beiträge bietet. Besonders beachtenswert ist dabei ein stets kritischer Bezug zu einer Reihe bereits veröffentlichter Arbeiten über das Phänomen, die größtenteils zur bis dato noch unvollständigen Heptalogie erschienen sind, wobei eine Reihe früherer Ansätze und Argumentationen kritisch hinterfragt und gegebenenfalls auch ergänzt werden. Ein bedeutender Faktor dieses Sammelbandes ist dementsprechend seine Publikation nach Erscheinungsdatum des letzten Bandes. Die Vollständigkeit der Saga ermöglicht somit einen besseren Blick auf die einzelnen Bücher und die Charakterentwicklungen des Protagonisten und einiger Nebencharaktere. So zeigt zum Beispiel Maria Nikolajeva in ihrem Beitrag, wie sich die Figur des Severus Snape erst im letzten Band vollständig in ihrer Komplexität entfaltet und sich im Kontrast zu der vorhergehenden ambivalenten, wenn nicht negativ behafteten Charakterisierung als durchaus heldenhaft erweist.

Der Sammelband beschäftigt sich mit den einzelnen Facetten des Heldentums innerhalb der literarischen Tradition, weist die Entwicklung des Heroischen und der Helden innerhalb der Heptalogie nach und nimmt dabei auch Bezug auf ambige Nebencharaktere. Im ersten der drei Hauptabschnitte wird der Oberbegriff des Heroismus im Kontext einiger ausgewählter literarischer Genres, deren Einfluss auf die Heptalogie erkennbar ist, kritisch hinterfragt. Im zweiten Teil wird unter verschiedenen Gesichtspunkten und in Verbindung mit den filmischen Adaptionen die Entwicklung des Protagonisten zum Helden untersucht, während der dritte Teil auf heroische Vorbilder und den Heroismus ausgewählter Nebencharaktere eingeht. Obwohl das Spektrum der behandelten Themen sehr vielfältig ist und einige bisher eher außer Acht gelassene Aspekte betrachtet, bleibt das Thema des Heldentums durchweg Anknüpfungspunkt und sorgt für eine gewisse Geschlossenheit der abwechslungsreichen und gut recherchierten Beiträge. Die Auswahl ordnet das Werk nicht nur in seine literarische Tradition der Jugend- und Populärliteratur ein, sondern beleuchtet auch die filmischen Adaptionen der Harry-Potter-Reihe bis zum vorletzten Band näher und versucht damit auch ein stückweit, die Faszination des Phänomens Harry Potter bei gleichermaßen Jung und Alt zu erklären.

Das Buch strebt somit eine Annäherung an die verschiedenen Konzeptionen des Heroischen an, die zumeist in den Genres des Epos, des Ritterromans und des Abenteuerromans präsent sind und die in der Harry-Potter-Heptalogie heraufbeschworen und für gewöhnlich mit einem simplistisch dargestellten maskulinen Rollenbild verbunden werden. Dabei werden auch geschlechtsspezifische Theorien herangezogen, beispielsweise die Aufteilung in männliche und weibliche Traditionen innerhalb der Schauerliteratur, bei der die maskuline Handlung üblicherweise die Überschreitungen sozialer Tabus und eine Identitätskrise umfasst, während die Heldin der femininen Handlung vom patriarchalischen Unterdrücker dominiert wird und eine Wiederherstellung der Ordnung erst durch eine Identifikation der Heldin mit dem Antagonisten erreicht werden kann. Beide Handlungskonventionen werden am Beispiel des Protagonisten Harry Potter nachgewiesen. In dem Kapitel von Karley Adney aus dem letzten Abschnitt wird zudem versucht, Harry Potter als psychologisch androgynen Charakter darzustellen, was aufgrund von veralteter Sekundärliteratur im Hinblick auf die Geschlechterforschung jedoch leider nur bedingt überzeugt.

Als Einstieg des Sammelbandes werden die Harry-Potter-Romane auf ihren Status als Heldenepos im Kontext der Postmoderne untersucht. Dabei wird besonders die Relevanz eines zeitgenössischen Bezugs unter Verwendung aktueller Medien neben dem universellen mythischen Gehalt des Heldenepos betont, ohne die das Epos grundlegend an Bedeutung für die Leserschaft verlieren würde. Eine solche Stellung wird stichhaltig an der Heptalogie nachgewiesen, obwohl die Wirkung der Harry-Potter-Reihe im Hinblick auf die Fangemeinde natürlich bereits für sich spricht. Der zeitgenössische Bezug wird zudem in Nadine Böhms Beitrag zur Erscheinung des ersten Bandes *Harry Potter and the Philosopher's Stone* (1997) hergestellt und mit der britischen Identitätskrise der 90er Jahre in Verbindung gesetzt, wobei Böhm das Harry-Potter-Phänomen zur Identitätsbildung und als quasinostalgischen Ausblick, sowie potenzielles Mittel zum Krisenmanagement und Glaubensersatz der Zeit herausarbeitet. Ein weiterer interessanter Beitrag von Rita Singer führt die Struktur der einzelnen Harry-Potter-Romane sowie die gesamte Heptalogie auf den aus der mittelalterlichen Literatur bekannten Topos der Psychomachia zurück, die den von christlicher Moral geprägten allegorischen Kampf zwischen verkörperten Tugenden und Lastern darstellt, womit auch ein Stück weit die unreflektierten christlichen Anklagepunkte gegen die Bücher aufgrund einer angeblichen Verführung zum Okkultismus und Heidentum widerlegt werden.

Der dritte Hauptabschnitt geht auf die Entwicklung des Heldentums anhand der Nebencharaktere ein, wobei unter den weiblichen Vertretern Hermione Granger ausführlicher behandelt wird und entgegen konventioneller Kritiken an dem von Granger vermittelten Frauenbild ihre Entwicklung zur selbstbewussten intelligenten jungen Frau nachgewiesen wird. Aber auch Severus Snape als der wohl komplexeste aller Charaktere wird hier auf seinen bis zum letzten Band *Harry Potter and the Deathly Hollows* (2007) eher fragwürdigen und höchst ambivalenten Heldenstatus kritisch untersucht, nicht zuletzt im direkten Vergleich zu Albus Dumbledore mit dem Fazit, dass mit Vollendung der Heptalogie der Heldenstatus zwischen den beiden Schulleitern eine unerwartete Wendung erhält, wenn nicht fast komplett umgekehrt wird. Dementsprechend wird Snape von Maria Nikolajeva als wesentlich höher gestellter Held verortet, der durchweg die Rolle des lieblosen und verachteten Lehrers und Verbündeten Voldemorts vorgeben muss und dessen Taten und ständiger Zwiespalt erst posthum gewürdigt werden.

Zusammenfassend kann gesagt werden, dass der vorliegende Sammelband trotz vorhergehender weitreichender Untersuchungen und Analysen des Phänomens wieder etwas Neues zum Mythos Harry Potter beiträgt und interessante Ansätze bietet – von mythischen und historischen Aspekten bis hin zur Intertextualität, wobei hier Einflüsse von romantischen bzw. viktorianischen Romanen ebenso belegt werden wie solche der zeitgenössischen Populärliteratur und filmischer Werke. Gerade aufgrund dieser weitreichenden intertextuellen Bezüge der Heptalogie erscheint das Phänomen Harry Potter als ein offenbar unerschöpfliches Thema, zu dem *Heroism in the Harry Potter Series* – gerade weil es die gesamte Heptalogie im Blick hat – neue Perspektiven und Einblicke liefern kann.

FRANZISKA BURSTYN

Manlove, Colin. *The Order of Harry Potter: Literary Skill in the Hogwarts Epic*. Cheshire, CT: Winged Lion Press, 2010. 199 pp., $ 14,99.

Colin Manlove, seit vielen Jahren einer der prominentesten Kommentatoren der Fantasy Fiction[1] und älteren Inklings-Mitgliedern vielleicht noch in Erinnerung durch seine Teilnahme am C. S. Lewis-Symposium 1998, hat sich nun auch ausführlich zu dem wohl wichtigsten Fantasy-Werk der Jahrtausendwende geäußert. *The Order of Harry Potter* ist ein im heutigen akademischen Betrieb in mancher Hinsicht ungewöhnliches Buch: Unter Verzicht auf Theoriediskussionen und sparsam im Rekurs auf Sekundärliteratur, gibt es eine sehr persönliche und gerade deshalb anregende Antwort auf die Frage, weshalb die Harry-Potter-Heptalogie ein herausragendes Meisterwerk der Fantasy Fiction sei, wert, in einem

---

[1] Autor u. a. von *Modern Fantasy: Five Studies* (1975), *The Impulse of Fantasy Literature* (1982), *C S Lewis: His Literary Achievement* (1987), *Christian Fantasy: From 1200 to the Present* (1992), *Scottish Fantasy Literature: A Critical Survey* (1994), *The Fantasy Literature of England* (1999) und *From Alice to Harry Potter: Children's Fantasy in England* (2003, rez. im Inklings-Jahrbuch 22).

Atemzug mit anderen großen Werken von Tolkien, Lewis, Peake und Le Guin genannt zu werden.

In guter angelsächsischer Tradition hält sich Manlove nicht mit theoretischen Überlegungen auf. Gestützt auf seine immensen Kenntnisse der fantastischen (und natürlich auch der klassischen) englischsprachigen Literatur, zelebriert er ein *close reading*, in dessen Verlauf er dem Leser mal einleuchtende, mal recht spekulative, stets aber bedenkenswerte Beobachtungen und Assoziationen anbietet.

In der Einleitung schildert Manlove seine Konversion vom Potter-skeptischen Saulus zum Rowling-begeisterten Paulus und erklärt das Ziel seines fast 200 Seiten starken Essays: "to show that the Harry Potter stories work as the best kinds of literature work, as an ordered vision with the style both mirroring and commenting on the content" (8). Es geht ihm also darum, den Wert der Harry-Potter-Bücher nicht nur an ihrer moralischen, philosophischen oder religiösen Botschaft festzumachen, sondern auch an ästhetischen Kriterien wie Form, Ambiguität und Komplexität.

Zu diesem Zweck setzt er sich zunächst einmal mit den von anderen Kritikern bereits konstatierten (oder behaupteten) christlichen Inhalten der Harry-Potter-Bücher auseinander, indem er sie in einem ersten Schritt mit Werken der Inklings-Schriftsteller Charles Williams, C. S. Lewis und J. R. R. Tolkien vergleicht, um sich dann "the larger question of how [Rowling] is a writer of Christian fantasy" (28) zuzuwenden. Zum einen zieht er in diesem Kontext Parallelen zu Spensers *Faerie Queene*, zum anderen setzt er sich mit den Thesen John Grangers auseinander, der in mehreren Büchern nicht nur christliche, sondern auch spezifisch alchemistische Symbolik aufzuzeigen bemüht ist. Obgleich Spekulationen selbst nicht abgeneigt, distanziert sich Manlove von Grangers Methode, "to pick out items that serve his purpose and throw the rest away" (40) und belässt es lieber beim Konstatieren von Ambivalenzen: Rowlings "books are and are not Christian" (40) und spiegeln damit "her own uncertain relationship with her God" (42).

Kapitel 3 greift den Vergleich Rowlings mit Enid Blyton auf, der häufig bemüht wird, wenn es darum geht, ihre enorme Beliebtheit selbst bei sonst lesefaulen Kindern zu kommentieren. Dass der Vergleich nicht gerade zum Vorteil Blytons ausgeht (obwohl Manlove sich hier mit dem Konstatieren von Unterschieden begnügt und Werturteile meidet), wird niemanden überraschen, der sich mit beiden Autorinnen beschäftigt hat. Manloves Ausführungen sind gleichwohl lesenswert, denn sie enthalten viele scharfsinnige Beobachtungen – etwa wenn er den Harry-Potter-Büchern "narrative democracy" (63) attestiert oder feststellt, dass die Welt Harry Potters, ganz im Gegensatz zu der der Fünf Freunde, "inherently unstable" (74) und "abrasive in character" (80) sei: "Where Blyton gives us a fairly conventional image of a pastoral idyll, everything about Hogwarts disconcerts" (80).

Problematischer ist das folgende Kapitel, "Did Harry Dream it All?" (83–115). Ausgehend von der richtigen Beobachtung, dass die Harry-Potter-Bücher konsequent personal, d. h. aus der Perspektive der Hauptfigur erzählt werden, spielt Manlove mit dem Gedanken, das ganze Werk als Tagebuch Harrys zu betrachten ("Each of the seven books is a diary", 89), ja sogar, im nächsten Teilkapitel, "as also a series of dreams of Harry's" (96). Seien die Träume anfangs noch vorwiegend "wish-fulfilment fantas[ies]" (98), so würden sie in den späteren Bänden zunehmend zu Albträumen. Dass dergleichen Gedankenspiele, so faszinierend sie sein mögen, vom Text nicht gerade nahegelegt werden, ist Manlove sehr wohl bewusst (vgl. 101); für legitim hält er sie gleichwohl. Aber Manlove findet ohnehin allerorten Widersprüche, Brüche und Ambiguitäten: "Everything both is and is not" (109) – in seinen Augen, und ganz im Einklang mit der Ästhetik des *New Criticism*, ein sicheres Zeichen für literarische Exzellenz.

Ebenso typisch für Manloves Umgang mit dem Text ist seine Suche nach Ober-Begriffen, die als einigende Klammern dem Kunstwerk allen Ambiguitäten und Brüchen zum Trotz ästhetische Geschlossenheit verleihen. Eine solche einheitsstiftende Idee sieht er im Begriff der Veränderung, des Wandels ("Change"): Im Kapitel "Changes – Good, Bad, and Indifferent" untersucht er die Vielfalt der Situationen auf der Ebene der Handlung, die Entwicklung auf der Ebene der Figuren (Harry wächst nicht nur körperlich, sondern auch charakterlich, in demselben Maße wie sein Widersacher Voldemort geistig und moralisch schrumpft) und, parallel zur Entwicklung Harrys, die wachsende stilistische Komplexität auf der sprachlichen Ebene. In Kapitel 6 macht er "The Song Behind Each Book" – weniger poetisch ausgedrückt, spezifische Themen und Motivkomplexe – ausfindig. In *The Philosopher's Stone* zum Beispiel gibt "a theme of desire" (152) den Ton an, in *The Chamber of Secrets* "the note is one of continual frustration" (156), in *The Prisoner of Azkaban* dominiert der Eindruck von zwei parallelen Realitäten (158), usw. Konsequent macht es sich das letzte Kapitel zur Aufgabe zu zeigen, wie aus den "Seven Songs – One Symphony" (186) entsteht, wobei Manlove nochmals Parallelen zu Spensers *Faerie Queene* zieht und die Heptalogie schließlich, einem schon in früheren Büchern gerittenen Steckenpferd folgend, als "an Anglo-Saxon fantasy" (194) identifiziert.

Der Rezensent sieht solche pauschale Kategorisierungen mit einiger Skepsis, dem abschließenden Urteil aber schließt er sich gerne an. "[The Harry Potter books'] characterisation is excellent", Rowlings "powers of invention are considerable", ihr "portrayal of a personal and spiritual development [...] is well-handled"; nicht zu vergessen ihr "humour and wit" (197), der vor allem die frühen Bände würzt, und, nicht zuletzt, die Komplexität des Gesamtaufbaus: "The organisation of the books, the way they find a place for their creations in a larger design, is particularly impressive" (198). Man mag das alles auch vorher schon so empfunden haben, aber was Manloves Studie lesenswert macht, ist die Fülle von Beobachtungen am Text, mit denen diese Werturteile überzeugend belegt werden.

DIETER PETZOLD

VERMISCHTES

Gewalt in der Kinderliteratur

Kullmann, Thomas, ed. *Violence in English Children's and Young Adult's Fiction.* Aachen: Shaker Verlag, 2010. 213 pp., € 49,80.

Gewalt begegnet uns tagtäglich, wenn nicht unmittelbar, dann zumindest in den Medien. Da unsere Welt nicht gewaltfrei ist, spiegeln sich verschiedene Ausformungen von Gewalt zwangsweise auch in der Kinder- und Jugendliteratur. Der Fachbereich Englisch der Universität Osnabrück hat sich im September 2009 im Rahmen einer Konferenz mit diesen Büchern auseinandergesetzt und dabei die Darstellung von und den Umgang mit Gewalt in englischen Kinder- und Jugendbüchern näher untersucht. Thomas Kullmann versammelt in *Violence in English Children's and Young Adult's Fiction* 12 Beiträge, die sich mit unterschiedlichen Aspekten von Gewalt beschäftigen. Untersucht wurden dabei sowohl Märchen und Fantasy Fiction als auch realistische Texte, die sich etwa mit dem Irlandkonflikt, dem Zweiten Weltkrieg und AIDS in Südafrika auseinandersetzen. Auch die viktorianische und edwardianische Abenteuergeschichte ist vertreten.

Jeder der Beiträge gibt einen guten Einblick in sein Thema. Übereinstimmend kommen die Verfasser zu dem Ergebnis, dass Gewalt, selbst wenn sie zunächst scheinbar idealisiert wird (etwa in Eva-Maria Muhles Beitrag über den Osteraufstand 1916, der die Bereitschaft junger Menschen zeigt, für ihr Land bis zum Äußersten zu gehen), nie bis zum Schluss als akzeptierbar oder positiv dargestellt wird. Die jugendlichen Protagonisten zerbrechen letztendlich an der Gewalterfahrung, wie besonders Peter Osterried in seiner Analyse von Myron Levoys Roman *Alan and Naomi* darlegt. Werden die kindlichen Protagonisten gewalttätig, dann aus dem Wunsch nach Gerechtigkeit (wie in Thomas Kullmanns Beitrag über die Abenteuergeschichte des 19. und frühen 20. Jahrhunderts) oder aus Selbstverteidigung. Willkürliche Darstellung von

Gewalt, wie man sie etwa in Lemony Snickets *A Series of Unfortunate Events* findet, wird, wie Frederike Rathing schreibt, so stark übertrieben, dass sie kaum wahrscheinlich ist; Grausamkeit, die so weit geht, dass Väter ihre Kinder ermorden, wird im Märchen durch Schönheit und Kunst geschwächt, die Gewalt dekonstruiert, so Davood Khazaie in seiner komparatistisch angelegten Untersuchung eines Märchenmotivs, das sich in Persien, England und Deutschland gleichermaßen findet. Ein erstaunlich hoher Anteil von Texten befasst sich mit Gewaltdarstellungen in phantastischen Texten. Anne Klaus untersucht Tolkien und Pullman näher, Sabine Burkhardt befasst sich besonders mit Harry Potter und Darren Shan, Masoumeh Javadifar schreibt über Gewalt und Toleranz und Dominik Becher über die Riesen im englischen Märchen. Dass die Darstellung von Gewalt in phantastischen Texten nicht gleichbedeutend mit Eskapismus ist, belegt Stefanie Krüger in ihrem Beitrag über "Violence in Archaic Worlds". Sie interpretiert die Romane von George MacDonald, J. R. R. Tolkien, C. S. Lewis, Ursula K. Le Guin und Peter Dickinson als kritische Abbildungen negativer Verhaltensmuster der realen Welt.

Eine etwas andere Herangehensweise haben Ellen Grünkemeier in ihrem Text über Gewalt und Versöhnung in südafrikanischen Jugendbüchern und Karin Kokorski in ihrem Beitrag über symbolische Gewalt. Beide zeigen, wie Gewalt erlebt wird und wie auch nicht körperlich ausgeübte Gewalt die Opfer zerstören bzw. zu einem vorzeitigen Reifeprozess zwingen kann, der ihnen ihre Kindheit nimmt.

So interessant und sorgsam bearbeitet ich die einzelnen Aufsätze finde, so überrascht bin ich doch über die Zusammensetzung. Alles in allem scheinen mir die gewählten Themen doch sehr weit weg – lange her, wie der Osteraufstand von 1916 oder der Zweite Weltkrieg, von großer räumlicher Distanz, wie die Probleme in Südafrika, oder gar fern von unserer extrafiktionalen Realität, wie die zahlenmäßig deutlich überlegenen Beiträge zu Märchen und Fantasy Fiction, selbst wenn die dort thematisierte Gewalt Parallelen zur Lebenswirklichkeit der Leser aufweisen mag. Was in meinen Augen fehlt, sind viel nähere Themen: Mobbing in der

Schule, Sadismus und brutale Quälereien unter Jugendlichen, häusliche Gewalt, Missbrauch, Vernachlässigung als Form von psychischer Gewalt. All diese Themen gibt es in der englischsprachigen Kinder- und Jugendliteratur, mitunter ist die Darstellung von Gewalt so drastisch, dass man sich als erwachsener Leser fragt, ob sie für Jugendliche wirklich zumutbar ist (wie z. B. in Blake Nelsons *Paranoid Park*).

Es ist natürlich immer eine heikle Sache, ein Buch für das zu kritisieren, was es *nicht* ist oder beinhaltet – doch in diesem speziellen Fall wurde dem Band vom Herausgeber selbst eine Fragestellung übergeordnet, die sich meiner Meinung nach anhand der behandelten Texte nicht wirklich beantworten lässt: Was bewirkt fiktionale Gewalt beim kindlichen und jugendlichen Leser; ist er in Gefahr, traumatisiert zu werden? Wird er zu einem kritischen Umgang mit Gewalt ermutigt oder regt die dargestellte Gewalt zu Nachahmung an? Ich denke, dass bei allen in diesem Band vorgestellten und analysierten Texten eine zu große Distanz zur Lebenswirklichkeit der Leser besteht, als dass man von Traumatisierung oder möglicher Nachahmung sprechen könnte. Vor diesem Hintergrund wäre eine Fortsetzung, wie Thomas Kullmann sie selbst in seinem Vorwort anregt, wünschenswert. Entweder von der Universität Osnabrück selbst oder, wie von Kullmann vorgeschlagen, von anderen Forschern. *Violence in English Children's and Young Adult's Fiction* ist auf jeden Fall eine gute Grundlage dafür.

MAREN BONACKER

Eine kurze Geschichte der englischen Kurzgeschichte

Jarfe, Günther. *Die moderne britische Short Story: Eine Einführung.* Grundlagen der Anglistik und Amerikanistik 34. Berlin: Erich Schmidt Verlag, 2010. 260 S., € 19,95.

Etwa seit den achtziger Jahren ist eine Reihe von Überblicksdarstellungen zur Geschichte der britischen bzw. englischen *Short Story* erschienen. Insofern klingt es etwas 'vollmundig', wenn auf dem

Umschlag von Günther Jarfes *Einführung* festgestellt wird, dass es "bis heute an einer differenzierten Gesamtdarstellung der modernen britischen *Short Story* fehlt, die [...] ihre gattungsgeschichtliche Entwicklung seit dem Ende des 19. Jahrhunderts im Überblick vorstellt und erläutert" und dass dieses Buch es sich zum Ziel gesetzt hat, "diese Lücke zu schließen". Wenngleich Jarfe einige einschlägige Publikationen nennt, so ist es doch bedauerlich, dass er darauf verzichtet hat, die 'konkurrierenden' Werke genauer vorzustellen und sich gegen sie abzugrenzen.

Jarfe spannt den Bogen von Thomas Hardy bis in die Gegenwart. Nach einer kurzen Erörterung der Frage "Was ist eine *Short Story*?", die ihren Ausgangspunkt bei Edgar Allan Poes theoretischen Ansätzen hat, stellt er Hardys Kurzgeschichten als Prototypen traditionellen Erzählens im Sinne realistischer Schreibweisen vor, von denen sich die modernen Schreibweisen durch "thematische und formale Neuerungen" (15) absetzen. *Short Stories* aus dem Bereich der *science fiction* und der *crime fiction* werden ausgeschlossen, "weil sie nach dem Verständnis des Verfassers nicht zum Kernbestand der Gattung gehören" (7). Wie sich dieses Verständnis begründet, erläutert Jarfe jedoch nicht. Die Begründung hätte wohl auch einige Schwierigkeiten bereitet angesichts der Tatsache, dass *crime fiction* und *science fiction* in vielfältiger Weise im Fundus der modernen *Short Story* vertreten sind. Aufmerksamkeit hätte auch die populäre, für ein literarisch weniger versiertes Lesepublikum bestimmte *Short Story* verdient, die in der Erzählliteratur des 20. Jahrhunderts einen festen Platz hat.

Als die beiden Grundtypen der modernen *Short Story* werden die *plot story* und die *slice-of-life story* an Texten von Maugham und Mansfield vorgestellt. Darauf folgen Erläuterungen zur Genese der britischen *Short Story*. Die anschließenden Blöcke ("Die Anfänge der modernen *Short Story*", "Die modernistische *Short Story*", "Die nachmodernistische *Short Story*", "Die postmoderne *Short Story*") eröffnen jeweils mit der knappen Erläuterung dominanter Gruppenmerkmale. Im "Ausblick" am Ende des Buchs beobachtet Jarfe als Tendenzen in der *Short-Story* der Gegenwart die "Rückkehr zum Realismus", "unbestreitbare Professionalität", "ein Übergewicht der Inhaltsseite", zudem einen "künstlerischen Anspruch, der sich in bescheidenen Grenzen hält" (235). Die Hauptkapitel schließen jeweils mit kurzen, prägnanten Zusammenfassungen.

In den Unterkapiteln wird eine Reihe bedeutender Autoren behandelt. Jarfe liefert kurze Werkeinführungen, bevor er auf einzelne Erzählungen eingeht, die ihm repräsentativ im Hinblick auf seine Klassifizierungen und auf die jeweils spezifischen Themen und Erzähltechniken erscheinen. Dabei akzeptiert er es, dass bei manchen Erzählungen die Gefahr besteht, in einen zu engen Rahmen gepresst zu werden.

Bei Stevenson etwa steht die Abenteuergeschichte im Mittelpunkt, bei Kipling das Thema des Kolonialismus, bei Virginia Woolf der "Blick auf das Innenleben", bei Joyce die "Aspekte der Paralyse", bei Sillitoe "der anti-bürgerliche Standpunkt", bei McEwan der "depravierte Ich-Erzähler", bei Rushdie die "postkoloniale Fabulierfreude". Zu den behandelten Autoren gehören auch Crackanthorpe und D'Arcy, Pritchett und Greene, Wilson und Lessing, Josipovici und Carter. Andererseits bleibt eine ganze Reihe großer Erzähler unberücksichtigt bzw. unerwähnt, unter ihnen Lawrence, Forster, Huxley, Amis, Sinclair, Fowles.

Jarfe geht in der Regel recht ausführlich auf die Inhalte der behandelten *Stories* ein und bringt ausgiebige Textzitate, wohl auch aus der Erwägung heraus, dass viele seiner Leser nicht hinreichend mit den Texten vertraut sind. Insgesamt haben seine Analysen den Charakter des *close reading*, bei dem das etwa seit dem *new criticism* etablierte begriffliche Instrumentarium der Textbeschreibung benutzt wird und bei dem sich das Interesse vor allem auf die zentralen Themen und Motive, die Figuren und Figurenkonstellationen, die Erzähler und Erzählverfahren, nicht zuletzt Eröffnungs- und Schlusstechniken richtet. Ein Sachregister sowie ein Namen- und Werkregister ermöglichen einen schnellen Zugang zum Buch.

Stilistisch tendiert Jarfe immer wieder zu floskelhaft-kolloquialen Formulierungen, wie sie im mündlichen Vortrag – etwa einer Vorlesung – vorkommen mögen, in einem Fachbuch aber eher stören: Da geht es um "erlebte Rede, wie sie im Buche steht" (60) oder um einen Erzähler, der eine "Masche" hat (17); Autoren treiben mit der Fiktionalität "ihre Spielchen" (188); ein Vorfall "schlägt [...] wie eine Bombe ein" (231), usw., usw.

Alles in allem ist Jarfes didaktisch konzipierte *Einführung* gleichwohl ein informatives Lehr- und Lernbuch, das problematisierende Fragestellungen freilich eher meidet. Gerade deshalb ist es sicherlich eine nützliche Hilfe für Anglistikstudentinnen und -studenten bei der Erarbeitung und Vertiefung eines faszinierenden, klar konturierten Spezialgebiets und liefert auch dem literarisch interessierten *general reader* willkommene Anregungen.

ARNO LÖFFLER

Das lange Leben des Don Quijote

Detmers, Ines, und Wolfgang G. Müller, Hg. *Don Quijotes intermediale Nachleben / Don Quixote's Intermedial Afterlives*. Trier: WVT Wissenschaftlicher Verlag Trier, 2010. 350 S., € 34,50.

Das Phänomen, dass fiktionale Figuren der Literatur in anderen literarischen Formen sowie in anderen Medien re-produziert werden, ist vermutlich fast so alt wie die Literatur selbst. Ein eindrucksvolles Beispiel für das Fortleben von Klassikern stellt Miguel Cervantes' 1605/1615 erschienener Roman *Don Quijote* dar, der wie alle ganz großen Meisterwerke die Phantasie der Literaten und Künstler immer aufs Neue beflügelt hat.

Wie die Herausgeber in ihrer Einleitung klarstellen, ist der Sammelband *Don Quijotes intermediale Nachleben* keineswegs die erste wissenschaftliche Beschäftigung mit diesem Thema. Anders als in früheren Darstellungen geht es hier jedoch nicht einfach um einen historischen Überblick über das Material, sondern darüber hinaus um das genannte Phänomen an sich und insbesondere um die übergreifende Frage nach den Faktoren, die bei der Umgestaltung einer literarischen Figur wirksam werden: um "intermedial profilierte Interfiguralität" also, womit "jene semio-ästhetischen Veränderungen und/oder Sinnverschiebungen [...], die sich [...] beim Transfer eines zuvor verbalsprachlich fixierten Textsubstrats in ein anderes Medium' [...] ergeben" (9) gemeint sind. Auf 350 eng bedruckten Seiten entfalten die 16 Beiträge dieses Sammelbandes – entstanden im Rahmen eines DFG-geförderten Forschungsprojekts an der Universität Jena – ein beeindruckendes Panorama der "Wiederbelebungen" Don Quijotes und seines Gefährten Sancho Pansa während der letzten 400 Jahre in der westlichen Welt, von Spanien über Frankreich, England, Deutschland bis Russland und die USA. Wir erleben, wie der Ritter von der traurigen Gestalt in der Musik (was die Opernbühne einschließt), im Theater, bei fürstlichen Festaufzügen, in Skulpturen, Gemälden, Buchillustrationen, ja sogar politischen Karikaturen, in konventionellen Romanen und in Graphic Novels, in Bearbeitungen für Kinder (von Nacherzählungen über Bilderbücher und Comics bis zu Computerspielen) und im Film immer aufs Neue umgestaltet, umgedeutet und so wiederbelebt wurde und wird.

Getreu dem übergreifenden Programm des Projekts sind die Beiträge bemüht, die historischen und ästhetischen Bedingungen des jeweiligen Mediums, in die Cervantes' Erfindung 'übersetzt' wurde, mitzureflektieren. Neben die Auseinandersetzung mit den eigentlichen Objekten (Texten, Bildern, Filmen usw.) tritt also die Beschäftigung mit medientheoretischen sowie geistes- und gattungsgeschichtlichen Grundlagen, was zu einem gewissen Problem wird, wenn man sich nicht mit der Analyse von Fallbeispielen begnügen, sondern gleichzeitig auch der Fülle des Materials Rechnung tragen möchte, wie zum Beispiel in dem über 40 Seiten langen Beitrag von Friedrich Geiger und Oliver Huck über "Don Quijote in der Musik". Andererseits sind solche Hintergrundinformationen für das Verständnis der Texte ja notwendig und auch willkommen, selbst wenn es dabei gelegentlich zu Überschneidungen kommt. So enthält zum Beispiel Kurt Müllers Beitrag über *Don Quixote in England*, eine Komödie des späteren Romanciers Henry Fielding aus dem Jahre 1733, einen Überblick über die Don-Quijote-Rezeption in England – ein Thema, das auch Paul Goetsch in seinem Aufsatz behandelt, diesmal unter Einschluss von Buchillustrationen, um den Kontext für Charles Dickens' Umgang mit dem Don-Quijote-Stoff in seinen *Pickwick*

Papers zu explizieren. Auch Astrid Lohöfer geht in ihrem Beitrag über Don-Quijote-Skulpturen zunächst u. a. auf die akademische Rezeption des Romans ein, und Ines Detmers stellt ihrer Analyse von "Re-Aktualisierungen der Don Quijote-Figur in postmodernen Graphic Novels" (302ff.) eine kompakte Theorie und Geschichte dieser neuen Gattung voran. Auch Franziska Hug sieht sich genötigt, zuerst einen historischen Abriss der französischen Don-Quijote-Rezeption zu erstellen, bevor sie sich mit den einschlägigen Gemälden und Zeichnungen Honoré Daumiers beschäftigt.

Um die Bildende Kunst geht es im Übrigen noch in einigen weiteren Beiträgen. Gerhard R. Kaiser behandelt die Illustrationen Gustave Dorés vor dem Hintergrund der Literatur, aber auch der materiellen Reproduktionsbedingungen des 19. Jahrhunderts, und Wolfgang G. Müller betrachtet speziell Darstellungen des lesenden Quijote, die das Spannungsfeld von Realität und Fiktion thematisieren. Die Don-Quijote-Ikonographie ist durch diese und viele andere Illustrationen so etabliert, dass sie zum europäischen Gemeingut und damit, weitgehend sinnentleert, zum Spielgut geworden ist, wie die Beiträge von Dirk Vanderbeke ("Don Quixote in politischen Karikaturen") und Ina Schabert ("Lese-Logos") eindrucksvoll vor Augen führen.

Allen Beiträgen gerecht zu werden, ist an dieser Stelle aus Raumgründen unmöglich. Wollte man ein Resumé aus den überaus reichhaltigen Erkenntnissen ziehen, so wäre es vielleicht die Beobachtung, dass sich in den vielfältigen Gestaltungen der Don-Quijote-Figur ein ständiger Wandel der Rezeption spiegelt. Diese sich immerfort verändernde Rezeption wiederum ist einerseits Ausdruck der Mentalität und geistigen Befindlichkeit der jeweiligen Epoche und gründet andererseits auf den Ambivalenzen, die schon den Originaltext auszeichnen, den man aufgrund seiner Ironie und metafiktionalen Struktur auch als den ersten postmodernen Roman lesen kann. Cervantes' Held, der sich an der Realität reibende Phantast, ist "both, ridiculous fool and tragic hero" (Lohöfer, 79), Solipsist und Utopist, Symbolfigur für die Machtlosigkeit und zugleich für den Triumph des Geistes.

Insgesamt stellt der Band eine wenn nicht systematische, so doch eindrückliche Einführung in die Studienfelder der Intermedialität dar – und natürlich auch eine Fundgrube für die unendlich vielen Gestaltungen einer Ikone der Weltliteratur, deren Gebrauchswert allerdings durch bessere bzw. größere Illustrationen und einen Index noch hätte gesteigert werden können.

DIETER PETZOLD

Surrealismus, Futurismus, Spiritismus

Bertrand, Aloysius. *Gaspard de la Nuit: Phantasien in der Manier Callots und Rembrandts.* Aus dem Französischen von Jürgen Buchmann, mit einem Essay des Übersetzers. Leipzig: Reinecke & Voß, 2010. 143 S., € 11,90.

Krutschonych, Alexej. *Phonetik des Theaters.* Übersetzt, eingeleitet und kommentiert von Valeri Scherstjanoi. Leipzig: Reinecke & Voß, 2011. 79 S., € 10,00.

Pytlik, Priska, Hg. *Spiritismus und ästhetische Moderne – Berlin und München um 1900.* Tübingen/Basel: Francke, 2006. 723 S., € 98,00.

Ein kleiner Leipziger Verlag wagt es, einen Autor herauszubringen, von dessen Werk einst der Verleger gerade mal zwanzig Exemplare verkauft hatte. Das war ein Jahr nach dem Tod des früh Gestorbenen, den man vielleicht als Symbolisten bezeichnen könnte, lange bevor diese Richtung sichtbar wurde. Aloysius Bertrand ist eines der großen Rätsel der frühen Moderne. Er wurde 1807 geboren und starb mit 34 Jahren an TBC. Sein Hauptwerk ist *Gaspard de la Nuit*, das nun wieder auf Deutsch vorliegt. Die Ausgabe im Insel-Verlag von 1978 ist längst vergriffen. Bertrands Prosagedichte avancierten bald zu einem Geheimtipp unter den Avantgardisten. Insbesondere Baudelaire nahm sich seiner an, Victor Hugo pries den Rätselhaften und viele andere bis zu den Surrealisten sollten folgen. Die Gattung des Prosagedichtes nahm hier erstmals Gestalt an, mit großen Folgen für Baudelaires Stücke über das moderne Paris und für Rimbauds *Illuminationen*. Bertrand benutzt alte Bilder und Metaphern, ein mittelalterliches Bildreservoir, und dreht es so lange, bis es eine schräge, moderne Richtung bekommt und so zum Spiegelbild der eigenen Zeit avanciert. Die gotische Nacht ist die Quelle der Visionen des nächtlichen Kaspar, das alte Paris öffnet seine Mitternachtskammern und entlässt die Gespenster in die Zukunft. Mit Jürgen Buchmanns Essay, der die Texte einordnet, hat man einen Schlüssel an der Hand, mit dem man die Mansarden und Untergeschosse Bertrands betreten kann.

Auch bei Bertrand sind Wortspiele wichtig, doch werden sie im Werk des russischen Avantgardisten/Futuristen Alexej Krutschonych zum Dreh- und Angelpunkt seiner *Phonetik des Theaters*. Gut daher, dass diese Ausgabe zweisprachig ist. Der 1886 als Bauernsohn in der heutigen Ukraine geborene Krutschonych wird neben den zwei anderen Manifestschreibern Chlebnikov und Majakowski meist vergessen. 1912 veröffentlichte er seine "Ohrfeige für den öffentlichen Geschmack" als Manifest des russischen Futurismus. Was in der *Phonetik* zu lesen ist, ist allerdings nicht ein schulmäßig erfassbares Russisch, sondern die Sprache der Zukunft: saumnisch: "Nur der Unsinn gibt der Zukunft den Inhalt". Damit sind wir wiederum den viktorianischen Unsinnsdichtern wie Lewis Carroll nahe, der mit seinem "Jabberwocky" den Archetyp aller Nonsenspoesie erfand. Möge sie als Archäopteryx weiterhin fliegen und die Menschen in ihren starren Welten beflügeln und berauschen.

Wenn Nonsens die eine Seite der Moderne ist, dann ist das Geheimnis ihre andere Seite. Priska Pytlik, die vor einigen Jahren mit einem Buch über *Okkultismus und Moderne* (Paderborn 2005) hervorgetreten ist, legt mit ihrem opulenten Werk *Spiritismus und Moderne* nun eine reichhaltige Dokumentensammlung nach, die sich allerdings auf die kreativen Orte München und Berlin beschränkt. Wie umfangreich müsste eine Materialsammlung sein, die die anderen Hauptstädte des Okkultismus, Paris, Prag und London, einbezöge, von Moskau ganz zu schweigen? Auch Leipzig würde eine Menge hergeben, wie die Arbeiten des Religionshistorikers Mürmel belegen. Interessant an der vorliegenden Sammlung ist die Breite der Diskussion, die um 1900 alle Gesellschaftsschichten erreichte: Ist der Mensch unsterblich, und wie ist das zu beweisen? Wie kann es dann in der Kunst sichtbar gemacht werden? Gibt es ein Leben nach dem Tod, und wie kann ich damit zu Lebzeiten kommunizieren? Das automatische Schreiben, das in den Surrealismus mündet, ist wiederum eine Entdeckung der Spiritisten. Die Frage des Mediums stellt sich auch als Frage nach dem Künstler als Medium. Die größten Wissenschaftler und Autoren haben sich an diesen Debatten beteiligt, wie der Band mit seinen Zeugnissen nachweist: Max Brod ebenso wie Wilhelm Bölsche, Fontane, Rilke, Werfel, Breton, Döblin, Panizza, Wedekind, Thomas Mann und Georg Simmel. Andere sind erwartbar: Gustav Meyrink oder Ludwig Klages und Theodor Däubler. Für Großbritannien ließe sich ein ähnliches Spektrum aufziehen, angeführt von W. B. Yeats und Sir Arthur Conan Doyle. Man schaut auf diese Zeit mit einem gewissen Neid, denn heute würden sich die wenigsten so weit hinauslehnen und die ersten und letzten Fragen stellen. Man zieht sich lieber auf die Evolutionsbiologie oder Neurologie zurück, statt über Gott und das Universum, das Leben, den Tod und die Unsterblichkeit zu philosophieren. Für wen ist dieses Buch? Es ist für alle, die sich für Mentalitätsgeschichte interessieren, für Religionsgeschichte und dafür, wie wir heute wurden, was wir sind, und wohin möglicherweise der Weg gehen könnte. Denn die Fragen, die damals aufgerissen wurden, sind bis heute nicht beantwortet.

ELMAR SCHENKEL

Walter Benjamin und Mircea Eliade

Lindner, Burkhardt, Hg. *Benjamin Handbuch: Leben – Werk – Wirkung*. Stuttgart: J. B. Metzler, 2011. 720 S., € 19,95.

Müller, Hannelore. *Der frühe Mircea Eliade: Sein rumänischer Hintergrund und die Anfänge seiner universalistischen Religionsphilosophie. Anhang mit Quellentexten*. Münster: LIT Verlag 2004, 329 S., € 29,90.

Walter Benjamins Werk erlebt derzeit wieder eine gewisse Renaissance. Man stellt fest, dass einiges, was in unserer Zeit politisch oder auch in den Medien passiert, dass einige Denkrichtungen von ihm immer noch Impulse erhalten, während die seiner Zeitgenossen und zeitweisen Mitstreiter Ernst Bloch oder Theodor W. Adorno schon in einen Dornröschenschlaf versinken. Warum ist Walter Benjamin bis heute lebendig geblieben? Ich denke, weil er sich nicht auf ein paar Formeln verkürzen lässt, was bei Bloch oder Adorno schon der Fall ist. Ihre Gedanken, ihre Haltungen zu bestimmten Fragen lassen sich voraussagen, hat man einmal ihren Denkalgorithmus erfasst. Das geht bei Benjamin nicht. Er ist zu vielgestaltig, auch widersprüchlich, er hatte zu viele Interessen und konnte nicht nur Ambiguitäten ertragen, sondern auch selbst so manche erzeugen. Er war Marxist mit religiösen Interessen, Jude mit einem Hang zur Kabbala und Soziologe, der mit die Grundlagen der Frankfurter Schule legte, zu der er aber nicht gehören sollte. Seine Habilitation wurde ihm verweigert für eine Studie zum barocken Trauerspiel, die bis heute nichts an ihrer Faszinationskraft eingebüßt hat. Als Schriftsteller kultivierte er das Prosagedicht, das bei ihm zum Denkbild wurde, etwa in *Einbahnstraße* oder *Berliner Kindheit um Neunzehnhundert*. Bis heute befruchtet er Medientheorie und Kunstanalyse mit seinem Aufsatz über die "Reproduzierbarkeit des Kunstwerks im technischen Zeitalter". Er war Sprachphilosoph, Dichter und Literaturkritiker. Seine Archäologie der modernen Kultur, wie er sie vor allem in dem monumentalen Passagenwerk anhand der Stadt Paris freilegte, ist unvergleichlich und hat viele weitere Projekte hervorgerufen. Sowohl in Germanistik wie in Romanistik, in allgemeiner Literaturtheorie oder in der Übersetzungstheorie als auch in Religions- und Sprachphilosophie und Theologie hat Benjamin seine Spuren hinterlassen. Dass er sich auf der Flucht vor den Nazis in den Pyrenäen umbrachte, hat seinem Leben eine Tragik verliehen, die man oft rückwirkend in seine Texte zu lesen gewillt war.

Einen Grundplan von Leben und Werk liefert das *Benjamin Handbuch*, und zwar zu einem günstigen Preis. Benjamin-Spezialisten haben hier Artikel zum Leben, zur Bibliographie und zu den wichtigsten Werken geliefert – darunter Axel Honneth, Burkhardt Lindner, Gert Mattenklott und Sigrid Weigel. Auch die eher randständigen Arbeiten Benjamins wie die zum Radio, zur Photographie und zur Kindheitskultur werden berücksichtigt, ebenso die Briefe und Aufzeichnungen, die Beziehungen zum jüdischen Religionsphilosophen und Freund Gershom Scholem, zu Brecht, Adorno und Horkheimer. Das Buch ist ideal für den Einstieg und die Orientierung, aber auch bestens geeignet als dauerhafter Begleiter einer Auseinandersetzung mit dieser vielköpfigen und vielarmigen Figur namens Walter Benjamin.

Nicht ganz so vielseitig, aber doch zumindest janusköpfig war Mircea Eliade, und zwar in doppelter Hinsicht. Berühmt wurde der aus Rumänien stammende Gelehrte als Religionshistoriker und -philosoph zunächst in Frankreich, später in Chicago. Gleichzeitig – und das hat Inklingsleser immer schon interessiert – schrieb er phantastische Romane und Erzählungen. Seine Studien zum Yoga, zur Ewigen Wiederkehr, zur Symbolik des Zentrums und zum Schamanismus bilden immer noch einen Standard, auf den heute Bezug genommen werden muss. Auch seine monumentale Religionsgeschichte seit der Steinzeit ist immer noch beste Lektüre. Gegen Ende seines Lebens schlug jedoch die Vergangenheit zurück, die er erfolgreich ausgeblendet zu haben schien. Während seiner Jahre in Rumänien (1907–1940) stand er den Faschisten und Antisemiten um die Eiserne Garde nahe, insbesondere einem sehr einflussreichen Philosophen namens Nae Ionescu. Da sich in den letzten Jahrzehnten (Eliade starb 1986) zahlreiche Legenden bis hin zum Kriminalroman um ihn entwickelt haben, ist es sinnvoll, einmal die wichtigsten Dokumente aus seiner rumänischen Zeit zu versammeln. Das hat Hannelore Müller getan, indem sie ein Porträt Ionescus erstellt und dessen Einfluß auf Eliade genau nachzeichnet. Sie zeigt auch, wie Eliades religionshistorischer Ansatz aus dem Denken Ionescus hervorgeht. Diese Verzahnung von Politik und Philosophie ist in einem umfangreichen Anhang an Eliades eigenen Texten nachzulesen. Welch gefährlicher Nährboden der Nationalismus sein kann und wie er fortwirkt bis in die höchsten Gipfel kreativer Leistungen, kann hier anschaulich erlebt werden, aber auch, was an Gift neutralisiert und anderen, besseren Ideen zugeführt wird. Denn wer Eliades religionsphilosophische Schriften liest, wird und kann kein Nationalist werden, dazu ist das Konzept viel zu universalistisch, ausgestattet wie es ist mit einer Neugier auf und Achtung vor allen Kulturen dieser Welt. Menschlich bleibt der Eindruck einer Janusköpfigkeit bestehen, die philosophisch-historisch aufgehoben ist.

ELMAR SCHENKEL

Anthroposophie

Majorek, Marek B., Hg. *Rudolf Steiners Geisteswissenschaft und die Naturwissenschaft.* Basel: Futurum, 2011. 260 S., € 24,80.

Steiner, Rudolf. *Die Welt der Bienen: Ausgewählte Texte.* Hg. und kommentiert von Martin Dettli. Dornach: Rudolf Steiner Verlag 2010. 248 S., € 19,90.

Belyj, Andrej. *Verwandeln des Lebens: Erinnerungen an Rudolf Steiner.* Aus dem Russischen von Swetlana Geier. Basel: Futurum, 2011. 470 S., € 24,80.

Vögele, Wolfgang G., Hg. *Der andere Rudolf Steiner: Augenzeugenberichte, Interviews, Karikaturen.* Basel: Futurum, 2011. 403 S., € 18,80.

Die Verwissenschaftlichung der Welt schreitet voran und die Anthroposophie hat es immer schwerer, sich in ihr zu platzieren. Ihre praktischen Erfolge in Pädagogik, Heilpädagogik, Landwirtschaft und Medizin werden zwar teils anerkannt, andererseits gesteht man ihr aber keinen Ort im Raum der Wissenschaften zu. Nicht förderlich dabei ist das riesige Werk des Begründers der Lehre. Rudolf Steiners Schriften sind unübersichtlich, weitverzweigt, editorisch schwer zu erfassen, mal Vorträge, mal Bücher, mal Mitschriften. Da erstaunt es zunächst, wenn man in Marek B. Majoreks Sammlung seiner Äußerungen zur Naturwissenschaft liest, dass Steiner ursprünglich Naturwissenschaftler und Mathematiker war und dass er unter anderem Goethes naturwissenschaftliche Schriften herausgegeben hat. Es wäre an der Zeit, dass ein nicht-anthroposophischer Wissenschaftshistoriker einmal unvoreingenommen Steiners Beiträge zu diesem Gebiet untersuchen würde. Hier ist ein Anfang gemacht.

Entscheidend ist natürlich der Sprung von der Wissenschaft der Materie zur Wissenschaft des Geistes, und den werden die meisten nicht mitmachen wollen. Denn Steiner sah seine Anthroposophie als eine Verlängerung der Wissenschaften in die Geisteswelt hinein. Immerhin war er sich bewusst, wie sehr die Wissenschaft zum modernen Menschen gehört und dass keine Glaubenslehre mehr daran vorbeikann. So bildet die Evolution einen wichtigen Teil des anthroposophischen Denkens, auch wenn es sich von Darwin oft abgrenzt.

Steiner hatte zu allem etwas zu sagen, das ist ein weiteres Problem. Als Laie muss man öfter den Kopf schütteln zu den Dingen, die er im Buch über die Bienen von sich gibt. Es wäre interessant zu wissen, wie Imker ein solches Buch lesen würden. Oder aufgeschlossene Biologen. Einmal behauptet er, der Mensch bilde fortwährend Vorformen von Quarz, die sich vom Kopf nach unten bewegen. Wie könnte das in eine moderne Aussage transponiert werden und ginge es denn? Steiner wirft Fragen auf, so über den Bienenstock als ganzes Wesen, der von Liebe durchdrungen sei. Vor Steiner muss man entweder kapitulieren oder ihn sich zur Lebensaufgabe machen.

Letzteres machte der russische Dichter und Romancier Andrej Belyj (1880–1934), ein Begründer der russischen Moderne (mit dem Roman *Petersburg*). 1912 kam er in das anthroposophische Mekka, das Dornach heißt und bei Basel liegt. Dort lernte er Steiner und seine Anhänger kennen, arbeitete als Schnitzer und Nachtwächter bis in die Kriegszeit hinein. Aus nächster Nähe beobachtete er das Geschehen und den Meister und schrieb darüber ein bewegendes und anregendes Buch, übersetzt von Swetlana Geier. Dornach und der Doktor, das waren für ihn dasselbe, das Goetheanum eine "sichtbare Verkörperung des Individuums des Doktors". Der liess es sich nicht nehmen, zu den Schnitzern hinaufzuklettern und an der Kuppel des "Tempels" mitzuarbeiten. Ein verrücktes Unternehmen, wie so viele in dieser Zeit, in den Alpen, im Tessin, in Bayern und anderswo, wo russische und europäische Künstler und Denker zusammenkamen und die ästhetisch-philosophisch-musikalischen Grundlagen des 20. Jahrhunderts legten.

Belyjs Aufzeichnungen sind von Respekt geprägt. Das kann man über die Augenzeugenberichte, die in *Der andere Rudolf Steiner* gesammelt sind, nun beileibe nicht sagen. Es ist ein Zeichen dafür, dass die Anthroposophie sich öffnet oder zumindest keinen monolithisch-dogmatischen Block mehr darstellt, wenn solche zum Teil sehr kritischen und despektierlichen Zeugnisse in einem anthroposophischen Verlag erscheinen. Eine neue Generation hat sich der Lehre bemächtigt und stellt sie zur Diskussion, einschließlich ihres Meisters. So wird dem Band als Motto ein Zitat des respektlosen Arno Schmidt vorangestellt, der fordert, dass auch die anderen einmal gehört werden müssen, denn bislang gab es nur die weihevollen Stimmen der Verehrer. Dabei kann Steiner eine Menge vertragen, er selbst hat vieles mit Humor und Gleichmut genommen, was ihm entgegenschwappte. Man darf auch nicht vergessen, dass er in jungen Jahren selbst der Bohème angehörte und der Karikatur aufgeschlossen war. So entsteht unter den kritischen, parodistischen, verständnislosen oder kalten Blicken der anderen, der Nicht-Anthroposophen, ein höchst lebendiger Steiner, Guru und Mensch, Bühnenfigur, Schelm und Prophet. Arthur Schnitzler hat etwas gegen Wundermänner, beginnt dann aber doch Steiner zu lesen. Stefan Zweig fand ihn aufregend und großartig, aber auch bedrückend. Albert Schweitzer empfand eine tiefe Freundschaft, Einstein erkannte Unsinn, Hesse hielt seine Schriften für ungenießbar und Tucholsky sah, dass alles aus zweiter Hand stammte. Karl Kraus, Franz Blei und Gustav Meyrink schrieben Satiren auf den "Dr. Schmuser". Steiners Erscheinung und Rede polarisierte, und das wird hier schön dokumentiert. Interviews mit Steiner und zahlreiche eingestreute Kommentare des Herausgebers geben dem Band eine historische Tiefendimension. Bevor sich eingefleischte Anthroposophen die Haare raufen, sollten sie bedenken, dass mit diesen Berichten Steiner endlich in der Gesellschaft wieder angekommen ist. Denn einst war er mitten drin und man hat es ihm gezeigt. Wir sollten uns weiter mit dieser Ikone des 20. Jahrhunderts beschäftigen und nicht nur aus historischen Gründen. Die Turbulenzen des 21. Jahrhunderts finden möglicherweise Erklärung in seinen Werken.

ELMAR SCHENKEL

Ein Freund der Inklings: Stephen Medcalf

Medcalf, Stephen. *The Spirit of England: Selected Essays of Stephen Medcalf*. Edited by Brian Cummings and Gabriel Josipovici. London: Legenda 2010. 306 S., £ 45,00.

Das eine oder andere Inklings-Mitglied mag sich noch an Stephen Medcalf erinnern, der an einer unserer Konferenzen teilnahm, jene über Chesterton in Leipzig, an seine ehrfurchtgebietende, aber unprätentiöse Gelehrtheit und seine Englishness. 2007 ist der Autor und Professor der Universität Sussex verstorben, im Alter von 70 Jahren. Er gehört zu jenen Geistern, die, obwohl sie kein Standardwerk oder überhaupt ein großes Werk hinterlassen haben, dennoch mit einer Art postumer Festschrift geehrt werden. Die Herausgeber deuten im Vorwort an, warum: es war seine Ausstrahlung, sein Wissen, seine Kollegialität, sein nonkormes Auftreten, sein rednerisches Charisma, aber eben auch seine Englishness. Wiewohl er fast alle Kontinente bereist hat und sich überall in der Welt zuhause fühlte, galt seine besondere Liebe jedoch England und dem Englischen. Dabei war er kein Nostalgiker, sondern stand, wie die Herausgeber schreiben, eher in der Tradition der großen romantischen Wanderer von Coleridge bis Cobbett und ihrer Nachfolger Belloc, Chesterton oder Charles Williams. Er wurde 1936 in Romford/Essex geboren, studierte am Merton College in Oxford, dem College Tolkiens, moderne Sprachen und Literaturen sowie Klassische Sprachen. Einer seiner Lehrer war der Inkling Hugh Dyson, einer seiner Mitstudenten A. D. Nuttall. Iris Murdoch hat einmal gesagt, Nuttall und Medcalf seien die zwei brillantesten Studenten gewesen, die sie jemals gehabt hatte. Nach einer Zeit als Lehrer kam Medcalf an die Universität Sussex, der er bis zu seiner Emeritierung treu geblieben ist.

Die versammelten Aufsätze stellen einen repräsentativen Querschnitt durch das umfangreiche und kaum gesammelte Werk des Autors dar und zwar in einer chronologischen Folge von der römischen Literatur ausgehend (Vergils Einfluss auf die englische Literatur) bis zur modernen Lyrik Betjemans, Sissons und Hills. Für *Inklings*-Leser dürfte vor allem der grundlegende Essay über die Leistung von G. K. Chesterton von Interesse sein sowie "The Coincidence of Myth and Fact", in dem es um die Diskussion der Inklings geht, inwiefern die Eucharistie ein realisierter Mythos ist. Medcalf war mit William Golding befreundet, und so findet auch dieser Platz in der Sammlung. Von Shakespeare bis Kipling und Eliot reichen die anderen Autoren, und immer geht es um zentrale Fragen der Bildlichkeit, des Mythos, des religiösen Gehalts oder der Beziehung zur Antike. Hervorzuheben ist der Essay über den unvergleichlichen P. G. Wodehouse, dessen Englishness nicht zu übertreffen ist. Medcalf gibt uns ein Bild von der Person, von seinem sprachlichen Stil und seinem Humor, den er gelegentlich als geradezu metaphysisch empfindet. Das Bild trägt den Titel: die Unschuld. Unter diesem Zeichen endet auch der Band, der abgeschlossen wird von einem autobiographischen Text: "Things New Born" – Medcalf berichtet, wie er 1983 eines Tages ein Baby in einer Telefonzelle fand und es retten konnte. Gut zwanzig Jahre später traf er es wieder, als ausgewachsene Frau. Von solchen und literarischen Wundern berichtet das Buch, es sollte in vielen Inklings-Bibliotheken stehen und durch die Hände vieler Freunde der englischen Kultur gehen.

Elmar Schenkel

Besprechungen: Vermischtes

Das Geheimnis ist immer und überall

Kroker, Nadja Anne, und Elmar Schenkel, Hg. *Die Macht des Verborgenen: Über das Geheimnis in Kunst, Natur und Politik.* Frankfurt: Peter Lang, 2011. 187 S., € 39,80.

'Geheimnis' ist eines jener Alltagswörter, über die wir selten nachdenken, obwohl (oder gerade weil) sie eine ebenso intensive wie diffuse Aura besitzen. In der utilitaristisch-verschulten Universitätslandschaft unserer Tage ist für dergleichen kein Platz: Umso erfreulicher, dass sich die Universität Leipzig den Luxus einer 'Studium universale'-Vorlesungsreihe leistet, in deren Rahmen auch so 'nutzlose' Themen wie dieses behandelt werden und das Ergebnis sogar in Form einer Publikation einer breiteren Öffentlichkeit zugänglich gemacht wird.

Mit der Kernbedeutung des Begriffs: 'Information, die Mitmenschen vorenthalten wird' arbeitet im Grunde nur ein Beitrag ausschließlich. Hans-Christian Treptes "Das Geheimnis von Katyń" befasst sich mit dem Massaker an rund 15 000 polnischen Gefangenen durch die sowjetische Armee im Frühjahr 1940 und illustriert den unglaublichen Zynismus, mit dem politisch motivierte Gräueltaten geleugnet wurden (und werden, könnten wir hinzufügen) und die Beflissenheit, mit der solche Lügen toleriert werden, wenn es opportun erscheint.

Andere Beiträge assoziieren 'Geheimnis' mit 'Rätsel' und betrachten den Umgang damit als künstlerisches Spiel. So zum Beispiel Sabine Lenore Müller, die drei Filme untersucht, in denen das zentrale Geheimnis – offensichtlich der Motor jeden Krimis – gerade nicht aufgelöst wird, wodurch die Medialität des Film ins Bewusstsein gerufen werde und wir erfahren, "dass wir selbst die potentiellen Opfer der Intrige bewegter Bilder sind" (83). Deutlicher noch demonstriert der Beitrag des vom Naturwissenschaftler zum Künstler mutierten "HAEL YXXS" (der Band verrät das Geheimnis dieses Pseudonyms nicht), wie die Kunst die 'Geheimnisse' dieser Welt darstellen kann, indem sie spielerisch die abstrakte Welt der Zahlen sinnlich erfahrbar macht.

Damit befinden wir uns bereits im Dunstkreis jener Bedeutungsschicht, der sich die meisten Beiträge verschrieben haben: Sie meinen mit 'Geheimnis' eine von der Wissenschaft (noch) nicht gelöste Frage oder auch (die Übergänge sind fließend) etwas, das sich der rationalen Erklärung prinzipiell entzieht und uns so (weltlich gesprochen) in Erstaunen versetzt oder (religiös gewandt) als 'Arkanum' oder 'Mysterium' erschaudern lässt – jedenfalls uns mit unserer eigenen Begrenztheit und Endlichkeit konfrontiert. In diesem Sinne sind auch Höhlen (deren architektonisch-künstlerische Faszination im 19. Jahrhundert Karl Kegler analysiert) 'Geheimnisse', ebenso wie die Entwicklung der Eizelle (Katharina Spanel-Borowski) oder der Mond, den Elmar Schenkel in seinem blitzgescheiten Abschlussbeitrag als "Katalysator menschlichen Verstandes" (176) identifiziert – als jenes Objekt, das uns, gerade weil es durch die moderne Wissenschaft und Raumfahrt "entzaubert" wurde, vor Augen führt, "dass wir mit unserem Bewusstsein fremd sind in dieser Welt" (181).

Um "Entzauberung" geht es auch in dem Beitrag von Dominik Becher, "Vom verlorenen Geheimnis der Feen" (133–52). Das Thema 'Feen in Märchen, Sage und Fantasy Fiction' böte – besonders wenn 'Feen' wie hier vage als Überbegriff für übernatürliche Wesen unterschiedlicher Gestalt verwendet wird – Stoff für mehr als eine Dissertation; doch Becher schafft es, uns auf zwanzig Seiten eine lehrreiche (wenn auch nicht ganz geradlinige) Reise durch die Geschichte der literarischen Feen zu bieten, von den klassischen Fata und Parzen bis zu Eoin Colfers Feenpolizei: ein Prozess der zunehmenden Verweltlichung, von der Schrumpfung und zugleich Politisierung der Feen bei Shakespeare und Drayton über die Allegorisierung bei Kingsley und die Verkitschung im späteren 19. Jahrhundert sowie Tolkiens heroischen Bemühungen um eine Rehabilitierung bis hin zur postmodern-ironischen Vermenschlichung bei Rowling und Colfer.

Dass 'Geheimnis' viel mit der Struktur unserer Sprache und also des Denkens – genauer: deren metaphorisch-metonymischem Wesen – zu tun hat, legt Elmar Schenkel in seinen höchst anregenden "Überlegungen zum Geheimnis" schon am Anfang des Bandes dar. Kein Wunder, dass Jürgen Ronthaler in seinem Parforceritt durch die englische Literaturgeschichte allüberall Geheimnisse als Energiequellen literarischer Meisterwerke ausmacht und Märchen durchtränkt sind vom "Geheimnis der Zahlen" (Kathrin Pöge-Alder). Schließlich kann auch die Wissenschaft durch die Lösung von Fragen nur immer wieder neue Geheimnisse sichtbar machen, wie Ernst Peter Fischer demonstriert, und selbst ein scheinbar so banales Phänomen wie die Macht bleibt der Soziologie noch immer ein Geheimnis (Andreas Anter).

Was vermitteln die zwölf Beiträge (von denen übrigens ein Drittel von Inklings-Mitgliedern stammt) letzten Endes? – Ein Zyniker könnte antworten: Dass uns der Begriff unter den Händen zerfließt, wenn wir danach greifen. Was sich aber auch positiv wenden lässt: Der Band führt uns die Vielgestaltigkeit des Begriff vor Augen und zeigt uns zugleich, von welch elementarer Bedeutung er für das menschliche Denken und das menschliche Miteinander ist. Von einem Sammelband eine in sich geschlossene Lehre zu erwarten, hieße die Quadratur des Kreises zu verlangen. Belassen wir es dabei, dass das Wesen des Geheimnisses eben für uns immer – *was* bleiben wird? – Genau: ein Geheimnis.

DIETER PETZOLD

Was ist das Glück?

Reusch, Siegfried, Hg. *18 Antworten auf die Frage nach dem Glück: Ein philosophischer Streifzug*. Stuttgart: Hirzel, 2011. 232 S., € 19,90.

Ist Glück ein fragloser Zustand, wie es die konventionelle Vorstellung des Märchens will? Manche Menschen werden aber erst glücklich, wenn sie Fragen stellen können oder entdecken; auch die Offenheit oder Unlösbarkeit der Fragen muss nicht ins Unglück führen. Jedenfalls aber kann man Fragen über das Glück stellen. So geschehen in dem von Siegfried Reusch herausgegebenen Band. Wir erleben ja seit einigen Jahren eine Glückskonjunktur – allerdings nur in der Medien- und Bücherwelt. Das Thema scheint alle andere Werte verdrängen zu wollen, denn am Ende wollen wir alle glücklich sein. Reusch hat Philosophen und Philosophierende (wobei letztere meist interessanter, weil offener sind) gebeten, sich auf einigen Seiten Gedanken über ihre Glücksvorstellungen zu machen. Rüdiger Safranski erschließt sich Lebenskunst in Fortsetzung Nietzschescher Gedanken, Reinhold Messner setzt auf die rein individuelle Sinnsuche, die immer die Grenzen auslotet und so auf das Eigentliche zurückgeworfen wird. Besprochen werden auch Philosophen, die entweder das Glück propagierten (Marcuse) oder es sich durch Widerspenstigkeit eroberten, wie etwa E. M. Cioran oder Max Stirner. Ein Lesebuch mit vielen Anregungen. Eine gute Maxime, die man daraus mitnimmt, stammt nun doch von einem Philosophen, dem Stuttgarter Emeritus Günther Bien: "Glück ist nicht das Ziel, sondern der Lohn."

ELMAR SCHENKEL

WEITERE EINGEGANGENE SCHRIFTEN

Die bunte Welt der Rituale. Zusammengestellt vom Sonderforschungsbereich "Ritualdynamik" Universität Heidelberg. Heidelberg: Winter, 2010. 60 S., € 14,00. – Das etwas andere Bilderbuch: In neun Kapiteln und mit Hilfe vieler Illustrationen erklären Wissenschaftler jungen Lesern, was es mit Ritualen auf sich hat — im täglichen Leben und vor allem in den Religionen der Welt.

Castells, Manuel. *Communication Power.* Oxford: Oxford UP, 2009, pb. 2011. 571 pp., £ 12,99. – Ein in jeder Hinsicht gewichtiges Werk zum Verhältnis von Kommunikation und Macht im Zeitalter der digitalen Netzwerke.

Fastitocalon: Studies in Fantasticism Ancient to Modern. Vol. 1, issue 2 (2010). Trier: wvt, 2010. 112 pp., € 15,00. – In dieser zweiten Nummer der von Thomas Honegger und Fanfan Chen herausgegebenen Zeitschrift beschäftigen sich sechs Beiträge mit "Immortals and the Undead"; hinzu kommen zwei kurze "Notes", die bisher unbekannte Quellen zu Stokers *Dracula* sowie die "Neglected Fantasists" James Dickie und C. Bryson Taylor vorstellen.

Handke, Barbara. *First Command: A Psychological Reading of Joseph Conrad's "The Secret Sharer" and* The Shadow-Line. Glienicke/Berlin/Madison, WI: Galda Verlag, 2010. 120 S., € 52,00. – Die von Elmar Schenkel betreute Leipziger Arbeit betrachtet die beiden inhaltlich auffallend ähnlichen Erzählungen Conrads unter Bezugnahme auf die Tiefenpsychologie C. G. Jungs als autobiographisch inspirierte Reifungsgeschichten.

Kollewe, Caroline, und Elmar Schenkel, Hg. *Alter: unbekannt: Über die Vielfalt des Älterwerdens. Internationale Perspektiven.* Bielefeld: transcript Verlag, 2011. 276 S., € 29,80. – 13 Beiträge diskutieren "Bilder des Alterns" in Kunst und Literatur, betrachten "alternde Gesellschaften" in Deutschland und außereuropäischen Ländern und untersuchen, wie "Körper, Geist, Seele" sich im Alterungsprozess verändern.

Schenkel, Elmar, Hg. *Englisches Leipzig: Eine Spurensuche von A bis Z.* Leipzig: Edition Hamouda, 2010. 300 S., € 10,95. – Die Verbindungen zwischen Großbritannien und Leipzig sind so umfangreich und vielfältig, dass es Elmar Schenkel und seinem Team von StudentInnen – Teilnehmer an einen Seminar "Angelsächsisches Leipzig" – tatsächlich gelungen ist, jeden Buchstaben des Alphabets für ein Stichwort zu verwenden. Das Ergebnis: 27 höchst interessante und zugleich kurzweilige Artikel, die allesamt den Weltstadtcharakter der Sachsenmetropole belegen.

DIETER PETZOLD

DIE BEITRÄGER

ADAM BARKMAN: Assistant Professor of Philosophy at Redeemer University College at Ancaster, Ontario. His current research interests include the intersection between philosophy and popular culture and the interaction between western and eastern philosophies.
Adresse: Redeemer University College, 777 Garner Road East, Ancaster, Ontario L9K 1J4, Canada
E-mail: Adam_Barkman@hotmail.com

DOMINIK BECHER: Studierte Anglistik, Theaterwissenschaften sowie Allgemeine und Vergleichende Literaturwissenschaft in Leipzig und Glasgow. Derzeitige Tätigkeit: Wissenschaftliche Hilfskraft des Studium universale, Universität Leipzig; Arbeit an Dissertation: "Magicians and Scientists in Children's Literature" bei Prof. Schenkel.
Adresse: Köbisstraße 8, 04317 Leipzig
E-mail: dbecher@rz.uni-leipzig.de

MAREN BONACKER: Leitet seit August 2006 die Kinder- und Jugendbibliothek in der Phantastischen Bibliothek Wetzlar. Sie hat in Gießen Anglistik und Romanistik studiert und promoviert im Fachbereich Anglistik bei Prof. Dr. Borgmeier über den Artus-Mythos in der Kinder- und Jugendliteratur. Freiberuflich arbeitet sie für verschiedene Fachzeitschriften und Kinderbuchverlage.
Adresse: Sonnenweg 4, 35578 Wetzlar
E-mail: Maren.Bonacker@web.de

FRANZISKA BURSTYN: Studium der Anglistik und Theaterwissenschaft an der Universität Leipzig und an der Roehampton University in London. Zur Zeit Lehrauftrag am Institut für Anglistik an der Universität Leipzig. Publikation zum Schlaraffenland-Mythos in der englischsprachigen Kinderliteratur. Interessenschwerpunkte: Kinder- und Jugendliteratur, Shakespeare, Theater-Anthropologie und Essen in der Literatur.

Adresse: Oststraße 61, 04317 Leipzig
E-mail: Franziska_Burstyn@live.de

RUDOLF DRUX: Professor für Neuere deutsche Literaturgeschichte und Allgemeine Literaturwissenschaft an der Universität zu Köln. Forschungsschwerpunkte: Deutsche Literatur vom Frühbarock bis zum Nachmärz und des 20. Jahrhunderts; Gattungspoetik, Metaphorologie und Motivforschung; Wechselbeziehungen von Dichtung und Musik, Poetik und Rhetorik, Literatur- und Technikgeschichte, bes. am Beispiel des technisch reproduzierbaren Menschen zwischen Fiktion und Wirklichkeit. Zu diesen Gebieten zahlreiche Aufsätze und Buchveröffentlichungen.
Adresse: IDSL I, Universität zu Köln, Albertus-Magnus-Platz, 50923 Köln
E-mail: rdrux@web.de

UWE DURST: Privatdozent für Allgemeine und Vergleichende Literaturwissenschaft an der Universität Stuttgart. Dissertation zur Theorie der phantastischen Literatur, Habilitationsschrift zu subordinierten wunderbaren Ereignissen in realistischen Texten und im 'Magischen Realismus'. Arbeiten zur parahistorischen Literatur, zum Spiel im Spiel, zum Volkslied und zum Film. Weitere Forschungsinteressen: Russischer Formalismus/Strukturalismus, Realitätssystem, Realismustheorie, thematisches Material, Lyrik des Barock.
Adresse: Schwieberdinger Str. 61, 70435 Stuttgart
E-mail: UweDurst@web.de

MARIA ELISABETH FLEISCHHACK: Studium der Anglistik und Ägyptologie an der Universität Leipzig. Zur Zeit Promotion an der Universität Leipzig zum Thema "The Representation of Ancient Egypt in Victorian and Edwardian Fiction". Interessenschwerpunkte: Shakespeare, Viktorianismus, Fantastische Literatur, Ägyptenrezeption, Literaturverfilmungen und schottischer Film.
Adresse: Waldstrasse 85, 04105 Leipzig
E-mail: mahrai@aol.com

Die Beiträger

THOMAS FORNET-PONSE: Studierte Katholische Theologie (Diplom), Philosophie (Magister) mit Nebenfächern Fundamentaltheologie und Alte Geschichte in Bonn und Jerusalem und promovierte in Salzburg in Fundamentaltheologie und Ökumene. Derzeit tätig am St. Jakobushaus in Goslar und Promotion Philosophie. Forschungsinteressen: Philosophische und theologische Hintergründe bei Tolkien und anderen (Fantasy-)Autoren, ökumenische Fragestellungen, jüdisch-christlicher Dialog sowie grundlegende fundamentaltheologische Fragestellungen.
Adresse: Orleansstr. 58, 31135 Hildesheim
E-mail: fornet-aquin@gmx.de

SUSANNE GRUSS: Promotion zu feministischem Schreiben bei Michèle Roberts und Angela Carter (*The Pleasure of the Feminist Text: Reading Michèle Roberts and Angela Carter*, Rodopi 2009). Zur Zeit wissenschaftliche Assistentin an der Universität Erlangen-Nürnberg. Forschungsinteressen: Feminismus und Gender Studies, zeitgenössische Literatur (insbes. Neoviktorianismus), Adaptation (insbes. Film), Drama der frühen Neuzeit.
Adresse: FAU Erlangen-Nürnberg, Institut für Anglistik und Amerikanistik, Bismarckstr. 1, 91054 Erlangen
E-mail: Susanne.Gruss@angl.phil.uni-erlangen.de

KARL HEPFER: Studium der Fächer Englisch, Französisch und Italienisch in Tübingen. Dissertation über J. C. Powys. Lehrertätigkeiten im Ausland und in Hamburg (heute pensioniert), Übersetzer von Kinder- und Jugendbüchern.
Adresse: Lehmsahler Landstr. 167, 22397 Hamburg

ADELHEID KEGLER: Studium der Philosophie, Germanistik und Kunstgeschichte in Köln. Studiendirektorin a. D. am St. Ursula-Gymnasium Brühl. Forschungen zu George MacDonald, David Lindsay, den Brontës, S. T. Coleridge, C. S. Lewis, Neuplatonismus, neuzeitliche Gnosisrezeption.
Adresse: Christophstr. 24, 50670 Köln
E-mail: adelheid@kegler-worldwide.de

TILL KINZEL: Privatdozent für Neuere Englische und Amerikanische Literaturwissenschaft an der Technischen Universität Berlin; lehrt z. Zt. anglistische und amerikanistische Literatur- und Kulturwissenschaft an der Technischen Universität Braunschweig. Publikationen u. a. über Allan Bloom und Leo Strauss, Philip Roth, Michael Oakeshott, Nicolás Gómez Dávila sowie Gotthold Ephraim Lessing. Forschungsschwerpunkte: Jüdisch-amerikanische Literatur, Aufklärung, Anglo-amerikanische Seeliteratur, Literaturtheorie und Philosophie, Intertextualität, transnationale Rezeptionsforschung, Dialogliteratur, Literaturdidaktik.
Adresse: Von-Stauffenberg-Str. 22, 33102 Paderborn
E-mail: Till.Kinzel@gmx.de

JOANNA KOKOT: Professor of literature at the University of Warmia and Mazury, Olsztyn (Poland). Her current research interests include the English popular literature at the turn of the 19th and 20th century.
Adresse: Katedra Filologii Angielskiej, Uniwersytet Warmińsko-Mazurski, ul. Kurta Obitza 1, 10–725 Olsztyn, Poland
E-mail: marmurka@interia.pl

JULIANE KREPPEL: studierte Germanistik, Philosophie und Kunstgeschichte in Tübingen, Bonn und Köln. Promotion in Köln (2008) über Poetik und Politik in bundesrepublikanischen Gedichten der 1970er Jahre. Zur Zeit ist sie als wissenschaftliche Mitarbeiterin am IDSL I der Universität zu Köln tätig. Forschungsschwerpunkte: Deutsche Literatur des 19. und 20. Jahrhunderts (insbesondere metapoetische Literatur, politische Literatur und Wechselbeziehungen zwischen Literatur und bildender Kunst).
Adresse: Universität zu Köln, Institut für deutsche Sprache und Literatur I, Albertus-Magnus-Platz, 50923 Köln
E-mail: juliane.kreppel@web.de

STEFAN LAMPADIUS: Studium der Anglistik, Germanistik und Kommunikations- und Medienwissenschaft in Leipzig und Auckland (Neuseeland) und Aufbaustudium Deutsch als Fremdsprache am Herder-Institut. Zur Zeit Promotion an der Universität Leipzig

Die Beiträger

zum Thema "Artificial Humans in English Science Fiction Literature of the 20th Century". Wissenschaftlicher Mitarbeiter (Literatur und Kulturstudien) am Institut für Anglistik der Universität Leipzig. Interessenschwerpunkte: Wissenschaft und Religion in der Literatur, Phantastik, Identitätsbildung in literarischen Texten.
Adresse: Eilenburger Str. 41, 04317 Leipzig
E-mail: lampadius@rz.uni-leipzig.de

ARNO LÖFFLER: Bis Oktober 2005 Professor für Englische Philologie (Literaturwissenschaft) an der Universität Erlangen-Nürnberg; seither im Ruhestand. Forschungsschwerpunkte: Museales Sammeln und Gedächtniskunst in der Renaissance; nicht-narrative Prosa des 17. Jahrhunderts; Jonathan Swift; Beziehung von Roman und Satire; Kurzgeschichte; Literatur des Fin de Siècle.
Adresse: Rudelsweiherstr. 4b, 91054 Erlangen
E-mail: arno.loeffler@gmx.de

CATRIONA MCARA: Doctoral candidate at the University of Glasgow. Her research interests include the intersection between Surrealism and the fairy tale, contemporary research-based practice, taxidermy, and text/image relationships more broadly.
Adresse: History of Art, 8 University Gardens, University of Glasgow, Glasgow, G12 8QH
E-mail: c.mcara.1@research.gla.ac.uk

JANA NITTEL: Seit April 2010 Universitätslektorin für Literatur- und Medienwissenschaften im Studiengang English-Speaking Culture/Englisch an der Universität Bremen; promovierte 2007 an der Roehampton University London. Forschungsschwerpunkte: Konstruktion von Männlichkeitsbildern in der britischen Literatur des 20. Jahrhunderts, Geschlechterforschung, genrespezifische Entwicklungen in der Kriminalliteratur und im Kriminalfilm, Science Fiction unter kulturgeschichtlichen Aspekten sowie postkoloniale und transkulturelle Perspektiven in der Reiseliteratur der englischsprachigen Kulturen.
Adresse: FB 10; English-Speaking Cultures; Postfach 330440; 28334 Bremen
E-mail: jnittel@uni-bremen.de

JOHN S. PARTINGTON: Dr Partington is an independent researcher, an historian of socialist thought and the British labour movement. He has published six books; five concerning H. G. Wells and one focussing on the life, music and thought of Woody Guthrie. He is currently researching the reception and influence of Clara Zetkin in Britain during her lifetime. He works as a training administrator in the railway industry.
Adresse: Flat 1, 195 Oxford Road, Reading RG1 7UZ, United Kingdom
E-mail: j_s_partington@hotmail.co.uk

DIETER PETZOLD: Bis Oktober 2007 apl. Professor für Englische Philologie (Literaturwissenschaft) an der Universität Erlangen-Nürnberg; seither im Ruhestand. Forschungsschwerpunkte: Nichtmimetische Erzählformen, Kinder- und Jugendliteratur, Literatur der Jahrhundertwende.
Adresse: Parkstr. 6, 91336 Heroldsbach
E-mail: dieter.petzold.@gmx.net

JOHANNES RÜSTER: Nach dem Studium von Anglistik und Theologie in Würzburg und Erlangen sowie der Promotion zum Thema "Gottesbilder in der englischsprachigen Fantasy und Science Fiction" derzeit Gymnasiallehrer im Nürnberger Raum. Besondere Forschungsinteressen: Interaktionspotential von Religion/Religiosität und nichtmimetischer Literatur, Science Fiction und Fantasy im Kinder- und Jugendbuch. Dazu diverse Publikationen.
Adresse: Wildenfelsweg 16, 90411 Nürnberg
E-mail: johannes@ruester.info

ELMAR SCHENKEL: Prof. für englische Literatur an der Universität Leipzig, Übersetzer und Schriftsteller.
Adresse: Institut für Anglistik, Universität Leipzig, Beethovenstr. 15, 04107 Leipzig
E-mail: schenkel@rz.uni-leipzig.de

CHRISTIAN SCHNEIDER: Studierte Anglistik und Romanistik an der Friedrich-Alexander-Universität Erlangen-Nürnberg. Er promoviert zum Thema "Das Spannungsfeld 'Natur – Zivilisation' in ausgewählten Werken der heroic fantasy" und ist selbständig tätig als

Die Beiträger

Dozent für Rhetorik- und Sprachkurse. Seine Interessenschwerpunkte liegen im Bereich der phantastischen Literatur und der Populärkulturforschung.
Adresse: Harm 15, 90596 Schwanstetten
E-mail: christianschneider@gmx.de

JOSEF SCHREIER: Dr. phil. Wissenschaftlicher Bibliothekar i. R. an der Diözesanbibliothek Aachen. Neben den Inklings interessiert ihn vor allem das geistesgeschichtliche Phänomen Romantik, Religionsphilosophie, Musikgeschichte.
Adresse: Christian-Böttcher-Str. 3, 52156 Monschau-Imgenbroich
E-mail: Josef.Schreier@gmx.de

MAIKE VAN DELDEN: Studium der iberoromanischen Philologie, Germanistik und Allgemeinen Sprachwissenschaft an der Universität Bonn. Zurzeit Promotion an der Universität Bonn zum Thema "Theorie der Neophantastik", Interessenschwerpunkte sind lateinamerikanische Literatur, Phantastik, Literatur der Moderne und Postmoderne, Sprachphilosophie und Metapherntheorie.
Adresse: Magdalenenstr. 1, 53121 Bonn
E-mail: maikevandelden@hotmail.com

KATI VOIGT: studierte Mathematik und Anglistik auf gymnasiales Lehramt und Magister an der Universität Leipzig. Zur Zeit ist sie als wissenschaftliche Hilfskraft am Anglistik Institut in Leipzig tätig und promoviert zum Thema "The Science in Time Fantasies for Children and Young Adults". Ihre Interessenschwerpunkte sind Kinderliteratur, Mathematik in der Literatur und die Vierte Dimension in Raum und Zeit.
Adresse: Manetstraße 25, 04109 Leipzig
E-mail: Voigt-Kati@gmx.de

STEFAN WELZ: lehrt Englische Literatur des 19. und 20. Jahrhunderts sowie Neuere Englische Literaturen an der Universität Leipzig und ist als Übersetzer tätig.
Adresse: Institut für Anglistik, Universität Leipzig, Beethovenstr. 15, 04107 Leipzig
E-mail: welz@rz.uni-leipzig.de

PERSONENINDEX

Abbott, Edwin A. 124
Allen, Grant 186, 188
Alpers, Hans Joachim 255, 259, 260, 262, 265, 267

Ballantyne, Robert Michael 169
Barkman, Adam 344
Barlow, Steve 91
Bates, Henry Walter 72
Batory, Dana Martin 329
Bear, Greg 91, 92
Becher, Johannes R. 222
Belyj, Andrej 375
Benjamin, Walter 372–375
Berndt, Katrin 354
Bertrand, Aloysius 370
Birtwistle, Harrison 207
Blériot, Louis 20, 27
Blackwell, Su 115
Blackwood, Algernon 52
Blumenberg, Hans 217, 219, 221
Bradbury, Ray 133
Buchan, John 155, 166

Calvin, David 318
Campbell, Liam 340
Carroll, Lewis (d. i. Charles Lutwidge Dodgson) 324–329
Carter, Lin 256, 258, 264, 265
Castagna, Valentina 350
Cervantes Saavedra, Miguel de 367–370
Chapman, Vera 206
Chaucer, Geoffrey 197
Churchill, Winston S. 147, 155, 168–185
Conrad, Joseph 161
Cornell, Joseph 110
Crichton, Michael 91, 93

Cummings, Brian 378

Dante Alighieri 28
Darwin, Charles 70, 72, 89
Davis, Richard Brian 324
Dawkins, Richard 95
Dawson, Charles 86, 89
de Camp, L. Sprague 255, 256, 258, 264, 265, 269
Detmers, Ines 367
Dodgson, Charles Lutwidge *siehe* Carroll, Lewis
Doyle, Arthur Conan 10–195, 329–333
Doyle, Innes 146, 165
Doyle, Kingsley 165
Doyle, Louise 157, 187
Doyle, Richard 105, 117
Dubs, Kathleen 333
Dvorkin, David 134

Einstein, Albert 132, 134
Eliade, Mircea 372–375
Ernst, Max 105, 111

Farmer, Tessa 116
Fechner, Gustav Theodor 123, 130
Fenn, George Manville 169
Freeman, R. Austin 51
Freiligrath, Ferdinand 222, 223
Freud, Sigmund 111
Froud, Brian 116

Gardner, Edward L. 100–120
Gide, André 219
Goethe, Johann Wolfgang v. 215, 218, 220, 224, 229, 319–324
Griffiths, Frances 100–120
Gutzkow, Karl 214

Personenindex

Haeckel, Ernst 23, 82, 85
Haggard, Henry Rider 51–53, 142–167
Hall, Robert Lee 134
Harsent, David 207
Henty, George Alfred 169, 176
Herder, Johann Gottfried 215
Hewlett, Maurice 104
Hinton, Charles Howard 124
Hodgson, William Hope 52
Hoffmann, Ernst Theodor Amadeus 217, 219, 220
Houdini, Harry 11, 15, 110, 115, 123
Howard, Robert E. 253–273
Huxley, Thomas Henry 71, 77, 84, 89, 94

Illger, Daniel 308

Jarfe, Günther 364
Josipovici, Gabriel 378

Kafka, Franz 20, 27
Kaščáková, Janka 333
Kehr, Eike 336
Kipling, Rudyard 142–167
Kroker, Nadja Anne 380
Krutschonych, Alexej 370
Kullmann, Thomas 362

La Mettrie, Julien Offray de 228
Lankester, Ray 60, 78, 88
Le Guin, Ursula Kroeber 268
Lear, Anne 134
Leckie, Jean 157, 190
Leiber, Fritz 254, 258, 265
Lewis, Clive Staples 232–252, 344–349
Liddell, Alice 328
Lindner, Burkhardt 372
Lovecraft, Howard Philipps 269
Lyell, Charles 77

Machen, Arthur 108, 117

Majorek, Marek B. 375
Manlove, Colin 358
Marx, Karl 222, 223
Masterman, Charles 163
McAra, Catriona 318
Meckel, Christoph 274–290
Medcalf, Stephen 378–379
Minkowski, Hermann 131
Moorcock, Michael 254, 268
Morgan, Edwin 291–305
Müller, Hannelore 372
Müller, Wolfgang G. 367
Murdoch, Iris 208

Otten, Karl 222

Page, Will A. 22
Plantinga, Alvin 236, 239, 241, 247, 248
Poe, Edgar Allan 21
Ponsor, Y. R. 207
Pytlik, Priska 370

Reusch, Siegfried 382
Roberts, Michèle 350–354
Rowling, Joanne Kathleen 354–361
Rzeszotnik, Jacek 308

Schenkel, Elmar 380
Schlegel, August Wilhelm 215
Schmeink, Lars 308
Shaftesbury, Anthony A. C. Earl of 214
Shelley, Mary Wollstonecraft 224, 226, 227
Skidmore, Steve 91
Skorniakova, Kristina 319
Spencer, Herbert 77, 85, 89
Spiegel, Simon 311
Spinrad, Norman 267
Steiner, Rudolf 375
Steveker, Lena 354
Stoker, Bram 51–53
Stucken, Eduard 206
Sturridge, Charles 114
Suvin, Darko 315

Tennyson, Alfred Lord 78
Todorov, Tzvetan 311
Tolkien, John Ronald Reuel
 333–343

Vaucanson, Jacques de 228
Verne, Jules 22, 76, 78
Vögele, Wolfgang G. 375

Wallace, Alfred Russel 72, 75, 89
Wallace, Edgar 155
Weismann, August 60, 70
Wells, Herbert George 14, 22, 131,
 329–333
Winchester, Simon 327
Wright, Elsie 100–120

Yeats, William Butler 205

Inklings
Jahrbuch für Literatur und Ästhetik

Herausgegeben von Dieter Petzold

Die Bände 1-10 sind im Verlag H.-W. Stier, Lüdenscheid, erschienen, die Bände 11-27 im Brendow-Verlag, Moers.

Band 28 Multimediale Methamorphosen. Die produktive Rezeption der Inklings im 21. Jahrhundert. Internationale Tagung vom 1. bis 3. Oktober 2010 in Nürnberg. 2011.

Band 29 Der andere Conan Doyle. Internationale Tagung am 20. und 21. Mai 2011 in Leipzig. 2012.

www.peterlang.de